THE PENGUIN CLASSICS

FOUNDER EDITOR: (1944-64) E. V. RIEU

PRESENT EDITORS:
Robert Baldick (1964-72), Betty Radice, C. A. Jones

DEMOSTHENES, the great Greek orator, was born in Athens in 384 B.C. He studied rhetoric and judicial procedure under Isaeus and success in private legal cases led to public prosecutions and ultimately to a political career. His quarrel with Aeschines, a politician whose policies he bitterly opposed, was a conspicuous feature in a life which ended with Demosthenes' impeachment and retirement from public life. He died in 322 B.C.

AESCHINES was born *c.* 390. His early career was spent in the armed forces, where he served with distinction. His political career began under the aegis of Eubulus, *c.* 357. Aeschines' attempt to remove Demosthenes from public life proved to be his own downfall. He eventually retired to Rhodes, where he practised as a rhetor.

A. N. W. SAUNDERS was born in 1900 and educated at Rugby School, and later at New College, Oxford, where he obtained a first in Mods and Greats. He was Senior Classical Master at Rugby School until 1965, when he retired. He is also the author of *Roman History, Extracts and Outlines, Imagination All Compact* and *Greek Political Oratory* (Penguin Books, 1970).

T. T. B. RYDER, who was born in 1930, and educated at Eton and King's College, Cambridge, is Reader in Classics at Hull University. He is the author of *Koine Eirene: General Peace and Local Independence in Ancient Greece* (1965) and was Executive Editor (Ancient History) for the *Dictionary of World History* (1973).

G000245939

DEMOSTHENES
AND
AESCHINES

Translated by

A. N. W. SAUNDERS

Introduction by

T. T. B. RYDER

PENGUIN BOOKS

Penguin Books Ltd, Harmondsworth, Middlesex, England
Penguin Books Inc., 7110 Ambassador Road, Baltimore, Maryland 21207, U.S.A.
Penguin Books Australia Ltd, Ringwood, Victoria, Australia
Penguin Books Canada Ltd, 41 Steelcase Road West, Markham, Ontario, Canada

—

First published 1975
Translation copyright © A. N. W. Saunders, 1974
Introduction copyright © T. T. B. Ryder, 1974

—

Made and printed in Great Britain by
Hazell Watson & Viney Ltd,
Aylesbury, Bucks
Set in Monotype Fournier

CONTENTS

Foreword 7

Map 8-9

Introduction 11

THE TREATY

I. The Prosecution: Demosthenes 55

II. The Defence: Aeschines 141

THE CROWN

I. The Prosecution: Aeschines 191

II. The Defence: Demosthenes 259

Appendix 331

Chronological Table 333

Bibliography 335

FOREWORD

THE original title of the first pair of speeches in this volume, here called *The Treaty*, was *Peri parapresbeias*, literally 'On misconduct as ambassador', which in some editions appears in the Latin *De falsa legatione* or in English as *On the Embassy*; they are numbered XIX in the works of Demosthenes and II in those of Aeschines: *The Crown* is the usual translation of *Peri tou stephanou*, the Greek title of Demosthenes XVIII (Latin *De corona*); Aeschines III, which it answers, was entitled *Kata Ktesiphontos*, *Against Ctesiphon* (Latin *In Ctesiphontem*).

The translations are by Mr Saunders, the introduction by Dr Ryder; the notes are the work of both.

Dr Ryder wishes to acknowledge his gratitude to Mr J. C. G. Strachan, who read the introduction and made valuable suggestions.

The texts used are the Oxford text of Demosthenes, the Teubner text of Aeschines. Some textual points have been noticed in the Appendix.

The sections into which the text is divided appear at the head of each page. Reference is made to these in the summaries of each speech, and in the notes.

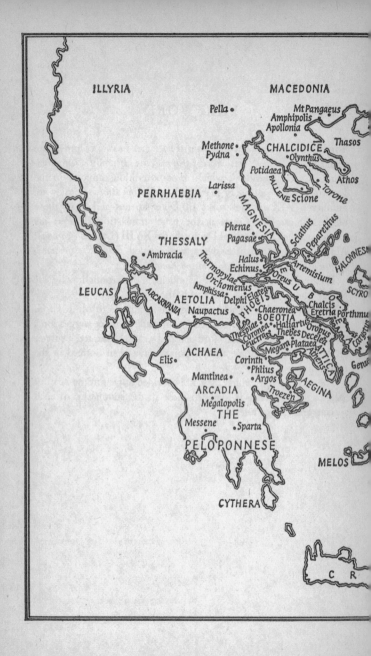

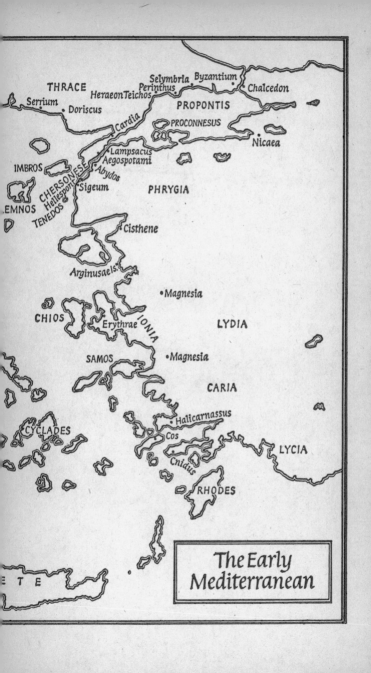

THRACE
Serrium
Doriscus
HeraeonTeichos
Selymbria Byzantium
Perinthus
Chalcedon
Cardia
PROPONTIS
PROCONNESUS
Nicaea
Lampsacus
Aegospotami
Abydos
PHRYGIA
IMBROS
CHERSONESE
Sigeum
Hellespont
EMNOS
TENEDOS
Cisthene
Arginusae Is.
Magnesia
CHIOS
Erythrae
IONIA
LYDIA
SAMOS
Magnesia
CARIA
Halicarnassus
CYCLADES
Cos
LYCIA
Cnidus
RHODES
ETE

The Early
Mediterranean

INTRODUCTION

1. The Speeches and History

THE four speeches in this volume form two pairs, each consisting of an accusation and the defence to it, the only such pairs in the surviving works of the Greek orators; two confrontations in a single personal rivalry which played an important role in the last years of the Athenians' unsuccessful resistance to Philip of Macedon and in the first years of their reluctant subservience to him and his son, Alexander the Great. Demosthenes, the most celebrated and therefore the best preserved Greek orator of antiquity, was the leading anti-Macedonian politician; Aeschines was but one of his chief opponents, but virtually the only one of whom any work survives,[1] although his three extant speeches can hardly be representative of a busy career of speaking, in law-courts, at political meetings and on diplomatic missions abroad.

Arguments between Demosthenes and Aeschines must have been commonplace in the popular assembly open to all citizens, where all matters of public policy were debated and decided, but the two preserved took place in the law-courts. The processes of law, however, were organized on the same democratic principles as the Athenians' political institutions. There was no Public Prosecutor's office and it was left to individuals to bring charges for actions against the community as well as for those against individuals. Little authority was given to the chairman, a minor official chosen by lot, who had no power to enforce rules of evidence, to rule on points of law or to sum up, and the verdict was delivered by a large jury (in these cases probably of over a

---

1. The speeches of Deinarchus and Hyperides against Demosthenes, the former extant, the latter partly preserved on papyrus, belong to his trial in 324. Deinarchus was a professional speechwriter, and the identity of his client is unknown; Hyperides was an anti-Macedonian politician who had earlier been an associate of Demosthenes.

thousand) empanelled from the 6,000 citizens selected annually by lot for this duty.[2] In these circumstances any case involving prominent politicians was bound to be decided as much on political as on legal grounds, and was likely to bring under scrutiny the whole of the protagonists' public careers and not simply the episode which was the subject of the charge. So in the first of these two cases (heard in 343 B.C.) Demosthenes accused Aeschines of *parapresbeia*, misconduct as ambassador in the second delegation of ten which was sent to Philip of Macedon in 346 B.C. to procure his ratification of the recently agreed Peace of Philocrates, but his speech and Aeschines' reply are concerned with the whole story of the negotiations leading to that Peace, its conclusion and immediate consequences. In the second case the defendant was not Demosthenes, but Ctesiphon, who was accused in 336 B.C. under the procedure known as *graphê paranomôn* of making an illegal proposal that Demosthenes should be publicly crowned for his services to the state. But Aeschines frankly admitted that the accusation was politically inspired and aimed at Demosthenes, for to two technical grounds for a charge of illegality he added the third,[3] that Ctesiphon had proposed to include a false statement in a decree of the people, that is his citation of Demosthenes' services to the state. He thus explicitly brought within the scope of the trial (which did not take place until 330 B.C.) the whole of Demosthenes' political career and the whole question of the policies of the Athenians towards Macedon before and after the establishment of Macedonian supremacy in Greece in 338 B.C.; and Demosthenes' defence of Ctesiphon is very much a defence of his own life's work.

It is clear, then, that these four speeches are sources of great importance for the history of the Athenians' fatal struggle with Macedon; and this importance is enhanced, and the understanding of the speeches made more difficult, by the comparative scarcity of other material. Most of what there is consists also of speeches, most of them by Demosthenes (chiefly the political speeches delivered to

2. On Athenian legal institutions and procedure see R. Flacelière, *Daily Life in Greece at the Time of Pericles* (trans. Green, London, 1965), pp. 228 ff., and the article by D. M. MacDowell on *Dikasterion* in the Oxford Classical Dictionary (2nd ed., 1970), pp. 342–3.

3. Aeschines, *Crown*, 50 (p. 205).

the Athenian assembly which are included in the earlier Penguin volume, *Greek Political Oratory*) and a few by other orators, principally anti-Macedonians such as Lycurgus, Hyperides and Hegesippus, the presumed author of Pseudo-Demosthenes VII (*On Halonnesus*). There are also political pamphlets and 'open letters' by the veteran rhetorician, Isocrates, who came to favour a compromise with Macedon and died aged 98 soon after the Macedonian victory at Chaeronea in 338 B.C. Other literary sources are the relevant parts, brief and rather confused, of Books XVI-XVII of the World History of Diodorus Siculus (first century B.C.), Plutarch's *Lives* (*c.* A.D. 100) of Demosthenes, Phocion (an Athenian general and politician not committed to uncompromising hostility to Macedon) and Alexander the Great, and Arrian's account (second century A.D.) of Alexander's conquest of Asia. All these three used some contemporary material, but the most reliable, Arrian, is the one least concerned with Greek affairs, while the others are so sketchy that they fail to record the vast majority of incidents discussed or alluded to by the orators.

It is, then, largely from the speeches themselves that we have to build up our picture of the historical events they discuss and form judgements of the merits of their arguments and of the policies and actions of those who delivered them; and this is a situation which a historian cannot find easy. It need hardly be said that political speeches present many hazards to anyone who seeks to construct the true record of events, especially if, as is usually the case in this period, only one side of the argument has come down to us. It is true that in the two trials with which this volume is concerned both sides can be heard, but often only to increase the general uncertainty; the two versions of some episodes in the not too distant past are so discordant that one or other speaker must be trying to escape with untruths which, though he presumably thought them plausible, should, one feels, have been too much for the gullibility of any audience. It is not always easy to tell which of the two is the culprit; moreover we are left wondering how often either speaker indulges in similar misrepresentations on occasions where the argument of the other is not available.

The absence of expert and authoritative control of the courts' proceedings no doubt made misrepresentation of the past easier, but the degree of credulity at times assumed by speakers is surprising in a comparatively small community which was so politically conscious and enjoyed such extensive participation in public affairs; the more so as it evidently kept remarkably detailed records of public business, such as resolutions of the Council or decrees of the People. These records indeed are frequently cited by our speakers and might be expected to have provided the solid foundations for their arguments. But, since the documents were not shown to the jurymen and only selected extracts were read out, the true sense of the evidence could well be twisted, as Aeschines seems to do in *Treaty*, 62 (p. 156), where he says that the allies' decree required the Athenians to wait for the other Greek ambassadors, whereas he has quoted the decree, as well as having had it read out, in c. 60 (p. 156) to the effect that the Athenians should wait for the return of *their own* ambassadors from the other Greek states;[4] and, as the trial was usually continuous and completed on one day, there was little time for an opponent to refute from the documents a false argument which had previously been unknown to him. More important for our purposes, the documentary evidence has not been preserved with the speeches. Extracts from alleged documents are included in the manuscripts of Demosthenes, *Crown*, but these have been shown to be spurious, perhaps the work of some reader of the speech who had indirect knowledge of genuine documents of the period (though not the ones which Demosthenes in fact adduced).[5] They were discredited first on internal grounds, because they do not fit the contexts in which they appear (the discrepancies not being the sort likely to be produced by adroit misrepresentation) and are in some cases stylistically inappropriate; and then by a demonstration that letters in the margins of one manuscript of the speech mark what in an earlier version were a hundred lines of text, a method of enumeration which, calculations suggest, antedated the inclusion of the documents.[6]

4. See also Demosthenes' remarks about Aeschines' selective quotation of laws in *Crown*, 121 (p. 286).

5. See the introduction of the G. A. and W. H. Simcox edition of the *Crown* speeches, pp. xciv–cxi.

6. See 'Stichometry in the Manuscripts of Demosthenes', Appendix VIII in W. W. Goodwin's edition, pp. 350–55.

Leaving aside this apparent readiness of orators to mislead and of their listeners to be misled, the historian is also faced with some uncertainty about how much of the preserved version of the speech is what the listeners actually heard. There is no doubt that some alterations were made before publication. There are, for example, two passages in Aeschines, *Treaty*,[7] where he refers to statements which he says have been made by Demosthenes in his speech, but which do not occur in our version of it. The most likely explanation (but not the only one possible) is that Demosthenes omitted them when he subsequently edited his speech. By contrast, it seems very probable that Aeschines inserted into the published version of his *Crown* speech, at chapters 37–9 (pp. 202–3ff.), an attempt to answer Demosthenes' contemptuous dismissal (*Crown*, 121, p. 286) of his detailed argument based on a law regulating the proclamation of citizens as worthy of a crown.[8] Again, Demosthenes at *Treaty*, 196–8 (p. 104), has probably retained in the published version the full text of a story about his opponent, which according to Aeschines, *Treaty*, 153 (p. 181), the jury refused to allow him to complete. Moreover, in addition to these particular suggestions of later revision, there is the consideration that both of Demosthenes' speeches here seem to be rather longer than the normal time allowance would have permitted.[9] But, granted that the orators' purpose in publishing their speeches was primarily political – to reiterate their cases before the educated public, it is arguable that such a published version needed to be more accurate than the spoken, for its statements were open to more prolonged and careful scrutiny.

In the sections which follow an attempt is made to trace the history of the Athenians' involvement with Macedon from the beginning of Philip II's rule. Those who wish to proceed at once to the immediate background to the *Treaty* speeches should turn to section 5, The Peace of Philocrates (p. 25).

7. Chapters 10 (p. 145) and 124 (p. 172).
8. See Goodwin's 'Remarks on the Argument of cc.120, 121' in his Appendix I, pp. 313–16.
9. The point is made by G. Mathieu in his introductions to the speeches in the Budé editions (Démosthène, *Plaidoyers politiques*, vols. 3 and 4, Paris, 1956 and 1958).

2. *The Athenians in 360* B.C.

In 404 B.C. Athens surrendered to the Spartans, their chief enemies in a series of wars which had started in 459. The year before, they had lost their last fleet and the naval power which had been the basis of their strength and prosperity over the previous seventy-five years. Now they were compelled to dismantle the most essential of their fortifications and to become subject-allies of the victors, renouncing at once their democratic institutions in favour of a narrow and tyrannical oligarchy, the Thirty Tyrants, whose power was bolstered by a Spartan garrison.

In the forty-five years between then and the appearance of Philip as regent of Macedon, the Athenians had certainly made a remarkable economic and political recovery. In 403 democracy was restored and the Spartan garrison removed. The Corinthian War (395–387) broke the Spartan naval empire which had replaced the Athenian and enabled the Athenians to regain full independence. They were able to survive another period of Spartan dominance in Greece (386–379) and in 378 began the formation of a new naval alliance, the Second Athenian Confederacy, to support Thebes against Sparta. Athenian successes at sea contributed to the decline of Spartan power; but then the Thebans defeated the Spartans at Leuctra in 371 and subsequently entered the Peloponnese, invaded Spartan territory and brought an end to Spartan rule of Messenia, which for three and a half centuries had formed the economic basis of Spartan power. The Athenians now changed sides and assisted the Spartans and others in frustrating Theban hopes of dominating Greece, which were finally extinguished with the death of the greatest Theban general and statesman, Epaminondas, at Mantinea in 362.

A general peace treaty followed, of the kind called Common Peace by the Greeks, based on the principle of independence for all states. This principle the Athenians had been professing to defend since the formation of the naval Confederacy, and they had actively opposed what they had presented as unjust interpretations of it put forward first by the Spartans and then by the Thebans. The conclusion of this peace treaty, then, after the failure of both

Spartans and Thebans to dominate Greece, should have given the Athenians a period of ascendancy. But they were soon to face the secession of some of their leading allies in the Confederacy and then to find themselves virtually without support in the first part of their struggle with Macedon.

This long-term failure of Athenian foreign policy is not to be explained solely by the chronic selfishness and the war-weariness of the Greek states. Militarily Athens was as exhausted as any state. The people had been beguiled by successes into overestimating the city's real strength, while overlooking the important role played by other states in its recovery; they owed much more than they admitted to the generosity of the Spartans in allowing the restoration of democracy in 403, to their Greek allies, and not least to the Persians in the victories of the Corinthian War, to the initiative of the Thebans in defying Spartan rule in 379 and to the growth of their military power in the 370s, and finally to the opposition of the Arcadians to Theban domination and to the failure of the Persians to back with arms or money their support of the Common Peace proposed by the Thebans in 367. Thus even before 362 the city was beginning to seem less capable of helping its friends and harming its enemies.

Diplomatically too, it is clear, some Athenians had not learned the lesson of the failure of their fifth-century empire, and, although moderate leaders were notably successful in restraining the new imperialists, it would not be surprising if other Greeks still remembered the old. Indeed such memories were probably stimulated by certain Athenian lines of action, which, though evidently accepted by the allies in the Confederacy in time of war with mainland enemies, could well cause greater alarm if continued after the peace treaty. Thus, persistent but fruitless attempts to capture their old colony at Amphipolis on the Strymon were probably intended at first, and accepted, as measures to counteract Theban influence in Thessaly and Macedon; but they continued after 362, and were no more successful. To the allies it was not the only evidence that Athenian policy was both ill conceived and ineffective. It was thus scarcely a good moment for the Athenian state to face a new and dangerous challenge.

3. The Accession of Philip and the
Origins of his Quarrel with the Athenians

When Philip became regent of Macedon in 359 and soon after king, there was little to suggest that the Athenians should hesitate to incur his displeasure. Macedon seemed to be backward, weak and divided. It was still ruled by kings such as self-assertive Greeks had sloughed off centuries before; the kings indeed, though they claimed descent from Greek heroes, were not normally recognized as Greek, still less their subjects. Their military power had never seemed very significant, and they had appeared on the stage of Greek international politics in minor roles which brought them scant respect. Perdiccas II had joined in the Peloponnesian War, but had changed sides with bewildering frequency and little effect. Amyntas III had encouraged the Spartan expedition against Olynthus in 382, but later became an ally of Athens. Since his death in 369 there had been a series of kings, who had been the objects of the competing interests of the Athenians and the Thebans. The last of them, Perdiccas III, had made an alliance with Athens and then abandoned it, before perishing in a catastrophic defeat at the hands of the Illyrians, who with the Paeonians were Macedon's perennially hostile northern neighbours. His infant son, Philip's nephew and ward, was challenged by no fewer than five pretenders. One of these, Argaeus, had the support of the Athenians; to them it must have seemed to be still the same old game, still played for relatively insignificant stakes; some not too reliable help against Amphipolis if they backed a winner, little to lose and another chance no doubt in the near future if they did not.

Philip, however, was exceptional. In 359 he bought off his barbarian enemies and defeated Argaeus, the challenge of the other pretenders evaporating; in 358 he turned on the Illyrians and the Paeonians and soundly defeated them; in 357 he besieged and captured Amphipolis and took by treachery Pydna, a city of the Athenian Confederacy on the Macedonian coast. From Amphipolis he was able to extend his power eastwards and win control of the important gold and silver mines on Mount Pangaeus, from which he is said before long to have obtained 1,000 talents per year (as much as the annual revenue of imperial Athens at the outbreak of the Peloponnesian War); with this new wealth he was able to back with generous bribery his diplomatic skill and to pay his army. By now or soon after he carried out a reorganization of the Macedonian army which both helped to unify a hitherto disjointed nation and provided him with the means of establishing a permanent superiority over his northern neighbours and in time of dominating Greece; by the time he had to fight a serious land war in Greece he had a cavalry force larger and more efficient than that of all the Greek city-states south of Thermopylae together, and also a body of well-trained heavy infantry, the famous Macedonian phalanx, which was the best of its kind in the peninsula.

The Athenians, of course, could not appreciate these developments for some years. In the winter of 359–358 they had made peace with Philip after he had released without ransom the Greek mercenaries captured with Argaeus, and they could well have been already thinking of using his help against Amphipolis, when Philip began to move against that city in 357. At all events they rejected a plea for help from some Amphipolitan envoys and overtures for an alliance from the Chalcidians, who were alarmed by Philip's activity, and accepted his promise that he would give them the city when he took it, apparently agreeing in return to hand over Pydna (despite its status as a free ally in their Confederacy).[10] The makers of this ignoble bargain underestimated both Philip's ambition and his power, for it rested on the suppositions that he would be happy to see Athenian power established on the Strymon, that having taken Amphipolis he could not take Pydna too, and that the Athenians did not need allies in Chalcidice.

Philip probably felt that the failure of the Athenians to help him take Pydna freed him of his obligation to hand over Amphipolis, but the Athenian people, who were in general ignorant of their leaders' side of the bargain and whose desire to recover their

10. For Amphipolitan envoys see Demosthenes, *Olynthiac* I, 8 (*Greek Political Oratory*, p. 200); for the Chalcidians (Olynthians) and for Philip's promise see *Olynthiac* II, 6 (ibid., p. 206); for the Athenians' undertaking see Theopompus, Frag. 30 (F. Jacoby, *Fragmente des griechischen Historiker*), who says that it was given by the Council of 500 without the knowledge of the Assembly. For a sceptical view of the episode see G. E. M. de Ste Croix, *Classical Quarterly*, N.S. XIII (1963), pp. 110–19.

former colony has been rightly judged an obsession,[11] no doubt regarded his retention of it as a betrayal. But the sources do not clearly reveal what action they took; at this time Aeschines and Demosthenes were barely starting their political careers, and the beginnings of the struggle with Philip are not discussed in the speeches contained in this volume. The fact that Aeschines twice refers to the first part of the struggle with Philip (down to the peace of 346 B.C.) as the war over Amphipolis[12] suggests that the Athenians now declared war, but it is possible that they did so only after Philip's attack in 356 on Potidaea, where they had a garrison and which they tried too late to succour, or even that no formal declaration was ever made. If they did commit themselves to war on the evidence of Philip's retention of both Amphipolis and Pydna, the decision was certainly a bold one, coming at a time when, although recently successful in detaching the Euboean cities from Thebes, they were at least threatened with, if not actually involved in, serious trouble with some of their maritime allies; for the secession of Chios, Cos and Rhodes from the Confederacy, which led to the so-called Social War, took place in 357. Yet it would be too simple to say that the war was only about Amphipolis and Pydna (and perhaps Potidaea) and therefore avoidable; it does not now seem likely that a pacific Athens would have curbed Philip's ambitions to eliminate Greek influence in the environs of Macedonia and it is quite possible that some Athenians then already saw him as a serious danger, even if most still regarded him as a nine-day wonder.

4. The First War between Athens and Philip

The resistance of the Athenians to Philip's expansion was severely handicapped by their involvement in the Social War. In the first place the secession of three important islands from the Confederacy, although encouraged and assisted by the Persian vassal king Mausolus of Caria, was surely due to significant grievances and could not but seem an important failure and a serious condem-

11. By G. L. Cawkwell, *Journal of Hellenic Studies*, LXXXIII (1963), p. 51.

12. *Treaty*, 70 (p. 158), *Crown*, 54 (p. 207). It is possible that Aeschines is not simply descriptive here, but is obliquely condemning the war as one begun for a triviality.

nation of Athenian policies in the Confederacy. In the second the Athenians' unsuccessful attempts to coerce the rebels not only diverted their attentions from Macedon, but left them even more severely weakened than before; for, although they made prodigious efforts by sea and did stop the spread of the secessionist movement,[13] they were so impoverished that they had to hire their army out to a rebel Persian satrap and, when the Persian king threatened war, were compelled to make peace with the rebellious allies and recognize their independence.

While the war was in progress, the Athenians had tried belatedly to help Potidaea against Philip (356), but had taken no other military action against him. They had, however, joined an alliance with the Paeonians and the Illyrians and with Cetriporis, king of western Thrace, whose territories Philip was threatening.[14] But they could do nothing to help these new allies. By summer 355 Philip had defeated Cetriporis and was threatening Neapolis, a member of the Confederacy on the Aegean coast about thirty miles beyond the Strymon. The end of the Social War did not bring a great increase of Athenian effort. When Philip besieged Methone, the last Athenian position on the Macedonian coast, in winter 355–354, no relief arrived until too late and a squadron stationed at Neapolis could not save Abdera and Maroneia, two members of the Confederacy along the coast to the east.

The failure in the Social War seems indeed to have led to a reappraisal of Athenian foreign policy. Isocrates, who earlier in his *Panegyricus* (380) had advocated a panhellenic war against Persia under the joint leadership of Athens and Sparta and in his *Plataicus* (373) had urged the Athenians to exert their authority as leaders of the Confederacy by forcing the Thebans to respect Plataea, now published his pamphlet *On Peace*, recommending the maintenance of peace with Persia and the dissolution of the remains of the Confederacy; Athens's aims abroad were to be pursued by diplomacy, not with arms. This suggestion was not likely to commend itself to the Athenian people, who at about this time

---

13. Aeschines' account of seventy-five allied cities lost (*Treaty*, 70, p. 158) is gross exaggeration.

14. An inscription, M. N. Tod, *Greek Historical Inscriptions*, vol. II (Oxford, 1948), no. 157, records the decree proposing this alliance.

were being restrained from provoking a war with Persia by, among others, Demosthenes in his first public speech, *On the Symmories* (*Oratio* XIV). But the men who seem to have won control of Athenian policies at this time – Eubulus and others, with whom Aeschines was to be closely associated – did embark on a programme of financial retrenchment and of avoiding unnecessary foreign adventures. The Theoric Fund, which was to figure prominently in Athenian politics, was probably set up by them and intended not primarily as a means of distributing the state's money to the poor but as a way of preventing its use on dubious enterprises foisted on the assembly by irresponsible demagogues.[15] In foreign affairs pleas for help from Megalopolis (353), which was threatened by Sparta, and from Rhodians exiled by the oligarchy installed by Mausolus of Caria (351) were rejected, although Demosthenes, apparently unconcerned with the threat of Philip, strongly supported them, with speeches which survive.[16] The Athenian leaders also seem to have avoided any direct involvement in another Greek inter-state conflict, the so-called Third Sacred War, which had broken out in 356. The previous year the Thebans had tried to use against the Phocians, their subject-allies since 370, the machinery of the Amphictyonic League, the religious association, chiefly of central Greek states, connected with the shrine at Delphi. The Phocians under Philomelus had defied the Amphictyonic decree, seized Delphi itself and defeated the Thebans, who in 356 persuaded the Amphictyonic Council to declare a Sacred War against them. Philomelus's reply was to seize the temple treasures of Delphi and to raise over 10,000 mercenaries, with which he defeated not only the Thebans again, but also their Locrian and Thessalian allies. Thus the Thebans were being distracted and weakened at the time when they too might have been looking with concern at Macedon, which they had tried to keep under their influence in the 360s (Philip indeed had been their hostage), and were in time driven into a position where they saw Philip as their saviour. The Athenians, who had striven to reduce

15. For the Theoric Fund and for Eubulus' policies and achievements in general, see G. L. Cawkwell, *Journal of Hellenic Studies*, LXXXIII (1963), pp. 47–67.

16. Orations XVI (Megalopolis) and XV (Rhodes); see *Greek Political Oratory*, pp. 173–87.

Theban power since the battle of Leuctra in 371, had made an alliance with the Phocians in winter 357–356, but such was the elasticity of Greek international relations that this alliance, if not activated, need not lead to war with the Thebans; Eubulus and his friends prudently remained inactive.

They were not, however, unaware of the threat from Philip. Inscriptions attest an impressive programme of ship-building, while in 352 two expeditions were sent to oppose the Macedonian advance at places where it seemed to be threatening Athens's vital interests. In 354, Philip had marched south at the request of the Thessalian League to attack Pherae in southern Thessaly; he had besieged and captured Pagasae, the port of Pherae, an Athenian squadron arriving too late to save it, but had then been defeated by the Phocians, enemies of the Thessalian League in the Sacred War. In 352 Philip returned, defeated the Phocians, took Pherae, and gained control of all Thessaly; the Athenians were again too late to help Pherae, but they did send a force of 400 cavalry and 5,000 citizen infantry to hold the Pass of Thermopylae and stop any further Macedonian pursuit of the Phocians, which would bring this hostile army dangerously near the borders of Attica. The decree celebrating the success of this expedition was proposed by Diophantus, very probably a close associate of Eubulus.[17] A few months later Philip, after making an alliance with Athens's enemy Cardia in the Chersonese (the Gallipoli peninsula), was besieging Heraion Teichos on the Propontis (Sea of Marmora) uncomfortably close to Athens's corn-supply route from the Black Sea. Again the Athenians decided to send a substantial expedition, but Philip fell ill and abandoned the siege, and the expedition was no longer necessary.

Thus Philip's threats in these two sensitive areas receded, but there was some justification in Demosthenes' criticism in the *First Philippic*, delivered in 351, that the Athenians had surrendered the initiative to Philip and merely reacted, often too late, to his moves, relapsing thereafter into inactivity.[18] It is another matter whether

17. See Demosthenes, *Treaty*, 86 (p. 77).

18. Oration IV; see *Greek Political Oratory*, pp. 188–98. Demosthenes cites Potidaea, Methone and Pagasae as places which the Athenians were too late to save (c.35, p. 195).

his remedy, the maintenance of land and sea forces constantly available to be rushed to places threatened and to harass the Macedonian coast, was financially practicable, despite his assertions and detailed exposition of the costs involved. It depended too on the readiness of Athenian citizens to serve and this was at least doubtful; at all events his proposals were not accepted.

Philip's decision in 349 to end his policy of alliance and friendship with Olynthus and the Chalcidian League, to whom he had given Potidaea in 356, created a new situation. Here was a chance to acquire Greek allies on the borders of Macedon, if only the Athenian people were willing to let bygones be bygones, to accept the Olynthian request for help and to send it promptly. Demosthenes in his three *Olynthiac* speeches[19] argued strongly the case for sending help and urged that it be swift and powerful. In the event the Athenians did send three expeditions, but the first two were very largely drawn from the existing mercenary squadron maintained in the north Aegean, while the third, which did include citizen hoplites and cavalry, was too late to save Olynthus in late summer 348; moreover in early 348 the Athenians sent an army to Euboea, against Demosthenes' advice,[20] and soon after three of their leading generals, and presumably a fleet, were engaged in some unknown activity in north-western Asia Minor. Criticisms of the Athenians for lack of urgency here should perhaps be tempered by the obvious importance of Euboea and by the possibility that the Athenian leaders (still, clearly, Eubulus and his group) thought it risky to commit citizen troops on the distant territory of a recently hostile state, which perhaps seemed in no immediate danger of defeat; there is indeed evidence that Philip's final thrust at Olynthus succeeded with surprising speed, being accelerated by treachery there and elsewhere.[21]

The fall of Olynthus was followed by its destruction and the enslavement of its people and by the virtual incorporation of Chalcidice into the Macedonian realm. Eubulus and his friends

19. Orations I–III; see *Greek Political Oratory*, pp. 199–220.

20. See Demosthenes, *On the Peace*, 5 (*Greek Political Oratory*, p. 223). This was the campaign in which Aeschines distinguished himself – see his *Treaty*, 169 (pp. 184–5), and *Crown*, 86–8 (p. 216).

21. See G. L. Cawkwell in *Classical Quarterly*, N.S. XII (1962), pp. 122–40.

evidently felt that this was an opportunity to convince other Greeks of the common danger from Philip; Eubulus proposed an attempt to win allies in the Peloponnese, Aeschines supported him in the assembly and served on a delegation to the Arcadians at Megalopolis.[22] There Philip's agents were already at work and the Arcadians, whose plea for an alliance with Athens had been rejected five years earlier despite Demosthenes' advocacy, were unmoved; no new allies were forthcoming. This diplomatic isolation together with their military impotence put the Athenian people and their leaders in a receptive mood, when Philip in winter 348–347 began to talk peace.

5. The Peace of Philocrates

If it is not surprising that the Athenians should have responded to peace overtures at this stage, it is harder to explain why Philip began to make them. It may be that his ambitions for power in Greece were limited and that he would still have preferred Athens's alliance to her hostility. Certainly he did insist that the peace treaty be supplemented by an alliance. But on the other hand there is no evidence that he had made any earlier attempt to end hostilities since the Amphipolis affair in 357, and his attitude during the negotiations did little to counteract the impression which must have been created by his treatment of Olynthus. In particular he showed himself unwilling to compromise over two areas, Thrace and central Greece, where he had not yet achieved his immediate objectives and where his chief enemies, in Thrace the prince Cersobleptes and in central Greece the Phocians, were allies of Athens. No peace could be acceptable to Philip which afforded them the protection which the Athenians wanted them to have and which they had in fact given the Phocians by blocking Thermopylae in 352.

What in the end happened was that a peace was concluded which did give Philip a free hand in these areas, though public opinion at Athens was somehow beguiled into believing that the Phocians in particular would be preserved. Within a few weeks, Philip had

22. Demosthenes, *Treaty*, 10–11 (p. 59) and 303–6 (p. 130) and Aeschines, *Treaty*, 79 (p. 161).

not only completed the subjugation of the part of Thrace ruled by Cersobleptes, but also penetrated Thermopylae and reduced the Phocians to surrender. The illusions of the Athenian public were thus rudely shattered and thereafter the politicians tried hard to deny responsibility for the peace and its consequences and to fix it on their rivals.

Demosthenes and Aeschines were both fully involved in the negotiations and the debates, but Aeschines had been so wildly wrong in his predictions of Philip's subsequent actions that Demosthenes was able to carry the attack to him in the form of an accusation of treachery. So Demosthenes in his *Treaty* speech, which he delivered when this accusation was tried in 343, has most to say about the events immediately following the conclusion of the peace; but he also made brief references to Aeschines' part in the negotiations and the debates (cc. 12–16, pp. 59 ff.). Aeschines in his defence made a lengthy counter-attack on Demosthenes' part in these negotiations and debates (*Treaty*, 14–68, pp. 146 ff.); thirteen years later in the *Crown* case he repeated and in some ways elaborated these criticisms (cc. 58–72, pp. 208 ff.), provoking only a short reply from Demosthenes (*Crown*, 17–24, pp. 264 ff.). Our record of what happened is indeed a tangled one; but an attempt must be made to unravel it.

The first positive reaction of the Athenians to Philip's peace-feelers was the unanimous approval by the assembly of a proposal of Philocrates that Philip be invited to send a delegation to Athens. This was probably early as the winter of 348–347, but Philo-crates was charged with having made an illegal proposal and the assembly's decree had to be suspended pending trial of the charge. When the trial took place, Philocrates was overwhelmingly acquitted, but no action seems to have been taken at once on his original motion. It may not, however, have been long before Aristodemus the actor, who had been sent to Philip to ransom some Athenian citizens captured at Olynthus, returned with more messages of peace and goodwill from him (some time after mid-summer 347, when Demosthenes began a year's service on the Council). Aristodemus's report was well received, and Philo-crates now proposed that a delegation of ten be sent to Philip to discuss peace; Philocrates himself as well as both Aeschines and Demosthenes were appointed to serve on it. Aeschines, who recounts these events in *Treaty*, 13–19 (pp. 145 ff.), and *Crown*, 62–3 (pp. 209 ff.), says that it was Demosthenes who defended Philocrates and moved that a crown be conferred on Aristodemus on his return from Macedonia. There seems no reason to doubt him, and it would not be surprising if Demosthenes, whose faith in his countrymen's war effort was obviously shaky, had decided that peace was needed and better soon than later. Demosthenes says (*Crown*, 21, p. 265) that Aeschines and Eubulus also backed Philocrates' proposal, and it seems likely that it enjoyed general support.[22a] Indeed, the arguments for peace were growing stronger, for, although Philip had done nothing very spectacular in 347, he had sent some troops to fight the Phocians, and then in early 346 the chances of keeping him out of central Greece were further diminished. The Phocian authorities had agreed to hand over to the Athenians certain positions around Thermopylae, and Proxenus was sent with a force to occupy them, but the commander on the spot refused to comply.[23] This rebuff was probably known at Athens before the delegation left for Macedonia in February 346.[24]

The object of this first delegation was to explore Philip's intentions and, if they seemed friendly, to arrange for him to send ambassadors of his own to Athens with full powers to negotiate. Demosthenes later explicitly excluded Aeschines' conduct on this delegation from his accusations (*Treaty*, 93, p. 80), but Aeschines still spoke at length about it, not only ridiculing Demosthenes' speech before Philip, but giving a long account of his own (*Treaty*, 22–43, pp. 147 ff.); he told how he was (quite reasonably) criticized by Demosthenes for bringing up such matters as the return of Amphipolis, which, though still yearned for by the Athenian public, was hardly a subject of negotiation acceptable to Philip; but Philip took no offence and praised him for his speech, so that Demosthenes had later to eat humble pie. At all events, the

22a. Aeschines indeed says (*Treaty*, 13, p. 145) that it was passed *nem con.*
23. Aeschines, *Treaty*, 132–4 (p. 174).
24. See G. L. Cawkwell, *Revue des études grecques*, LXIII (1960), pp. 427–33.

delegation returned home (on about 28 March) with a favourable report, bringing a letter from Philip and the news that he was preparing to send ambassadors to negotiate.

The situation at Athens was now complicated by the fact that other diplomatic delegations were out in Greece in a further attempt to persuade the the neutral cities to join in the war or at least to take part in any peace treaty that might be made. It is Aeschines who at *Treaty*, 57 (p. 155), tells us about these delegations, but Demosthenes' denial in *Crown*, 23 (p. 266), that any such had been sent hardly tallies with his original statement in *Treaty*, 16 (p. 60), that ambassadors from the Greek states, whom the Athenians had sent for, were present during the subsequent debate in the assembly about the peace.

An important aspect of Aeschines' counter-attack on Demosthenes in 343 was his accusation that his opponent had frustrated the purposes of these diplomatic missions to Greece by bringing on the debate in the assembly on the peace terms, before the other Greeks could be involved (*Treaty*, 57–62, pp. 155 ff.). Aeschines supports his argument by citing a decree of the council of the allies in the naval confederacy which recommended the Athenians to wait for the return of the envoys from the Greek states before debating peace terms and a decree proposed by Demosthenes fixing definite and early dates for the debate (15 and 16 April). Although these decrees, which were read out in court, are not extant and there is some suggestion of verbal sleight-of-hand in the detail of Aeschines' reasoning, his argument, which he repeated in *Crown*, 64–8 (pp. 209 ff.), is more convincing than Demosthenes' blank denial in 330 (*Crown*, 23, p. 266) that any Athenian envoys had been sent out. Demosthenes follows this denial by remarking that the other Greek states had long before been proved useless, a remark which shows why at this stage in 346 he still believed in the advantages of as early a peace as possible. The Greek states were no more likely, he thought, to join in the war against Philip now than they had been in 348–347; and, if some of them were prepared to subscribe to a Common Peace treaty, which was apparently the aim of the naval allies and probably of Eubulus and Aeschines,[25] it was doubtful in view of their lukewarm attitude whether this was a

25. See G. L. Cawkwell, *Revue des études grecques*, LXIII (1960), p. 435.

better sort of treaty for Athens than a bilateral treaty with Philip. Moreover, Demosthenes may already have calculated – what Philip's subsequent diplomacy and actions make clear – that he for his part would not accept the sort of general restriction on his expansionist activity which a Common Peace treaty would impose.

The Athenian people supported Demosthenes in this argument, and the debate on the terms duly opened on 15 April. The two orators present a very confusing picture of what happened in it. Prosecuting in 343, Demosthenes concentrated on what he presented as a sudden change of front by Aeschines between the proceedings of the 15th and those of the 16th, so sudden indeed that bribery was the only explanation. On the first day, he says, Aeschines was all against the peace terms proposed by Philocrates as being dishonourable for Athens, but in favour of *a* peace, whereas on the second he urged the people to forget their glorious past and to abandon allies who had not done the city any good (*Treaty*, 13–16, p. 60).

Aeschines' first reply to this charge (*Treaty*, 65–6, p. 157) is that it is impossible, for Demosthenes' own decree (which he has already had read and now adduces again) laid down that there was to be discussion only on the first day allocated for the debate and only voting on the second; Demosthenes has therefore made two speeches out of one. Aeschines later admits that he expressed the opinions ascribed by Demosthenes to his second speech and defends them on the grounds that he spoke at a time when other speakers were invoking past history and ignoring present safety; what he had urged the people to do was not to forget past glories, but to remember past failures too and their causes and to apply their lessons to the present (*Treaty*, 74–7, p. 160). Aeschines also produced a witness who testified that he had been shown by Demosthenes a draft decree, which he was prepared to propose, embodying the same terms as those moved by Philocrates (*Treaty*, 64 and 67–8, p. 158).

When Aeschines took up the question of this debate in 330, he introduced a new element into his argument. He asserts that before the debate a resolution of the Council of the naval confederacy was presented, which he first summarizes and then causes to be read out in full as evidence (*Crown*, 69–70, p. 211). This resolution is clearly not the same as that which Aeschines had already adduced in his argument about the timing of the debate, but shows the allies altering their position in recognition of the fact that the Athenians had decided not to wait for any move from the other Greeks, as the allies had recommended, but to negotiate and debate peace terms as soon as possible; they now propose that any Greek state that wished should be permitted within three months to have its name included in any treaty negotiated.

Aeschines claims that on the first day of the debate he himself supported this resolution, as did all the other speakers, and that at the end of the day the general impression was that peace would be made in accordance with it; but on the next day, he asserts, Demosthenes prevented further discussion and, after producing one of Philip's delegates, Antipater, as witness (duly primed by himself) – probably to testify that Philip would not accept the terms discussed the previous day – enabled Philocrates to propose the acceptance of the terms which were in the event agreed between Athens and Philip (*Crown*, 71–2, pp. 211 ff.). Demosthenes in his defence makes no specific reply to these charges and indeed goes straight on from arguing about whether the Greek states had or had not been invited to the peace conference to discuss the affair of the second delegation sent to obtain Philip's ratification of the terms (*Crown*, 25, p. 266), and, despite Aeschines' failure to mention it in 343, the existence of this resolution of the allies should not be doubted. Indeed it explains Demosthenes' references in *Treaty*, 15 and 144 (pp. 60 and 90), to the resolution of the allies, which he claims to have supported.

It is clear, however, that the resolution of the allies was not the only proposal before the people when the debate began. Demosthenes in his speech in 343 (*Treaty*, 14, p. 60) quotes the opinion which Aeschines expressed on the first day of the debate about Philocrates' proposal, and it must be assumed that Philocrates had put down a motion containing terms for the peace. It is well known that Philocrates proposed the final decree embodying the terms of the peace as concluded (hence the title, Peace of Philocrates); both Aeschines (*Crown*, 54, p. 207) and Demosthenes

(*Treaty*, 291–2, p. 127) are agreed on this point. But it is evident that this proposal which was accepted was not the same as Philocrates' original proposal; for that, Demosthenes says (*Treaty*, 159, p. 94), contained a clause which explicitly excluded both the Phocians and the city of Halus, a state which, like the Phocians, had some claim to be regarded as an ally of Athens but was not a member of the Athenian naval confederacy; whereas the terms finally agreed made no mention of the Phocians and Halus (Demosthenes, *Treaty*, 159 and 321–2, pp. 159 and 134–5 ff.), leaving the allies of the Athenians undefined.

At first, it seems, opinion ran strongly against Philocrates and in favour of the alternative proposal of the allies. Aeschines' claim to have spoken in support of the allies (*Crown*, 71, p. 211) is confirmed by Demosthenes' account of him attacking Philocrates (*Treaty*, 14, p. 60); and Demosthenes' similar claim (*Treaty*, 15 and 144, pp. 60 and 90) is supported by Aeschines' statement that all the speakers on the first day agreed with his own view. Perhaps this opposition goaded Philocrates into saying that only his terms were acceptable to Philip. At any rate the feeling against his proposal became, under the influence of the popular speakers, a feeling against any kind of peace and in favour of continuing war; and Aeschines was forced to speak again, not now against Philocrates' proposal of what seemed dishonourable terms, but against the extremists on the other side who wanted war. This was the speech which Demosthenes criticized in *Treaty*, 15–16 (p. 60), for its inconsistency with Aeschines' previous utterances, and which Aeschines defended in his *Treaty*, 74–7 (pp. 159 ff.), his explanation of it showing that he was arguing for peace against war rather than for one set of peace terms against another.

Exactly when Aeschines delivered this second speech is not clear. Demosthenes says that it was at the second meeting on the second day; and, despite Aeschines' assertion (*Treaty*, 65, p. 157) that there were no speeches on the second day, because the original decree had provided for voting only, it is eminently possible that the prescribed procedure was abandoned and that the debate continued.

Demosthenes says that he himself was still at this stage of the debate supporting the proposal of the allies (*Treaty*, 15, p. 60);

but, if so, he very quickly changed his mind, presumably because he became aware that Philip would not accept anything like the allies' proposal and wanted a free hand over Halus and the Phocians (an aim which he had evidently concealed from the delegation that visited him in Macedon a few weeks earlier). On this assumption Aeschines' story, in *Treaty*, 67-8 (p. 158), and *Crown*, 71-2 (p. 211), of Demosthenes' subsequent conduct makes sense: when Philocrates' original motion to exclude Halus and the Phocians was put to the vote and defeated, Demosthenes was ready to put forward in its place an amended version still very different from the allies' proposal; Philocrates in fact produced a similar amendment himself, but Demosthenes hastened its acceptance by bringing in Antipater as witness to Philip's views. On the other hand, there does not seem any reason to reject Demosthenes' assertions that both Aeschines and Eubulus also supported the amended proposal, Eubulus arguing that the only alternative was a strenuous war-effort (*Treaty*, 150, p. 92; 178, p. 99; 291, p. 127); or his claim that other speakers (he says Aeschines and his friends) were working to overcome public anxiety over Halus and the Phocians, though with less strikingly direct methods than he, by suggesting that Philip was unwilling to include the Phocians in the peace only because he did not wish to offend his Theban and Thessalian allies, but would meet Athenian wishes once the peace had been secured (*Treaty*, 321-2, p. 134). It is clear enough that, when peace was agreed, public opinion at Athens was satisfied that the Phocians were protected; and more than likely that, while some politicians, including probably Aeschines, shared this belief, others, such as Demosthenes, had no illusions about Philip's real intentions.

A few days after the debate in the Athenian assembly the same ten men who had formed the first delegation to Macedon were appointed to go again in order to receive the oaths of Philip and his allies ratifying the agreement. The Athenians and their allies gave their oaths at Athens to the Macedonian envoys. For this purpose the allies of Athens were limited to the members of the naval confederacy, but not without some argument, for, although no attempt seems to have been made to include the Phocians, Critobulus, a representative of the Thracian prince Cersobleptes,

demanded his inclusion and found some popular support. Cersobleptes had been an ally of Athens but had never joined the
confederacy. Each orator accused the other of being instrumental
in debarring Critobulus, and it is likely that the two cooperated.
Demosthenes' position was evidently based on the realistic assessment that Philip would not countenance Cersobleptes' inclusion;
his promise not to invade the Chersonese during the negotiations
implying an assumption of a free hand elsewhere in the area;[26] and
in Aeschines' eyes Philip's supposed goodwill in the matter of the
Phocians had to be fostered.

The events of the second delegation, however, led to a funda-
mental divergence of view and action between the two orators,
which became clear on their return to Athens and, as has been
said, formed the basis of Demosthenes' subsequent prosecution
of Aeschines. Here, the picture of what happened is clearer,
because Demosthenes' account of the delegation's conduct in
Treaty, 150–73 (pp. 92 ff.), and of the immediate consequences
in *Treaty*, 17–66 (pp. 60 ff.), is not seriously challenged by
Aeschines.[27]

Demosthenes wanted the delegation to sail at once to Thrace
where Philip was known to be and obtain his oath. His purpose,
he says, was to put Philip to the test as soon as possible, so that, if
after ratifying the terms he continued his advance in Thrace, the
people at Athens might become less trusting and take precautions
against an attack on the Phocians through Thermopylae (*Treaty*,
152, p. 92). This purpose certainly accords with what has been
conjectured above about Demosthenes' view of the situation. The
other delegates, Demosthenes adds, refused to agree, and he had to
obtain an order from the Council on 29 April to make them set
sail. After that they lingered in Euboea and made a slow land
journey through Thessaly, arriving at Pella, the Macedonian
capital, twenty-three days after leaving home, but even so had to
wait twenty-seven days for Philip. Aeschines' reply is that the

26. Aeschines tells in *Treaty*, 81–6 (pp. 162 ff.) of Demosthenes' actions and
arguments here and says that Demosthenes accused him of debarring Critobulus, although there is nothing to that effect in Demosthenes' speech.

27. Demosthenes narrates these events more briefly in *Crown*, 25–7 (pp.
266 ff.) and 30–36 (pp. 267 ff.).

delegation would have been too late to do any good in Thrace, because Cersobleptes had been finally defeated on 21 April; but he is significantly silent about the date on which this news reached Athens and how far it could have influenced the delegation's plans (*Treaty*, 89–92, p. 164).

Demosthenes makes other criticisms of the delegation's lack of enterprise in obtaining the oaths of Philip's allies and of the way its members spent their time in Macedon, but says nothing on the matter singled out by Aeschines for detailed treatment in his reply, the formal meeting of the delegates with Philip (*Treaty*, 102–18, pp. 82 ff.). Aeschines criticizes Demosthenes' part in it, on the grounds that he flattered Philip and dwelt on his own support for Philocrates and the peace; and represents himself as telling Philip to respect the traditions of the Delphian Amphictyony, punishing only individual Phocians for their sacrilege rather than indulging the Thebans' desire for mass vengeance. Demosthenes, it seems, was trying to win Philip's ear and to make him give his own oath and make his allies give theirs with the same urgency shown by the Athenians in the peace negotiations. Aeschines' continued delusions about Philip's real aims no doubt encouraged the king to dissimulate further and to make it easier for the credulous to avoid recognizing the truth. The delegates made no objection when Philip formally excluded the Phocians from his oath,[28] and it could well have been their complacency rather than Philip's money[29] which caused them to linger again, so that by the time they returned to Athens on 7 July Philip and his army were at Thermopylae.[30]

Back at Athens, Aeschines and his friends were eloquent with optimistic accounts of the benefits Philip would confer on the city. Demosthenes tried to counter them and succeeded in convincing the Council of the real dangers of the situation,[31] but on 10 July the Assembly would not hear him and not only believed everything Aeschines told them but accepted with enthusiasm a letter from Philip which made no mention of the Phocians, the recent object

28. Demosthenes, *Treaty*, 44 (p. 67).
29. Alleged by Demosthenes, *Crown*, 32 (p. 268).
30. Demosthenes, *Treaty*, 58 (p. 71).
31. Demosthenes, *Treaty*, 18 (p. 61) and 31–2 (p. 64).

of their concern.[32] Demosthenes thus failed to persuade the Athenians to grasp what he later maintained (*Treaty*, 123, p. 86) was a last chance to secure Thermopylae against Philip, but he had said enough to ensure that, when the public realized the truth, his own position would be above criticism.[33]

The truth was not long obscured. A third delegation, on which Demosthenes refused to serve and from which Aeschines after being nominated excused himself on grounds of ill health, was appointed to meet Philip at Thermopylae and inform him of resolutions passed in his favour by the people, but its members travelled no farther than Chalcis. There they heard that the Phocians, apprised by envoys of their own of the attitude of the Athenians, had capitulated to Philip, who had affirmed his solidarity with the Thebans. The delegation decided to return home, and one of their number, Dercylus, brought the first news of the disastrous turn of events directly to a meeting of the Athenian assembly. Panic followed, and the people voted to put Attica on a war footing in anticipation of imminent invasion.[34]

The people sent out again this same delegation, Aeschines now included. Exactly what it was charged to do neither orator makes clear, but it was evidently to be on hand while Philip decided the fate of the Phocians. This decision he entrusted to the Amphictyonic Council which had originally declared the Sacred War against Phocis; and its severity, about which Demosthenes is eloquent (especially *Treaty*, 64–6, p. 72), is attested by Diodorus Siculus (16, 60).

Demosthenes (*Treaty*, 128–30, p. 87) accuses Aeschines of joining in Philip's triumphal feast, but evidently some of his colleagues disapproved of his action, as they were prepared to bear witness to it, and the delegation took no part in the deliberations of the Amphictyonic Council. The Council voted to give Philip the two seats on it previously filled by the Phocians and the

32. Demosthenes, *Treaty*, 23–4 (p. 63) and 34–41 (p. 64); see also G. L. Cawkwell, *Revue des études grecques*, LXXV (1962), pp. 453–9.

33. Demosthenes' detailed account of these proceedings gives the lie to Aeschines' attempt (*Crown*, 80–1, p. 214) to put his opponent's criticism of his fellow delegates' behaviour after the news of the Phocian surrender.

34. Demosthenes, *Treaty*, 121–7 (pp. 85 ff.) and 59–60 (p. 73); *Crown*, 36 (p. 268), confirmed by Aeschines, *Crown*, 80 (p. 214).

right of precedence in consulting the oracle at Delphi which had been granted to Athens in the previous century.[35] The Athenian people's mood is shown by their decision not to send the usual delegation to the Pythian Games, over which Philip now presided (at their regular time, September 346).[36] Indeed, it seems that, relieved of their fear of imminent invasion, they were reluctant to accede to a direct request from Philip that they should recognize his election to the Amphictyonic Council. When Aeschines supported this request, he was howled down;[37] and in a situation where probably only he could impose restraint, Demosthenes delivered his speech *On the Peace*,[38] urging the people not to provide Philip and the Amphictyons with an excuse for war. What the Athenian people actually did is not known, but at least Philip was satisfied, and when he and his army in due time returned home he was still at peace with the Athenians and nominally their ally. But the Athenians in general were thoroughly disillusioned, and it was now unlikely that they would ever accept a real reconciliation with him, even if he wanted one.

6. The Treaty Case

It cannot have been long after the debate at Athens on Philip's demand for recognition of his Amphictyonic status that the members of the second delegation to Macedon were called on to present their accounts to the Board of Auditors (the *logistai*). When they did so, Demosthenes and one of his associates, Timarchus, formally charged Aeschines with misconduct on the delegation.[39]

Aeschines was able to put off the trial by bringing a successful charge of immorality against Timarchus, who in 345 was condemned and deprived of his citizenship. Aeschines' prosecuting speech was later published and is the only one of his works which survives beside the two speeches in this volume. He says in it that

35. On the Phocians' seats see Diodorus 16, 60; on Athens's loss of precedence, Demosthenes, *Treaty*, 327 (p. 135).

36. Demosthenes, *Treaty*, 128 (p. 87).

37. Demosthenes, *Treaty*, 111–13 (p. 83).

38. Oration V; see *Greek Political Oratory*, pp. 223–7.

39. See the second hypothesis (ancient introduction) to Demosthenes, *Treaty*, s.10.

Demosthenes was writing the defence and was likely to bring up the matters over which he and Timarchus had brought their charge; but, if Demosthenes spoke, the speech has been lost and we have no means of knowing how far the jury was subjected to (and rejected) political arguments.

Demosthenes at any rate persisted with his prosecution of Aeschines, but it was not heard until late in 343. Earlier in that year two other relevant trials had taken place. First, one Antiphon was arrested on Demosthenes' orders for plotting with Philip to set fire to the Peiraeus dockyards, released on Aeschines' intervention, but rearrested on the orders of the Areopagus, condemned and executed;[40] then, Philocrates was prosecuted by Hyperides for misconduct on the delegation to Macedon, condemned, and escaped death by exile.[41] Hyperides was soon after appointed by the Areopagus to plead Athens's case before the Amphictyonic Council in a dispute over the sacred island of Delos, after Aeschines had first been nominated by the assembly, and pleaded it successfully.[42] Thus, when Aeschines' trial came up, the omens must have been unfavourable to him; but he was acquitted, though by the very narrow margin of thirty votes from a jury which probably numbered over a thousand and may have been as large as 1,501.[43]

It is certainly fair to conclude that there is no convincing evidence of Aeschines' corruption in the documents available to us, however misguided his actions and erroneous his judgements on the events of 346; and perhaps the capacity of Athenian jurors to judge a case fairly on the relevant evidence is generally underestimated. Perhaps, too, Aeschines' attacks on Demosthenes' responsibility for the Peace of Philocrates carried some weight,[44] and it may have told in Aeschines' favour that, unlike Philocrates, he could produce eminent citizens, such as Eubulus and Phocion, to support him in court.[45] We should in any case be wary of

40. Demosthenes, *Crown*, 132–3 (p. 289).
41. Aeschines, *Treaty*, 6 (p. 144), and *Crown*, 79 (p. 213).
42. Demosthenes, *Crown*, 134–5 (p. 289).
43. Pseudo-Plutarch, *Lives of the Ten Orators*, 840C.
44. See Pickard-Cambridge's introduction to his translation of Demosthenes, *Treaty* (*Demosthenes' Public Orations*, pp. 146–7).
45. Aeschines, *Treaty*, 184 (p. 188).

assuming that Demosthenes' failure to secure a verdict of guilty shows any great softening of the Athenian people's attitude to Philip. Nothing that he had done in the three years since the crushing of the Phocians seems to have had this effect.

True, he had offered to cut a canal through the Thracian Chersonese to protect Athens' sallies there from the Thracians, but he had made no concessions to Athenian demands that he surrender strongholds in Thrace taken since the Peace. Nearer home he had again interfered in the Peloponnese in support of factions opposed to Athenian interests; and in 344 Demosthenes had persuaded the people to send a delegation there, headed by himself, to counteract his influence, but it was unsuccessful. On the other hand, Philip had not used his control of Thermopylae to make direct military threats to Athens and there are several references to Macedonian diplomatic activity at Athens in the Attic year 344–343, some of it evidently aimed at improving relations between the two states.

First, the *hypothesis* or introduction to Demosthenes' *Second Philippic* connects the speech with the presence of delegations from Philip and from his Peloponnesian associates complaining about Athenian support of Sparta. Second, a part of Didymus' commentary on the *Fourth Philippic* mentions a delegation from Philip 'concerning peace' coinciding with one from Persia which unsuccessfully sought an Athenian alliance, evidently for the reconquest of Egypt. Finally, Hegesippus in his speech *On Halonnesus*[46] and Demosthenes in *Crown*, 136 (p. 289), refer to a mission sent by Philip consisting of Python of Byzantium and representatives of all his allies with an offer to amend the Peace of Philocrates.

Separate calculations of the chronological locations of these three events tend to concentrate them in late 344, and it is arguable that the three Macedonian missions are to be identified as one.[47] But even if they are not, most is known about the visit of Python and its consequences, and it is clear that the proposal which he is said to have brought and the Athenian reaction to it are the most important in the history of relations between Athens and Philip. Nothing written on the *Second Philippic* says how the debate ended

46. No. VII in the Demosthenic Corpus.
47. See Cawkwell, *Classical Quarterly* N.S. XIII (1963), esp. pp. 121–6.

to which it was a contribution, and it is impossible to evaluate the Athenians' refusal to help the Persians.

Python was a skilful orator and his proposal was attractive. Years later Demosthenes claimed (*Crown*, 136, p. 289) that Aeschines supported Python, but he himself recalled the people to their senses.[48] Certainly their answer to Philip's offer, though it kept the door open to negotiations, was not really conciliatory. Of their two suggestions, one, that the Peace of Philocrates be extended into a Common Peace to cover all Greeks, was certainly more acceptable to Philip now than similar proposals had been in 346 and he professed himself ready to accept it; but the other, that the clause in the Peace of Philocrates which gave to each side 'what they held' should be replaced by the stipulation that all should possess 'their own territory' was not likely to commend itself to Philip, as the Athenians still laid claim to Amphipolis and Potidaea and to Cardia, his ally in the Chersonese, and wanted also to discuss the question of Olynthus and the Chalcidian cities. A delegation headed by the anti-Macedonian Hegesippus, from whose speech to the people referred to above we derive our knowledge of the Athenian offer, was given an unfriendly welcome by Philip, and negotiations broke down for the moment.[49] Soon after these events further ammunition was provided for Philip's critics at Athens when he was thought to have backed an attempt by his supporters, Perillus and Ptoeodorus, to seize power in Athens's nearest neighbour, Megara; the attempt was frustrated, perhaps with Athenian help.[50]

7. The Renewal of the War and the Macedonian Victory

Despite the failure of Python's mission to produce a cooperative response from Athens, Philip left his offer to amend the peace terms on the table. They were not finally rejected until after a

48. If there was only one Macedonian mission, this speech would be the *Second Philippic* (Oration VI; see *Greek Political Oratory*, pp. 228–34).

49. Demosthenes, *Treaty*, 331 (p. 136).

50. Demosthenes, *Treaty*, 204 (p. 105), 295 (p. 128), 334 (p. 137).

debate in early 342, to which Hegesippus's *On Halonnesus* was a contribution. This speech shows that there was a good deal more to this debate than the question mentioned by Aeschines (*Crown*, 83, p. 215): whether the Athenians should accept as a gift from Philip the disputed island of Halonnesus or demand formal recognition of their right to it, as Hegesippus and, according to Aeschines, Demosthenes insisted.

Philip's actions were still giving Demosthenes and his friends justification for mistrusting him. When Hegesippus spoke, he had recently campaigned in Epirus, and the belief that he was threatening Ambracia led the people to send Demosthenes there on a diplomatic mission[51] and a force to Acarnania, its southern neighbour, though whether before or after the debate on Philip's offer is unknown. In addition there were probably increasing reports of Macedonian activity in Euboea. Such reports seem to have been already circulating at the time of Aeschines' trial,[52] and later in this year 342 the Macedonians intervened on the island to establish their supporters in power at Eretria, opposite north-east Attica, and at Oreus.[53]

Anxiety about Philip's plans seems to have spread beyond Athens. Demosthenes and others, including Hegesippus, made a tour of various Peloponnesian states; Demosthenes' claim in the *Third Philippic*, c. 72 (*Greek Political Oratory*, p. 262), that it was successful is confirmed by a list given in a scholiast's note on Aeschines, *Crown*, of allies won by Athens in 343–342 and by an inscription recording an alliance with Messene in July 342.

Demosthenes thus had further evidence to offer of Philip's threat and some successes to claim for his policy of resistance to it, when in early 341 a new letter came to Athens from Philip containing this time not an offer but a demand. Diopeithes, an Athenian general who had been sent with a body of settlers to help secure the Chersonese, had attacked both Cardia, Philip's ally there, and also Philip's conquered territory in Thrace; Philip now complained that he had transgressed the peace and demanded satisfaction. In

---

51. Mentioned in Demosthenes, *Crown*, 244 (p. 311).
52. Demosthenes, *Treaty*, 87 (p. 78), 204 (p. 105), 326 (p. 135).
53. Referred to by Demosthenes, *Crown*, 71 (p. 275).
54. Oration VIII: see *Greek Political Oratory*, pp. 235–48.

his speech *On the Chersonese*[54] Demosthenes urged the people not to accede to this demand and was confident enough of their general view of Philip to defend Diopeithes' actions as necessary contributions to a war already being waged against him. Diopeithes was not recalled and soon afterwards Demosthenes delivered his *Third Philippic*,[55] denouncing Philip's conduct since the peace and calling on the Athenians to prepare ships and armies with citizen troops and to seek allies among the Greeks.

This speech has been widely acclaimed as a masterpiece, and it certainly seems to have moved the Athenians to action. Soon after, probably in May 341, an alliance was made with Chalcis in Euboea on Demosthenes' motion, and an expedition which liberated Oreus was sent to the island.[56] Demosthenes and the Chalcidian leader, Callias, then visited the Peloponnese, where the Achaeans were won over and plans for a combined military effort set in motion;[57] and on their return a formal alliance was arranged between Athens and a new union of Euboean cities, which was itself completed when an Athenian force under Phocion expelled Cleitarchus, the tyrant of Eretria.[58] Demosthenes meanwhile visited Byzantium, long estranged from Athens, but now threatened by Philip (as Demosthenes had warned in *On the Chersonese*, 14), and obtained an alliance with it.[59] He also won over Abydos, another old enemy, while his associates subsequently negotiated a reconciliation with Rhodes and probably with Chios, both former allies which had seceded in the Social War of 357–355. Thus in this year Demosthenes established an almost irresistible hold on the Athenian people and justified his policies with diplomatic and some military success. It is not surprising to learn that he was publicly crowned for his services at the Great Dionysia of March 340 –

55. Oration IX: see *Greek Political Oratory*, pp. 249–63.

56. For the alliance, see Aeschines, *Crown*, 91–3 (p. 217); for Oreus, Demosthenes, *Crown*, 79 (p. 276). Both are in Philochorus, Frag. 159.

57. Aeschines, *Crown*, 95–6 (pp. 217 ff.).

58. For the alliance, see Aeschines, *Crown*, 100–1 (p. 219); for the expedition, Philochorus, Frag. 160–61. On Euboea at this time see P. A. Brunt 'Euboea in the time of Philip II,' *Classical Quarterly* XIX (1969), pp. 245 ff.

59. Referred to by Demosthenes, *Crown*, 88 (p. 278) and 244 (p. 311), and by Aeschines, *Crown*, 256 (p. 257).

with a citation, according to his own statement in *Crown*, 83 (p. 277), identical with that later proposed by Ctesiphon.

In his account of the Anaxinus affair (*Crown*, 223–4, p. 250), which probably took place at about this time, Aeschines says that he was on the point of prosecuting Demosthenes when it occurred. He does not specify the proposed charge, but elsewhere, in *Crown*, 91–105 (pp. 217 ff.), he accuses Demosthenes of having taken bribes from Callias of Chalcis, from Cleitarchus of Eretria and from Oreus, to secure for them alliances with Athens on favourable terms. In particular he criticizes Demosthenes for allowing these Euboean cities not to rejoin the naval confederacy and pay financial contributions to Athens, but to set up their own system by which Eretria and Oreus paid contributions to Chalcis. Aeschines thus makes Demosthenes out to be depriving the city of revenues it had not enjoyed since 348 and misrepresents his liberal policy of allowing the Euboeans to form their own federation. He ends by citing as proof of Demosthenes' corruption a decree of the people of Oreus providing for the payment to him of a talent with interest; but a bribe was unlikely to be enshrined in a public decree or involve interest, and it is probable that Demosthenes had earlier lent the sum to the city.

Aeschines might have been on sounder ground if he had criticized Demosthenes for risking open war with Philip at a time when he still had ready access to central Greece and friendly relations with Thebes. It is possible that Demosthenes was calculating on obtaining the alliance with Thebes which he was later able to negotiate in 339; more likely that he had simply a conviction that Philip must be opposed, with some faith in the ability of Athens to withstand a siege, if necessary.[60]

Philip, however, made no move in 341. In 340 he embarked on a campaign in Thrace which by late summer brought him close to the Hellespont and the Bosphorus and Athens's important trade route to the Black Sea. He then attacked first Perinthus, an independent Greek city on the north shore of the Propontis (Sea of Marmora), and then Byzantium. As he started these attacks, he sent a letter to Athens which amounted to a declaration of war.[61]

60. See Cawkwell, *Classical Quarterly*, N.S. XIII (1963), pp. 207–8.
61. This letter is preserved as No. XII in the Demosthenic Corpus.

The Athenian reply was to tear down the stone on which the Peace of Philocrates was inscribed and to send an expedition to the threatened area. Philip could take neither place and withdrew.

Philip's troubles did not end there. In winter 340–339 he was wounded fighting the Scythians, while in Greece itself his strategic superiority was suddenly put in doubt when the Thebans expelled his garrison from Nicaea in the pass of Thermopylae and took the place over. It seems that his ability to threaten Attica with invasion was gravely diminished and he must now face the prospect of a long war fought round the shores of the north Aegean against an enemy more determined and better supported than in the years before 346.

At this point a dispute arose in the Amphictyonic Council, which, it is generally agreed, afforded Philip an opportunity after all to apply his military superiority in central Greece. This affair is discussed in some detail by both Aeschines (*Crown*, 107–29, pp. 220 ff.) and Demosthenes (*Crown*, 145–52, pp. 292 ff.). Both agree that a speech of Aeschines, who was one of the Athenian delegation, was largely responsible for stirring up the Amphictyons to action against Locrian Amphissa which led to the declaration of a Sacred War. Aeschines claims that he made the speech to forestall a proposal by the Locrians to fine Athens fifty talents for making a dedication insulting to the Thebans; Demosthenes says that there was no such Locrian proposal and that Aeschines was bribed by Philip. To some,[62] corruption has seemed the only explanation of what was otherwise reckless folly on Aeschines' part, but perhaps he calculated that the Locrians would give in without a fight or that the Athenians would be able to take the lead in any war; he later claimed that they were prevented from doing so only by Demosthenes, who persuaded the people not to send delegates to the special meeting of the Amphictyons which condemned the Locrians and voted for war.

Be that as it may, the Amphictyons without the Athenians and the Thebans, who had also boycotted the special meeting, could make little headway, and at their regular meeting in autumn 339 the delegates decided to call on Philip for help. This meeting is

62. e.g. Goodwin, *Demosthenes, De Corona*, pp. 286–7.

reported by Demosthenes (*Crown*, 151–2, p. 293) but not by Aeschines, whose narrative breaks off just before this unhappy dénouement.

The strategic significance of the Amphictyonic invitation to Philip was that he could now bypass Thermopylae and enter central Greece by the direct route from Lamia in Thessaly to Cytinium in Doris, north of Amphissa. This route Philip now followed, but on reaching Doris he suddenly turned east and after a rapid march seized and fortified Elatea near the border of Boeotia and the main route to Thebes (September 339). This move was a clear threat to the Thebans aimed at constraining them to enter the war against Athens. In a passage of vivid description (*Crown*, 169–79, pp. 296 ff.) Demosthenes tells of the panic which news of Philip's action caused at Athens and how he persuaded the people to send him to Thebes to seek an alliance. The Thebans, it is true, had recently been showing some signs of hostility to Philip, but it was nevertheless a great triumph for Demosthenes that he was able to persuade them in face of obvious military danger to forget the bitter enmity of the past, and one of which he was justly proud (*Crown*, 188, p. 299, and 211–14, pp. 304 ff.). Aeschines' criticisms (*Crown*, 141–5, pp. 229 ff.) of the terms of the alliance as being too favourable to the Thebans overlook the fact that there was strong pressure on them to maintain what had been almost throughout Philip's reign their basic policy of friendship with him and hostility towards Athens.

Little is known of the campaigns of the next few months. Demosthenes (*Crown*, 216, p. 305) speaks of a battle by the river and a winter battle in which the Athenians and their allies were evidently victorious, but their locations are unknown. In March 338 he was again probably publicly crowned at the Great Dionysia.[63] This recognition may have preceded Philip's defeat of the western army of the Greeks and capture of Amphissa, but even after that the Athenians promptly rejected offers of peace and were prepared to fight on even if the Thebans gave way; the Theban leaders, it seems, were at one point wavering, but were probably fortified by a visit from Demosthenes.[64]

63. Demosthenes, *Crown*, 222–3 (p. 307).
64. Aeschines, *Crown*, 148–51 (pp. 230 ff.).

Late in this summer of 338 the two main armies met at the western entrance to Boeotia near Chaeronea. Philip was completely victorious and his victory decisive. But it had not been a foregone conclusion; Demosthenes' diplomacy had produced a formidable array of citizen hoplites, and the likelihood that the disparity was chiefly in generalship[65] should make us wary of taking the defeat as an unqualified condemnation of Demosthenes' opposition to Philip.

It was evidently not taken as such by the Athenian people. After a brief panic they rallied to the encouragement of Lycurgus and Hyperides and of Demosthenes, who had fought at Chaeronea and escaped. Emergency measures were taken against invasion; Lycurgus saw to the raising of funds and Demosthenes to the repair of fortifications.[66] Philip meanwhile had subjected Thebes, putting a garrison in the city, restoring his exiled friends and freeing the Boeotian cities from Theban control. But instead of moving against Athens he offered terms which were accepted; the Athenians were to be free allies of Philip, though they had to surrender the Chersonese and wind up the naval Confederacy. Macedonian supremacy was clear and was to be reinforced by the new Common Peace treaty which Philip organized in the winter of 338–337 after invading the Peloponnese and settling matters there to the advantage of his friends; a treaty guaranteeing the independence of all the Greek states, and accepted by all except Sparta, to be supervised by a new council of the Greeks, devised by Philip and likely to do his will, and by a Hegemon who was Philip himself, the whole settlement backed by the ultimate sanction of Macedonian military force, visible to all in the garrisons stationed at Thebes, at Chalcis and on the citadel of Corinth. Thus Philip sought to embody his settlement of a conquered Greece in a form that had grown out of the traditions of city-state independence.[67]

65. Demosthenes' hints, at *Crown*, 194 (p. 300) and 245 (p. 312), that the generals were deficient are regarded by Pickard-Cambridge, *Demosthenes*, p. 387, as 'perfectly justified'.
66. Demosthenes, *Crown*, 248 (p. 312), and Lycurgus, *Against Leocrates*, 37 ff.
67. On this treaty and the organization it set up (often misnamed the League of Corinth) see Ryder, *Koine Eirene*, pp. 102–5.

The Athenians, however, were unimpressed and continued to entrust their affairs to the politicians who had opposed Philip before Chaeronea. Demades, Aeschines and probably Phocion had been their principal negotiators;[68] Demosthenes was hardly suitable and was away from Athens when peace was made, probably on a mission about the corn-supply and not, as has been alleged, out of terror.[69] But on his return he was the one chosen by the People to make the funeral oration over the dead of Chaeronea,[70] and in 337 he was again in charge of fortifications and also of the Theoric Fund (the Festival Fund, which amounted to the reserve fund of the state). He was attacked in the law-courts, but always acquitted.[71] The people agreed with his refusal to accept Macedonian domination as irremediable.

8. *The* Crown *Case*

Early in 336 one of Demosthenes' political associates, Ctesiphon, proposed to the Council that he be publicly crowned again at the Great Dionysia for his particular services as commissioner for the walls and for his general merit 'because he continually says and does what is best for the people'.[72] Demosthenes' reputation had so well survived the city's defeat that Ctesiphon's proposal was passed by the Council.[73] But, before it could be presented to the Assembly, Aeschines served notice of a prosecution of Ctesiphon for making an illegal proposal. This prosecution was not, in fact, heard until 330.

The procedure of an indictment for making an illegal proposal to the Assembly (*graphê paranomôn*) seems to have originated in the second half of the fifth century, after the Areopagus (Council of Elders) had been deprived in 462 B.C. of its functions as the guardian of the laws. The Athenian people, while eagerly asserting

68. On Aeschines' role see Aeschines, *Crown*, 227 (p. 250), and Demosthenes, *Crown*, 282 (p. 320); on Demades see Demosthenes, *Crown*, 285 (p. 320).

69. See Demosthenes, *Crown*, 248 (p. 312).

70. Demosthenes, *Crown*, 285–8 (pp. 320 ff.).

71. Demosthenes, *Crown*, 249–50 (pp. 312 ff.).

72. Part of the citation is quoted by Aeschines, *Crown*, 49 (p. 205); see also 236–7 (p. 253).

73. Demosthenes, *Crown*, 9 (p. 262), 118 (p. 285).

their right to make the state's decisions on any and every matter in the Assembly, still acknowledged the sacred immutability of certain basic laws (which in general they ascribed to the early sixth-century law-giver Solon), and believed that these laws should not be altered or infringed even by decrees of the Assembly. They had grown to resent the right of the Areopagus, composed of ex-archons (drawn from the richer citizens) serving for life, to make the decisions when laws and decrees conflicted. But the *graphê paranomôn* procedure left the decision in the people's hands. Any citizen could indict a proposal as illegal, and the proposal was then held in abeyance until the question was tried by the popular court, after time for reflection and with the full deployment of relevant arguments.

It was inevitable that this procedure should come to be used as a political weapon, with politicians bringing prosecutions on technical grounds in order to frustrate their opponents' proposals. But it could be a two-edged weapon. Normally not more than a year was allowed to elapse before the case was heard, and the prosecutor had to rely for his success on a withdrawal of public support for the proposal which he wished to block; for technicalities were not by themselves likely to deflect Athenian jurors, however well chosen. Moreover a prosecutor who failed to secure one fifth of the votes at the trial was liable to certain penalties.

It is a fair guess that the indictment of Philocrates' proposal about peace with Philip in 348 (see above, p. 26) was brought on technical grounds, and it served to hold it up for the better part of a year without its failure, as far as we know, involving anyone in penalty. Aeschines' prosecution of Ctesiphon also sought to invalidate his proposal on technical grounds, namely that it was illegal to propose that anyone be crowned who still held public office and had not been subject to scrutiny by the auditors, and Demosthenes was still commissioner for the walls and for the Theoric Fund, and that it was illegal to award a crown at the Dionysia.[74] But the main burden of Aeschines' attack in his speech six years later was on that part of the citation which praised Demosthenes' general services to the state, and this must surely have been his intention, and known to be, from the first. Similarly,

74. Aeschines, *Crown*, 9–48 (pp. 195 ff.).

Demosthenes, who had a poor case on the technical points, must always have intended to defend Ctesiphon by seeking to justify the citation.

It is fair to ask why Aeschines brought the prosecution at this time and why, having brought it, he did not press it to a trial sooner. The first question may not in fact be a problem. This could have been just one more in the series of prosecutions to which Demosthenes says he was subjected after the city's defeat. But if a reason is sought why Aeschines should at this time have felt that the tide of opinion was running in his favour to the extent that a jury might within a few months condemn a proposal which now seemed likely to be passed, it may be that Philip's proclamation of and preparations for a panhellenic war against Persia were beginning to turn the tide of opinion.[75] The assassination of Philip and the expectations it aroused in Greece of turmoil in Macedon would then be sufficient explanation of Aeschines' failure to press the case this year.

It is possible that the defendants could exercise some influence on the timing of a trial of this sort; but beyond doubt the effective decisions to continue delaying the trial over a further five years must have rested with Aeschines and his friends, as did the final decision to bring it on in 330, which is ascribed to them by Demosthenes (*Crown*, 308, p. 326). One must conclude that to them it was only in 330 that the political situation seemed favourable. In 336 Alexander had made his presence felt in Greece and won expressions of loyalty from the cities, but in the following year a false rumour of his death in Thrace put Greece in a ferment and Thebes revolted, only to be rapidly besieged and destroyed by him. The Athenians had shared in the excited hopes of liberty and had in fact encouraged the Thebans and given them arms, but they had avoided commitment to war and narrowly escaped the wrath of Alexander, who also dropped a demand for the surrender of Demosthenes and other hostile orators. The atmosphere of alarm and outrage at Alexander's treatment of Thebes can have seemed no more suitable for Ctesiphon's trial than that of anti-Macedonian expectation which had preceded it. Then in 334 Alexander crossed to Asia to attack the Persian empire, and Demosthenes and his

75. See Cawkwell, *Classical Quarterly*, N.S. xix (1969), pp. 167–9.

friends could enjoy and encourage hopes that he would be defeated.

His victory at Issus in late 333, though not decisive, must have dimmed these hopes; and there could have been good reasons for thinking that a last chance had come when the Spartans, led by King Agis, attempted to raise Greece against Macedon in 331. Alexander had probably already embarked on a campaign into the Euphrates–Tigris valley (which later led to his victory at Gaugamela) and Antipater, his regent in Macedon, was engaged in dealing with a revolt in Thrace; and with the Spartans successful in their first encounter with Macedonian forces and with Athens's own dockyards packed with triremes as never before, it must have seemed a fine opportunity. But the Athenians rejected an appeal for help from Sparta; within a few months Alexander was decisively victorious at Gaugamela and had overthrown the Persian empire, and by early summer 330 Sparta was crushed.

Defiance of Macedon must then have seemed to many a more than ordinarily forlorn cause. Moreover, Aeschines' confidence on this score was surely further increased by the fact that Demosthenes, after at first encouraging the Spartans, had himself finally recommended the people not to help them. Whether he backed down because he saw that the people would not support him, as Plutarch says,[76] or because his nerve failed him and he dare not risk bringing on the city the fate of Thebes, as Aeschines' account suggests (*Crown*, 165–7, pp. 235 ff.), is uncertain, though the latter seems more likely. The same question-mark hangs over his actions four years earlier, when Thebes had risen: were the Athenians then reluctant to commit themselves to the Theban cause despite Demosthenes' pleading or in response to his sudden caution? In both episodes Demosthenes had either failed to carry his policy or had failed to live up to his proclaimed ideals. It is significant that Demosthenes has nothing to say about either in his *Crown* speech; after the second he might plausibly be thought to be slipping. At all events, the hearing of the charge against Ctesiphon was arranged for the late summer of 330 with sufficient notice for visitors from all over Greece to flock to hear the orators on an unprecedented scale.[77]

76. *Life of Demosthenes*, c.24.
77. Aeschines, *Crown*, 56 (p. 207).

Aeschines, however, reckoned without the basic loyalty of ordinary Athenians to Demosthenes and without Demosthenes' eloquence. The number of the jurors is unknown – either 1,501 or 2,001 is a likely guess, but more than four fifths of them voted to acquit Ctesiphon. Aeschines was thus subject to the penalty of a fine of 1,000 drachmas and of loss of the right to bring such prosecutions in the future. He was so disgusted that he left Athens and afterwards lived mostly in Rhodes. There he taught rhetoric and in his later years the teacher in him got the better of the politician; he is said to have read his *Crown* speech to an audience on Rhodes and, when they expressed amazement that he had lost the case, to have said to them: 'You would not be surprised if you had heard Demosthenes replying to it.'[78]

Demosthenes, meanwhile, enjoyed his triumph and was duly crowned at the Great Dionysia of 329. Although he still longed for liberation, he was still wary of a war with Alexander. In 325–324 Alexander's governor of Babylon, Harpalus, made off to Greece with 6,000 mercenaries and 5,000 talents from the treasury. Demosthenes spoke against a proposal to make common cause with him, and it was probably this further example of his lukewarmness that prompted his former associate Hyperides to join in prosecuting him for embezzling some of Harpalus' money; some of Hyperides' speech survives together with a short one written by Deinarchus for another prosecutor. The rights and wrongs of this case do not concern us here, but Demosthenes was condemned, fined and imprisoned, only to make his escape into exile. The next year (323) Alexander died, and the Athenians, encouraged this time by messages from Demosthenes, joined in a general rising of the Greeks against Macedon in what is known as the Lamian War. After early successes the Greeks were defeated in 322. The Athenians lost their freedom and had to accept a Macedonian garrison and the rule of a Macedonian-backed oligarchy; Demosthenes, with Hyperides and other orators, was condemned to death and on the island of Calauria off the Peloponnesian coast opposite Attica on the 16th of the fourth Attic month (probably mid-October) 322 B.C. he forestalled execution by taking poison.[79]

78. Pseudo-Plutarch, *Lives of the Ten Orators*, 840 D-E.
79. Plutarch, Demosthenes, 29–30.

9. Conclusion

It is impossible to make a final judgement on Demosthenes' career and policies. One can but indicate the headings of discussion.

First, was Aeschines perhaps right in suggesting that Philip could be trusted and that his attitude towards Athens was a great deal friendlier than Demosthenes made out? In support of this view of Philip there can be offered some of his actions, his initiative in the peace negotiations of 348–346, his offers to amend the Peace of Philocrates in 344–342 and his readiness to grant terms to Athens after Chaeronea; and perhaps, too, the attitude to him of Isocrates, as shown in his *Philippus*, published in 346 soon after peace had been made, and in his subsequent *Letters to Philip*. But Isocrates' judgement could have been warped by extreme old age and by a desire to see in Philip the means to Greek unity; and these actions of Philip could have other explanations, the first two as the means to establishing without warfare an arrangement between himself and Athens in which he was bound to be the increasingly dominant partner, the third as the avoidance of a tiresome siege of a still defiant enemy. Moreover, as has been seen, Philip's other actions provided ample excuse for Athenians to mistrust him.

Second, even if Demosthenes was right to think that Athens had to oppose Philip to survive as an independent state, might it have been a hopeless struggle from the beginning? Weakened by earlier wars and largely unsupported by other mainland Greeks until the last few years before Chaeronea, had Athens any hope of defeating a man who had fashioned a new type of army much stronger than the city-state levies and more reliable than their Greek mercenaries? In a sense there is no arguing with the verdict of Chaeronea; but, as has been seen, the coalition eventually assembled against Philip, largely through Demosthenes' efforts, was a formidable one, and the course of events in 340–338, even of the battle itself, do not suggest that Philip's final success was easy or inevitable. Again, clearly the Greek failure in the Lamian War of 323–322 does not of itself condemn the optimism of Demosthenes and others who after 338 encouraged the Athenians to look forward to liberation.

Third, if Demosthenes' policy was both necessary and possible, was his judgement always for the best in the promotion and execution of it? Here, not all the city's mistakes, and certainly not those made on the field of battle, can be laid at his door, but there can be argument about certain episodes in which he did have some influence, such as the failure to test adequately through negotiations Philip's intentions in offering to amend the Peace in 344–342 and the decision not to help the Spartans in 331.

Whatever may seem to posterity to be the more probable answers to these questions, the result of the *Crown* case shows that the vast majority of Demosthenes' fellow-citizens believed that he had in general been right. They would understand how in later centuries people fighting to defend their freedom against a conqueror have come to find in his speeches an expression of their own fears and hopes, an impulse to greater effort and inspiration in adversity.

THE TREATY

I. THE PROSECUTION: DEMOSTHENES

Summary of the Speech

I. Introduction. Plea against intimidation. Procedure and arrangement of the defence. 1–8.

II. The main charge. Corruption proved by Aeschines' change of front. 9–66.

Aeschines as opponent of Philip (9–16) and as his supporter in company with Philocrates after the first delegation (17–28). The effect on Phocis (29–30) not commended at Athens on the evidence (31–3). The effect at Athens. Philip's letter and the evidence of a plot for the destruction of Phocis (34–63). The misery of Phocis (64–6).

III. Comments on charges and on possible pleas of the defence. 67–149.

Value to Philip of traitors (67–87). Defence pleas anticipated and countered (88–101). Proofs of Aeschines' corruption (102–20). His conduct after the third delegation and his deserts (121–33). A political plea countered (134–49).

IV. Narrative. The second delegation. 150–77.

Events after the agreement of 16 April. Misconduct of the delegation in regard to signing (150–68). Demosthenes concerned in ransoming captives (169–73). Aeschines' private association with Philip (174–7).

V. The charges recapitulated with various comments. 178–255.

Recapitulation (178–81). Further pleas forestalled (182–91). Aeschines' character shown by (i) a party in Macedonia, (ii) his antecedents, (iii) the contrast with those of Demosthenes and his conduct (192–214). Further irrelevancies anticipated (215–33). Aeschines' malice exposed in reference to the entertainment offered to Philip's representatives, and to his speech against Timarchus (234–42) and illustrated by poetical references seen as appropriate (243–55).

VI. Conclusion. General inferences. 256–end.

Moral deterioration since Solon (256–87). The implication of treachery. Apostrophe to Eubulus. The evil of political corruption (288–99). Aeschines' change of front and his deserts again described (300–34). The charges recapitulated once more (315–36). The danger from Aeschines' vocal capacities (337–41). Peroration (342–3).

GENTLEMEN of the jury, the interest aroused by this case and the lobbying which has taken place over it are presumably well known to you. You saw the tiresome objections and the approaches that were made over the names to be included in your number. I shall ask from you all something which may be expected without asking, that you shall allow no personal preference or individual bias to outweigh the justice of the issue or the oath you have sworn before coming into court. You should reflect that this issue is your concern and that of Athens, while the insistent demands of advocates are dictated by selfish motives; the law empanelled you to prevent these and not to open the door to corrupt practice. Thus most honest people, even after their accounts[1] have been passed, invite continual inquiry into their conduct. But of Aeschines the reverse is true. Before approaching this court or making any report on his proceedings, he has got rid of one[2] of the jury and goes round with threats against one or two others. This is to introduce a most unwarrantable and undesirable political practice. If a participant in public affairs is to put intimidation in the place of justice and engineer the elimination of accusers, your proceedings will be devoid of all effect.

Therefore, while I am entirely confident of proving him guilty of a whole list of serious offences, which render him liable to extreme penalties, I have none the less one anxiety which I will put before you without concealment. It seems to me that cases which

1. All holders of office had at the end of their tenure of office to submit an account of it, which was examined by auditors chosen by lot from the Council. If there were any question a legal case could be brought, as in this instance against Aeschines.

2. i.e. Timarchus, prosecuted by Aeschines and convicted shortly before the present case. The speech of prosecution is the only extant speech of Aeschines besides those translated in this volume.

come before this court are as much affected by temporary circumstances as by facts, and the time which has elapsed since the conference may have made you either forget the offences committed or feel them to be out of date. The way in which I think it would be right for you to view the events and assess them is what I now propose to describe. You should make a deliberate judgement what are the activities of which an account ought to be exacted of the state's representative at a conference. You should recall first the reports he has made, next his recommendations, his terms of reference, the sequence of events, and throughout the question of his freedom from corrupt influence. Why? Because it is his reports which govern your deliberations, whose effectiveness depends on their accuracy. You credit the advice of your representatives with greater reliability, because you regard it as based on knowledge of the facts relevant to their mission. So justice requires that their recommendations shall not be proved to have injured your honour or your interests. Indeed your instructions as to what was to be said or done, your explicit orders for their conduct, should have been carried out. Next, why the order of events? Because it often happens with events of importance that there comes a single crucial moment, and if it is treacherously let slip and passed to the enemy, it can never be recovered by any sort of means. Finally, on the question between corrupt and incorrupt conduct, profit made to the injury of the country would, I know, be universally regarded as a matter for the greatest resentment and indignation. But it was not so defined by the law, which merely forbade corrupt practices on the assumption, I imagine, that such corruption, once accepted, precludes for the future even reliable political judgement. If, then, I can provide clear and certain proof that Aeschines failed to give accurate reports, that he prevented my true statements from reaching the public, that his recommendations were directly opposed to the country's interests, that he failed entirely to carry out his instructions as a member of the conference and squandered critical opportunities which cost the country dear on numerous occasions, and finally that all this was due to corrupt practices undertaken in company with Philocrates, then you should find a verdict of 'guilty', and exact a penalty adequate to his conduct.

If I fail in whole or in part, you may regard me as the guilty one and acquit him.

I have a number of other serious charges to bring against him as well as these, which would doubtless fully deserve strong feeling against him. But before I say anything else I want to recall something most of you will no doubt remember, the political position Aeschines adopted from the first and the public attacks on Philip he thought it advisable to make. This will show that it is his original public actions and words which give the proof of his venality. Aeschines was the first man in Athens, as his public utterances[3] show, to realize Philip's designs against the Greek states, and his corrupt dealings with certain leading men in Arcadia, with Ischander son of Neoptolemus to understudy him. Aeschines approached the Council, addressed the Assembly on this subject and carried a motion to send representatives all over Greece and urge a general meeting here to consider war with Philip. He returned from Arcadia with accounts of the long and brilliant speeches he said he had delivered to the Thousand at Megalopolis in the cause of Athens against Hieronymus, Philip's supporter, including a diatribe on the unwarrantable damage done not merely to particular states but to Greece as a whole, by the acceptance of Macedonian bribery. After this activity of his and the clear indication it won him, the motion for a deputation to be sent[4] to Philip about peace was successfully urged by Aristodemus, Neoptolemus, Ctesiphon and the others who brought unjustifiable reports from Macedonia. Aeschines now joined them, not as a party of betrayal of Athenian interests nor of confidence in Philip, but in the part of a watchdog over the rest. His speeches which I have mentioned and his hostility to Philip led everyone to think of him in this way. At this point he approached me and agreed to share a common policy on the deputation, and urged at length that we should unite in precautions against that infamous, unscrupulous character, Philocrates. Till

3. This diplomatic mission was soon after Philip's capture of Olynthus in late 348 B.C.

4. In winter 347 B.C. Aristodemus was an actor and friend of Aeschines, who gives further details of his mission to Philip at *Treaty*, 15–19 (pp. 146–7). This Ctesiphon, who subsequently served as one of the delegation to Philip, is not to be identified with the defendant in the *Crown* case.

his return here after the first conference[5] I personally failed to realize the bribery and corruption which lay behind his proceedings. Apart from his previous statements which I have narrated, he spoke at the first meeting of the Assembly on the subject of peace, and opened with a preamble which I think I can quote word for word. 'Had Philocrates spent years', he said, 'wondering how he could best maintain opposition to peace, I don't think he could have found a better way than this resolution. In my view this peace is one which I would never urge upon Athens so long as one Athenian is left alive. Peace, however, I maintain must be made.' It was short and reasonably sweet. That is what he said on the first day in the hearing of everyone. But the day after, when peace was to be finally decided, when I supported the decision of the allies[6] and acted to secure fair and just terms, when there was a general desire for this and a general determination not to listen to a word from the despicable Philocrates, there he was on his feet again, speaking in agreement with Philocrates in words which I most seriously and solemnly declare deserved the death penalty several times over. He called upon us to forget our ancestors, to discard all mention of past victories by land and sea, and said he would pass and draft a resolution that Athens should give up assistance to any Greek state from which she had not received assistance herself. It was an outrageous and shameless performance, which he had the nerve to make in the hearing, under the very nose of the representatives of Greek states who had been summoned at his instigation before he descended to corruption.

Next, gentlemen, you shall hear what happened after his election to the conference[7] for the formal conclusion of the terms of peace, when he squandered opportunities to the detriment of Athenian interests, and you shall learn of the antagonism which

5. On the 18th of the Attic month Elaphebolion, about the middle of April 346 B.C.

6. This resolution included the provision that any Greek state that wished should be permitted to join in the peace treaty within three months. It is quoted by Aeschines in *Crown*, 69 (p. 211 below) and was read in full as evidence there. See Introduction, p. 30.

7. i.e. on the return of the delegates from the second delegation to Philip to administer to him the oath of fidelity to the treaty just negotiated. The date is 6 July (13 Scirophorion) 346 B.C.

arose between him and myself from my efforts to prevent it. When we returned from this conference for the conclusion of the Peace, which is the subject of the present inquiry, the situation at our entry to the Council was that not a single item, great or small, had been realized, of all the gains mentioned and expected when peace was made. We had been hoodwinked in every particular, because this junta had taken action in the opposite sense, and played their part in the conference in contravention of the stated instructions. Here I am going to enter on facts which are known to many, because the Council was full of ordinary onlookers. I spoke and told the Council the true story. I accused Aeschines and enumerated all the details from the first hopes suggested by Ctesiphon and Aristodemus, and, after peace had been agreed, the speeches made by Aeschines and the effect they had on the country. I then came to the final points (about Phocis[8] and Thermopylae[9]) with the advice not to abandon our position, not to risk what happened before and be buoyed up by hope after hope and promise after promise till we finally succumbed altogether. This recommendation was agreed by the Council.

When it came to the Assembly, and the subject had to be put to the People as a whole, our friend was the first of all to address the meeting – and I most strongly urge you to follow me in recalling the truth of what I say, because this is what did such damage and destruction to our whole cause. He said not a word by way of describing the events of the conference or the discussion in the Council and whether he disputed the truth of my statements. The nature of the speech he made and the flattering statements in it were of a kind to carry away the whole meeting. He said he came bearing Philip's agreement to everything that Athens wanted, in regard to the Amphictyonic Council[10] and everything else. He

8. For the role of Phocis in the negotiations for peace, see Introduction, p. 25ff.

9. The main pass from the north into central Greece, which Philip had to force in order to attack Phocis or Thebes, and which an Athenian force had successfully manned against him in 352 B.C. See note 34, p. 77, below.

10. The Amphictyonic League was an ancient association for the protection of the sanctuary of Apollo at Delphi. Athens and Sparta were members, but it was formed largely of states in central Greece. The 'Sacred War' between Thebes and Phocis had opened with Thebes using the Amphictyonic machinery

described a long attack which he claimed to have made to Philip against Thebes, and gave the headings of it. He added a reckoning that as a result of the part he had played in the conference Athenians could expect within two or three days without taking a step away from home, without any military or other trouble, to hear that Thebes was under siege and detached from the rest of Boeotia,[11] and that Thespiae and Plataea were being reconstituted and the Delphic dues exacted, not from Phocis, but Thebes, in retribution for the move to capture the sanctuary. He had pointed out to Philip, he said, that the sacrilege was as much a matter of instigation as the physical act, and for this he had had a price put on his head at Thebes. He also said he had heard from certain quarters in Euboea, where there was anxiety and consternation at the friendly feeling between this country and Philip. They were quoted as saying to the delegation that they very well understood the terms on which we had made peace with Philip, and fully realized that Athens had agreed to let Philip have Amphipolis in return for an agreement that Euboea[12] was to be handed to Athens. There was also a further arrangement he said he had made, which he was not then prepared to divulge because of ill will against him on the part of some of the delegates. This was a hint at Oropus.[13] All this naturally added to his reputation. He had looked the part of an understanding statesman and a man of note, and he stepped down with an impressive flourish. I was next, and I said I had no knowledge of all this, and made an attempt to say something on the lines of my report to the Council. The two of them, Aeschines and Philocrates, stood on either side of me and shouted interruptions and finally ridicule. The audience laughed, refused to listen, refused to accept anything except Aeschines' account. I admit it

---

to condemn Phocian sacrilege. Philip was therefore able to pose as the protector of the Amphictyonic League in his attack on Phocis.

11. Thebes constantly sought a position of supremacy over the rest of the cities of Boeotia, who as constantly sought to resist it. Plataea and Thespiae in southern Boeotia had been destroyed by Thebes between 373 and 371 B.C.

12. For the role of Amphipolis and Euboea in the dispute between Athens and Philip, see Introduction, pp. 19ff.

13. A small region at the eastern end of the border between Attica and Boeotia, probably seized by Athens after the victory over Thebes in 506 B.C., but recovered by Thebes in 366 B.C.

seemed to me pretty reasonable on their part. With the expectation of having it all so good, who would ever have tolerated either denial of it or accusations levelled at their proceedings? Everything else was unimportant compared with the expectations and hopes which had been implied. Any opposition must be mere malice and ill will, while this was a golden prospect for Athens beyond belief.

Why do I make this the first subject to recall, the account of this debate? First and foremost, gentlemen, I wanted to prevent any of you who might hear some detail of my account of the past which seemed conspicuously regrettable from expressing astonishment and saying, 'Why didn't you say so and point it out at the time?' I wanted you to remember the promises that were made by these two, promises given on every occasion, which precluded so much as a word on the other side, and to remember the magnificent announcement made by Aeschines, and realize that this is to be added to all the rest of the wrong he has done the country, that at the time when she ought to have received accurate information it was kept from her, and she was fobbed off with deliberately misleading hopes and promises. This, as I said, is my first and principal reason for describing the incident. The second is equally important. I want you to recall Aeschines' political position when he was still immune from corruption, the defensive, distrustful attitude he took towards Philip, so as to compare it with the sudden change to trust and friendship. Then if his public pronouncements were realized in a satisfactory outcome for Athens, you may regard his attitude as the fruit of a genuine pursuit of Athenian interests, but if the facts proved to be diametrically opposed to his statements, and resulted in deep disgrace and serious danger to our country, you may realize that the change has been due to self-interest on his part and the distortion of truth by corruption.

Since I have been led to discuss that debate, I should like first of all to point out how his activities lost us control of the Phocian position. You must not suppose, gentlemen of the jury, if you consider the importance of the issues involved, that the accusations and charges brought forward are too big for such a figure as Aeschines. You should reflect that any man, whoever he was, whom you put in this position of control over the sequence of events, who chose, as he did, to misrepresent the situation and mislead the country for his own profit, would have been responsible for equally disastrous results. You may often appoint officials of low competence, but this does not mean that the affairs for which as a nation we are held responsible are necessarily of low importance. Far from it. The destruction of Phocis was the work of Philip, but these were his accomplices. You must realize this and ask whether, to the extent to which questions of the preservation of Phocis were in the scope of the conference, it was they who were the cause of its ruin and destruction, not whether Aeschines himself destroyed it. How could he?

Now give me the resolution[14] passed by the Council on my report and the evidence of the mover of it on that occasion. This will prove that I am not dissenting from a report which I then passed unchallenged, but that on the contrary I at once set about making my accusation and predicted the result. Observe, too, that a Council which had not been kept from hearing the truth from me passed no commendation of the other two, and did not think fit to invite them to the Prytaneum.[15] This has never before been the fate of any delegate since Athens has existed, not even of Timagoras,[16] who was condemned to death by the vote of the Assembly. But it was the fate of Aeschines and Philocrates. Read the evidence first and then the resolution.

(The evidence and the resolution are read.)

This contains no commendation and no invitation to the delegates from the Council. If Aeschines claims the opposite, he must display his evidence, and in that case I will withdraw. But he cannot. Now if we all played the same part in the conference, the

14. One function of the Council was to prepare motions for consideration by the Assembly, who would not normally proceed without this preliminary resolution.

15. i.e. for the dinner given by custom to a delegation for a successful performance of its functions. The Prytaneum, on the north side of the Acropolis, may have been the headquarters of the Prytaneis before the Tholos was built for them. Later it was used for some homicide cases, but also for some public occasions, such as these dinners.

16. Timagoras was executed as a traitor after a delegation to Artaxerxes at Susa in 367 B.C. in which he agreed to humiliating terms refused by his colleague, Leon.

Council are justified in refusing commendation to all alike. If on the contrary some delegates conducted themselves correctly and the rest the reverse, it must be due to the unprincipled that the meritorious have been involved in the dishonour which was inflicted. Then how can you most easily tell which is the villain of the piece? Remember whose is the original accusation of these proceedings. It is clear that all the real culprit needed was to hold his tongue and elude detection without involving himself in any account of what happened. But the man whose conscience was clear realized the risk to himself if it appeared that silence made him look like an accomplice in misconduct. Well, I myself brought the original accusation, and none was brought against me.

This, then, was the resolution of the Council. When the Assembly met, Philip was already at Thermopylae.[17] This was the first unjustifiable step, to have put Philip in control of the position, so that at a moment when we should have heard the report, then deliberated on it, and then taken what action was decided, the news was that here was Philip already and it was hard to say what to do. To make matters worse, this resolution of the Council was not read to the Assembly at all. No one heard it. Instead Aeschines made an oration to the effect which I have just described, and enlarged on all the outstanding benefits which he claimed to have persuaded Philip to accept and which formed the reason why he had had a price put on his head at Thebes. The result was that members of the Assembly who had first been horrified at Philip's arrival and enraged with the delegates for not reporting it now turned as mild as anything in the expectation of everything they wanted, and refused to hear a word from me or anyone else. After this Philip's letter was read. This had been composed by Aeschines on the side,[18] and proved to be nothing more nor less than a written defence of his party's illegal actions in so many words. It includes the statement that they wanted to approach the Greek states and receive the oaths of ratification, but Philip prevented them and detained them to help in the reconciliation of Halus with Pharsalus.[19] He appears as sponsor for all their misdemeanours, which

17. 10 July 346 B.C.
18. This allegation is most unlikely to be true.
19. Two communities in Thessaly. Philip had controlled Pharsalus since

he attributes to himself. About Phocis and Thespiae and all Aeschines' pronouncements there is not a syllable. The way in which this was done was not mere chance. Their proceedings gave ground for a penalty against them for not carrying out or organizing what the original decree instructed. Philip accepts the blame, and there was no chance of penalizing him. But his attempts to delude and overreach Athens were the subject of Aeschines' announcements, which were designed to forestall any accusation or criticism of Philip then or later, since none of it was contained either in this letter or in any other communication from him.

Now read the letter written by Aeschines and sent by Philip. Observe that it takes the form which I have pointed out.

(The letter is read.)

There you have it, gentlemen. Charming and considerate, isn't it? But as to Phocis and Thebes and the rest of Aeschines' pronouncements – not a sound. There is not a word in it that rings true, as you will see in a moment. According to Philip these two were kept to help secure a settlement for Halus. Yet the settlement she got was that her people were expelled and the place depopulated. As for the prisoners, despite his supposed eagerness to find what he could do for our satisfaction, apparently he never thought of ransom for them. On the other hand I went there with a talent for this, as has been several times shown in evidence. The evidence shall be repeated now. It was to deprive me of the credit for my public spirit that Aeschines urged Philip to include this item. The most important point of all is that the earlier letter[20] which we received contained the words, 'I would have made an explicit statement of my intended benefit to Athens, had I had clear knowledge of a guaranteed alliance'. Yet as soon as the alliance was made, the second letter professes uncertainty as to what can be done for our satisfaction, including what he had himself promised. He must have known, unless there was double dealing. However,

---

352 B.C. Halus was still free when the peace was negotiated, but Philip insisted on being left a free hand with it (see Introduction, pp. 31 ff.).

20. i.e. when the first delegation returned from Macedonia before the debate about the peace.

in proof that this is what he wrote, take this extract from the first letter and read it, from this point.

(An excerpt from the letter is read.)

Thus before securing his peace he agrees that, if an alliance is included in the terms, he will make proposals which will be beneficial to Athens. When both his demands have been met, he says he doesn't know what he can do to give us satisfaction, but if we tell him, he will do anything which does not involve compromising his honour or his reputation. He takes refuge in these pretexts, so that, in case we actually offer a reply or are led to make a proposal, he has a line of retreat.

At that time and hour the possibility remained of refuting all this and giving true information, had not the talk of Thespiae and Plataea and immediate retribution upon Thebes stolen the truth from us. Yet if what was needed was to report all this for the deception of Athens, the announcement was sensible, though if it was really meant to be carried out, silence would have been better. If the business had reached a stage when even knowledge of it would have done no good to Thebes, why didn't it take place? If it had been forestalled by the knowledge, who divulged it? Wasn't it Aeschines? Oh no, it was never part of his intentions or hopes, so he must be absolved of the charge of causing a leak. The aim was to mislead Athens by means of this pronouncement and make her refuse to hear the truth from me, and to lead to a little peace and inactivity while the decree for the destruction of Phocis carried the day. That was the reason for laying it on so thick, that was what lay behind all his oratory.

I heard all this propaganda he put out, and I was quite certain of its falsity. I'll tell you why: first because, when Philip was about to take the oath ratifying the peace, Phocis was put down by our friends here as not included,[21] when it was reasonable to omit mention of her if she was to be preserved; secondly from the

21. A clause excluding Phocis from the peace had been deleted in the Assembly, but as it was clear that Philip would not make a peace which included Phocis, leading Athenian politicians must have been aware that she would be excluded in Philip's definition of 'the Athenians and their allies' (see 159 below, p. 94), whatever the ordinary public expected. See Introduction, p. 32.

silence of Philip's delegates about all this and about Philip's letter as well. It was Aeschines who mentioned it. On this evidence, then, I rose to speak and tried to controvert it, but as I could get no hearing I stopped and contented myself with declaring by way of protest that I knew nothing about it and had no part in it, and added that I did not believe it. The last phrase led to some violent abuse, and I added, 'And be sure that, if any of this comes off, you bestow the honour and glory and the decorations on Aeschines and Philocrates instead of me, but in the opposite case you turn your resentment on them. I retire from both.' 'No,' replied Aeschines, 'you needn't retire, so long as you make no claim then.' 'I'll certainly do nothing so unjustifiable,' I said. Then up jumped Philocrates with a taunt, 'It's hardly surprising, gentlemen, that Demosthenes and I don't agree. He drinks water and I drink wine', and everyone laughed.[22]

Now consider the draft decree proposed and entered by Philocrates. It reads magnificently as it stands. But when account is taken of the circumstances under which it was proposed and the undertakings offered with it, it is obviously nothing more nor less than a betrayal of Phocis to Philip and Thebes with her hands tied behind her back. Read the draft, please.

(The draft decree is read.)

You see the text of it, gentlemen of the jury, and how overflowing with ostentatious panegyric it is. 'The terms of peace and alliance shall be the same as for Philip and his descendants' and 'a vote of thanks is due to Philip for his undertaking to act in accordance with justice'. He gave no undertaking at all, so much the reverse as to say that he didn't know what he could do to secure your satisfaction. The man who made these undertakings on his behalf was Aeschines. Philocrates made use of your enthusiasm for Aeschines' pronouncements to introduce into the draft decree the words 'and in the event of any failure by Phocis to carry out her obligations and transfer the sanctuary to the Amphictyonic League, the people of Athens will take action against any state attempting to prevent it'. Thus, gentlemen, we stayed at home and made no military move, the Spartan delegates went off realiz-

22. cf. Demosthenes, *Philippic II*, 30 (*Greek Political Oratory*, p. 233).

ing the trick that was being played, and there were no other members of the Amphictyonic League left except Thessaly and Thebes. At that point he brought a measure in the suavest possible terms for the transfer of the Delphic sanctuary by proposing its conveyance to the Amphictyons. What Amphictyons? There were none except Thebes and Thessaly. Nothing was said about summoning an Amphictyonic Congress or waiting to convene one, nothing of an expedition under Proxenus[23] to Phocis or mobilization of Athenian forces or anything of that sort. There were two letters from Philip addressing Athens.[24] Yes, but not to suggest action. Of course not. Had this been intended, he would not have written at such a time as to forestall the chance of an Athenian expedition. He would not have prevented my attempt to sail back here.[25] He would not have given Aeschines orders to say what he did, making the chance of Athenian action very slight. The aim was that we should imagine his intentions to coincide with our hopes, and make no adverse decision, that Phocis should be led by your expectations to abandon defence or resistance and in despair put herself in his hands. Now read Philip's dispatches.

(The letter is read.)

This letter does call upon Athens, and none too soon, you may say. But if it was genuine, what course was appropriate for Aeschines and Philocrates, except to agree to an Athenian expedition and an immediate call to Proxenus, who was known to be in the district? It is obvious that what they did was the opposite. Not unnaturally. Their attention was not on the text of the dispatch. They had inside knowledge of the idea which lay behind it. This was what dictated their cooperation and the backing they gave it.

23. Proxenus, the Athenian admiral was sent to Thermopylae at the time of the Phocian appeal for Athenian aid in 347–346 B.C., and was rebuffed by Phalaecus, the Phocian leader, who had broken with the government and had taken over the pass. This incident is described in Aeschines' reply (*Treaty*, 132–4, pp. 174–5 below).

24. After the second delegation had returned to Athens. Athens was now Philip's ally, besides being a member of the Amphictyonic League.

25. Demosthenes repeats this assertion below at 323 (p. 134). Philip probably justified his refusal by the action of Demosthenes' colleagues in voting against sending to Athens a dispatch he had written (see below 174, p. 98).

When news reached Phocis of the attitude in the Assembly, when they had in their hands the decree of Philocrates and the report of Aeschines and the promises he had made, there was no hope for them in any direction. Just think of it. There was a party among them which mistrusted Philip, and sensibly enough, but they were lured into trusting him. Why? Because they held the view that even if they were misled by Philip ten times over never would Athenian representatives dare mislead the people of Athens, so that Aeschines' announcement to the Assembly must be true, and it was Thebes and not Phocis that was due for destruction. There was another party which was in favour of defence at all costs. But they too had their sting drawn by the persuasion that Philip was on their side, and, if they refused, Athens, which they looked to for assistance, would be against them. Some of them also thought that there might be regrets at Athens at having agreed the peace with Philip. To these an Athenian treaty with Philip and his descendants was sufficient proof for them to give up hope of Athens altogether. That is the reason why these people combined all this in a single decree. And this I regard as the greatest injury of all which they did to Athens. To draft a peace with a mere mortal man who owed his power to circumstance and make it a vehicle of undying shame to this city, to deprive her, besides all else, of every benefit that chance might offer, and to carry degradation to such excess as to extend the injury not only to Athenians of their day, but to all who might ever live in future times, must surely be thought to pass beyond every extreme of iniquity. Indeed this is an addition you would never have tolerated, the clause 'and his descendants', had you not put your trust in Aeschines' promises, whose acceptance by Phocis caused her destruction. And it was her surrender to Philip, her unresisting submission to his will, which was the exact opposite of the undertakings made for her by Athens.

For clear proof that this was the manner and these people the cause of the destruction of Phocis, I will deal in detail with the chronology. Any dispute of the facts may be made within my time allowance. The peace was made on 16 April,[26] and our journey

26. The Greek dates here are 19 Elaphebolion and 13 and 17 Scirophorion. On the dating of the events referred to in this passage and in 60 below see Introduction, pp. 33–4.

to take the formal oath of ratification took a full three months, throughout which time Phocis was still uninjured. We returned here after the conference on 7 July, by which time Philip was at Thermopylae and advertising intentions to Phocis none of which was believed there. This is certain because otherwise they would never have approached Athens. The meeting of the Assembly took place after this, and that was when the whole position was lost by the lying statements and deliberate deception practised by Aeschines and Philocrates. This was on 11 July. I reckon it must have been four days later when news from Athens reached Phocis. Phocian representatives were here, and the nature of the coming report from our delegates and of the decree to be made in Athens was of the first importance to them. So it was on the 14th, we must suppose, that Phocis had news of the Athenian attitude, four days later. Then come the 15th, 16th, 17th, and that was the day of the treaty and the final doom of Phocis. The proof of this is that the 22nd was the day when the Assembly met at the Peiraeus on the question of the dockyards. It was then that Dercylus arrived from Chalcis with the news that Philip had made all arrangements in the Theban interest, and this was five days after the treaty. This takes you down to the 22nd, which makes it the fifth day after. Thus the dates I have given you and their own reports and the motions proposed are final proof of their complicity with Philip and their responsibility for the destruction of Phocis. Furthermore, the fact that not one of the cities in Phocis was captured by siege or by armed force, but all on an agreement for their utter destruction, is the strongest indication that their fate was due to persuasion from Athens of Philip's intention to preserve them. It is not as though they had no knowledge of him. Now show us the alliance of Phocis with Athens and the enactment whereby they pulled down their walls, and it will be easy to compare the then existing relations with Athens and those to which they were led by the damnable proceedings of these persons. Read them, please.

(Text of the alliance between Phocis and Athens.)

This was the relation previously existing between Phocis and Athens, one of friendship, alliance and mutual assistance. Their fate after the removal of this assistance by Aeschines you can now hear. The next document, please.

(Text of the agreement between Philip and Phocis.)

Note the wording, gentlemen: 'an agreement between Philip and the people of Phocis', not of Thebes and Phocis, or Thessaly and Phocis, or Locris or any other existing state. Again 'Phocis to hand over its cities to Philip': to Philip, not Thebes or Thessaly or anyone else. Why? Because the statement had been made to us by Aeschines, that Philip had moved down for the preservation of Phocis. Their trust was in Aeschines. Upon him their eyes were fixed. It was he with whom peace was being agreed. Read the rest. Then realize the contrast between the trust they gave and the fate they underwent. Was that the same, or anything like the same as Aeschines stated? Read it, please.

(Decree of the Amphictyonic Council.)

Never in the history of our times, nor, I believe, of earlier periods, were more appalling, more devastating events known. Yet events of such a description and prominence as these were the work of one man, by the aid of these two, despite the existence of the city of Athens and her tradition of leadership of the Greek states and her intolerance of such proceedings. The way in which the unhappy country of Phocis was destroyed can be seen not merely from the decrees but from the action that was taken, and it is a subject terrifying and piteous to contemplate. When we made our recent journey to Delphi, we could not help seeing it all, ruined houses, walls thrown down, a country bereft of active inhabitants, confined to a few old women, small children and pitiable old men. No description could approach their present miseries. And yet the vote they passed against Thebes about our own country,[27] when our liberty was at stake, that is on your lips, as I can hear. What vote, then, gentlemen, do you suppose our ancestors, if they had knowledge of this, would cast about the perpetrators of the destruction of Phocis? I think they would feel they could stone them with their own hands and be free of guilt.

27. In 404 B.C., after the surrender of Athens.

Is it not scandalous, or any stronger word you like, that the people who saved us on that past occasion, who gave the vote that brought us salvation, should themselves suffer the opposite fate at the hands of men like these, should be allowed without a glance of pity to endure sufferings unparalleled in the history of Greece? Who is responsible? Who engineered the deception? Aeschines.

There is a great deal, gentlemen, which could lead us to congratulate Philip with justification on his good fortune, but there is one thing most of all which is matter for congratulation. And I most solemnly declare that I can think of no one else in our time of whom this can be said. The capture of great cities, the reduction of large stretches of land to his control, all this is matter for envy, no doubt, and lends distinction. It must. But there are more men than one who could be credited with it. One thing is unique, an advantage no other human being has ever enjoyed. What is that? The ability, when he needed traitors to serve his ends, to find even more abandoned traitors than he wanted. What else could be thought of men who at Philip's most critical moment could make statements for his benefit which it passed his own powers of mendacity to write down, even in a letter, or give a subordinate to report, and could hire themselves to do so for the deception of Athens? Antipater and Parmenio,[28] even under that despotic master and without the prospect of meeting Athenians again, secured exemption from being the instruments of our delusion. But these other deceivers, Athenian citizens from the very citadel of liberty, her appointed representatives and men who must of necessity meet her citizens and look them in the face, must live among them throughout their lives and face their criticism of their own conduct, yet undertook to deceive them. Could any man be more base of spirit, more abandoned in wickedness?

I want to show you that he is also formally subject to execration, and that neither morality nor religion allows such falsehood as

28. Antipater was later left to govern Greece and Macedonia by Alexander the Great, when he invaded Asia, and was regent for his successors until his death in 319 B.C. Parmenio was a leading general under Philip and Alexander, fought in the latter's great battles against Persia and was executed in 330 B.C.

his to go unpunished. So I ask for the form of execration[29] provided by law to be read to you.

(Form of execration.)

This is the form of prayer read at the opening of every Assembly as laid down by law, and at sessions of the Council. It is impossible for Aeschines to plead ignorance of it. He was a clerk in the state service, second class, and a subordinate officer to the Council, and was concerned to dictate the statute to the herald. So we should be acting with monstrous inconsistency if enactments or demands made to the gods on our behalf were to be neglected when it is under our control to carry them out, or if a man upon whom your prayers have invoked total destruction with his whole family and household should now be released. It cannot be allowed. Delinquents who escape detection are left to the retribution of the gods. Those whom we have ourselves caught ought not to be left to them.

I understand that the lengths to which he is likely to go in unashamed and brazen falsehood extend to denying everything he has done, his report, his promises, his deception of Athens, as though his trial were to be in some other court, and not this one, in which it is all well known, and to turning the accusations on Sparta, on Phocis, on Hegesippus.[30] This is simply ridiculous, or rather it is downright contempt of court. The claims he will now make about Phocis or Sparta or Hegesippus, that they rejected Proxenus, that they are guilty of sacrilege, or any other accusations he may make, all concern events which had taken place before the return of this delegation, and were no obstacle to the rescue of Phocis, as is claimed. By whom is it claimed? By Aeschines. There is no question of 'but for Sparta', or 'but for the rejection of Proxenus', or 'but for Hegesippus' or 'but for' this or that other circumstance Phocis would have been preserved. This was not

---

29. Aristophanes, *Thesmophoriazusae*, 331, is modelled on the curse, which formally opened meetings of Council and Assembly, on any who attempted to subvert the constitution.

30. Hegesippus had proposed the Athenian alliance with Phocis in 355 B.C. (see Aeschines, *Crown*, 118, p. 223 below). The reference to Phocis is to the rebuff of Proxenus in 346 (see note 23 above) when Sparta was evidently also at fault (see 76–7 below, p. 75).

how his report ran. He passed all this without a word and expressly stated that before his return he had persuaded Philip to preserve Phocis, to disestablish Boeotia[31] and to adopt a course which would favour Athens. This would have been completed in a few days, and this was the reason why a price had been put on his head in Thebes. You should therefore refuse to accept actions taken by Sparta or Phocis and concluded before this report, or to tolerate mention of them, or allow attacks on Phocian lack of principle. It was not for her valour that we saved Sparta, nor for that that we rescued Euboea[32] even while we called down imprecations on her, nor the numerous other states we have been the means of saving. It was because it was in our interest, as it is in the case of Phocis now. What offence on the part of Phocis or Sparta or of our own country or anyone else after the statements made by Aeschines caused the miscarriage of what he undertook on that occasion? Ask him that. He will have no reply to it. No more than five days covered all these events, his false statements, our belief of them, the reception of the news at Phocis, her surrender and her destruction. Which makes it perfectly clear that the destruction of Phocis was a matter of deliberate falsehood and a carefully hatched plot. All the time that Philip was prevented from activity by the peace moves but was still mobilized, he was making approaches to Sparta with promises to do everything she wanted. This was to prevent Phocis from securing her assistance by means of Athenian support. But when he arrived at Thermopylae, when Sparta had realized the trick and withdrawn, he used Aeschines as a decoy for the delusion of Athens. Otherwise Athens might grasp that his activities favoured Thebes, and he might be reduced to a period of delay and hostilities and time-wasting, with Phocis on the defensive assisted by Athens. He wanted to gain universal control without opposition. And he succeeded. Therefore you must not allow Philip's deception of Sparta and Phocis to enable Aeschines to escape the penalty for his delusion of Athens. To do so would be a perversion of justice.

Now if he claims, as a counterweight to Phocis and Thermopylae

31. See note 11, p. 62, above.

32. i.e. Sparta from Thebes in the years after the defeat at Leuctra in 371 B.C., Euboea also from Thebes in 357.

and all the other losses this country has sustained, that the Chersonese[33] is still subordinate to her, I most strongly urge you, gentlemen of the jury, not to tolerate nor to add to the injuries we have
sustained over the conference by allowing the fabrication of an
added stigma arising from the defence in the suggestion that we
engineered a profit under the counter at the expense of the survival
of our allies. This is not true. It was after peace was made, when
the Chersonese was secure, while Phocis still had four months to
survive, that Aeschines' false statements eventually brought her
down by deluding Athens. And even now you will find that the
Chersonese is in greater danger than it was. Do you suppose it
would have been easier to bring Philip to justice for offences
against the Chersonese before he had secured his advantage over
Athens or now? Far easier before, I suggest. So what is the extra
value of the Chersonese at a time when the dangers and anxieties
of her potential attacker are removed?

There is something else too which I hear he intends to produce,
that he wonders why he is being accused by Demosthenes, but by
no one at all from Phocis. I had better forewarn you how this
matter stands. Of the Phocians in exile the best, I imagine, and the
most reasonable, driven as they are from their country and brought
to so dire a fate, remain inactive. None of them would make their
country's disasters a ground for private enmity. Others, who
would do anything for money, have no one to provide it. I
personally wouldn't give anyone a halfpenny to support me by
making an outcry about his miseries. The truth itself, the very
facts cry out to tell you. The people of Phocis itself are in a pitiable
state of suffering in which legal remedies at the Athenian investigation of accounts are not an issue. The issue for them is slavery.
They are in mortal terror of Thebes and of Macedonian mercenaries, whom they are forced to maintain, disarmed as they are and
separated into villages. Do not let Aeschines make this claim. Make
him demonstrate that Phocis is not in ruins, or that he did not
promise that Philip would preserve her. This is the real substance
of the questions at the investigation: 'What action has been taken?'

33. Now the Gallipoli peninsula, then important for the Athenian corn route
from the Black Sea. Athens had controlled the peninsula in the fifth century
and regained it in 357 B.C.

and 'What report did you render? If a true one, you go free; if a false one, you are punished.' The absence of Phocian representatives proves nothing. They were treated in such a way, in part by you, as to be unable either to cry for help to their friends or to resist their enemies.

In addition it is easy to prove that, apart from the loss of good name and reputation caused by the affair, Athens has been involved in considerable danger from it. It can be no secret that the Phocian war and the Phocian command of Thermopylae at once gave us security against Thebes and the certainty that neither the Peloponnese nor Euboea or Attica could be invaded by Macedon. This security, which Athens enjoyed, both geographical and political, has been surrendered to the mendacious and misleading persuasion of Aeschines and his supporters. It had the sanction of armed force, of years of warfare, of the alliance of large cities and considerable territory, and now we have shut our eyes and let it fall in ruin. In vain was the previous Athenian move to Thermopylae,[34] made at a cost of over two hundred talents, if you count the private expenditure of its members. In vain were our hopes about Thebes. But numerous and disastrous as have been the services he has rendered to Philip, the affair which has shown the most unashamed contempt of Athens and of us all, let me tell you, is that, when Philip had all through decided to act towards Thebes as he did, Aeschines reported the opposite. He made plain your dislike of these intentions, thereby causing Theban relations with Athens to deteriorate and improving them with Philip. Could he have done anything more offensive?

Now take the decree of Diophantus[35] and Callisthenes[36] and

---

34. In 352 B.C., when Philip moved towards Thermopylae after defeating the Phocian force in Thessaly (see note 9 above). On the implication that Athenian hoplites had to keep themselves, see A. H. M. Jones, *Athenian Democracy*, p. 31.

35. Diophantus of Sphettus was a leading Athenian politician, referred to twice again in this speech (198, 297, pp. 104 and 128 below). The occasion of this decree was the successful occupation of Thermopylae mentioned in the previous note.

36. This decree evidently authorized the evacuation of the countryside of Attica and the withdrawal of the population behind the walls. See also 125 below, p. 86.

read it. It will prove that when Athens acted as she should she was felt both at home and abroad to deserve civil and religious celebrations, but after being deluded by these people it was a matter of bringing women and children in from the fields and of a vote to conduct the feast of Heracles within the walls, and that in time of peace. It makes me feel astonished that a man who never even gave religion its traditional honour can possibly be left unpunished. Now please read the decree.

(The decree is read.)

On that occasion, gentlemen of the jury, your decree was worthy of the circumstances. Now read the next one.

(The second decree is read.)

Such was the decree on that occasion, a decree caused by Aeschines and Philocrates. It was not what we expected at the beginning either of the peace or of the alliance, nor even when we were induced to add the phrase 'and his descendants' to the text. We had hopes of astonishing benefits which they were to accord us. Since then you know well enough the alarm we have felt at the news of Philip's power and Philip's mercenaries at Porthmus or Megara[37]. But the fact that they are not yet on the threshold of Attica is not one to encourage idleness. If these people have enabled him to do this at will, we should keep it in mind, direct our attention to the danger and vent our hatred and our retribution on the man who gave Philip this power.

Now I am quite sure that Aeschines will avoid a relevant discussion of the actual charges. He will attempt to draw you as far as possible from the facts by describing the benefits everyone derived from the peace, and the miseries of the war. He will turn it into a general eulogy on the blessings of peace and make that his defence. But in fact this constitutes a further condemnation of him. If the cause of such benefit to others was also the cause of such extensive trouble and danger to Athens, what is one to say of it

37. Porthmus was the port of Eretria in southern Euboea, where Philip later assisted in the overthrow of democracy (in 342 B.C.). At Megara an attempt to introduce a force of Philip's mercenaries was defeated in 343.

except that the corruption these people employed turned success into disaster? 'Well, isn't it the peace that gives you three hundred triremes and all that equipment and wealth,[38] which is so much profit and will continue to be so?' That is what he may say. Your reply to it should be that the peace has made Philip's position far easier too, by the wealth of equipment, territory and revenue which he has gained. We had some gains too. But in the field of affairs and alliances which enables most states to possess advantages for themselves or for stronger neighbours, our position has been lost to us by corruption and invalidated, while Philip's has largely increased in power and importance. It is not equitable if Philip is to develop in both directions because of the activities of Aeschines and Philocrates, in the acquisition both of allies and of resources, while the benefits which the peace would in any case have brought us are to be set against what they have corruptly surrendered. Our gains are not a compensation for such losses. By no means. They would have been ours in any case, and the rest too, had it not been for this party.

In a word, gentlemen, you would presumably call it justice that if endless disasters had befallen Athens without being due to Aeschines the resentment should not fall on him, and similarly that any good done by another hand should not save him. You should consider the events for which he stands responsible, and afford him both your gratitude, if that is what he deserves, and on the other hand your indignation, if it is that. How, then, are you to make a just appraisal? You can do so if you refuse to allow him to confuse all the issues, the failures of strategy, the course of the war with Philip, the benefits of peace, but regard them all on their merits. Was there a war with Philip? There was. Is there any charge against Aeschines on that, any accusation anyone has to make against him on the conduct of it? None at all. On this score, therefore, he is acquitted, and need make no reference to it. It is the questions in dispute about which the defendant is required to provide witnesses and show evidence. He should not obscure the

38. An Athenian economic recovery had, in fact, taken place chiefly in the years between the Athenian war with the allies (355) and the peace with Philip (346 B.C.). An inscription of 353–352 B.C. records 349 triremes available to the fleet.

issue by a defence which is irrelevant. So he must not mention the war, because he is not being accused about it.

Next, then, we were persuaded to make peace. Correct. We sent representatives, and they brought a delegation here to conclude the peace. Once again is there any charge against Aeschines? Is there any claim that it was he who introduced measures for peace, or that he acted illegally in bringing the other delegates here? None. Therefore he has no call to make any reference to Athens's part in the peace conference. It was not his responsibility. 'Well, then,' I may be asked, 'in that case what possible ground have you for the accusation?' This ground, gentlemen: that at the meeting of the Assembly, not on the question whether to make peace, which had been decided, but on the question of the terms on which it was to be made, Aeschines opposed the course of honour,[39] and for corrupt motives supported the corrupt proposal. Then, when elected to take part in the meeting on formal ratification, he abandoned every item of the instructions given him, and caused the ruin of Athenian allies whose survival was maintained during the war, and in the process was guilty of deliberate falsehood to an extent never paralleled before or since. From the beginning to the time at which Philip had access to the debate, Ctesiphon and Aristodemus[40] took the lead in the deception, but when it came to actual business they handed over to Philocrates and Aeschines, who accepted the task and brought the whole country to disaster. And after that, as he has to render an account and undergo judgement for his conduct of affairs, like the damned, unprincipled character that he is, and a mere clerk at that,[41] he will make his defence as if he stood for peace. This is not in order to cover more ground than the accusation – that would be insane – but because he realizes that while his actual proceedings contain nothing commendable at all, nothing but misconduct, a plea in defence of peace has anyhow a nominal claim to the title of beneficence. As to the peace, gentlemen, I am afraid, I am very much afraid, we may wake up to the realization that it has been made at a heavy rate of compensation.

39. i.e. the demand for the inclusion of Phocis and Halus.

40. See above, 12 (p. 59) and below, 315 (p. 133).

41. Aeschines was secretary to Aristophon and Eubulus, and became clerk to the Assembly.

The sections of it upon which we could rely for security have been betrayed by these people, I mean Phocis and Thermopylae. All the same it was not his doing that we made peace. What I am going to tell you is curious, but it is absolutely true. If there is a man here who is pleased at the peace, it is to the high command, which is universally condemned, that he may feel due gratitude for it. If it had been conducted as we desired, we would not have tolerated so much as a mention of peace. It was the strategy which caused the peace, but it was the corruption of these politicians which has caused its menacing, untrustworthy, precarious character. It is vital, therefore, that you should keep Aeschines off the peace, and put him on the right track, on the subject of his own actions. It is not Aeschines who is on trial for the peace. Certainly not. It is the peace which has been brought into disrepute by Aeschines. The proof is this. Had peace been made without any subsequent deception of Athens or any disaster to our allies, it would have done no damage to anyone apart from its inglorious character. Though this too could be put down to Aeschines for his association with Philocrates, nothing irreparable would have happened. As it is, there is a great deal, and it is Aeschines who is to blame for it.

The damnable, dishonourable conduct of these people, and the damage and destruction they caused, are presumably well known to everyone. I myself have no desire to use underhand methods of information in this business or to ask you to do so, and if it has all been due to stupidity or naïveté or any other form of ignorance, I willingly acquit Aeschines and advise you to do the same. None the less, none of these excuses is appropriate to politics or to a just cause. No one takes to public affairs on official instruction or compulsion. When a man is sufficiently persuaded of his ability to come forward, we act as good sense and humane feeling dictate, we accept him with friendly good will, we elect him to public position and trust him with the conduct of affairs. A man who succeeds earns greater kudos and has the pull over others for that reason. If he fails, will he offer pretexts and excuses? Justice precludes this. It would not give sufficient satisfaction for allies who have been killed or for their women and children or anyone else to know that it was my folly – to avoid saying his – that had caused it. Not by any means. However I urge you to absolve Aeschines from such terrible, overwhelming mismanagement, if it is folly or ignorance of any sort which has led to the damage he has done. If on the other hand it is misconduct in the corrupt acceptance of bribery, and the facts themselves are clear proof of it, you should by rights inflict the death penalty, or, if you stop short of execution, you should make a permanent and public example of him. Consider now the proof of the facts I offer, and the justice of it.

Aeschines must explain his statements of that time on the subject of Phocis, Thespiae and Euboea if we are to believe that he did not sell his services and create misconception on purpose. There are only two alternatives. Either he heard Philip make these promises in so many words, or, if not, he was duped by the magic of Philip's benevolence and these were mere hopes he got from him. There is no third possibility. Either of these should have led him to an unequalled detestation of Philip. Why? Because his association with Philip has left him in the extreme of disaster and disgrace. He has deceived Athens, he has been discredited and he is on trial. If he had a fraction of his deserts, he would have been subject to criminal prosecution long ago. As it is, it is due to the easy credulity of Athens that he is only subjected to the investigation of his accounts, and that at a moment of his own choosing. Well, is there a man here who has ever heard a word of accusation against Philip on the part of Aeschines? Is there anyone who has witnessed a word in refutation of him? No one at all. Every man in the street in Athens has been quicker to make accusations of Philip, though none has any private wrong to complain of. What I expected him to say, if he was not corrupt, was, 'Gentlemen, I throw myself on your mercy. I was too trusting, I was duped, I made an error which I acknowledge. But, gentlemen, beware of this man. You cannot believe him. He will trick you. He is immoral. You see how he has treated me, how he has deluded me.' But I do not hear a word of this sort, nor do you. Why? Because he has not been misled or deluded. It is bribery and corruption which led him to say what he did and to betray us to Philip. To him he has done a square deal as a hired employee, but as an Athenian delegate and citizen he is a traitor who deserves the death penalty over and over again.

This is not the only proof that his statements were entirely corrupt. Quite recently[42] a deputation from Thessaly accompanied by Macedonian representatives arrived in Athens with the claim that Philip should be made a member of the Amphictyonic League. The man who should have been the strongest opponent of this demand was Aeschines. Why? Because Philip's actions had been the opposite of Aeschines' announcements. These had been that Philip was to fortify Thespiae and Plataea, that he would not destroy Phocis, but would put an end to Theban intransigence. Actually Philip has added to the power of Thebes, he has utterly destroyed Phocis, he has not fortified Thespiae and Plataea, but has brought Orchomenus and Coronea[43] to complete slavery as well. Could there be any greater reversal? Well, Aeschines has said nothing against it. He has not opened his mouth or spoken a word of objection. And this is not all, bad as it is. He has voiced his agreement, the only man of the whole population of Athens to do so. Even Philocrates dared not do that, and he is reprehensible enough. But Aeschines did. There was a general outcry, and he was shouted down. He left the platform with a sneer for the benefit of the Macedonian representatives to the effect that there were plenty of people to shout, but not enough to fight when it was needed – you remember the incident – as though he were himself outstanding as a soldier, one supposes.

Again, if we had no proof of bribery against any of the delegation, and the truth had not been open for all to see, the last resort would have been torture and that sort of thing.[44] But as Philocrates not merely acknowledged it publicly on several occasions, but made it absolutely clear by his dealings in the corn market, his building operations, his talk of going abroad, whether officially or otherwise, by his imports of timber and ostentatious money transactions at the bank, it is hardly open to him to claim that he received nothing, when he admitted it himself and gave proof of it. Can we then suppose anyone so devoid of either sense or decision

42. In 346 B.C.

43. Cities in western Boeotia which had been freed from Theban control by Phocis. See note 11 above.

44. i.e. the torture of slaves. To us this seems both barbarous and useless. But it is often mentioned by Greek authors as a means of arriving at the truth (see *Greek Political Oratory*, p. 68, note).

as to allow Philocrates[45] to make the gain while he takes the disrepute and the danger, and instead of accepting examination among men of innocence and integrity, to quarrel with them and ask to be impugned as an associate of Philocrates? It seems impossible. A correct view will find in all this powerful and clear proof of corruption.

Last, but not least, among the proofs of Aeschines' venality is this which I now ask you to observe. You are aware no doubt that the other day, when Hyperides indicted Philocrates, I rose and complained of one item in the indictment, that Philocrates should have been made responsible for so many heinous offences, and the other nine of the deputation for none. I denied that it was true. Philocrates would have been nothing by himself, I claimed, in the absence of his accomplices. To avoid making claims of 'guilty' or 'not guilty', I said, but to let actual facts provide the proof of complicity or the opposite, I proposed that it should be open to anyone at will to stand up and attest publicly the fact that he was not involved in Philocrates' proceedings nor approved of them. Anyone doing this I would exculpate. I think you must remember that. Well, no one appeared or presented himself. Each of the others had some pretext for this. He was not liable to examination, or perhaps he was not there, or he was related to the accused man. None of these applied to Aeschines, who stands so committed to his corrupt practice (which it is clear is not confined to the past, but offers fresh proof that if he escapes now he will be in Philip's service against Athens) that to avoid speaking a single syllable against Philip he refuses acquittal even if offered it, and prefers to accept disrepute, legal action, anything, at Athens rather than do anything to displease Philip. But what does this association with Philocrates and this anxiety in his interest amount to? Even if his conduct of the conference was as splendid and as valuable as is possible, but combined with the admission of corrupt practice, as it was, this one feature should have been a thing for the honest delegate to shun with all possible caution, and protest his own innocence of it. Aeschines has not done this. Can there be any

45. Philocrates was indicted by Hyperides for corruption early in 343 B.C., shortly before Demosthenes' indictment of Aeschines, and was condemned and compelled to leave Athens.

doubt of all this, gentlemen? Does it not cry out to proclaim that Aeschines has been subject to corruption, that he continually discards principle for money, and that it is not due to folly or ignorance or mischance?

'What evidence of corruption is there against me?' he will ask. This is the really telling point.[46] The facts, Aeschines, are the most reliable test of all. It cannot be said or objected that they are subject to persuasion or ingratiation on anyone's part. The character you have given them by your betrayal and corruption they are shown on examination to maintain. But there is additional evidence too — your own. Answer me this before the court. You cannot say it is lack of experience which makes you unable to find an answer. A man who can undertake such novel cases of a theatrical kind and without witnesses at that, and win them against time[47] must obviously be a skilled speaker.

There is a whole series of heinous offences which stand against the name of Aeschines and imply a depraved character. I think you share this view. But there is nothing more serious, nothing which more clearly shows on the face of it that he is corrupt and has sold his integrity, than what I now intend to put before you. The third time the task was being undertaken of sending representatives to Macedon on the basis of the impressive and extensive undertakings made by Philip,[48] Aeschines and I were chosen together with most of the rest of the same delegation. I formally cried off at once. There were loud shouts for me to go, but I refused. Aeschines had been elected. When the assembly adjourned, his party got together and discussed whom to leave in Athens. Everything was still in the air and the future quite uncertain, and all kinds of discussions and rumours were current in the market place. They were afraid an extraordinary meeting might be summoned at which

46. See Appendix, p. 331.

47. Demosthenes again refers to Aeschines' career on the stage, combining it with a reference to the time allowance for speakers, which was normally limited, as apparently in this case. See Aeschines' reply (*Treaty*, 126, p. 173 below).

48. After Aeschines' report of Philip's plans for attacking Thebes, it was resolved that, if Phocis refused to surrender Delphi to the Amphictyons, Athens would take steps against her, and a delegation was sent to inform Philip of this resolution.

the truth might be learnt from me and a motion passed in honourable terms in defence of Phocis and the position lost for Philip. Once a motion was passed and the slightest glint of hope remained, Phocis might have been saved. Had not Athens been duped, it was impossible, quite impossible that Philip should remain at Thermopylae. There were no supplies of corn, as the war had prevented sowing, and none could be imported as long as Athenian ships were there in command of the sea, while the cities of Phocis were numerous and hard to capture without a long siege. If he could capture as much as a city a day, there were still twenty-two of them. This being so, to ensure that Athens should not be undeceived they left Aeschines here. Resignation without adequate reason was a serious matter which gave rise to grave suspicion. 'What? After giving the news of all these tremendous benefits, do you mean to say you're not going on the conference to bring them home?'[49] But it was vital to stay behind. How could it be managed? He made a pretext of illness, and his brother got hold of Execestus, who was a doctor, and then went to the Council and declared on oath that Aeschines was ill, and was himself appointed to the delegation.

Five or six days after the destruction of Phocis Aeschines' pay was stopped, as anyone else's would be. Dercylus crossed from Chalcis and brought news to an Assembly held at the Peiraeus of the destruction of Phocis. Like him Athenians were naturally appalled and horrified at the news. There was a decision to bring women and children in from the country districts, an order to bring the frontier posts into readiness, fortify the Peiraeus and hold the festival of Heracles[50] in the city. At this point, at a moment of such clamour and confusion in Athens, our clever schemer with the wonderful voice went off without any instruction from Council or People, on a deputation to the perpetrator of the mischief. There was no word of the illness which had given a pretext for his resignation, no reference to a different appointment in his place, no mention of the enactment by which such proceedings are stated to be punishable by death, no suggestion of the scandal of first announcing that a price had been put on his head

---

49. Aeschines replies to this in his speech (*Treaty*, 94, p. 165 below).
50. Normally held outside the city.

at Thebes and then waiting till Thebes had acquired all Boeotia and now gained control of the territory of Phocis as well. He just walked into the middle of them, straight into the Theban camp. He was so devoid of good sense, so engrossed in the corrupt profits of his bribery, that he blandly took the journey without turning a hair.

This was bad enough, but there was much worse that he perpetrated after he got there. Members of this jury, like everyone else in Athens, looked on the fate of the unfortunate people of Phocis as so cruel, so appalling, as to refuse to send even the Council officials to the Pythian games,[51] and allowed their traditional representation to lapse. Aeschines, however, appeared at the thanksgiving celebrations for success in the war which were solemnized by Thebes and Philip. He was present at the banquet, taking part in the religious ceremonial performed by Philip in triumph over our allies' lost fortifications, their territory and their armament, now taken from them. He took part in the jubilations and songs of triumph and drank Philip's health.

There is no question of my giving one version and he another. The facts of his resignation are given in the public records in the temple of Demeter under official control, and there is specific reference to him by name. As regards his actions in Macedonia, evidence against him will be given by his fellow delegates who were there. It is their account which I received, not having been a party to the delegation, from which I resigned. Now read the decrees and call the evidence.

(The decree is read and the evidence heard.)

What prayer to the gods at this service do you suppose was offered by Philip or by the Theban delegates? Must it not have been a prayer for power and victory in war for themselves and their allies, and damnation to Phocis? If so, that is the prayer Aeschines took part in, an imprecation against his country which it falls to you to turn to his own destruction.

Very well. He left Athens in contravention of a law which imposes the death penalty for doing so. On his arrival his actions are shown to have deserved the same penalty over again. And his

51. Held at Delphi in September 346 B.C.

previous behaviour and his conduct of the delegation in the Macedonian interest would bring him to the scaffold with full justification. I therefore invite you to consider what sentence will meet his deserts, will appear an adequate equivalent for all these offences. It must be thought a dishonour that the whole people, that everyone in Athens, should publicly proclaim their condemnation of the results of the peace, should refuse to participate in the festival of the Amphictyons and cast black and suspicious looks on Philip for impious, damnable proceedings which were as unjust as they were disastrous to us, and yet should come to court to give judgement on the actions which led to them, under oath publicly administered, and acquit the man who is the cause of all these disasters and has been found in the very act. Every man in Athens, every man in Greece, would be justified in crying shame upon you, in the knowledge of your indignation against Philip for ending the war by buying a peace in the political market, which is an excusable offence, while you acquit Aeschines of such shameful and corrupt conduct, when the law imposes the extreme penalty for it.

It may be that we shall hear this sort of plea from them, that a repudiation of the proceedings of the delegates to the conference will open bad relations with Philip. If this is true, personally I can think of no stronger reason for accusing Aeschines. If the leader who has paid to secure the peace has risen to such formidable power that Athenians disregard justice and their sworn oaths to consider how they can please him, what can be inflicted on the people responsible for his power, to give them their deserts? However, I believe it can also be shown that the beginnings of a more valuable friendship will in all probability emerge from their punishment. You must realize this, that Philip does not feel contempt for the city of Athens. It is not because he thinks less of us than of the people of Thebes that he has shown a preference for the latter. He has learnt a lesson from them. He has been told what I once mentioned in the Assembly and was not contradicted, that democracy is the most uncertain thing in the world, as unpredictable and as unstable as a wave of the sea, and as liable to the sudden influence of chance. Individuals may come and go, without pursuing or recollecting the general good. What he needs is some friends to conduct and control Athenian affairs in his interest, as he would himself.[52] Once this is contrived he will get anything he wants from Athens. Well, if he had learnt that the promoters of this opinion had been brought to a violent death the moment they returned, he would have taken a leaf out of the King of Persia's book. What was his method? He was taken in by Timagoras[53] to whom he gave forty talents, it is said. When he learnt that Timagoras had met his death in Athens, and had not even been able to make good his own life, let alone the services he had promised, he realized that the receiver of the money could not fulfil the contract. Consequently he restored Amphipolis to Athenian control, after previously assigning to it alliance and friendship with himself, and abandoned the practice of bribery for the future. This is what Philip would have done, had he learnt of punishment inflicted on his friends, and will do, if it happens in the future. But when the news he hears is of their speeches, their high reputation, their judgements of others, what can we expect? That he will deliberately spend a lot of money when he could manage with less, that he will seek the favour of the world when one or two people would be enough? It would be insane. It was no free choice he made to cultivate Thebes. Of course not. He was led to it by the conference. I'll tell you how. He was received by Theban representatives at the same time as by our own. He offered them a bribe, and a considerable one, according to their account. The Theban representatives refused to accept it. After this there was a ceremony and a dinner, at which Philip drank with them and treated them with general consideration, offered them various presents, prisoners for instance, and finally tried to bestow gold and silver plate on them. The Thebans were by way of rejecting everything, and never committed themselves. Eventually one of their delegation, named Philo, made a speech which might better have been made by Athenian than by Theban representatives. He said he was delighted to see Philip's generous and considerate attitude towards his delegation. However, Thebes was already on terms of friendly association with Philip even without these presents, and urged that he might transfer his interest to their affairs, on which he

---

52. See Appendix, p. 331.
53. In 367 B.C.; see note 16 above.

was engaged at the moment, and turn to suggestions of value to both Thebes and himself, in which case their whole city as well as the delegation would be greatly in his debt. You should in fact remember what the result of this was for Thebes, what happened to her, and regard objectively the nature of this refusal to sell one's interests to the enemy. She secured in the first place peace after her labours and miseries and her defeat in the war, secondly the utter ruin of her enemies in Phocis, whose walls and towns were destroyed. But this is not all. In addition she gained Orchomenus, Coronea, Corsia, Tilphosaeum[54] and as much Phocian territory as they wanted.

That was the outcome of the peace for Thebes, and no one could ask for more. And what about the Theban delegates? All they got out of it was the credit of having secured this for their country. But this, gentlemen, stands high in the history of nobility and renown, and this is what Aeschines and his associates sold for money. Compare now the outcome of the peace for the people of Athens and for the Athenian representatives, and consider what parallel there is between the result for the city and for these individuals. For Athens the result was divorce from her entire[55] possessions and her allies alike, and a sworn undertaking to Philip to thwart any other attempt to recover them, and to look with enmity upon anyone who might wish to transfer them to her, and with friendship and cooperation on the man who robbed her. To this Aeschines agreed, and the proposal was drafted by his coadjutor, Philocrates. I won my point the day before, and carried a proposal to our representatives to confirm the decision of our allies[56] and summon Philip's delegation. But Aeschines got it adjourned to the following day and induced the meeting to accept Philocrates' proposal, which included this and a number of still more disastrous clauses. Such was the outcome of the peace for Athens. It would be hard to find anything more dishonourable. And what was the fortune of the delegates who brought it about?

54. On Orchomenus and Coronea see note 43 above. Corsia was in southwest Boeotia on the Corinthian Gulf, Tilphosaeum a mountain near Lake Copais.

55. A gross exaggeration.

56. See note 6 above.

I omit most of it, because you saw it yourselves, the houses, the timber, the wheat, endless possessions and farm property in the territory of the allies, which brought in an income of a talent to Philocrates and half that amount to Aeschines. Surely it must be thought scandalous and intolerable that the ruin of your allies should have been turned into profit for your delegates, and that the peace which brought to the country which sponsored them the ruin of their allies and the loss of their possessions, and turned their glory to dishonour, should have loaded the party in the delegation which was responsible for it with added wealth and prosperity, with property and opulence, in place of the extreme of poverty. But in proof of the truth of my statement please call the Olynthian witnesses.

(The evidence of witnesses is heard.)

I should not be surprised if he goes so far as to say that it was impossible to make an honourable peace such as I demanded because of the misdirection of the war by the commanders. If he takes this line, I insist that you reply from your memory of events by asking whether it was Athens he had gone to represent or some other city. If it was another, which he is prepared to maintain won the war and enjoyed skill in generalship, there was some justification in accepting bribery. But if it was our own Athens, what justification can there be for openly accepting added presents for his services in connection with losses made by the city which sent him to represent her? Justice demands that the same treatment should be accorded to the official delegates as to the city which they represented. Then there is another point, gentlemen of the jury. Which do you take to have been the greater success in the war, that of Phocis over Thebes or that of Philip over Athens? I am quite sure it was that of Phocis over Thebes. Phocis held Orchomenus, Coronea and Tilphosaeum, she had cut off their force at Neon, caused 270 casualties at Hedulaeum,[57] setting up a trophy, and established her superiority in cavalry. Thebes had been beset by a whole Iliad of troubles. Nothing of this sort was true of our country, and it is to be hoped it never will be. This

57. Neon was a city in Phocis east of Mt Parnassus, Hedulaeum a mountain north of Lake Copais. The incidents are otherwise unknown.

was the worst feature of the war against Philip, that we were unable to inflict on him the damage we should have liked, though we enjoyed complete freedom from injury ourselves. Why was it that the same peace enabled Thebes, so defeated in the war, both to regain her own possessions and to add her enemy's to them, while we ourselves lost in the peace what we had preserved in the war? Because Theban interests were not sold by the Theban delegates, as ours were by Aeschines and Philocrates.[58] The truth of this will be more clearly shown by what follows:

When this peace, the Peace of Philocrates, to which Aeschines expressed his agreement, was finally concluded, when Philip's representatives had given their concurrence by taking the oaths – before which nothing irreparable had been done – it was a dishonourable peace and a disgrace to Athens, but there were to be tremendous concessions to offset this. At this point I insisted on a suggestion which I impressed on Aeschines and Philocrates, to sail to the Hellespont, to avoid losing control of the situation, and to prevent Philip from seizing any more key points there in the interval. I knew perfectly well that any losses due to the change from war to peace can never be made good by the indolent. No one who has ever been induced to make peace on the main issue has been prepared to go to war again for things left in uncertainty. Here possession is nine points of the law. Now apart from this I didn't think the country could fail to make one of two gains, if the expedition were made. Either we should make our appearance and compel Philip's ratification, in which case he would surrender to Athens what he had appropriated and keep his hands off anything else, or any failure on his part would be at once reported in Athens. In that case his rapacity and perfidy in these remote and unimportant instances would give a line on the important ones nearer home – Phocis and Thermopylae – over which we should not lose control. And if he did not steal a march on us there and Athens were not misled, her position would be secure and justice would be done her without demur. I thought I had reason to suppose this could be attained. So long as Phocis was entire, as she then was, and in control of Thermopylae, Philip would have had no threat to menace us with which could have induced us to forgo any of our

58. See Appendix, p. 331.

rights. He was not in a position to make an attack on Attica, which a land movement or a naval victory would have won him. On the other hand any illegal practice on his part could be met on ours by an instant closure of the ports, which would cause a shortage of money and supplies and again reduce him to a state of siege, and make him, instead of Athens, dependent on the advantage of peace. Now, that this is no figment of *ex post facto* imagination, but a genuine piece of foresight made at the time is proved by this: at the time when there was no meeting of the Assembly left,[59] because they had all been used already, but Aeschines and his friends were still waiting in Athens and had not yet gone, I drafted a decree as a member of the Council, that under powers conferred by the People on the Council the delegation should leave with all possible speed, and that Proxenus, as strategus, should convey them wherever it was discovered that Philip then was. The proposal was made explicitly in these words, as I give them. Now read the decree.

(The decree is read.)

So I made them go – against their will, as their subsequent actions prove. When we arrived at Oreus[60] and contacted Proxenus, they didn't sail off and carry out their instructions, not they. They proceeded on a circuitous route, and before arriving in Macedonia we had spent twenty-three days. The rest of the time we hung about in Pella,[61] waiting for Philip to arrive, and including this we had been fifty whole days on the journey. The interval was spent by Philip in the capture of Doriscus,[62] Thrace and its fortified posts, the Sacred Mount, and the control and organization of the whole position in the district. This was in time of peace under the

59. The Assembly was bound to hold four statutory meetings in each 'prytany', and did not exceed this number unless specially convened by the Council. A prytany was one tenth of the year, the period during which the fifty members of one tribe (Prytaneis) served as executive committee.

60. Oreus was at the north-western tip of Euboea, facing Thessaly.

61. Pella was the principal city of Macedon, about twenty-four miles north-west of the modern Salonica. See Aeschines, *Treaty*, 108, p. 168, and *Crown*, 160, p. 234 below.

62. These are places of uncertain location in south-east Thrace on Philip's way to the Chersonese and the Hellespont. He was engaged in taking them from the native king, Cersobleptes.

terms of the treaty. During this time I made repeated comments, and in general said all I could, at first in the way of official exhortation, then of information to the ignorant. Finally I abandoned all restraint, and addressed them as corrupt traitors. The open opponent of every speech of mine and every decree was Aeschines. Whether the same view was approved by the rest of the delegation is yet to be seen. At present I say nothing, I make no accusation against anyone. Nor is anyone under any compulsion at the present time to show his good intentions. It can be left to his own conduct, his actual freedom from participation in any of the wrong that was done. That this was dishonourable, serious and corrupt, you have all realized. The names of those involved will be clear from the facts.

It is claimed that it was during this time that the oath of ratification was taken by the allies, and other necessary formalities carried out. This is not so at all. The delegation had been away three whole months at the cost of a thousand drachmae of public money in expenses, without any administration of oaths to anyone either on the way there or back. The oaths were sworn at the Castor and Pollux inn (anyone who has been to Pherae will know it) while Philip was on his way back with his army, at great cost to Athenian honour and prestige. But there was nothing Philip could have thought of greater value than this way of doing it. These people had been unable to get the peace terms worded as they set out to do, with the phrase 'except Halus and Phocis', and Philocrates had been forced by the Athenian people to excise the words and include explicit reference to 'Athens and her allies'. So Philip didn't want the oath taken in this form by any ally of his. They would not align themselves with him on terms of his present appropriation of your possessions, and the oath would confirm their case. Nor did he want witnesses to undertakings on his part on which the peace was likely to depend, or a public demonstration that it was not Athens which had been worsted in the war, but Philip who had wanted peace, and was prepared to make concessions to get it. In his desire to avoid a general demonstration of all this he did not want the delegation to go anywhere. They gratified his wishes by an ostentatious and ingratiating display of deference to him. Now, when the charge is brought home against them, when they are convicted of squandering valuable time, of casting away the position in Thrace, of failing to carry out any of their country's instructions or preserve her interests, and of issuing perjured statements, how can it be consistent with a reliable and conscientious court of justice that Aeschines should secure an acquittal? As evidence of the truth of my statements read first the decree, to prove the obligation to administer the oath, then Philip's letter, and then Philocrates' decree and that of the People of Athens.

(The decree, letter and subsequent decrees are read.)

I now call witnesses present at the time to prove that we should have found Philip on the Hellespont if my demands had been agreed to and the city's orders in the decree obeyed.

(The evidence of witnesses is heard.)

Now read the other piece of evidence, Philip's reply to Eucleides,[63] who arrived later.

(The evidence is read.)

The next point I want to make is that they cannot even deny that their actions were aimed at Philip's advantage. When the first delegation left for the peace conference, a herald was sent in advance to secure our safe conduct. On that occasion, as soon as they reached Oreus they refused to wait for the herald or spend any unnecessary time. Halus was under siege, but they sailed across there. Parmenio was also occupied with a siege, but they went to him next, and left there to travel through the enemy lines to Pagasae. On they went and finally met the herald at Larissa. That shows the eagerness and the speed with which they went on their way. On the other hand after the peace had been made, and they had complete safety for their movements and instructions from Athens to make all possible speed, they were not concerned to hurry the land journey or to take to the sea. Why? Because on the first occasion it was speed that was in Philip's interest, now it was the waste of as much time as possible before the ratification was sworn. Again to prove the truth of my statement, take this evidence.

63. Eucleides was sent to protest against Philip's action in attacking the territory of Cersobleptes.

(The evidence is read.)

What clearer proof could there be that the proceedings were conducted entirely in Philip's interest than their inertia when it paid Athens to hurry, and their haste on the same journey when it paid her to make no move at all without the herald?

Now during the time when we were hanging about at Pella I want you to realize what course of action each of us chose to take. Personally I set about seeking out and redeeming prisoners, and I thought it right to spend money of my own for the purpose, and asked Philip to let us ransom them out of funds devoted to our own entertainment. You shall hear in a minute what Aeschines' continual practice was. What was the object of Philip's frequent offers of money to the delegates? I want you to realize this as well. Philip was sounding us. How? By communications sent to each of us privately with considerable offers of money. When he failed with one or other of us – I need not specify my own instance, since facts and actual conduct are evidence enough – he concluded that a present in common would be accepted without demur. It would confer indemnity on those who had been corrupted, if all had some small share in a common present. He therefore made the offer on the pretext of hospitality. As I put a stop to the proceeding, Aeschines' friends made a fresh distribution of it in their own favour. When I asked Philip to spend the money on the prisoners,[64] he couldn't very well condemn them or say 'it is in the hands of so and so and so and so', or avoid the expenditure I asked for. So he agreed, but postponed payment to the Panathenaea, when he said he would send it. Now read the evidence of Apollophanes, and then of the other eye-witnesses.

(The evidence is read.)

Now let me tell you about those prisoners whose release I myself secured. All the time we spent at Pella before Philip arrived, some of the captured who were on bail distrusted my ability to persuade Philip, and said they would secure their own ransom without being indebted to Philip for it. Accordingly they proposed to

64. i.e. Athenian prisoners captured at the fall of Olynthus, whose ransom Demosthenes worked for.

borrow three minae or four or whatever it was for their ransom. So when Philip agreed to release the rest, I collected the ones I had lent money to, told them what had happened, to prevent their feeling they had had the worst of the bargain by their hurry and by making their own arrangements for their ransom though they were not well off, and made them a present of their ransom money. Read the evidence which substantiates this.

(The evidence is read.)

The amount of money I spent or gave as a free gift to Athenian citizens who had been in misfortune is now clear. Now Aeschines may say, 'Well, Demosthenes, if it is as you say, if I entered into an agreement with Philocrates and from then on you knew our proceedings were unjustifiable, why did you associate yourself with the later deputation for the formal ratification instead of withdrawing from it?' In answer to this you must remember that I had given my undertaking to the prisoners I ransomed to bring the money and do all I could to rescue them. It would have been a disgrace to go back on my word and fail Athenian citizens in their time of disaster. On the other hand, to go all the way there privately after withdrawing from the deputation would have been both improper and unsafe. Had it not been for the desire to rescue these people I would not have associated with delegates of their kind at any price. I'd rather have died. Look what happened later. I was twice elected on the third delegation[65] and twice withdrew. Besides, on this expedition I opposed them at every turn. When I was my own master, this was the way I conducted myself. When they were in a majority and carried their wishes, the result was disaster. Yet all might have been as successful as my proceedings were, had my advice been followed. I am not so futile or unthinking a character as to give away money when I could see others were being paid it, out of pure public spirit in the interest of Athens, and at the same time disapprove of what could have been achieved without expense and with far greater benefit to Athens. And in absolute truth, gentlemen, this might have been the case. The fact is that they were too strong for me.

Put Aeschines' achievements against mine, and those of Philo-

65. See 122 above, p. 85.

crates too. The comparison will make the point clearer. First, then, they put Phocis and Halus outside the treaty, also Cersobleptes, in contravention of the decree and the agreement with Athens. Secondly, they attempted to upset and alter the decree which was the basis of the conference. In addition they included a clause to make Cardia[66] a Macedonian ally, they countermanded the report I drafted to send to Athens, and sent a disingenuous concoction of their own. Then our admirable Aeschines asserted that I had promised Philip to bring down democratic rule in Athens because I protested at these proceedings, which I not merely thought dishonourable, but feared might cause my own ruin on their account. Yet all the time he was maintaining private intelligence with Philip without a pause. I pass over most of it. But here is one occasion. One night at Pherae, Dercylus was on the watch over him instead of me, keeping my servant there, and he caught Aeschines coming out of Philip's quarters. He told the servant to let me know and to remember it himself. Finally Aeschines was unprincipled and shameless enough, when we were on the move night and day on our return, to remain behind with Philip. The evidence for this consists first in my own written account, to which I shall testify under the oath and sanction of official accounts. In addition I shall call the other deputies individually, and require them to agree to the alternative, and either add their declaration or declare on oath their inability to do so. If they do the latter, I shall give clear proof of their perjury to this court.

(The evidence is read.)

You see the trouble and unpleasantness which bedevilled the whole time I spent abroad on the conference. How do you suppose they conducted themselves at the actual place where they drew their pay, in view of their behaviour here in the presence of the court which has power either to do them honour or to inflict punishment on them?

66. Demosthenes unfairly blames his colleagues for allowing Cardia to take the oath among the allies of Philip. Cardia, consistently hostile to Athens, had been made a special exception when the rest of the Chersonese was given up to Athens by Cersobleptes as early as 357 B.C., and had probably been Philip's ally since 352. Demosthenes' complaint had been made by implication in *On the Peace* (25) and is repeated in *On the Chersonese* (66).

I now want to recapitulate the charges from the beginning, to show that I have fulfilled the undertakings I made at the opening of the speech. I proved that Aeschines' reports were without foundation and aimed at deception. Here I have referred to the actual facts, not to statements. I have proved that he was responsible for the official refusal to listen to my true account, which was discredited because of the undertakings and pronouncements made by Philip, and that he advocated a policy the very reverse of right, that he opposed the peace terms offered by the allies and agreed to those of Philocrates, that he threw away valuable opportunities in order to prevent any movement to Phocis if we had wanted it, and was responsible for a number of other unjustifiable actions during the absence of the delegation, for the betrayal of Athenian interests to secure his own, for receiving bribes and for every sort of enormity. This I undertook to prove at the outset, and I have proved it. Consider what follows from it. The next point to be put before you is quite straightforward. You took the oath to vote in accordance with the laws and decrees of the People and the Council of Five Hundred. But it is proved that Aeschines' conduct as a delegate has been wholly opposed to these laws and decrees and to right. Therefore he must be found guilty by a jury of sound sense like yourselves. If we had nothing else against him, there are two offences which merit the death penalty. He has betrayed to Philip not only Phocis but Thrace as well. No one could point to two districts of greater value to Athens than Thermopylae on land and the Hellespont by sea. Both of these he and his companions have damnably bargained away in defiance of right and to the detriment of Athens. The second of these alone, the abandonment of Thrace and its fortified posts, is an offence of which denunciation could be endless. How many have been condemned to death or to pay enormous fines on similar charges it would not be hard to demonstrate – Ergophilus, Cephisodotus, Timomachus, in the past Ergocles, Dionysius and others,[67] almost all of whom, I should say, have done less to injure Athens

67. Ergophilus commanded in the Hellespont in 363–362 B.C., Ergocles in the same area in 390–389, Timomachus in the Chersonese in 361, Cephisodotus in the Propontis in 359, Dionysius probably in the Hellespont in 387–386. All were Athenian naval commanders. Cephisodotus was thwarted by Charidemus, who forced him to a discreditable treaty, and was dismissed and fined.

than Aeschines. In the past, however, the citizens of Athens took careful precautions against danger, and used foresight. Nowadays anything which is not within the scope of present business, any trouble or drawback which is not immediate, is passed by. Afterwards random resolutions are passed demanding 'peace for Cersobleptes', 'hands off the Amphictyonic states', 'revision of the peace terms', and the like. None of these resolutions would have been needed if Aeschines had been prepared to sail straight away and do what was required of him. As it is, what could have been saved by sailing at once has been dissipated by insisting on a land journey, and what the truth could have secured has been lost by lying.

I understand it is likely that he will protest shortly at being the only speaker at the Assembly to be called to account for his statements. I dismiss the point that anyone should be thought responsible for speeches made under the influence of bribery, and put it to you like this. If Aeschines were a private individual and a great talker who got things wrong, no great insistence should be set on the letter of the law. You should be lenient and let it go. But if he was a delegate who in the conduct of his office was guilty of deliberate deception for corrupt ends, you should not pass it over or tolerate the plea that he ought not to be made responsible for his speeches. What else is there for which delegates ought to be made responsible? Delegates have not control of ships, soldiers, strategy, defences. They are not entrusted with these. But they are responsible for the choice of words and for the choice of occasions. As to the occasions of opportunity for Athens, if he did not squander them beforehand he is not guilty. If he did, he is. As to words, if his were truthful or valuable he may be acquitted, but if they were false, corrupt and disastrous he must be condemned. There is nothing worse than lying words to injure our country. Where one is politically dependent on words, how can the policy be sound if they are false? How can it be free of danger if they depend on bribery in the interests of the enemy? Nor does the choice of occasion depend on honesty anything like so much for oligarchs or tyrants as for Athens. With them everything is done on the instant, at the word of command. With us there is first a debate in the Council[68] and its recommendation to consider, which is not an affair to be carried out no matter when, but one of due notice to heralds and foreign representatives. Then we have to convene a meeting of the Assembly, again only at a time laid down by law. Next the right measure has to be carried and good policy win the day against ignorance and dishonesty. For these purposes, when the measure is decided and approved, time has to be allowed for democratic inefficiency to provide the means necessary to carry it out. And anyone who invalidates these procedures in a state like ours deprives us not merely of the procedures, but of the political action itself.

There is one ready road for all attempts at the deception of Athens, in the cry of 'disturbers of the country, who will not let Philip be our Benefactor'.[69] Against this I bring no arguments. I will just read you Philip's letters and remind you of the circumstances in which we have been led astray on each occasion. That will show you how the hackneyed phrase *ad libitum* applied to his benefits has been by-passed by his misrepresentations.

(The letter of Philip is read.)

That is the extent of the dishonour and the injury he has inflicted on the country. And then he goes round with the question, 'What about Demosthenes and his complaints against his colleagues in the delegation?' Well, this is inevitable, whether I like it or not, after being the target of your intrigues throughout the expedition, which has left me only two alternatives, either to be supposed a party to proceedings of that sort, or to lodge an accusation. I deny that I had any part in your proceedings on the conference. I declare that your conduct as a delegate was active and dangerous, while mine was devoted to the interests of Athens. Your associate on the delegation was Philocrates, and also Phryno. Your policies and preferences were the same. 'Have we not eaten their salt,' he

68. See 31, note 14 above.
69. 'Benefactor' was a title not infrequently bestowed on leading men of other cities (see Demosthenes, *Leptines*, 60) and may be alluded to in the text here. But I follow the Oxford text in taking *ad libitum* rather than the title itself to be the hackneyed phrase intended.

says, 'sat at their table, filled the cup of friendship?', trotting out these high-flown clichés as though it were not the wrong-doers but the righteous who had abandoned such claims. I know that the Prytaneis do sacrifice together on each relevant occasion, and join in the dinner and the loving-cup. That does not mean that the good follow the conduct of the bad. If they find one of their number at fault, they report it to the Council and People. It is the same with the Council, who hold an inaugural service, dine together and take part in communal libation and ceremonial. So do the *strategi* and virtually all officials. Does that mean an indemnity for all wrong-doers? Of course not. Leon brought charges against Timagoras after four years on the same delegation. So did Eubulus against Tharrex and Smicythus after sharing the same mess. So did Conon long ago against Adeimantus, who had been a fellow *strategus*.[70] Which were the offenders against the salt of hospitality and the cup of friendship on those occasions, Aeschines? The betrayers who had been guilty of corruption, or their accusers? Clearly the offenders, such as you, against the claims of public, not merely private responsibility.

To show you that these people have proved the lowest and most despicable of all who ever approached Philip not only in public but in private affairs, may I relate to you an incident which is not connected with the conference? After Philip's capture of Olynthus, when he was celebrating the games at Mount Olympus,[71] he collected all the artists he could to attend the ceremony and the general gathering, gave them a dinner and crowned those who had won prizes. He asked our friend, Satyrus the comic actor, why he was the only one not to put down any public request. Did he feel any want of public spirit in Philip himself? Had he detected any personal ill-feeling? Satyrus' reply, it is said, was that he didn't happen to want anything the others asked for, and what he would like to put down was the easiest thing in the world for Philip to do to please him, but he was afraid he might not be granted it. Philip told him to say what it was, and with a certain youthful extravagance declared he wouldn't refuse him anything. Satyrus then said that Apollophanes of Pydna had been a guest and a great friend of

70. After Aegospotami. See Xenophon, *Hellenica*, I, 7, 1.
71. A Macedonian festival held at Dium, in this case in 348 B.C.

his, but had been treacherously done to death, and his relations had taken his daughters away to Olynthus when they were children. 'Now,' he went on, 'since the capture of Olynthus they have been prisoners, and are in your hands, and of an age to be married. The request that I make to you is to hand them over to me. And I hope you will understand when I point out the kind of gift you will be giving me, if you do. I shall get nothing out of it. I shall give them each a dowry and find them husbands, and not allow them to meet with a fate which is beneath myself or their father.' At this the guests at the party gave a loud shout of applause, which shamed Philip into agreeing, although this Apollophanes had been one of the killers of Philip's brother, Alexander.

Let us draw a comparison between this party of Satyrus's and the party enjoyed by Aeschines in Macedonia. You will observe exactly how close the similarity is between the two. Our friends were invited by Xenophanes, whose father, Phaedimus, was one of the Thirty,[72] and went to the party. I did not. When they got to the drinks after dinner, their host brought in an Olynthian girl, who was pretty, but well brought up and a nice girl, as was shown by what happened. They first made her take something to eat and drink in the normal way, as far as I can gather from Iatrocles' account next day. But when things went further and they got warmed up, they told her to sit down and to sing. She was embarrassed, poor girl, and couldn't sing, so she refused. Then Aeschines and Phryno called it intolerable impudence for a damned bitch of an Olynthian captive to give herself airs. 'Send a slave,' they said, 'and get a whip', and a servant came with a strap. They were drunk and ready to get in a fury with anything, I suppose, and though she expostulated and burst into tears, the slave tore her dress across and lashed her several times over the back. She was beside herself with the pain and the treatment she had received, and she leapt up and cast herself at the feet of Iatrocles, and threw down the table as she did so. And if he hadn't rescued her, this drunken brawl would have been the death of her, because when a

---

72. i.e. the so-called Thirty Tyrants, the oligarchic clique who ruled Athens after its surrender to Sparta in 404 B.C. According to Aeschines (*Treaty*, 153 ff., p. 181 below) the jury actually refused to allow Demosthenes to finish this story, when the speech was made.

low brute like Aeschines gets drunk it is horrifying. The story of the girl reached the Ten Thousand[73] in Arcadia, was narrated here by Diophantus, whom I shall put in the witness-box on the subject, and was all over Thessaly in full.

He is quite conscious of his guilt, which is ineradicable. Yet he will dare to look you in the face and talk in his fruity voice of the life he has led. It sticks in my throat altogether. Do you suppose the jury don't know how you began by reading out the texts for your mother's incantations, how you spent your boyhood knocking about in the society of drunken revellers, how after that you were a junior clerk prepared to wink at any iniquity for a few drachmae, and finally of late you were content with a parasitic existence as a minor performer in someone's school of drama?[74] What sort of life can you lay claim to? Where have you lived it? Because it is obvious how it has been passed. And look at the liberties he presumes to take. Fancy his bringing accusations against others in this court for immoral practices! But that is enough. First take these depositions and read them.

(The evidence is read.)

That is the number and the nature of the offences of which his guilt has been proved. The list includes everything imaginable, bribery, flattery, impiety demanding execration, perjury, betrayal of his friends, all the greatest offences known. He will offer no defence against any of them. He will have no adequate or genuine defence to make. The line which I learn he does intend to take borders on insanity, but I suppose that for lack of any other justifiable plea fabrication becomes necessary. I hear he intends to claim that all the charges I am making apply to me equally, that I agreed to it all and took part in it, and have now suddenly changed my tune and started condemning it. In regard to the action that was taken no such defence is either justifiable or relevant, though some such charge might lie against me. If I have taken part in

73. The federal assembly of the Arcadian League. On Diophantus, see note 35 above.

74. These disreputable allegations are made again by Demosthenes, and must be regarded as normal currency in Greek forensic oratory. See Demosthenes, *Crown*, 129, and note, p. 288 below.

these actions, then I am a man of low character, but the actions
themselves are none the better for that. Very much the opposite.
However, I think I should demonstrate both how false this claim
will be, and what is the right line of defence in fact. The correct and
genuine defence is either to prove that the actions complained of
were never committed, or that they were in the interest of Athens.
Neither of these is possible for him. He cannot claim Athenian
interest for the destruction of Phocis, for Philip's control of
Thermopylae, for the added power of Thebes, for the presence of
an army in Euboea, for the intrigues against Megara[75] or for a
peace left unratified. The exact opposite was what he declared was
in her interest and would actually take place. Nor can he maintain
that this is not what happened, when your own first-hand knowledge disproves it. It therefore remains for me to prove that I took
no part in these proceedings. Do you wish me, then, to leave
everything else, the denials I have made in this court, the objections
I made during our absence from Athens, my continued opposition
throughout, and present the evidence of their own admissions to
prove that my conduct has been the precise opposite of theirs, and
in particular that they received payment to damage the country's
interests, while I refused to accept it? Look at this, then.

In the whole of Athens whom would you call the most conspicuous figure of unashamed contempt for morality? No one, I am
sure, even inadvertently, would name anyone but Philocrates.
And who has the loudest voice and the most audible delivery of
any? Aeschines, I am quite sure. And who is the man whom these
would call timid and apprehensive, though I should say cautious,
in front of a crowd? Myself. I have never caused any trouble,
never used force on protesting citizens. Now in all these meetings
of the Assembly, wherever these subjects have arisen, you have
heard from me constant attacks and accusations against these
two, and explicit charges of bribery and corruption in the affairs
of Athens. None of them has ever opened his mouth to contradict
me, or shown his face in public. What is the reason why the most
unprincipled and the most vociferous allow themselves to be thus
put down by the most diffident and soft-spoken? Because there is
strength in truth and weakness in a conscience aware of corruption.

75. On Euboea and Megara, see note 37 above.

This is what saps their courage, disrupts their vocal powers, stops their mouths and chokes them into silence. The last confrontation was at the Peiraeus[76] the other day, when Aeschines was refused membership of a deputation, and uttered loud threats of impeachment and actions against me and cries of 'Shame!' Yet all this sort of thing means long litigation. All that was needed was two or three simple words which would not be beyond a slave bought yesterday. 'Gentlemen, this is wicked. He is accusing me of what he has done himself. He says I have taken bribes, which is what he himself has done or been a party to.' But he said nothing of this sort. You have never heard him utter a word of it. He produced threats which were irrelevant. Why? Because he has a guilty conscience, and words of that kind defeat him. His ideas did not go to that length, because conscience cut them short. But there was nothing to prevent idle, slanderous abuse. However, the most telling thing, which is not a question of words but of action, is this. I was out to do what was right. I had been on two conferences, and wanted to give two accounts of my services. At this point Aeschines approached the auditors[77] with a number of witnesses to forbid my being called into court, as not liable to account. The thing was ridiculous. What did it amount to? Having produced his account of the first of the two, to which no objection was raised, he objected to appearing about the second, with which he is now concerned, on which all the offences were committed. My second appearance involved his appearing twice as well, and that was why he objected. This affair shows you two things quite clearly. The first is that Aeschines is self-condemned, which makes an acquittal a breach of the sanctity of your oath. The second is that all he says about me will be untrue. If he has anything true to say against me, we should have found him ready to criticize and probe it. He would certainly not be forbidding my appearance in court.

In proof of which call the next witnesses. Indeed, if he produces slanderous statements against me which do not bear on the conference, there are many reasons why you should refuse to listen to them. I am not on trial today, and I am not given any second time

76. Perhaps the episode referred to at 126 above, p. 86.
77. Responsible for scrutinizing the accounts of all magistrates who had handled public money.

allowance.[78] So this sort of thing is mere inability to say anything justifiable. No one on trial would choose attack, if he had any sound defence. And there is a further point, gentlemen. If I were on trial and Aeschines were my accuser with Philip as my judge, and I had no defence against my guilt and tried to abuse and vilify my accuser, do you think Philip could fail to be enraged at an attack on his benefactors in his presence? Then you must do no less than Philip, and compel Aeschines to confine his defence to the subjects at issue. Read the deposition.

(The evidence is read.)

Now my conscience was clear, and I thought it my duty to submit accounts and fulfil all legal requirements. Not so Aeschines. So how can it be said that our actions have been the same? How is it possible for him to make a charge before you which he has never made before? He cannot. Yet he will make the claim, and it is not unnatural. You know, of course, that ever since human beings have existed and cases been tried, no one has ever admitted the charge on which he has been found guilty. They lose all sense of shame, they will deny everything, tell lies, fabricate pretexts, anything rather than be penalized. You must not be misled by anything of this kind today. You must judge the facts from your own knowledge without bias either from his arguments or from mine, or indeed from the witnesses he offers, who are prepared to vouch for anything with Philip as producer for their performance. You will observe the readiness with which they offer their evidence. Nor must you be influenced by the volume of Aeschines' vocal effects or the feebleness of mine. It is not a competition in voice production or rhetoric that you have to judge today, if you look at it rightly. It is an occasion of disaster and dishonour, the unavoidable shame of which must be set on the right shoulders by the investigation of facts which are familiar to you. What facts are these which are known to you and which you need not be told? If the peace has given us all they promised, if we admit to such a depth of degradation that, untroubled by enemy invasion or naval blockade or any other anxiety, at a time when the cost of living was

---

78. There seems to be no information on the possibility of according a second time allowance to the defendant.

low and general conditions no worse than they were, we knew from foresight and from advance information that our allies were marked for destruction, if we knew that Thebes was to rise to power and Philip capture the position in Thrace, that bases were going to be rigged against us in Euboea and that all was to happen as it has indeed happened, and yet we made this peace without dissatisfaction, in that case you should acquit Aeschines, and you will avoid adding perjury to your many other ills, because in that case he has done no injury, and it is I who am senseless and demented in accusing him. But if the case is the exact opposite, if after numerous honeyed declarations that Philip favoured Athens, that he would preserve Phocis, check the intransigence of Thebes, and in addition offer to Athens benefits to outweigh Amphipolis, in the event of a peace settlement, and return Euboea and Oropus – if after such statements and promises as these they have used deception and treachery against us and almost stolen Attica itself from us, then you must condemn them. Do not add to the outrages you have undergone – I don't know what else I am to call them – nor reward the corruption they have used by bringing home upon yourselves the execration and the perjury which is theirs.

There is another question to ask, gentlemen of the jury. If they had committed no offence, why should I have wanted to accuse them? There is no answer to this. Is it enviable to make enemies? No, nor safe either. Had I taken some initial dislike to them? None whatever. What reason can there be, then? 'You were afraid for yourself, and so cowardice found you a way of escape.' I have been told that this is a claim he is making. But if there was nothing to be afraid of, if no offence had been committed, as you claim – if that is to be the argument, gentlemen, just ask yourselves this question. If the circumstances were such as to make me afraid for my skin on their account, what penalty ought the actual offenders to undergo? But in fact this is irrelevant. What *is* the reason for my accusation? Is it trumped up to levy blackmail, perhaps? But would it have suited me better to get the money from Philip, who is lavish and certainly as generous as any of them, and to enjoy his friendship and theirs (because they would have given it all right to an accomplice – they have no family feud against me, only the fact that I'm not an accomplice), or to cash in on their takings and be an enemy of theirs and Philip's? Besides, I should have paid a lot of money in ransom for the prisoners for the small return I should have got with their hostility to go with it. That won't do. I told the truth and kept clear of corruption, to maintain honesty and accuracy and leave my subsequent reputation clear, in the view shared by others of your number, that integrity would bring me the same credit, and that no gain would be a good exchange for my honour in Athens. My dislike of this party of people is due to their damnable misconduct which I witnessed at the conference, and the loss of my own position of honour owing to their corruption in the general discredit of the whole conference.

I now bring my accusation and appear at this investigation with an eye to the future and a desire to have it laid down by a case in court that my actions have been the opposite of theirs. And I am afraid, speaking with all possible candour, I am afraid of being innocently involved in their offences at a time of national despondency. It seems to me that the country has now lost all vigour and allows danger to remain in being, and despite disaster to others remains off her guard without thought for the numerous symptoms which bode ill for the state. Do you not regard the danger as desperate? – I am now led to give voice to all I had decided to leave unsaid. You know Pythocles, the son of Polydorus. I was on the best of terms with him, and till today there had been no ill-feeling between us. But now he consistently avoids meeting me, ever since he has gone over to Philip. If he is inescapably brought into contact with me, he jumps up at once, to avoid being seen in conversation with me. He goes round and round the agora in discussion with Aeschines. It is a terrible thing, gentlemen, that men who prefer to cultivate Philip's interests should be subjected to such precise observation of their practice in either direction as to feel it is just as though he were present in person and aware of everything they do even here, and they must make friends and enemies according to his choice. At the same time the rest who are oriented towards Athens, who desire Athenian respect and have not betrayed it, are confronted with this deaf and blind unawareness, which means that even in a court which knows all the truth I must stand on equal terms in the struggle with these execrable traitors. If you want to know the real reason for this, I will tell you, but I do claim immunity from resentment if I tell the truth. It is this. Philip is a single body and a single mind who wholeheartedly approves of all who do him good and dislikes all who do the reverse, while citizens of Athens first of all do not regard the good and evil that is done her as benefit or injury to themselves. There are many things which touch them more nearly, and often lead them astray – pity, envy, anger, the will to please, and much else. Anyone who avoids all these still cannot escape the dislike inspired by such a character. And the wrong involved in each such instance gradually coagulates as a source of general infection in the body politic.

Do not allow this to happen today. Do not let a man go free whose offences against you have been of such magnitude. Indeed, what in fact will be said of you, if you acquit him? A delegation went to Philip from Athens, and it included Philocrates, Aeschines, Phryno and Demosthenes. What happened? One of the four made no profit from the delegation, and paid ransom for the prisoners at his own expense. Another spent the money he made from the sale of Athens in acquiring the means for immoral practices and high living. One sent his son to Philip before he came of age,[79] that unspeakable character, Phryno. Another never disgraced either Athens or himself. One fulfilled state services in the financing of dramatic choruses and warships, and yet thought it right to add an extra voluntary expense rather than allow citizens to suffer hardship for want of it. The other was so far from rescuing any prisoner at his expense, as to provide prisoners for Philip by bringing a whole district with more than ten thousand infantry and a thousand cavalry from the forces of our allies[80] into his possession. What next? When the people of Athens caught them (and they knew them of old, of course) the ones who had accepted bribery and graft, who had brought shame on themselves, on the country and their descendants, they acquitted with the verdict that they were men of sense who set about political organization in the right way.[81] And what about their accuser? They called him a lunatic, ignorant

79. At 18 years old.
80. i.e. Phocis.
81. See Appendix, p. 331.

of politics and ignorant how to throw his money about. With this example before them, gentlemen, who will care to seek a name for justice or to perform public offices without gain, if he is neither to make anything out of it nor seem more reputable than others who have. It is not only their trial with which this court is concerned. You are also establishing a ruling on the question whether it is proper that all should seek illicit gain from assistance to their enemies when they conduct a delegation, or that they should make no gain, but assist their country and seek its interest without corruption. There is only one of all these items for which evidence is needed, the sending of Phryno's son. Bring the evidence of that, please.[82] Now Aeschines never brought Phryno to court for sending his son to Philip for discreditable purposes. But when you find a youth of unusual good looks who fails to foresee the suspicions to which such looks give rise, and lives an indecorous life thereafter, you at once pass judgement that he has been sexually corrupted.

Now let me say a word about the banquet and the decree, of which I ought to have made particular mention, but nearly forgot. When I proposed the preliminary motion arising from the first conference, and repeated it at meetings of the Assembly, at which the peace was to be discussed, before any statement had been made by Aeschines' party or any offence committed by them, I carried out the normal formalities, proposed a vote of thanks to them and invited them to the Prytaneum. Indeed I included Philip's representatives in the invitation, and in fact I provided a lavish entertainment.[83] I observed that they set considerable store by this sort of thing as evidence of prosperity and distinction, and unhesitatingly decided that I must emulate their ideas and show equal generosity. This will be referred to by Aeschines with the claim that I expressed gratitude to them and gave a dinner to the conference, without specifying the exact occasion. In fact it was before the injury to Athens was done, before the proved corruption of Aeschines' group, just after the first conference, when the report on its decision was due in the Assembly and before any indication that Aeschines would take the same line as Philocrates, or Philo-

82. The MS. text does not include the usual statement of the evidence nor any proof that it is forthcoming.
83. See note 15 above.

crates make the proposals he did. If he refers to this, remember that these occasions were prior to their offences. After them no friendly association took place between us. Now read the evidence of this.

(The evidence is read.)

He will perhaps be given brotherly support by Philochares and by Aphobetus.[84] There is a certain amount which can justifiably be said to both. We must use complete candour, gentlemen, and speak without reservation, and then we shall say: 'One of you, Aphobetus and Philochares, was a decorator of caskets and drums, and the other clerk of the second grade, very ordinary people. This is no reflection on you, but you were not quite the type for the *strategia*. Yet we raised you to offices such as membership of delegations, the *strategia* and other high-ranking positions. So if none of you had ever misconducted himself, we should not have been justified in showing gratitude to you so much as you to us, for passing over worthier claimants and adding dignity to you. If, however, any of you has actually committed misconduct in the offices with which you have been dignified, and misconduct of this kind, you are the more deserving of detestation rather than lenience. Very much more. Perhaps you will add pressure to your pleas, because you go in for loud utterance rather than modesty, and claim 'kindred blood' as justification. Gentlemen of the jury, you should not show deference to this, but reflect that such ideas may be proper to them, but you have to think of law, of the country, and above all of the oath taken when you were empanelled. You must look at any request any of them has made for lenience towards him in the light of the question whether it depends on proof of his misconduct or not. If it does, I agree, but if it is to be irrespective of this, then they are asking you to set aside your oath. Even if it is a secret, it will not escape your conscience, because the framer of the law was very well aware that if a corrupt vote is known to no litigant yet a wrongly directed vote will be known to the divine understanding of heaven. At that tribunal every man will do better to secure the hope of blessing for himself and his children by a right and proper verdict, than to earn himself

84. Brothers of Aeschines. See Aeschines, *Treaty*, 149 (p. 179).

the undeclared and obscure merit of gratifying a litigant so as to acquit a man who stands self-condemned. What clearer evidence can I provide, Aeschines, of the numerous grave offences in your conduct of the conference than your own? In supposing that you must involve in so signal a disaster anyone who sought to throw light on any of your acts as a delegate, you must have expected a terrible fate to descend upon yourself if the jury discovered your practices.

So if you are sensible, this will prove to have been to his cost, not because it is so signal a demonstration of his conduct but because by making this accusation he has used an argument which now recoils against himself. Principles which he laid down as right in his prosecution of Timarchus,[85] hold good in exactly the same form against himself. On that occasion his words to the jury were, 'Demosthenes will speak in his defence and will attack my proceedings on the delegation. Then, if what he says distracts you from the point, he will put on a display of insolence, and say to everyone, "Just see how I led the jury up the garden path, and got away with a discussion irrelevant to the subject."' That's not for today, please. Keep to the subject in dispute. In the case against Timarchus you were in a position to make any charges, any statements you chose.

Indeed, you even recited poetry to the jury, as you couldn't produce anyone to substantiate the charges you were bringing against the unfortunate fellow:

> No word is forever lost that the multitudes
> Report; the power of God is in it.[86]

Well, Aeschines, it is true in your case. Everyone declares that you took bribes for your part in the conference, so it holds good against you that 'no word is forever lost that the multitudes report'. Just consider how you can tell how many more your accusers are than his. Timarchus was barely known even to his neighbours, whereas you members of the peace conference are

85. See note 2 above.
86. Aeschines quoted this passage (from Hesiod, *Works and Days*, 761) in his speech *Against Timarchus* (129) and reverts to it in *Treaty*, 144, p. 178 below.

stated by everyone, Greek or otherwise, to have been bribed at it. So assuming that the saying in your passage is true, you stand condemned by the report of the many; and its soundness and divine character, and the penetration of the poet who wrote it, are axioms you yourself laid down.

Next he went through some dramatic verse which he had collected:

> The man who rejoices in evil company,
> I do not ask questions of him. I know him.
> He is like the company he rejoices in.[87]

He then goes on, 'A man who frequents the bird-market and goes around with Pittalacus' and so on 'you cannot fail to realize what character he must be assumed to have'. Well, I can adapt your passage against yourself, Aeschines, and if I quote it to the jury, it will be most appropriate. 'The man who rejoices (especially at a peace conference) in Philocrates' company, I do not ask questions of him. I know him. He took bribes like Philocrates, who admitted it.'

He tries, then, to insult others by calling them rhetorical or sophistic, but he shall be convicted of the same faults himself. The previous passage comes from Euripides' *Phoenix*, which was never performed by Theodorus or Aristodemus, to whom he played third, though Molon used to take the part, and perhaps other earlier actors. But Sophocles' *Antigone* has been acted frequently by Theodorus and Aristodemus. This contains lines which are admirably appropriate. He has often spoken them, and must know them well, though he omitted to quote them. You know, of course, that in tragic drama it is always the special privilege of actors of the third part to enter as tyrants carrying sceptres. Imagine this scene and observe the lines Aeschines as Creon is made by the poet to speak. He did not recite them to himself, nor to the jury, in reference to the delegation. Just read it.

---

87. From Euripides, *Phoenix*, now lost (Fr. 4), quoted at greater length by Aeschines in the speech *Against Timarchus*, 152. Pittalacus was a state slave of evil reputation, the subject of a long story told to discredit Aeschines' opponent in the *Timarchus* (54, 64).

From Sophocles' *Antigone*[88]

> There is no one whose soul and spirit and thinking
> You can learn in advance, until it is shown
> He has experience of law and government.
> To my mind the man who rules a whole city
> And sets his hand to counsels which are not righteous,
> But holds his tongue in silence, being afraid,
> Is the wickedest of men, now as of old.
> And he who sets a friend in higher esteem
> Than his own country is to me worthless.
> I declare before Zeus, whose vision is everywhere,
> I would not be silent if I saw doom
> Stalking upon my fellows in place of safety,
> Nor make an enemy of my country
> A friend to myself. She, I know,
> Is our salvation. Sail on her upright keel,
> And we shall make good friends for our voyage.

These were not lines Aeschines applied to himself in relation to the conference. Instead of his country he held the hospitality and the friendship of Philip in higher esteem and of higher profit. He threw away the wisdom of Sophocles, and, though he could see doom stalk in his path in the shape of the expedition against Phocis, he gave no warning, no notice in advance. On the contrary he helped to conceal it, he joined the destroyers and prevented

88. Sophocles, *Antigone*, 175–191. It would be natural to suppose that the part of Creon, far the longest in *Antigone*, would have been played by the first actor or protagonist. Pickard-Cambridge (*The Dramatic Festivals of Athens*, 2nd edition, p. 141) thinks that the categorical statement that Aeschines played the part may have been sheer invention. And it seems to us hard to credit Demosthenes' audience with such ignorance of the norms of Sophocles' day. However, one can see in the peroration of Aeschines' speech (*Treaty*, 171 ff.) how garbled an account of fifth-century history could apparently be accepted, and thus how blurred the details could become of traditions of a hundred years earlier, which were not systematically preserved. Furthermore the statement may be true of the Rural Dionysia as distinct from the tragic competitions of the City Dionysia. In the former, fifth-century plays were commonly revived in the fourth century, and in such performances as these a part which required ranting and little subtlety (Pickard-Cambridge, op. cit., p. 134) might have been given to the third actor. Alternatively our passage might be taken as irony at the idea of supposing that Aeschines could have played Creon, especially among the distinguished actors, such as Theodorus and Aristodemus, with whom he is associated.

the attempt to declare the truth. He did not remind himself that 'she is our salvation, and on her upright keel'; his mother performed her rites, carried out her purifications, won her keep from her clients to bring up these offspring till they were too much for her, while his father taught children to read, so I hear from older acquaintances, by the shrine of Asclepius, as best he could. Anyhow that was how he got a living. And the children got some money as second-grade clerks, subordinates in government offices, until eventually they were elected to the senior grade, with keep at the Tholus,[89] and finally from there Aeschines was sent on the delegation. He never considered any of this, never gave a thought to the upright keel of the ship of state. He scuttled and sank her, and did his best to make her over to the enemy. Is it not you yourself who are to be called sophistic and rhetorical? Yes, and unprincipled and wicked as well. You passed over the lines you often played and knew so well, and cast yourself for a part you never in your life performed, and produced it for the injury of a fellow-citizen.

Now turn to his remarks about Solon. He said that a statue of Solon was erected as a standing example of the restraint of orators of the period, with his cloak thrown back and no hand held out. This was in an abusive attack on Timarchus' impetuosity.[90] But we are told by people in Salamis that this statue has not been standing more than fifty years, whereas it is now 240 years since Solon's time,[91] so that neither the sculptor who made the figure nor even his grandfather could have been alive at the time. Anyhow, he told the jury this, and accompanied it with an imitative gesture. But far more valuable to Athens than this statue would have been an idea of Solon's mind and thought. This he did not imitate. Very much the reverse. After the revolt of Salamis from Athens and the decree forbidding on pain of death any motion to recover it, at his own risk Solon composed and sang an elegiac poem, by which means he recovered the island for Athens, and freed her of the stigma involved. Aeschines did the opposite to a place recognized as Athenian by Persia and all the Greek states,

89. On the Tholus see note 15 above.
90. See Aeschines, *Timarchus*, 26.
91. The date usually accepted for Solon's reforms is 594 B.C.

Amphipolis.[92] This he let pass out of our hands and surrendered in collaboration with Philocrates, who proposed the motion. A distinguished performance, wasn't it? He might have remembered Solon. This behaviour was not confined to Athens. When he went to Macedonia, he never even mentioned the place his delegation was concerned with. He stated this himself. You remember his words: 'I could also have mentioned Amphipolis, but I omitted[93] it to give Demosthenes a chance of speaking on the subject.' I got up and said he had never passed on to me anything he wanted to say to Philip. He'd rather have let one shed his blood than have a hand in his speech. Now please read this poem of Solon's. This will show Solon's hatred of men of his character.

No need to curb your hand in speaking, Aeschines, but in your conduct of the conference you should have. You held it out with the palm well uppermost,[94] and brought shame on your fellows, and now you talk big. Do you imagine that for these petty speeches, which you have studied and now uttered with full voice production, you can avoid punishment for offences of such extent and magnitude, even though you may walk about with a cap on, and cast abuse on me. Read it, please.

A poem of Solon[95]

> Never shall this our city fall
> Foredoomed by Fate and the gods' will.
> So great a daughter of so great a sire,
> Pallas Athene, ever guards and protects her.

92. For this recognition by the King of Persia in 367 B.C. that Amphipolis, the Athenian colony on the Strymon in Thrace which had broken with Athens in 424 B.C., rightly belonged to Athens, see 137, p. 89 above. And for the, role of Amphipolis in the quarrel between Athens and Philip see Introduction pp. 19–20.

93. Aeschines' summary (*Treaty*, 27 ff., pp. 149 ff.) of what he said on this occasion includes a good deal about Amphipolis.

94. Suggesting the desire for a bribe.

95. This (Solon 4, *Bergk*) is taken to be part of the poem uttered by Solon to urge the recapture of Salamis after its revolt from Athens and the enactment of death to anyone who proposed its recovery. The cap is a reference to the tradition later repeated by Plutarch (*Solon*, 8), according to which Solon recited the poem wearing a cap, to assist the impression that he was mad and improvising an inspired utterance.

On the text see Appendix, p. 331.

Yet is the folly of her folk lured
By gain to lay the great city low.
Her leaders seek evil, and are ready
To bow to insolence and to suffer ill.
They do not know how to check selfishness
Nor temper luxury and curb enjoyment.
They prosper in wickedness
And spare no riches, sacred or profane,
But seek theft and robbery, now here, now there,
Nor give heed to the foundations of Justice,
Who looks in silence on what was and will be,
And in her time will bring retribution to all.
It comes on all the city, the unescapable
Disease, the swift road to dread slavery.
Or else it wakes the sleeper to strife and war at home,
Which wastes the lovely age of youth.
For the city of delight is soon ravaged by enemies
In gatherings which give pleasure to the wicked.
These are the ills that beset the people;
And the poor come in number to foreign lands,
Sold in slavery and the chains of misery.
So the wickedness of a people comes into every home,
And the doors of the house will not hold it,
But high on the threshold it leaps and seizes them,
No matter if a man hide in the depths of his chamber.
This is the message my heart bids tell to Athens,
That great are the ills that lawlessness brings.
But lawfulness is order and right everywhere,
And often sets chains about the wicked,
Makes the rough smooth, checks the selfish, dims pride,
Withers the sprouting flowers of doom,
Makes crooked judgements straight, makes gentle
Unbridled acts, curbing the words of discord,
Curbing the wrath and pain of strife, and all
Under her reign is order and wisdom.

You hear, gentlemen, what Solon has to say of men of that kind and about the protection the gods give to Athens. I have always believed and sought to believe in the truth of the claim that the gods protect our city, and in a sense even these recent events seem to me a signal proof of divine benevolence. Think of it. A man who has committed a number of heinous offences as a delegate, and surrendered to the enemy districts in which the honour of the gods was the special duty of ourselves and our allies, disfranchised one who was willing enough to appear before the court in an accusation against him.[96] What for? To avoid pity or extenuation for his own offence. But even in the course of his accusation he chose to make an attack on me, and again threatened to bring a public indictment and the like. With what object? To cause me as little embarrassment as possible in my accusation of Aeschines, of whose acts of villainy I had the best knowledge, because I had followed them closely. But owing to his evasion up to the last moment he has been brought into court just at the time when in view of the immediate future, if nothing else, it was neither safe nor possible to allow further corruption on the part of Aeschines to go unpunished. One must always detest and penalize betrayal and bribery. But at this moment it is especially opportune and valuable to the whole of mankind.

Gentlemen of the jury, a dreadful plague has come upon all Greece, which is both dangerous in itself and demands much good fortune and much careful management on our part. Men of the greatest note in the cities of Greece, who claim to take the lead in public affairs, are most regrettably betraying their own liberty, and bringing on themselves slavery of their own seeking, by ingratiating talk of the friendship and companionship of Philip and the like, while the rest, including authoritative bodies throughout the states, who ought to be dealing out punishment or instant death to them, are so far from anything of the kind as to feel admiration and emulation, and wish they were the same themselves. It is this state of things and such emulation as this which in the case of Thessaly has in recent years brought down her leadership and general reputation, and is now making inroads on her liberty, since some of her strong points are now garrisoned by Macedon. This spirit has spread to the Peloponnese, where it is responsible for the massacres in Elis,[97] and has filled that unhappy people with such an access of maniacal frenzy that, to subdue each other and

96. i.e. Timarchus.

97. In 343 B.C. a pro-Macedonian party caused a massacre in Elis, killing many of Phalaecus' remaining mercenaries from Phocis, who had been hired to protect Elis.

gratify Philip, they degrade their own kith and kin, their own fellows, with the stain of bloodshed. Nor is that all. It has come to Arcadia and made havoc there. Now many of her population, who should feel the highest pride in liberty, like ourselves, because they are the only other original[98] inhabitants of Greece, are yet mad for Philip, are erecting a bronze statue of him, adorning it with garlands, and to cap it all, have voted to receive him in the Peloponnese, if he comes. It is the same in Argos.[99] And I solemnly declare, if one treats it with proper seriousness, that all this calls for no little caution, because this disease has gone round in a circle, and is here among us ourselves. So while there is safety, keep guard against it, and cast out from your number all who have introduced it. Otherwise take care, or you will fail to realize the wisdom of this plea till you have lost the means to act on it.

Athenians must keep clear in view the manifest and pitiable example of Olynthus, which owes her misery to nothing so much as this. The story is a clear instance to go by. When they were only possessed of four hundred cavalry, and amounted to a total force of no more than five thousand, since there was no unified Chalcidian body, they were attacked by Sparta with a large naval and land force – you realize that Sparta had territorial and naval supremacy at the time – yet in spite of the strength of their opponents they did not lose their city or any of its bastions. They fought a number of successful battles, killed three enemy commanders and ended by making their own political dispositions.[100] But as soon as certain of their number began to accept bribery, and the folly, or rather the ill fate, of the majority made them think these their most reliable representatives, when Lasthenes roofed his house with timber from Macedon, and Euthycrates raised herds of cattle which he had not paid for, and others of them similarly had sheep or horses, while the people as a whole, at whose expense all this was

98. Arcadians and Athenians claimed that they alone still lived where their ancestors had lived before the Dorian invasion.

99. In the year before he delivered this speech Demosthenes had been to Argos to try to counter Philip's readiness to assist Argos against Sparta (see *Second Philippic*, 9 – *Greek Political Oratory*, p. 231).

100. Demosthenes misrepresents the war between Sparta and Olynthus of 382–379 B.C. The Olynthian federation in Chalcidice was broken up and Olynthus itself was forced to become a subject-ally of Sparta.

going on, instead of being incensed and demanding the punishment of the guilty, looked on in envy and admiration and made heroes of them – when things began to reach this pitch, when bribery triumphed, then, although they had a thousand cavalry and their total strength was over ten thousand, although all the surrounding districts were their allies and they had the assistance of Athens with an army of ten thousand and fifty ships, and a citizen force of four thousand as well, all this could not save them. By the time war had lasted a year they had lost the whole of Chalcidice, and Philip was no longer waiting[101] for the instructions of the traitors, but was at a loss what to capture first. Five thousand cavalry were betrayed by their own leaders and captured by Philip with all arms and equipment, the greatest such capture in history. The men responsible could look unashamed at the light of day, at the country they knew as their own, in which they stood, at its sacred places, at its tombs and at the shame these events were to bring upon them. Such insanity, gentlemen, such paranoiac distraction, is wrought by bribery. You, then, you, the ordinary citizens of Athens, must show your sense, must not allow these things to be, but bring public retribution upon them. Indeed it would be beyond toleration that after passing frequent strong declarations against the Olynthian traitors you should fail before all the world to punish your own.

(The decree is read.)

That this decree against traitors and reprobates is both right and admirable, gentlemen, is the universal opinion among Greeks and non-Greeks alike. Since, then, bribery is the antecedent of such action and the one is the cause of the other, bribery is identified with betrayal. And if betrayal may be the betrayal of an opportunity or of a political position or of an army, the scope of a man's control is the scope of his power of corruption. All such cases deserve our detestation. But citizens of Athens are alone of mankind in being in a position to use national examples in this regard, and actively to follow the ancestors they rightly praise. You may not have occasion to imitate the battles, the campaigns, the acts of daring which made them famous. You may be yourselves at peace.

101. See Appendix, p. 331.

But their good judgement at least you can imitate. This is everywhere needed, and good judgement is never more laborious or more troublesome than bad. The time you sit in judgment is the same, and for every one of you to take a right view and a right decision is to make your country better and to act like your ancestors, to take a wrong one is to make it worse and demean them. What, then, was their judgment about this? Take this document, please, and read it. I want you to see that this is a situation in which you remain inactive where your ancestors passed penalty of death.

(An inscription is read.)

Gentlemen, you hear the words inscribed here. They record that Arthmius,[102] son of Pythonax of Zelea was declared an outlaw and enemy of the people of Athens with all his family. Why? For being the bearer of foreign gold into the Greek states. So we can see, apparently, that our ancestors took precautions to prevent anyone, Athenian or otherwise, from doing injury to Greece for money. We, however, take no care even to prevent it being done to our own city. Perhaps you suppose this is a chance inscription taken from no matter where. But in fact, though the whole of the Acropolis is sanctified and there is plenty of space on it, this inscription is placed on the right of the great bronze statue of Athena[103] set up by the city as a symbol of valour in the Persian wars from money presented by the Greek states. In those days so high stood justice, so great was the value set on the punishment of such acts as these, that one and the same position was thought suitable for the goddess's trophy of valour and the redress of such wrong as this. Nowadays we just laugh. We shrug our shoulders at the idea that Athenians should no longer be in such a position. It is my view, gentlemen, that it is not in one thing only that we should do well to follow an earlier age, but in all its actions through-

102. The decree is referred to in Aeschines, *Crown*, 258 (p. 258), and Demosthenes, *Third Philippic*, 42 (see *Greek Political Oratory*, p. 257). The occasion of it was a Persian delegation to Greece in about 460 B.C.

103. The statue of Athena Promachos on the Acropolis, no longer in existence. Demosthenes conceals the fact that the allies probably did not consent to their money contributions being used to beautify Athens.

out. You know well one story of the men of that time, the story
of Callias, the son of Hipponicus. It was he under whose leadership
the well-known peace was made which forbade the King of Persia
to advance within one day's journey of the sea, or sail a warship
inside the Chelidonian or the Blue Rocks.[104] But as he was found
guilty of corruption on his delegation, they almost killed him,
and at his investigation of accounts they fined him fifty talents.
Yet a prouder peace than that no man could point to in the history
of Athens before or since. But of that they thought nothing. They
reckoned it the worth of their own valour and the greatness of
Athens. But corruption, or the reverse, depended on the character
of the delegate. They expected honesty and not corruption of a
man who was to undertake public affairs. So traitorous and so
damaging did that age think corrupt dealing that it could not be
allowed to exist in any business, in any person. Now, gentlemen
of the jury, it is peace once again. This time you have seen it pull
down your allies' walls and build fine houses for your delegates,
you have seen it wrest from your city her possessions and heap
upon these men more than their wildest dreams could imagine.
But you have not yourselves brought about their death. You
demand a prosecution, and let words pass judgement on deeds of
wrong which all can see.

Now it is not only past history which affords examples to urge
you to retribution. In your own lifetime there have been numerous
instances of punishment for misconduct, of which I omit the
majority, recalling only one or two arising from delegations which
have been far less damaging than this one, but yet have led to the
death penalty. Take this decree and read it.

(The decree is read.)

By this decree, gentlemen, those Athenian delegates were condemned to death. One of them was Epicrates, who I hear from an

104. The Peace of Callias between Athens and Persia in 451 or 450 B.C. is
one of the most hotly debated topics in Greek history. Its existence was denied
in antiquity by the fourth-century historian Theopompus, and, since it is not
mentioned before 380 B.C. (by Isocrates in *Panegyricus*, 118 – see *Greek Political
Oratory*, p. 122), it is often thought to be the product of Athenian fourth-
century propaganda, which represented it in this and other passages as a
great triumph.

older generation was a man of considerable interest and value to Athens, a member of the party from the Peiraeus who restored the democracy,[105] and in other ways a man of the people. Yet none of these facts made any difference, and rightly. A fifty-per-cent honesty is not good enough for a man who claims a position in control of public affairs of that kind. It will not do to use a position of trust as a stepping-stone to misconduct on a larger scale. Complete integrity is what is needed. If, then, Aeschines and Philocrates have come short in any respect of the conduct which brought the death sentence on the others I have named, I urge you at once to inflict the same on me. Consider the wording: 'Inasmuch as their actions contravened the terms of the appointment.' This is the first charge. Did not Aeschines' party contravene them? Did not the decree run: 'to Athens and her allies', and they excluded Phocis? Again did it not run: 'to administer the oath to the magistrates in office in the Greek states', and they applied it only to those sent by Philip? Did it not preclude separate dealings with Philip, and they never stopped private relations with him? 'Some of them', it goes on, 'were convicted of making false reports to the Council.' Aeschines and his friends were actually convicted of it in the Assembly. On what evidence? Here is the telling point: on the evidence of the facts. Their reports were exactly reversed by the events in every case. 'And of false dispatches', the claim continues. So were these people. 'And of slander against allied states, and of bribery.' Instead of slander this was a case of complete destruction, which is surely a great deal more serious than slander. And as regards bribery, if they denied it the charge would have had to be substantiated. But as they admitted it, they should surely have been arrested.

Well, then, gentlemen, this being so, are you, the descendants of those figures of the past, some of whom are still alive, prepared to tolerate the thought that a benefactor of the people, one of the champions from the Peiraeus, Epicrates, should be expelled and penalized, and again not long ago that Thrasybulus, son of the

105. i.e. the group of refugees from the oligarchy of the Thirty Tyrants who under Thrasybulus entered Attica from Boeotia in 403 B.C. and seized first Phyle and then Peiraeus (see 280 below).

Epicrates had served on a delegation to Persia.

great democrat who came from Phyle to restore the democracy, should have incurred a fine of ten talents, or that the descendants of Harmodius[106] and your greatest benefactors, whose services to Athens have been rewarded with the right to take part in every ceremony, every offering and libation to the gods, who are the theme of your songs and awarded equal honour with the gods and heroes of legend, are you prepared that they should all have been subject to penalties imposed by law and allowed no lenience or remission, no benefit from weeping children who shared the benefactor's name or anything of that sort, and yet that a son of[107] Atrometus, the schoolmaster, and Glaucothea, the conductress of Dionysiac rituals, which have led to the death penalty for another priestess, that a man of that parentage, a man of no value whatsoever to Athens, either himself or his father or any of his family, should go free when you have caught him? Has there ever been a command in the cavalry, in the navy, or a campaign, the management of a play, a public service or tax or charity in his whole life which stands to his name as a benefit to his country? None the less, even if he had all these to his credit without that of integrity and uncorrupt service, death is what he deserves. And if he cannot be credited with either, can you fail to condemn him? Can you forget what he said in his speech against Timarchus, that there is no value in a state which has not the force to deal with offenders, or a political system in which lenience and private influence count for more than law; so that you should not feel pity for Timarchus's mother, who was only an old woman, or for his children or anyone else, but fix your attention on the certainty that if you are to let law and the constitution go unheeded you will never find pity for yourselves? Is that unhappy man to lose his rights for seeing the wrong that Aeschines committed, while Aeschines himself is granted indemnity?

If Aeschines demanded such retribution for offences of a private kind, what retribution ought a sworn jury to exact for offences

106. The occasion of the trial of Thrasybulus the younger is not known. He is to be distinguished from Thrasybulus of Collytus (Aeschines, *Crown*, 138, p. 228), but is probably the same Thrasybulus mentioned at 290 below (p. 127). Harmodius was celebrated as a tyrannicide because he and Aristogeiton murdered Hipparchus, brother of the tyrant of Athens, in 514 B.C.

107. i.e. Aeschines.

against the state of which he himself is proved guilty? We are informed that that trial will serve to improve the morals of the young. Then this one will do the same for politicians, who constitute the greatest political risk and ought to be seriously considered. So I want you to realize that the blow dealt to Timarchus was not due to consideration for the morals of your children. Their morals are secure, gentlemen, and heaven forbid that they should be in any need of correction from people like Aphobetus and Aeschines. No, it was due to Timarchus' resolution in the Council imposing the death penalty for the offence of transferring arms or naval equipment to Philip. Here is the proof. How long was Timarchus active in politics? A long time. Aeschines was in Athens throughout it without ever expressing disapproval or regarding this activity of his as reprehensible, until he himself made his journey to Macedonia and was corrupted. Now read the actual decree passed by Timarchus.

(The decree is read.)

So the proposer of a motion against conveying arms to Philip in time of war on pain of death has been disfranchised and dishonoured. He was accused by the betrayer to Philip of our allies' arms, who discoursed, if you please, about immorality, flanked by his two brothers-in-law, by that unsavoury character, Nicias, Chabrias' paid assistant in Egypt, and by the 'Brantub'[108] of evil repute, the comedian who needs no mask. And besides there in front of him was his own brother, Aphobetus. There was a flood of eloquence about immorality, but the stream of truth flowed the other way.

Indeed the dishonour brought on Athens by this reprehensible and libellous character I can leave to be exemplified by facts well known to you. In the past the decision of Athens was waited on by the Greek world. But now it is we who go about inquiring the decision of others, turning an eager ear to the news of Arcadia or

---

108. A nickname for Epicrates, brother of Aeschines (see Aeschines, *Treaty*, 150, p. 180). Bran is named as something worthless. Nicias is not otherwise known. Chabrias is an Athenian general first prominent in 388 B.C., who died in the Social War in 357. He served as a mercenary in Egypt in 380 on behalf of rebels against Persia, and again in 360 B.C.

of the Amphictyons, of Philip's intended movements, and whether he is dead or alive.[109] Is that not true? What worries me is not whether Philip is alive, but whether Athens's hatred and punishment of traitors is dead. My fear is not of Philip, if all is well with Athens, but of the possibility of unobstructed bribery on his part, of support for such conduct by once trusted Athenians, of speeches on his behalf where previously there has been nothing but opposition. There lies my fear. I ask you, Eubulus, how you stand. At the recent trial of Hegesilaus, your cousin, and of Thrasybulus, Niceratus' uncle, on the first vote[110] you refused when called, and in discussion of the sentence you had nothing to say in their favour, but asked the court to excuse you. So you are not prepared to speak for relations and close friends, but you are prepared to for Aeschines, although at Aristophon's prosecution of Philonicus, when he attacked your actions in the course of it, Aeschines supported his attack, and was ranked as an opponent of yours. You created a panic by declaring the need to man the fleet at Peiraeus, start war contributions and divert the Theoric Fund to military purposes,[111] or else vote for the proposals of Aeschines and his sordid associate, Philocrates, which resulted in a dishonourable peace instead of a fair one, while their subsequent misconduct ruined the country. And are you now reconciled with them? You hurled imprecations on Philip in public, and pledged your own children to your oath that you would like to see his overthrow. And are you now going to assist Aeschines? How is Philip to be overthrown, if you protect the man he bribes? Why

109. Demosthenes seems to be referring back to the winter of 352–351 B.C., when a rumour of Philip's death caused Athens to abandon preparation of a fleet to oppose him. See *Philippic I*, 10, in *Greek Political Oratory*, p. 190.

110. The first vote is the vote of guilty or not guilty, the second an assessment of the sentence.

111. The Theoric Fund had been created to provide the poor with the means of attending the national festivals, but it seems likely that it was used as a means of preventing politicians from using up financial reserves on ill-advised military expeditions. Although all surplus revenue was diverted to it, only a small proportion was in fact distributed. That a proposal to draw from it for military purposes was dangerous and drastic is shown by this passage and by Demosthenes, *Olynthiac I*, 19 (*Greek Political Oratory*, p. 202). See G. L. Cawkwell, 'Eubulus', *Journal of Hellenic Studies*, LXXXIII (1963), pp. 55 ff., and Introduction p. 22.

did you prosecute Moirocles for exacting twenty drachmae each from the contractors for the mines, and indict Cephisophon for embezzling sacred money because he was in arrear with the payment of seven minae into the bank, and yet, now that you're dealing with the people who have got the money, who admit it and have been convicted and caught in the act of working for money to the destruction of our allies, why do you not prosecute *them*, but actually demand their release? This is a bad business, and demands great foresight and precaution, whereas your previous prosecutions were trivial in comparison.

You can tell from this. Were there some people in Elis who misappropriated public money? Very likely. Had any of them any part in the downfall of the democracy? Not one. Well, were there such people at Olynthus, when it still existed? I expect so. Were they responsible for its fall? No. Or at Megara there must have been someone, don't you think, who feloniously embezzled public money? Has anyone been proved responsible for what happened there? No one. Who were the people who were guilty of such grave misconduct? People who fancied themselves as Philip's supporters and friends, people who longed for office, claimed positions of leadership and thought themselves superior to others. Wasn't Perillus prosecuted recently at Megara before the Three Hundred for a visit to Philip and defended in court by Ptoeodorus,[112] whose wealth, birth and reputation put him second to none in Megara, and sent back by him to Philip? After which one of them returned at the head of a force of mercenaries, while the other concocted a ferment at home? Something of the kind. There is nothing in the world which demands greater caution than allowing one man to rise above the general level. I would not have any man either remitted or consigned to disaster merely at one man's will. Where the facts prompt either good treatment or bad, the appropriate vote should be passed by the people's court. That is democracy. One might add that there have been many in Athens who have risen to power on occasion, Callistratus, Aristophon, Diophantus[113] and others earlier. In what field did they each become

112. Perillus and Ptoeodorus appear in Demosthenes, *Crown*, 295, in a list of traitors who had worked for Philip. They were active in Megara.

113. Callistratus was the most influential politician at Athens between the foundation of the Second Athenian Confederacy and his first trial in 366 B.C.

prominent? In the public Assembly. In the courts of justice no one has ever acquired a power greater than the laws and the juror's oath. It must be so today. You must not allow Aeschines such power. Precaution would be better than trust, which is the burden of a sacred oracle which I will read. Heaven always gives greater protection to the city than men of prominence. Read the oracles, please.

(The oracles are read.)

Listen, then, to the divine warning. If it has been given in time of war, it is the commanders of whom we are bidden to beware, if in time of peace, the statesmen. They are the leaders, they are the men we obey, the men by whom we may be misled. We are also bidden to unite the city in the way of general agreement, and not of favour to our foes. Is it, then, your opinion, gentlemen of the jury, that it would do more favour to Philip to release or to punish the author of such ills? To release him, I fancy. The oracle certainly bids us act to avoid favour to our foes. We are urged with one accord to punish any who have done service to our enemies by Zeus, by Dione, by all the gods. The plotters against us are outside, their accomplices within. The plotters are concerned to give bribes, their accomplices to accept them and to protect all who have done so.

However, it takes no superhuman intelligence to see that the thing most of all to be hated and feared is to have a leading statesman on familiar terms with the opponents of a people's policy. By what means did Philip gain control of affairs, by what means has he achieved the greatest of his successes? I put the question to you. By buying in the market where political gains were for sale, by corruption and inducement of leading politicians in the states. These were the means. Now you have it in your power today to make this inoperative, if you choose, if you turn a deaf ear to the support of such men as these, and show that the influence over you which they now claim is non-existent, and if you punish the traitor who has sold himself, and let the world know it. You would rightly be incensed, gentlemen, against anyone who had

---

Aristophon came to the fore through Timotheus's trial in 355 B.C. On Diophantus, see note 35 above.

acted in these ways, who had betrayed allies and friends and those opportunities on which success and failure everywhere depend, but against no one with greater force or greater justification than Aeschines. The man who set himself in the ranks of mistrust of Philip, who was the first and only one to see Philip as the common enemy of all Greece, and then deserted and was found on Philip's side, must surely deserve death many times over. And against the truth of this he cannot say a word. Who was it in the first place who brought Ischander here with an account of him as representing the friends of Athens in Arcadia? Who raised the cry that Philip had designs on Greece and the Peloponnese, but Athens was asleep? Who was the orator of those long, flowery speeches which quoted the decree of Miltiades and Themistocles and the oath administered to young men in the temple of Aglaurus? It was Aeschines who urged the dispatch of representatives[114] almost to the Red Sea with the message that Greece was threatened by a conspiracy of Philip's and the need for Athens was foresight for the preservation of Greece. It was Eubulus who drafted the decree, Aeschines who led the delegation to the Peloponnese. The discussions he took part in when he got there and the speeches he delivered he must no doubt know. His reports to Athens are well remembered, I know. In his speeches he frequently referred to Philip in the terms 'barbarian' and 'devil', and told us what satisfaction there was in Arcadia that Athens should be awake and aware. But what caused the greatest bitterness, he said, was this. On his departure he met Atrestidas on his way from Macedon, and there were about thirty women and children with him. He wondered at this, and asked a fellow traveller who it was, and what this cavalcade with him was doing, and was told it was Atrestidas returning with Olynthian prisoners as a free present from Philip. This he thought appalling. He was moved to tears at the degraded condition of Greece, that such suffering could be allowed to take place. He urged us to send a delegation to Arcadia to attack the Macedonian party there, and said he had heard from friends that if Athens took some notice and sent representatives this party would be punished.

That was the character of his speeches, which were laudable and

114. In 348 B.C. after the fall of Olynthus.

a credit to Athens. But he did not maintain this language when he went to Macedonia and met this enemy of his and of the country. Nothing of the kind. We were to forget our ancestry, forget our triumphs and the assistance we owed to others,[115] and as regards the suggestion to join the Greeks in discussing a peace with Philip it was surprising, he declared, that anyone should think persuasion necessary on a private issue of our own. Philip himself was astonishing, the most Greek of men, the finest of speakers, the kindest of people. But there were some extraordinary, ill-natured people in Athens who shamelessly abused him and called him a barbarian. Is it possible that the later speeches should have been spoken by the same man as the earlier, if he was not corrupted? Is there any man who could have felt such hatred for Atrestidas with his women and children and yet endured to follow the conduct of Philocrates in bringing free Olynthian women here for dishonourable purposes, a man so renowned for his revolting practices that there is no need for me to use opprobrious and unpleasant expressions about him. I need only mention Philocrates bringing these women with him for everyone here, even onlookers, to remember the rest of the story and to feel compassion, I am sure, for those poor, pitiable people, who received no pity from Aeschines and caused him no tears of regret for Greece at the cruelty they received among allies at the hands of Athenian delegates. But he will have his regrets, for the nature of his conduct of the conference, and perhaps he will be bringing his children and making them appear in court. If so, gentlemen of the jury, to balance the appearance of his children[116] you must remember how many of the children of your own people and your friends are wandering in poverty about Greece for the cruelty they have received on his account. They deserve your pity far more than the children of a father who wronged and betrayed them. You must remember that it was he and his friends who added 'and his descendants' to the terms of peace, and so deprived your children of all hope. Against his own tears of regret you should remember

---

115. A reference to Aeschines' speech in the debate in the Assembly about the peace terms. See Introduction, pp. 29 ff.

116. A standard Greek practice in court. Cf. Aristophanes, *Wasps*, 568 ff., and see below Aeschines, *Treaty*, 179, p. 187.

that you now have in your power the man who urged you to send your agents to Arcadia to attack the supporters of Philip. Now, gentlemen of the jury, you have no delegation to send to the Peloponnese, no long distance to travel or expenses to incur. You have only to advance to this platform, each man of you, and cast the vote which piety and justice demand on your country's behalf, against the man whose first public utterances invoked the names of Marathon and Salamis and the battles and the triumphs of those days, but suddenly changed, on his departure for Macedonia to the exact opposite, to demand silence and the neglect of ancestry and triumphs, of assistance to others or a common policy for Greece, almost to the destruction of our very walls. In all the history of Athens no words of greater dishonour have ever been spoken.

Is there a man in Greece or outside it so dull, so deaf or so antagonistic to our city of Athens that if he were asked, 'Tell me, is there any part of Greece, as it is now called and inhabited, which would own this name or be cultivated by the Greeks who now hold it, if those virtues had not been maintained on her behalf by the men of Marathon and Salamis, our ancestors?', he would say 'yes'? Not one, I am sure. They would agree that all would have been seized by the foreigner. Then are we to agree that men whose very enemies would not deny them this high praise and honour should be swept from the memory of you their descendants by Aeschines' desire of gain? From the dead most good things are withheld, but the honour which is accorded to noble deeds belongs in special possession to the men who so died. For envy no more stands in their way. By taking this from them he deserves himself to be deprived of honour, and this is the punishment you should exact on behalf of past generations. By the speeches he delivered this wicked man pillaged and tore in pieces the glory of our fathers, and what he said brought all they did to ruin. And it has made him a landowner, and a figure of self-importance. More still. Before he did all this injury to Athens, he admitted he had been a clerk, and was grateful for having been elected and showed himself a reasonable person. But since bringing 'unnumbered ills'[117] to the city he raises an eyebrow, and if

---

117. The Greek phrase, repeated at 337 (p. 138), suggests a reference to tragedy.

reference is made to 'Aeschines the ex-clerk' he is up in arms at once, and claims to have been insulted. He goes about in the market-place with his robe down to his ankles, adopting an impressive stride like Pythocles and puffing out his cheeks, one of Philip's close friends, please note, one of the class who want to disembarrass themselves of the common people and regard the present conduct of affairs as surrender to an uncontrolled wave of insanity. And this is the man who not long ago used to bow humbly at the Tholos.

I should now like to return to a summary of the way in which Philip overreached you with the assistance of these abominable accomplices. It is worth while to examine and contemplate the whole deception. In the first place he was anxious for peace because his territory was being pillaged by bandits, and the ports were closed, which lost him the benefit of the goods in them. He therefore sent those honeyed speakers to represent him, Neoptolemus, Aristodemus and Ctesiphon.[118] But when our delegation arrived in Macedonia, he at once bribed Aeschines to join that repellent character, Philocrates, in speech as well as action, and get round the well-intentioned members of the delegation. He wrote a letter to our government in terms which he expected to secure peace. All the same he couldn't gain any notable success against us without the destruction of Phocis. And this was not easy. Almost by chance his affairs had been brought to a point at which it was either impossible to attain any of his aims, or necessary to employ deception and perjury and make a general demonstration of his iniquity to the Greek and foreign worlds alike. If he accepted alliance with Phocis, and administered the oath to her together with Athens, it immediately became necessary to break the oaths sworn to Thessaly and Thebes. He had sworn to Thebes to assist the appropriation of Boeotia, to Thessaly to help re-establish her in the Amphictyonic Council. On the other hand, if he did not accept it – and he had no desire to – he felt sure we should not allow him through the pass. We should send a force to Thermopylae, as indeed we should have done had we not been misled. In that case he reckoned it would be impossible to pass through. He had no need of outside information of this. He had his own

118. See 12 and 94 above (pp. 59 and 80).

evidence. On his first conquest of Phocis, when he demolished their army and its leader and general, Onomarchus, and no one in the whole world, Greek or non-Greek, rendered any aid to Phocis except Athens, he not merely failed to go through the pass or to achieve any of his objects, he was unable even to approach it.[119] He knew with certainty, I imagine, that at a time when there were differences between him and Thessaly, when Pherae first refused to follow him, when Thebes was being worsted and had lost a battle and had a trophy raised, it was impossible to force the pass in the face of an Athenian expedition, and he would be likely to regret any attempt to do so, unless craft were added to his resources. How could he avoid downright falsehood or the appearance of breaking his word, and still achieve all he wanted? How could it be done? The answer was, if he could find agents to mislead Athens. In that case he would not be involved in a dishonourable business.

At this point Macedonian representatives forewarned Athens that Philip would not accept alliance with Phocis. But Aeschines and his party took up the discussion, and began making speeches to the effect that manifestly it wouldn't do for Philip to accept a Phocian alliance because of Thebes and Thessaly, but if he could get the position and the peace in his own hands he would then make the arrangement we should ask for. So on the basis of these hopes and inducements they contrived to get the peace from us without the inclusion of Phocis. But the further need for him was to forestall an Athenian expedition to Thermopylae, for which there were still fifty warships threatening the position, to prevent any move on Philip's part. How could that be dealt with? What further chicanery could be devised for this? A disruption of the time schedule by introducing a sudden check to proceedings, to make an expedition impossible, even if desired. This is what they are shown to have done, while I was unable to leave in time, as you have heard more than once, and even when I hired a boat,[120] I was prevented from sailing. It was also necessary that Phocis should trust Philip and commit herself deliberately, to avoid any interval

119. On the Athenian occupation of Thermopylae in 352 B.C. see above 18 (note 9) and 84–6 (note 34).
120. See on 51 above (p. 69).

during which a decree could be sent from Athens opposing it. So an announcement must be put out by Athenian representatives that Phocis was to be preserved. Then anyone who lacked confidence in Philip could put himself in their hands. Word should be sent to Athens to ensure that in the belief that their wishes were already granted they should make no adverse decision. Information and promises should be passed to them by Aeschines and his friends as coming from Philip, which would make it certain that any such resolution would not be acted on.

This was the method and these were the devices by which the most pitiable of mankind found their whole world brought to ruin. Instead of the reconstitution of Thespiae and Plataea news came of the enslavement of Orchomenus and Coronea.[121] Instead of the humiliation of Thebes and the reduction of her insolent pride our own allies had their walls razed to the ground, demolished by the Thebans, who according to Aeschines' account had been divided in pieces. Instead of the surrender of Euboea to Athens in exchange for Amphipolis Philip is building additional bases against us in Euboea, while his intrigues against Geraestus[122] and Megara continue. Instead of having Oropus made over to us we are making an armed expedition to defend Drymus and the district of Panactum,[123] which we never did while Phocis survived. Instead of the restoration of sacred rites to the Delphic sanctuary and the exaction of tolls in honour of Apollo, the original Amphictyons have been reduced to exile or expelled and their territory devastated, and an unheard-of, un-Greek population of Macedonians force their way into the Council, while any mention of the sacred treasures means that its author is thrown over the precipice, and his city deprived of her Delphic rights. To Athens it is all unfathomable. Philip has not broken faith, and yet has accomplished his every wish. Athens has seen every hope and prayer turned to the opposite. In semblance she is at peace, but she has fared worse than in war. And Aeschines and his friends have money in their pockets, and

---

121. On Thespiae and Plataea see 21 above (note 11). On Orchomenus and Coronea see 112 (note 43).

122. Near the south-east corner of Euboea.

123. For Oropus see note 13 above. Drymus and Panactum were small Athenian forts on the Boeotian border.

up till now have suffered no penalty. That it has all been the fruits of bribery, and that the price of it is in their possession, is clear to you, I suppose, for a number of reasons, and I feel some fear of doing the opposite of my intention, and in my eagerness to pin down every fact, irritating an audience which has full knowledge of them. However, I would ask you to listen to one more point. Is there any one of the representatives sent by Philip whose statue you would erect in the market-place? Or to whom you would award free board or any other of the recognized awards made to benefactors? I doubt it. Why? Not that Athenians are noted for ingratitude, injustice or selfishness, but because their actions were solely for Philip's benefit and not that of Athens, you would claim – and it would be both true and reasonable. Then do you suppose that Philip's view would be different from yours? Do you suppose he makes all these expensive presents to Aeschines and his friends for distinguished and just service to Athens on the delegation? Of course not. You see the reception he gave Hegesippus[124] and his fellow delegates. To give only one instance, he issued a proclamation banishing Xenocleides, the Athenian poet, for inviting them to his house, though they were from his own city. Speakers in the Athenian interest who say candidly what they think get this sort of treatment from him. Traitors who have sold themselves get treated as Aeschines has been. Does this fact require any other evidence, or any more cogent proof? Or can anyone blind you to what I have given?

I was told a very surprising thing by a man who met me outside the court just now, that Aeschines now plans to prosecute Chares,[125] and hopes to delude the jury by this means and by arguments of this sort. Now it is claimed that Chares has been brought to trial and found invariably reliable and attached to the interests of

124. Earlier in 343 Hegesippus had been sent to Philip to discuss his proposed amendment to the peace, but both the counter-proposals he took with him and his personal conduct offended Philip.

125. Chares had been commanding Athenian expeditionary forces since 366. He was conspicuous in connection with the recovery of the Chersonese in 357 and in the Social War (357–355), and led the expedition to Thermopylae in 352. He was unsuccessfully prosecuted after leading a mercenary force to help Olynthus in 349. He later successfully defended Byzantium (340), and was an Athenian commander at the battle of Chaeronea in 338.

Athens to the utmost of his power, but has failed on many occasions owing to the influence of corrupt intrigue against her. I do not lay too much emphasis on this, but I will go a long way in another respect. Grant that all that Aeschines intends to say about him is true. Even so it will be totally ridiculous for him to make this accusation. I make no charge against Aeschines for events of the war – that is the responsibility of the commanders – nor for the Athenian decision to make peace. Up to that point I acquit him entirely. What does that mean? Where does my accusation start? On his conduct during the peace negotiations in siding with Philocrates instead of with proposals on the side of right, in accepting bribes, afterwards at the second conference in manipulating the time schedule and failing to carry out any of his instructions, in deluding Athens and encouraging hopes of Philip's acceptance of our wishes and so bringing a catastrophe on us, and after that, when warnings were current against the man who had caused such unjustifiable injury, standing as his coadjutor. These are the charges I bring. These you must keep in mind, because a just and equitable peace, and delegates who had not descended to bribery and later to falsehood, would be something to which to accord even eulogy and decoration. If there has been an officer who has misconducted his command, he is not concerned in this investigation. But what commander caused the destruction of Halus, or of Phocis? Or the loss of Doriscus, or of Cersobleptes, or of the Sacred Mount or of Thermopylae? Who was it who made a highway for Philip through allied and friendly territory straight to Attica? Who brought Coronea, Orchomenus, Euboea out of our influence, and nearly did the same for Megara just lately? Who gave strength to Thebes? None of this long and heavy list was due to the commanders, nor was conceded in time of peace and made over to Philip by negotiation. All are due to Aeschines and his friends, and the bribery they accepted. If he attempts to evade these charges by resort to irrelevant considerations, this is the language with which you should meet him: 'This is not a military case. Your terms of reference are not of that sort. We do not want to hear tales of the guilt of others in regard to the destruction of Phocis, but proof of your own innocence. If Demosthenes was guilty of misconduct, why do you raise it now, when you refused at his investigation? That in itself is enough to condemn you. We do not want to be told how admirable or how beneficial a thing peace is. You are not charged with the existence of peace in Athens. Prove to us that it is not a shameful, dishonourable peace, that we were not the victims of gross subsequent delusion, leading to ultimate catastrophe. These are the facts for which you have been proved responsible. And finally, why do you continue in praise of the man who is behind it all?' Keep this grip on him, and he will have no reply. What he gives vent to will be a waste of words, mere voice production without substance.

Indeed his vocal powers perhaps need a word. I understand he sets great store by them, as a theatrical means of imposing on you. In my opinion it would be highly inconsistent on your part, if after howling him down and almost stoning him out of your theatres for his impersonation of the horrors of Thyestes and the Trojan war, till he gave up even playing a minor part, then, when he has changed his performance to the stage of public affairs of the greatest moment, and there too acted so disastrously and 'wrought unnumbered ills', you should listen to his utterance and uphold it. Impossible! You must not stoop to sheer folly, but you will remember that it is only a herald who needs assessment of his vocal powers. A delegate claiming to play a part in public affairs should show integrity and pride in the service of the state, equality in his relationship with her – as indeed I showed no respect for Philip, but I did for the prisoners, whom I rescued without the least hesitation. Aeschines grovelled before Philip, and sang extravagant praises of him, and paid no attention to the country. So when you see a shrewd intelligence or a commanding voice or any other talent in combination with honest ideas and public spirit, you should rejoice in it and follow the practice of it. It is valuable to all alike. But when it is to be found in company with bribery and dishonesty and a weakness for every source of gain, you should shut it out and listen to it with bitter opposition, because wickedness in the garb of power is a danger to the country. You have in view the troubles that have beset her since the days of Aeschines' elevation. Most human powers may be thought to stand for themselves, but that of speech is broken by an audience which stands against it. Such must be the hearing you give a man like this, wicked, corrupt and false in every word.

It is not only general considerations, observe, but relations with Philip himself which make Aeschines' conviction desirable. If Philip is ever reduced to the necessity of treating Athens justly, he will change his tune. At present he has chosen to cultivate a few friends by the delusion of the rest. If he finds that the few are broken, he will make future transactions through the majority, who are in control of affairs. On the other hand, if he continues in this unbridled disregard of right, you will have eradicated from the city the few who would act for him without limit, if you destroy this party of Aeschines'. If the people who expected punishment for such action, are treated with lenience, how do you suppose they will continue? Will Euthycrates, will Lasthenes,[126] will anyone be a blacker traitor? Can any man fail to be a worse citizen, when he sees that wholesale corruption leads to wealth, distinction and a quick way to friendship with Philip, while manifest integrity, with the expenditure of money to add to it, is left with trouble, unpopularity and sometimes jealousy? You must not allow it. Neither reputation, piety, safety nor anything else can make it desirable to acquit Aeschines. It needs retribution, to make him an example to the world, to Athens and to the rest of Greece alike.

126. Euthycrates and Lasthenes were Olynthians referred to as benefiting by their support of Philip. See 265 above, p. 120.

II. THE DEFENCE: AESCHINES

Summary of the Speech

I. Introduction. 1–11.

II. Preliminaries to the peace. 12–19.

Good feeling of Philip towards Athens (12–17). First movements initiated by Demosthenes and Philocrates (18–19).

III. The first delegation. 20–80.

Arrival in Macedonia (20–24). Aeschines' speech (25–33). Demosthenes' failure and Philip's reply to the delegation (34–9). Return journey (40–43). Meetings in Council and Assembly (44–69). Circumstances of the debate. Past history in explanation of the charge of having disparaged the greatness of the past (70–80).

IV. Cersobleptes and Phocis as the main subjects of accusation. 81–118.

Cersobleptes and the Chersonese. The charge that he was excluded from the peace. But dates prove that he was expelled before the second delegation (81–93). The third delegation (94–6). The second delegation. Narrative (97–100). Aeschines' speech to the delegation (101–7). The meeting at Pella. Servility of Demosthenes' speech (108–12). Aeschines' speech (113–18).

V. Replies to charges against Aeschines. 119–43.

That the humiliation of Thebes and assistance to Phocis were foretold (119–20); that Demosthenes was prevented from making a true report (121–3); that Aeschines had secret communication with Philip (124–30); that the destruction of Phocis was due to Aeschines (131–43).

VI. Minor charges. 144–70.

A quotation (144–5); defamation of Aeschines' character and

upbringing (146–52); story of a party in Macedonia (153–8); celebrations after the fall of Phocis (159–63); the charge of a reversal of policy (164–7); a sneer on military service rebutted (167–70).

VII. Peroration. Summary of Greek history with Demosthenes and the War party as the degrading conclusion. Final appeal to sentiment. 171–end.

MAY I request you, gentlemen, to be good enough to listen to me with sympathy in the realization of the great issues at stake for me, the extent of the charges to which I have to answer, and the technique and the ingenuities of my accuser, and also the savagery of a man who went to the length, in addressing a jury sworn to give equal weight to both sides in the case, of urging you not to listen to a word from the defendant. This is not due to indignation. Liars don't get angry with the victims of their slander, nor do speakers who are telling the truth try to deprive defendants of a hearing. Accusation carries no weight with an audience until the defendant has had a chance to plead and has proved unable to rebut the charges after they have been put forward. But I don't think Demosthenes likes fair argument. Nor is he prepared for it. Passion is what he has decided to elicit from you. And he has charged me with taking bribes. But he is not a very convincing accuser on that form of suspicion. If you are to appeal to passion on grounds of bribery, you really ought to be clear of it yourself.

My experience of listening to Demosthenes' accusations, gentlemen, has been that I have never felt so afraid as today, nor so incensed, nor so excessively delighted. I felt afraid, and indeed I am still very apprehensive that some of you may be brainwashed into a misconception of me by his conspiracy of malicious antithesis. I was beside myself with rage and indignation at his accusing me of drunken violence against a free Olynthian woman.[1] But I was delighted, when he embarked on this accusation, that you disallowed it, and I consider that I gained some reward for the moderation of my life. I therefore offer you my commendation and my warm regard for your reliance on the life lived by parties to a dispute rather than on accusations made by their enemies.

1. See Demosthenes, *Treaty*, 196 ff., pp. 103 ff., and Aeschines, 153 below.

However, I do not mean to decline defence on this charge. If any bystander – and almost all Athens is here – or if any gentleman of the jury is convinced that I have been guilty of any such action against the person not merely of a free individual, but of any individual whatsoever, I regard my life as not worth living. And if in the course of my defence I do not disprove it and demonstrate its falsity, and the damnable misrepresentation of the person who dared affirm it, even if I am shown innocent in every other respect, I invite a penalty of death.

There is another argument of his which I found both astonishing and appallingly unjustifiable. He asked you whether it is possible in one and the same city to pass sentence of death on Philocrates, because he stood self-condemned by refusing to await judgement, and to acquit me. On this assumption I think my acquittal would be justified. If self-condemnation by absence amounts to guilt, then denial of the charge and submission to law in the form of a jury amounts to innocence.

As to the rest of the accusation, gentlemen, I would ask you to bring up any point I may forget and omit, and question me about it, and make anything you want to know clear without prejudice in a spirit of mutual goodwill. I don't quite know where to begin, because of the contradictory nature of the charges. So please consider whether I am being reasonably treated. It is I who am being subjected to personal risk, but the greater part of the charges are against Philocrates, Phryno and the rest of the delegation, against Philip and the peace itself and against the policy of Eubulus,[2] in all of which I am being involved. According to the argument Demosthenes is alone in standing for the interest of Athens. All the rest are traitors. He has persisted in invective which is both untrue and abusive not only against me but against all the rest. He can hold a man in such contempt, and then turn round at a moment's notice and treat him like Alcibiades or Themistocles[3] with as high a reputation as any in Greece, and finally charge him

2. But cf. Demosthenes, *Treaty*, 336, p. 138. For Eubulus see Introduction, pp. 22 ff.

3. Leading Athenians of the Peloponnesian and Persian Wars, whose errors could have had, and in Alcibiades' case did have, terrible consequences.

with the destruction of the cities of Phocis, the alienation of the district of Thrace from Athens, and the expulsion from his kingdom of a popular Athenian ally like Cersobleptes. He embarked on a comparison of me with Dionysius, tyrant of Sicily, and showed the most vociferous eagerness in urging you to beware of me, and even related the priestess's dream[4] in Sicily. By whipping things up to this pitch he even grudged me the credit of his own misrepresentation, when he put down the results not to my arguments, but to Philip's armed force.

In facing this man's unashamed and wild exaggeration it is difficult to recall every detail and to reply at my own risk to unpredictable defamation. But I will begin at the point where I think what I have to say will be clearest and most within your knowledge, namely with the discussion of the peace and the election of the delegates. That will best enable me both to remember and to relate it, and you to grasp my account.

One occasion I think you will all yourselves remember, when the Euboean representatives discussed in the Assembly the question of peace terms between Athens and themselves, and said that Philip asked them to give the message that he desired a *rapprochement* and a peace. Not long afterwards Phryno of Rhamnus was captured by pirates during the Olympic truce,[5] according to the account he gave in protest. On his ransom and return here he asked for the election of a representative to go to Philip on his behalf in the hope of recovering the ransom. This was agreed, and Ctesiphon was chosen. When Ctesiphon returned from his mission he reported on his task, and added that Philip maintained that he regretted being at war with Athens, and would like to reach a conclusion of it. When Ctesiphon made this statement and spoke in addition of Philip's great good feeling, it was very well received by the Athenian people, who commended Ctesiphon. There was no opposition, and at once Philocrates of Hagnus offered to propose a decree, which was voted unanimously by the people,

4. Neither the comparison with Dionysius (tyrant of Syracuse 405–367 B.C.) nor the story of the dream appears in Demosthenes, who would have revised his original speech for publication. See Introduction, p. 15.

5. A truce was proclaimed shortly before the festival (July–August 348 B.C.) in order to allow all to take part without risk.

enabling Philip to send a herald and a delegation to discuss peace. Previously even this had met with some opposition, deliberately engineered, as the event showed. The proposal was indicted for illegality,[6] the name of Lycinus being attached to the indictment, and the penalty assessed at a hundred talents. After this the indictment was brought into court, and as Philocrates was ill he invited support – from Demosthenes, not from me. So our anti-Macedonian friend appeared, and spent a whole day in defence of Philocrates. The upshot was that Philocrates was acquitted, and the proposer of the indictment failed to obtain a fifth of the votes. This is well known to you all. About the same time came the fall of Olynthus,[7] and the capture there of a number of Athenian citizens, including Iatrocles, brother of Ergochares, and Eueratus, the son of Strombichus. An appeal was made by their relatives on their behalf and a request for assistance for them. Support was forthcoming from Philocrates, not from Aeschines. Aristodemus the actor was sent to Philip to represent them because of his acquaintance with him and the good relations won by his art. On returning from his mission Aristodemus failed for some business reason to approach the Council, and before he could do so Iatrocles himself returned from Macedonia, where he had been released by Philip without ransom. There was a good deal of annoyance at Aristodemus for failing to report on his proceedings, when they heard from Iatrocles the same message from Philip. Eventually Democrates of Aphidnae approached the Council with the proposal, which he carried, to call Aristodemus in. One of the Council was my opponent, Demosthenes. When Aristodemus appeared, he reported great good feeling towards Athens on Philip's part, adding that he would like an alliance. He did not confine his report to the Council, but repeated it to the Assembly. Demosthenes made no further difficulty, but proposed a crown of honour for Aristodemus.

After these proceedings Philocrates moved a resolution to appoint a delegation of ten to meet Philip on the subject of peace terms and points of common interest between him and Athens. At the election of delegates I was put forward by Nausicles, and

Demosthenes by Philocrates himself, whom he now accuses. And he was so eager to get to work that he put a motion to the Council with the object of allowing Aristodemus to join the delegation without being penalized, to send representatives to the cities in which Aristodemus was due to perform, and beg for a cancellation of his commitments. In proof of this please take the relevant decrees and read the deposition of Aristodemus, and also call the evidence of the persons to whom he made it. The jury will then know who it was who was Philocrates' boon companion, and who undertook to induce the Assembly to pay public money to Aristodemus.

(The decrees and deposition are read.)

The beginning of the whole business, therefore, did not originate with me, but with Demosthenes and Philocrates. On the delegation he was keen to join our party at meals. He did not say so to me, but to my companions, Aglaocreon of Tenedos, who was chosen from the allied states, and Iatrocles. He maintains that on the journey I urged him to joint action in mounting guard against the monster, Philocrates,[8] which is a pure invention. Why should I call for Demosthenes' aid against Philocrates, when I knew he supported him at the time of the indictment for illegality and was his nominee for the delegation? Besides we were not on those terms. The whole journey we were compelled to withstand Demosthenes' intolerable self-assertion. We held a consultation on the line we should take, and Cimon said he was afraid Philip would have the best of it in stating the rights of the case. But Demosthenes produced fountains of oratory which he claimed he would offer on the legal rights, on Amphipolis, on the opening of the war, which would stop Philip's mouth at once and have the business absolutely sewn up, and induce Athens to accept Leosthenes,[9] and Philip to restore Amphipolis to Athens.

To avoid going to great length on the subject of his aggressive style, as soon as we got to Macedonia we adopted an arrangement

8. See Demosthenes, *Treaty*, 13, p. 59.

9. Leosthenes, an Athenian admiral defeated in 361 B.C., was now in exile. On Amphipolis see Demosthenes, *Treaty*, 22, and Introduction, pp. 19–20.

among ourselves that when we met Philip the eldest should speak
first and the rest follow in order of age. As it happened Demosthenes
was the youngest, or so he said. When we were called in –
I should like you to pay special attention to this, because it shows
his extreme jealousy, his combination of apprehension and malice,
and the designs he harboured against his own associates both at
table and on the conference, which were beyond any normal
treatment of one's bitterest enemies. He says[10] he attached the
greatest importance to the city's salt and the table at which we sat,
though in fact he is not Athenian – let's face it – either by extraction
or by blood.[11] We, on the other hand, whose ancestral places of
worship and burial are in our country, whose habits and associations,
like yours, are those of free Athenians, as are our ceremonies
of marriage, our children and connections, we apparently deserved
your confidence at Athens, but as soon as we got to Macedonia
we suddenly became traitors, while the man who has no
single part of himself free of corruption poses as another Aristides
the Just,[12] and spits with anger at bribery.

Now I want to make clear to you the arguments which we put
forward as your representatives and those stated by that great
bulwark of Athens, Demosthenes. This will enable me to make my
defence against all the charges in series and in detail. And I must
offer my warmest possible gratitude to you, gentlemen of the
jury, for your silent and fair hearing of my case. It means that, if
in any instance I fail to rebut the charges, I shall have myself and
not you to blame for it.

When the older members had spoken for the delegation and our
turn came, what I had to say and Philip's reply to it have been
given accurately and in detail to the whole of Athens in the
Assembly, so I will now try to remind you by a recapitulation. I
first dilated on the good will and the benefactions which from long
tradition Athens rendered to Philip's father, Amyntas. I described
the whole series without omission, and then went on to benefits
which he could himself attest to having enjoyed. At the time when,

10. See Demosthenes, *Treaty*, 189 ff., pp. 101–2.

11. On Demosthenes' parentage see 78, 93 below and Aeschines, *Crown*,
172, p. 238.

12. Athenian leader at the time of the Persian Wars.

just after the death of Amyntas[13] and of Alexander, his eldest son, Perdiccas and Philip were children, and their mother Eurydice was betrayed by her nominal friends, the throne was occupied by Pausanias,[14] who was an exile, but an opportunist, and secured a good deal of support, and with a Greek force at his back took Anthemus, Therma, Strepsa and various other places. Macedonia was divided, the majority favouring Pausanias. At this juncture Athens voted a force under Iphicrates[15] against Amphipolis, which was then occupied and its assets enjoyed by its own citizens.

'When Iphicrates arrived in the district with only a few ships to start with, intending a reconnaissance of the position rather than a siege, he was sent for,' I said to Philip, 'by your mother, Eurydice, who according to the universal account of eye-witnesses put Perdiccas into Iphicrates' arms and you, as a little boy, at his feet, and said: "During his life, Amyntas, the father of these children, adopted you[16] as his son, and enjoyed great friendship with the city of Athens. So you come to be, as a person, brother to the children, and as an Athenian, our friend." She followed this with the most ardent appeal in your name and hers, and in that of her kingdom and her life. In response to this Iphicrates drove Pausanias out of Macedonia, and preserved the power for you.'

Next I spoke about Ptolemaeus, who was left as regent, and of his act of monstrous ingratitude, pointing out that in the first place he took the side of Amphipolis against Athens, and made an alliance with Thebes, when Thebes and Athens were in opposition,[17] and then Perdiccas after his accession went to war with Athens over Amphipolis. I then spoke of the forbearance of Athens despite her unjustifiable treatment, and mentioned her defeat of Perdiccas under Callisthenes[18] and the armistice which

---

13. In 370–369 B.C. The Greeks liked arguments from legend or past history, though they might seem futile. Isocrates is particularly fond of them, cf. *Panegyricus*, 54.

14. Member of a rival princely family.

15. Athenian general first prominent in 390 B.C. (see Aeschines, *Crown*, 243, p. 255) who fought against Spartans and Thebans and later in the Social War. He died in 353 B.C.

16. The date and occasion of this adoption are unknown.

17. In the year of Pausanias's expulsion, 368 B.C.

18. Probably in 363–362 B.C.

followed in the continued expectation that she would be accorded her rights. I tried to put an end to ill feeling by recalling that the execution of Callisthenes was not due to the armistice with Perdiccas, but to other reasons. Once again I did not hesitate to attack Philip by attaching to him the blame for the resumption of the war with Athens. I corroborated everything I said from dispatches and decrees from Athens and the terms of the armistice of Callisthenes. As regards the original ownership of the country and of the so-called Nine Ways[19] and the children of Theseus, one of whom, Acamas, is said to have received the district as his wife's dowry, then was the fitting moment to say all that and it was indeed said, but now perhaps one is forced to cut this account short. But those indications which did not appear in the ancient story, but came from events of our own time, were also among the points I included. A congress was arranged[20] between Sparta and the other Greek states, among whom was Amyntas, Philip's father. He sent a representative to record a vote for which Amyntas had full power, and he voted to assist the other states in regaining Amphipolis for Athens. Their common resolution and the names of its supporters were among evidence from the archives which I adduced. 'And what Amyntas resigned in the presence of all the Greek states not merely verbally, but by means of a formal vote,' I said, 'you, his son, cannot justifiably claim. And if your claim is based on capture in war, then, had you taken it among the spoils of a war against us, your possession of it would be valid. But if you took it from the people of Amphipolis, you hold territory which is not in fact theirs, but belongs to Athens.'

After this and more besides it came to Demosthenes' turn to address the conference. Everybody pricked up his ears in the expectation of hearing some oratorical masterpiece, because news had reached Philip himself and his friends, as we heard later, of the outstanding performance which had been advertised. This was the general attitude of the listeners, but the creature gave vent to a sort of murky opening, absolutely dying with fright, and after

19. The old name of the district of Amphipolis.

20. The occasion may have been the peace conference at Sparta in 371 B.C. or another peace conference held at Athens later in the year; or the conference at Athens in winter 370-369 at which the Spartans negotiated an alliance with Athens against Thebes.

carrying on the subject a very short way, suddenly dried up, couldn't go on, and lost the thread of his argument. Philip realized how it was with him, and encouraged him and urged him not to imagine it was like a stage performance or that it was anything disastrous, but to take his time quietly and recall and continue what he had to say. But once Demosthenes was upset and had lost the way in his notes he was unable to recover himself, and even at a second attempt the same thing happened again. Then, as there was complete silence, the herald told us to adjourn.

When we were by ourselves, our charming friend Demosthenes put on a frightful scowl and declared that I had done for Athens and her allies. I was astonished and so were the rest, and asked what he meant, and he asked if I had forgotten the condition of things at Athens and the sorry state of her people and their longing for peace. 'Is it the decrees which were passed that have put you on your high horse,' he said, 'and the fifty warships[21] which were never destined to be manned, that you make inflammatory speeches like that? They are less likely to change war into peace than peace into implacable war.' I was just beginning to answer this when we were summoned by the aides-de-camp. We entered and sat down, and Philip proceeded to reply to each argument in turn, but he paid particular attention, reasonably enough, to mine. There was hardly anything relevant, I fancy, which I had omitted, and my name was mentioned a great many times in his remarks. Demosthenes having come to such a ridiculous end didn't, I think, get a mention over anything. This made him choke with exasperation. But when Philip's remarks turned to politeness, and Demosthenes' malicious attack on me before the delegates (his claim that I should cause strife and dissension) fell to pieces, he was obviously beside himself to the extent that even when we were invited to a dinner he behaved disgracefully.

But on our way home from the conference he made himself unexpectedly pleasant to us one after the other. Expressions like 'monkey', 'sieve', 'doubleton' were outside my knowledge previously,[22] but under his initiation I learnt the whole vocabulary

---

21. See 133 below, p. 175 for the fifty ships voted for Proxenus.

22. We do not know the inner meaning of these terms, which are comparable with slang of this kind in other languages.

of crooked dealing. He went round to each of us in turn with undertakings to one man to raise a loan to aid him in his private affairs, and to another to get him on the board of the *strategia*. He hung on to me, congratulated me on my talent, complimented the speech I made, and was loud in praise to the point of embarrassment. When we all dined together at Larissa,[23] he made jokes against himself and the collapse of his speech, and talked about Philip as the most marvellous man living. I signified my agreement and added something to the effect that he had shown a good memory of what we had said, and Ctesiphon, who was the eldest of the party, made a great deal of his age and long experience, adding that in all this length of time he had never seen so pleasant and charming a person as Philip. At this our double-faced Sisyphus[24] clapped his hands, and said, 'All the same, Ctesiphon, you wouldn't say that in public to the people of Athens, nor would he' (meaning me) 'dare to tell an Athenian audience that Philip is a brilliant speaker with an excellent memory.' We were not quick enough to see the trap he was setting – you shall hear in a moment – and how he had made a sort of pact to which we were committed, that we would say this in public debate. He even made me a stringent request to say, and not forget, that Demosthenes also supported our demand for Amphipolis.

Up to this point my story is corroborated by the rest of the delegation, whom Demosthenes has continually denigrated and defamed in his accusation. But what he said on the platform in your presence you heard yourselves, so it will be impossible for me to mis-state it. But I do ask you to take the same care in listening to the rest of my account. I am sure every one of you is as eager to hear the story of Cersobleptes and the rights and wrongs about Phocis as I am to narrate them. But unless you hear what leads up to it, you will not be so well able to follow it. But if you grant me, as defendant and therefore at risk, to conduct my speech as I like, you will be able to preserve me, if I am innocent, on adequate grounds, and you will have a basis of agreed facts upon which to look at the arguments in dispute.

23. In Thessaly.

24. Sisyphus was renowned in mythology as a deceiver. The deceit in this instance is presumably to be found in the account of Demosthenes' remarks in 49 and 50 (p. 153 below).

When we returned here and made our report in summary form to the Council, handing over Philip's letter, Demosthenes commended us to fellow members of the Council, and swore an oath by Hestia[25] who stands in the Council, expressing gratification for the appointment of such a body whose loyalty and whose words made them worthy representatives of Athens. In regard to me he said something to the effect that I did not disappoint the hopes of my sponsors. To cap it all he proposed a crown of wild olive for each of us for his services to Athens, and an invitation to the Prytaneum for next day. To prove the truth of all that I have said, I ask the clerk to take the decree and the depositions of members of the delegation, and read them.

(The decree and depositions are read.)

Well, when we gave our account of the conference in the Assembly, Ctesiphon was the first to speak, and among other subjects he brought up what he had agreed with Demosthenes to say about Philip's manners and good appearance and his pleasantness at a party. Then after a few words from Philocrates and Dercylus I got up. After describing the conference as a whole, I turned to the subject I had agreed with the others to mention, and described Philip's ability as a speaker and his grasp of what had been said. I did not forget the arrangement with Demosthenes, that he was to deal with anything we omitted on the subject of Amphipolis. He rose last, after the rest of us. He put on his usual imposing manner, with one hand rubbing his head, and, seeing that the meeting accepted my remarks with approval, observed that he was surprised at the audience and the delegates alike wasting the time for discussion and advice, and spending it in mere talk on home affairs quite foreign to the purpose. 'I shall give you a demonstration,' he said, 'of how proceedings ought to be conducted.' With that he gave orders for the people's decree to be read. This was done, and he continued, 'These were our terms of reference, and we carried out these instructions as written down. Now please take the letter we brought from Philip.' This was also read. There was a general outcry, partly in praise of his admirable brevity, but

25. The Hearth, regarded as sacred in the Greek household and represented also in the Council chamber.

mostly against such unpleasantness and jealousy. He then went on, 'Just observe the succinctness with which I will cover the rest of the report. Aeschines thought Philip a good speaker. I did not. Divest him of his luck and give it to someone else, and you would get someone just as good. Ctesiphon thought him good-looking. I thought him no better than Aristodemus, the actor' (who was there as a member of the delegation). 'And he has been credited with a good memory. So have others. He was a good performer at a drinks party. Philocrates of our group was better. Someone else said it had been left to me to discuss Amphipolis. But this particular orator would not give up his own time to you or to me. No, this is all nonsense. I propose to move a resolution that an agreement be made with the herald who has come from Philip and the representatives who are coming, that on their arrival the Prytaneis call a two-day Assembly not only for the making of peace, but alliance, and that our delegation, if regarded as satisfactory, should receive the normal compliments and an invitation to the Prytaneum for tomorrow.'[26]

In proof of my statements take the decrees and read them, and that will show you, gentlemen of the jury, both his inconsistency and his jealousy, also his association with Philocrates over the business, and his scheming, disloyal character. Also, please, call my fellow delegates and read their evidence.

(The decrees are read.)

He not only moved these resolutions, but followed them in the Council by proposing a show for Philip's representatives at the Dionysia[27] when they arrived. Read this decree as well.

(The decree is read.)

Now please read the evidence of members of the delegation. This will show, gentlemen, that Demosthenes is incapable of speaking to further the interests of Athens, though against his own associates for dinner or ceremonial he is an expert.

26. See Demosthenes, *Treaty*, 31, note 15.
27. i.e. the great Dionysia festival in April 346 B.C.

(The evidence is read.)

Thus the close association over the peace discussions was not, you see, between me and Philocrates but between Demosthenes and Philocrates. I think you have been given sufficient assurance of what I said. As to the reports, you have your own knowledge, and the speeches made in Macedonia and the events of our return journey are attested by the evidence of members of the conference which I have called. You heard and remember the accusation recently made by Demosthenes, in which he began with my speech about the peace. Everything in that part of his accusation was untrue, but his strongest indignation[28] concerned the actual occasion. He states that this debate took place in the presence of the representatives sent to Athens by the Greek states at the instance of the people of Athens to enable us to unite for war with Philip, if need be, or for peace, if that were decided upon.[29] Look at the appalling, shameless deceit of the man on a point of great importance. If you consider the delegations sent out to the Greek states in connection with the war against Philip, the dates of their appointment and the names of the participants are in the public records. Even their persons are in Athens, not Macedonia. Foreign delegates are subject to the direction of the Council before they can address the people. And yet he states that the representatives of the Greek states were there. Now, Demosthenes, just stand up, in my time allowance, and name any of the Greek cities you like whose representatives you maintain were present on that occasion. Give us the text of the Council's directions to be read out. Call the Athenian representatives sent out to the Greek states. If they state in evidence that they were here and not abroad when Athens was engaged in peace negotiations, or if you can produce evidence of their appearance in the Council and of the decrees passed at the time you mention, I abandon my defence and accept the death penalty.

Now read the text of the resolution of the allies,[30] which contains

28. See Demosthenes, *Treaty*, 15, 16, p. 60. Here, however, Aeschines has made a volte-face from what he himself said in the speech *Against Timarchus*, 174, where he associates himself with Philocrates.

29. See Introduction pp. 28 ff.

30. i.e. the members of the Athenian Confederacy, whose *synhedrion* met at Athens. On their proposal see Introduction p. 28.

the specific decision that 'since the people of Athens are considering peace with Philip, and the delegates sent out by the people of Athens into Greece with a summons to the cities on behalf of the liberty of Greece have not yet returned, it is hereby enacted by the allies that on the return of the Athenian representatives and their report on their proceedings to the Athenians and their allies, the Prytaneis shall call two meetings of the Assembly in accordance with the law, and the Athenians shall devote these to a debate on the peace, and whatever is the decree of the people of Athens shall be adopted as the decision of the allies in common'. Now please read the decree of the Synod of the allies.

(The decree of the Synod is read.)

Now set against this the decree of Demosthenes which orders the Prytaneis after the City Dionysia and the session in the sanctuary of Dionysus to call two meetings of the Assembly, one on the fifteenth and the other on the sixteenth of April,[31] so as to determine the date and prearrange the meetings to take place before the return of the Athenian representatives from the Greek states. The decree of the allies, which I agree I also supported, only laid down discussion of peace, that of Demosthenes required discussion of alliance as well. Read the decree, then.

(The decree is read.)

Now you have heard both decrees, which convict Demosthenes of saying that the absent delegations were present and invalidating the decree of the allies when the Assembly wished to discuss it. They made their proposal to await the Greek delegations, but Demosthenes not only verbally urged against waiting, being the most shameless person and the quickest to change his ground, but used action and a decree as well, demanding an immediate decision.[32]

He has said that at the earlier of the two meetings after a speech

31. The Greek dates are 18 and 19 Elaphebolion. For the complex organization of the Greek calendar see Goodwin, *Demosthenes, On the Crown*, pp. 305–7.
32. See Introduction p. 28.

from Philocrates I got up and criticized the terms of the peace he proposed on the ground that it was dishonourable and beneath the greatness of Athens, but the day after I turned round and supported Philocrates, and was successful in carrying the Assembly with me by urging them not to pay attention to talk about the battles and the trophies[33] of our ancestors nor to assist the Greek states. The falsity of this accusation, and also its impossibility, is proved by various evidence, first his own, secondly that of the whole people, including you yourselves who remember it all, thirdly the sheer unconvincing nature of the statement, and fourthly by a distinguished individual in the political world, Amyntor, who was shown a draft decree by Demosthenes and invited to discuss the desirability of handing it to the clerk. This proposal was not opposed to that of Philocrates, but identical with it. Now please take and read the decree of Demosthenes, in which he is proved to have proposed that all who wished to should take part at the first of the two meetings, but that at the second the presiding officials should put the question to the vote without allowing debate, on which occasion he states that I supported Philocrates.

(The decree is read.)

So the decrees stand as they were originally written, but the words of detractors are uttered for the occasion, as it comes. According to my accuser my speech is divided in two, though according to the decree and to the truth it is one. If the *proedroi*[34] did not allow debate at the second meeting, I cannot have spoken then. And if my policy was the same as Philocrates', what would be the object of criticizing it the previous day before the same audience, and then after one night's interval supporting it? To gain credit myself, or to assist him? I couldn't do either. All I could do was to incur general unpopularity for nothing.

Now please call Amyntor of Herchia, and read his evidence. But I ought to describe in advance the terms in which it has been put down. 'Amyntor gives his testimony at the request of Aeschines, that at the time when the debate of the people of Athens was taking place on the question of alliance with Philip in accordance

33. See Demosthenes, *Treaty*, 16 (p. 60).
34. Presiding officers at meetings of Council or Assembly.

with the decree of Demosthenes, during the second of the two meetings, at which no speaking was allowed, and the decrees about the peace and the alliance were put to the vote, on that occasion Demosthenes sat beside him and showed him a decree headed with the name of Demosthenes, and discussed with him the question whether he should hand it to the presiding officials to put to the vote. It was a statement of the terms on which he proposed that peace and alliance should be made, namely on the same terms as those which Philocrates had proposed.' Now please call Amyntor of Herchia, and serve him with a *sub poena* if he fails to appear.

(The evidence is given.)

You have heard the evidence, gentlemen. I put the question whether in your opinion Demosthenes has been accusing me or whether the opposite is true, that he has accused himself in my name. But as he also casts aspersions on my speech, and disparages the arguments I put forward, I do not wish to run away from it or to deny anything I then said. I am not ashamed, but actually proud of it.

I also want to remind you of the circumstances of this debate. We first went to war for Amphipolis, with the result that our commander-in-chief in the war lost seventy-five allied towns which had been acquired by Conon's son, Timotheus,[35] and added to the combined allied synod. (I have preferred to speak with complete freedom, and let my survival depend on the liberty and truth of my account. If you take a different view, you must treat me harshly, but I am not going to hedge.) In addition, he received from the dockyards 150 warships, which he failed to bring home – as Chares'[36] accusers are always pointing out in court – and he

35. Aeschines, as often, is careless with history. About seventy cities joined the Second Athenian Confederacy between its foundation in 378 and 372 B.C., and Timotheus was prominent in Athenian operations until his disgrace in 373. After 371 there were defections from the Confederacy culminating in the Social War (357–355), but even after it a good number of allies remained loyal to Athens; and although Aeschines here treats this war as part of the war with Philip, he is clearly exaggerating. Timotheus had returned to active command in 366 and achieved some success, but in the Social War he was defeated at Embata (356) and fined 100 talents. See Introduction, pp. 20 ff.

36. On Chares see Demosthenes, *Treaty*, 332, p. 136 above.

spent 1500 talents, not on pay for the men, but on the set of self-advertisers he had as commanders, a collection of runaways from all over Greece like Deiares, Deipyrus and Polyphontes; and besides them, on his hired supporters by the platform and around the Assembly, who exacted a levy of sixty talents a year from the unfortunate islanders while they seized ships and Greek citizens from their own Greek waters everywhere. Meanwhile instead of gaining prestige and power for Greece our city's reputation was infected with the disease of piracy like that of Myonnesus.[37] Philip sallied forth from Macedonia, and no longer confined his war with us to Amphipolis, but was concerned with Lemnos, Imbros, Scyros, all possessions of ours. Athenian citizens were abandoning the Chersonese, admittedly our property, while Athens was compelled to call more extra meetings of the Assembly than the legally stated number[38] under conditions of panic and agitation. The position was so precarious and dangerous that Cephisophon of Paeania, one of Chares' boon companions, was compelled to move a resolution that Antiochus, the commander of the mercenary forces, should move in with all possible speed, discover the official head of the Athenian force, if possible, and inform him that the people of Athens was surprised that Philip should be marching to the Chersonese, an Athenian possession, while Athens herself did not so much as know the whereabouts of the commander and the force she had dispatched. In proof of the truth of this, I ask you to listen to the decree, and to cast your minds back to the war, and exact responsibility for the peace from the military leaders, not from members of the peace conference.[39]

(The decree is read.)

Such were the political circumstances under which the discussion of peace took place. Then the speakers of the established party, addressing the Assembly, made no attempt to consider the safety of Athens, but told us to turn our eyes to the Gates of the Acropolis, to remember the battle of Salamis and the tombs and trophies of our ancestors. Personally I maintained that certainly we should

37. Off the Thessalian coast.
38. See Demosthenes, *Treaty*, 154, note 59.
39. But cf. Demosthenes, *Treaty*, 336, p. 138 above.

remember all that, but we should also recall our ancestors' wisdom and beware of their mistakes and their unfortunate competitive spirit. 'Think of the battle of Plataea,' I said, 'of the struggle for Salamis, of the battle of Marathon and, at sea, of Artemisium, and follow the example of Tolmides,[40] who had a thousand picked Athenians under his command and successfully made his way through the middle of the Peloponnese, then at war with us. And beware of an expedition like that in Sicily, sent for the assistance of Leontini, when Spartan invasions of Attica had taken place and Decelea been fortified,[41] and later the crowning absurdity, when after being worsted in the war the people were offered a peace[42] by Sparta by which, in addition to Attica, Lemnos, Imbros and Scyros would be retained under legal democratic government, and they refused. They preferred to continue the war, though they had not the power, and Cleophon the lyre-maker, whom many remembered in chains, after being enrolled illegally as a citizen and then ruining the country by his system of money-distribution,[43] threatened to cut the throat of anyone who made any reference to peace. They finished by reducing the country to a condition in which she was thankful to have peace at the price of the loss of everything, of the destruction of the walls, of acceptance of a Spartan garrison and harmost[44] and the surrender of government to the Thirty, who put fifteen hundred Athenian citizens to death without trial' This was the sort of misgovernment which I own I urged the city to avoid, and instead to imitate the actions I mentioned just now. It was not from strangers that my own knowledge of it came, but from the closest of all sources. My father, Atrometus,[45]

40. In 458 B.C.

41. Aeschines refers to the Athenian expeditionary force sent to Sicily in the Peloponnesian War in 415 B.C. Decelea in Attica, some 14 miles north-east of Athens, was not, however, fortified by Sparta until 413 B.C., as a means of relieving Athenian pressure on Syracuse.

42. Sparta made offers of peace in 410 B.C. and in 406, the year before the decisive defeat of the Athenian fleet.

43. The diobelia, an allowance to poorer citizens, nominally to provide seats for the festivals, was instituted by Cleophon according to Aristotle, *Constitution of Athens*, 28.

44. The Spartan governor in each city taken over after the fall of Athens was called a harmost.

45. See also Demosthenes, *Treaty*, 281, and *Crown*, 130 (pp. 125 and 288).

whom you insult without any acquaintance with him or any knowledge of what he once was, and despite the fact that your own descent comes on your mother's side from the nomads of Scythia[46] – my father was exiled under the Thirty and took part in the restoration of free government. And my uncle, my mother's brother, Cleobulus, son of Glaucus of Acharnae, fought with the fleet under Demaenetus son of Buzygus against the Spartan admiral Chilon.[47] So it is the miseries of my own flesh and blood that ring in my ears as I listen to the story of Athens.

You also criticize my speech to the Ten Thousand[48] in Arcadia and my mission there. You call me a turncoat, though little better than a slave yourself, in fact almost branded a deserter.[49] What I did was to unite Arcadia, to the best of my power, with the rest of Greece against Philip. There was no one to assist Athens. They were all either waiting to see which way things went or joining Philip's campaign, while the speakers at home used the war to lead the dance of added daily expense, and I agree that I recommended the people to come to terms with Philip and arrange a peace. You call it a disgrace, as a man who never struck a blow in battle. But I call it a great deal more honourable than the war.

By rights, gentlemen, peace delegates should apply their attention to the occasion of their delegation, military commanders to the forces at their command. Statues are raised, promotions and honours and public banquets awarded, not for sending news of peace but for winning the battle. If official investigations are to be awarded to the delegates, and presentations to the commanders, you'll make war an implacable and unrelenting affair, because no one will be prepared to sit on a peace conference.

It remains for me to deal with the subject of Cersobleptes and of Phocis, and with the rest of the misrepresentations made against

46. See above 22, p. 148, and below 93, p. 165, and Aeschines, *Crown*, 171-2, p. 237

47. Probably during the Corinthian War, 395-387 B.C.

48. The federal assembly of the Arcadian League. Aeschines went there as one of a number of ambassadors sent to arouse the Greek states against Philip in the autumn of 348 B.C. See Demosthenes, *Treaty*, 304, p. 130 above.

49. In 348 Demosthenes had been compelled to return home from service in the field in Euboea to perform his duty as choregus, for which he had volunteered, and an attempt was made to treat this as a matter of desertion.

me as well. In actual fact, gentlemen of the jury, both on the first and on the second delegation I reported what I saw, as I saw it, and what I heard, as I heard it. What, then, comes under these two heads, what I saw and what I heard, in regard to Cersobleptes? I saw, and all the delegation saw, the son of Cersobleptes as a hostage in the hands of Philip. This is still the case. What happened was that, when we were engaged on the first conference, I returned here with the rest of the delegation while Philip moved towards Thrace, having agreed with us, however, that while Athens was engaged in the peace negotiations he would make no armed irruption into the Chersonese. Indeed on the day on which peace was voted here, no one gave a thought to Cersobleptes. But when we had been elected to the delegation to receive the oaths, but before we sailed on the second occasion, a meeting of the Assembly was held, at which Demosthenes, my present accuser, was allotted the post of presiding magistrate. At this meeting Critobulus of Lampsacus was present and stated that he had been sent by Cersobleptes, and claimed in his name the right to swear the oath to Philip's representatives, and at the same time to be included in the register of Athenian allies. After this Aleximachus of Pelex handed the presidents a decree to be read out, in which it was proposed that the newly arrived representative of Cersobleptes should take the oath among the allies of Athens. When it was read, as I think you all remember, Demosthenes from his place among the presidents said he refused to put the decree to the vote, since he would not break the peace with Philip, nor did he recognize as allies people who invaded the ceremony just as it started, when another meeting had been allowed for their purposes.[50] There was a general outcry and demands to the presidents on the platform, and so despite Demosthenes the decree was voted. In proof of this please call Aleximachus, the proposer of the motion, and Demosthenes' colleagues who presided, and read their depositions.

50. Demosthenes was no doubt afraid that the attempt to include Cerso-bleptes in an irregular fashion at the last moment might lead to the breakdown of the peace arrangements. Cersobleptes had been an ally of Athens, but had not joined the Confederacy. Athens's allies in the peace treaty were evidently limited to its members. Philip's promise not to enter the Chersonese implied his claim to freedom of action in Thrace.

(The depositions are read.)

So the man who just now wept in your presence at the mention of Cersobleptes is shown to have tried to exclude him from the alliance. After the adjournment of the meeting Philip's representatives began the administration of the oaths to Athenian allies in the hall of the *strategia*. My accuser has the temerity to tell you that I excluded Critobulus, Cersobleptes' deputy, from the ceremony in the presence of the allied representatives and after the vote of the people had been taken, with the strategi looking on.[51] How could I have had the power to do this? Or if I had, how could it have been kept quiet? If I were unprincipled enough to have done this, would you have allowed it, Demosthenes? Wouldn't you have let out a howl of indignation to fill the market-place, if you had seen me, as you have just asserted, forcibly ejecting a delegate from the ceremony? Ask the herald to call the strategi and the members of the synod, and listen to their evidence.

(The evidence is heard.)

Now isn't it scandalous, gentlemen, that anyone should attack a fellow citizen of his own, or rather, to put it correctly, of yours, and dare to utter such falsehood against him when his life is in danger? It was indeed reasonable that it was an ancestral practice in cases of homicide held at the Palladium[52] that the successful contestant should cut up the sacrificial victim and swear, as is still the established practice, that the jurors who had taken his side had given a vote which was true and just and had spoken no falsehood, and, if not, to call utter destruction upon himself and his family, and to pray for the jurors all that is good. This was good democratic practice, gentlemen, because even if none of you would wish to incur the contamination of justifiable bloodshed you would presumably take precaution against what is unjust, against depriving a man of life or property or rights, which has driven some to self-destruction or led them to execution. Will you, then, gentlemen, grant me pardon if I call him physically and mentally obscene like the words he utters, and then proceed to show the rest of his accusation about Cersobleptes to be demonstrably false?

51. This differs from the account given by Aeschines in *Crown*, 74, q.v.
52. A court dealing with unintentional homicide.

It is an admirable arrangement, and one of the highest value to victims of slander, that dates, decrees and the names on which they stand are preserved permanently in the public records. Now Demosthenes has stated[53] that the ruin of Cersobleptes' affairs is due to the fact that when I was leader of the delegation and the sun was on my side of the hedge he urged that we should go to Thrace, where Cersobleptes was under siege, and make a protest to Philip against it, but I refused, and that I and the rest of the delegates sat down at Oreus to secure consular posts there for ourselves. Now please listen to the letter sent by Chares to the people of Athens at the time, which indicates that Cersobleptes had lost his kingdom and the Sacred Mount[54] had been captured by Philip on 24 April. But that was the month in which Demosthenes was presiding in the Assembly on the 22nd.

(The letter is read.)

So not only did we spend the end of the month in Athens, but it was the following month that we started. I can offer the evidence of the Council for this. They have the decree ordering the departure of the delegation to administer the oath. Please read the decree of the Council.

(The decree is read.)

And with it read the statement of the date.

(The statement is read.)

That, then, is the statement that it was 3 May when the decree was passed. And how many days before my departure was it that Cersobleptes lost his kingdom? According to General Chares it was the previous month, if I am right in thinking that April is followed by May. So how could I have saved Cersobleptes, whose fall was before I left Athens? In that case can you believe in the truth of any statement about events in Macedonia or Thessaly made by a man who tells lies in the face of the Council, public

53. On this section see Demosthenes, *Treaty*, 150, 164, and *Crown*, 25 (pp. 92, 95 and 266).

54. The Sacred Mount had been held by Athens in the interest of Cersobleptes.

records, dates, meetings of the Assembly and everything? Why did you exclude Cersobleptes from the peace at Athens, and then feel pity for him at Oreus? Why do you bring charges of bribery now, when previously you submitted to the penalty imposed by the Areopagus for not pursuing an indictment for assault against your cousin, Demomeles of Paeania,[55] for the head injury which you yourself inflicted. And you parade an imposing style, as though the jury were ignorant that you are the bastard[56] son of Demosthenes the cutler!

Then you attempt to maintain that after crying off serving on the Amphictyonic[57] delegation I later misconducted it. You read one decree but omitted another. I was elected to the delegation in question, but I was unwell. I had shown the greatest eagerness in reporting the conference I had been on, and similarly now I did not refuse. I undertook to carry it out if I could, and, as the delegates were leaving, I sent my brother and nephew, and my doctor, to the Council, not to excuse me from going – it is illegal to decline a vote of the people in the Council – but to attest my illness. When the rest of the delegates heard the news about Phocis and turned back, a meeting was held at which I had recovered and was present. The people's decision was that the original delegation must go just the same in full, and I thought I ought to be quite candid towards the country. You make no charge against me in regard to this delegation, for which I submitted my account, but you pass to the one which concerned the ratification, for which I shall offer a clear and just defence. It is characteristic of you, as it is of all liars, to make alterations in the dates. But I prefer to narrate them in order and resume the beginning of the narrative of the conference for ratification.

First of all there were ten delegates, with the addition of one

---

55. Demomeles, the son of Demophon, Demosthenes' first cousin, was involved in the proceedings which Demosthenes had to take to recover his father's property in 364-363 B.C.

56. Demosthenes was called a bastard because his mother was of Scythian descent. See note 11 above.

57. Really to Philip, but concerned with the affairs of the Amphictyonic states (see Demosthenes, *Treaty*, 20, note 10 above). On the events of the third delegation see Demosthenes, *Treaty*, 121 ff., p. 85.

from the allies, making eleven in all. None of us wanted to share a table with Demosthenes when we started on the second expedition, nor to stay at the same inn on the way, because we knew that on the first occasion he had had adverse designs against us. No mention was made of the journey to Thrace.[58] The decree had not enacted this, but only the administration of the oath and the like. And there was nothing we could have achieved by making it, because the business about Cersobleptes had already taken place, as you have just heard, and there is no truth in Demosthenes' story, which is pure falsehood, a mountain of invention, because he has no true charge to bring.

He was accompanied by two servants carrying mattresses, one of which, according to his own account, contained a talent of silver. So his colleagues recalled his old nicknames. When they were children, a disgusting, immoral habit earned him the name of 'the pansy', but when he got a bit older and started bringing ten-talent suits against his guardians he was called 'the adder', and then when he was grown up the ordinary name for the dishonest was added, and he became 'the twister'.[59] He was going on the journey to ransom the prisoners, according to his own account at the time[60] as well as now in court, although he knew well enough that Philip had never exacted ransom from any Athenians in the war, and was told by all Philip's friends that if peace were made he would release the rest as well. So between a whole lot of hard cases he brought one talent, enough for one of them, and not a very affluent one then.

When we were in Macedonia, at a meeting held on the news of Philip's return from Thrace, the decree which formed the terms of reference was read out, and we reckoned up our commitments besides the administration of the oath. As no mention was made of the most important things, and the time tended to be spent on details, I made some observations which should be repeated to you. And I most solemnly urge you, gentlemen, to match the consideration you showed in giving the prosecution the hearing they demanded

58. To try to prevent Philip winning new territory before the treaty was ratified. See Demosthenes, *Treaty*, 150 (p. 92).

59. See Appendix, p. 331.

60. See Demosthenes, *Treaty*, 166 (p. 166).

by listening as methodically to the defence, and to maintain the attitude in which you received my earlier remarks at the beginning. As I said just now, gentlemen, I remarked at the meeting of the delegates that I thought we were shamefully neglecting the most important instructions we had received from the people of Athens. 'The administration of the oath, the discussion of other such matters and negotiation about the prisoners are subjects which I should say could have been carried out with a delegation of sub-ordinates invested with powers of representation. But a right decision of outstanding questions of importance,[61] so far as we or Philip can achieve it, requires delegates of some wisdom. I refer,' I said, 'to the expedition to Thermopylae which you know is in preparation. As to the accuracy of my estimate of this I can offer strong evidence. There is a Theban delegation here, and another from Sparta, and here are we with an official decree from Athens, with the direction "and the delegates shall do all in their power to improve the position". All the Greek states have an eye to the future. Had this country thought it desirable to make an explicit approach to Philip, urging him to curb Theban aggression[62] and rebuild fortifications in Boeotia, the demand would have been included in the decree. As it is, they left themselves a way of retreat in case of uncertainty in the event of a refusal, thinking it best to put the onus of decision on us. True public spirit should not appropriate the position of possible alternative represen-tatives of Athens, while deliberately avoiding the issue of Theban hostility. It was a Theban, Epaminondas,[63] who without any deference to Athenian prestige said explicitly in a speech before the body of Theban citizens that the gates of the Acropolis at Athens should be transferred to become instead the entrance to the Cadmeia.' While I was in the middle of this speech, Demosthenes gave a colossal shout, as all the delegates know. The reason is that besides everything else he's a pro-Theban. What he said was this: 'The man's an absolute figure of uncalled-for belligerence. Person-ally I confess to being timid and apprehensive about events in the

61. i.e. primarily the treatment of Phocis.

62. See Demosthenes, *Treaty*, 20.

63. Victor at Leuctra in 371 B.C. and chief architect of the Theban supremacy which perished with him at Mantinea in 362.

remote future, but I veto the proposal that we should set the Greek states about each other's ears. Non-interference on the part of this delegation of ours is what I think is wanted. Philip is going to Thermopylae, and I shut my eyes to it. I shall not be criticized for Philip's bellicose actions, but for any words of mine which are out of turn, or actions which are not in accord with instructions.' At the end the members of the delegation were asked a question, and each gave his opinion of what action was desirable. Now in proof of the truth of this call the other members of the delegation and read their statements.

(The evidence is read.)

Well, the delegations assembled at Pella, and Philip arrived. When the herald called the Athenian delegates, we did not speak in order of age, as we had on the first occasion, which is an arrangement commonly accepted as best in accordance with protocol. Demosthenes' blatant demand was allowed to hold the day. He declared he was the youngest, and therefore entitled to speak first, and refused absolutely to forgo this or to allow someone else – with a glance at me – to gain first access to Philip's ear and prevent the rest from speaking.

He began his speech with a slight reflection on his fellow delegates, when he stated that we had not come with entirely unanimous aims or opinions. He then enlarged on the services he had rendered to Philip, first his agreement with the decree of Philocrates,[64] when he was subject to a prosecution for illegality for his proposal that Philip be allowed to send representatives to Athens for peace talks. Secondly he read, clause by clause, the decree he had himself proposed for a safe-conduct for the herald and for Philip's delegation, and thirdly that for a discussion of peace terms in the Assembly on stated days. He added a corollary to this account to the effect that he was the first to curb the attempt to exclude peace negotiations, not by actual speech but by controlling the time sequence. He next introduced a new decree including alliance in the agenda for negotiation, and finally the decree giving the leading places at the Dionysia to Philip's representa-

64. See above 14, p. 146.

tives.[65] He also claimed to have given special consideration to them in the way of setting cushions for them and keeping a look out or a watch at night against jealous attempts to do violence to the credit he was acquiring. Then came what was really ridiculous and made his colleagues hide their heads, when he stated how he entertained Philip's representatives and on their departure hired pairs of mules for them and accompanied them on horseback without retreating into the darkness like others, but with a conspicuous show of deference to them. He then corrected impressions he had previously given with the words, 'I didn't comment on your good looks. Good looks belong principally to women. Nor did I credit you with soaking, which would be a word for a sponge, nor with a good memory, which I should regard as a quality of a laborious pedagogue.' To cut a long story short, the character of his remarks in the presence of the representatives of practically the whole of Greece were such as to give rise to considerable outbursts of amusement.

When he came to an end and the noise subsided, I had to follow this ill-bred exhibition of servile flattery. I had to say a word or two to start with in reply to his initial malicious attack on his colleagues. I said we had been sent as Athenian delegates, not to conduct our defence in Macedonia, but because our conduct had made us seem adequate representatives of our city. After a brief reference to the oaths which were the object of our journey, I passed on to the other instructions we had been given, because the outstanding oratory of the brilliant Demosthenes had made no mention of these essentials. I also referred to the expedition to Thermopylae, to Delphi and the sacred sites and to the Amphictyonic states, and urged Philip for preference not to use force, but arbitration and deliberation in settling these issues, but if this were not possible (obviously, because the army was there, already mobilized) I said that any deliberation on the subject of the religious centres of Greece ought to postulate a care for reverence and attention to expert understanding of tradition. At the same time I described from its inception the founding of the sanctuary

65. For these three decrees mentioned after that of Philocrates see above 54, 55, 61 respectively (pp. 154, 6).

and the first gathering of the Amphictyons, and read out their oaths, including the one which appears in the ancient statutes, that 'no city among the Amphictyonic states shall be made desolate nor cut off from spring water either in war or in peace, and any state which contravenes this law shall suffer invasion and the destruction of her cities, and anyone who either pillages the sacred treasure or is privy to such a deed or devises any act of damage to it shall be punished with hand and foot and word to the uttermost.' A devastating curse was added to the text of the oath. After reading this I said that in my opinion the destruction of the cities in Boeotia[66] ought not to be overlooked. To prove that there existed Amphictyonic states bound by this oath I enumerated twelve tribes, the participants in membership of the sanctuary: Thessaly, Boeotia (not Thebes alone), Doris, Ionia, Parrhaebia, Magnesia, Locris, Oeta, Phthia, Malia and Phocis. I pointed out that each of these had equal franchise, greatest and least alike, the member for Dorium and Cytinium having equal power with the representative of Sparta, because each tribe has two votes.[67] Similarly among the Ionian peoples Eretria and Priene are on a par with Athens, and the rest in the same way.

I showed that the original reason for this expedition was in accordance with religion and justice. But I maintained that the just course was that the Amphictyons should have assembled at the sanctuary and been allowed safe conduct and freedom to give their vote, and then justice should have been exacted from the people responsible for the seizure of the sanctuary, not for their countries, but from the actual individuals who had planned and carried out the action, and that states who handed over the guilty to judgement

66. See Demosthenes, *Treaty*, 20, 21 (p. 62) and note 11.
67. Aeschines gives eleven names for the twelve nations represented in the Amphictyonic Council, and it has been supposed that Dolopia has been omitted. Goodwin is of opinion that the missing name is that of Delphi. See Goodwin, *Demosthenes, On the Crown*, pp. 338–9. Each nation was represented by two 'Remembrancers' (ἱερομνήμων) who gave one vote each in the Council. But Doris, Locris and Ionia were divided, each division having one Remembrancer and one vote. Thus Athens was one division of Ionia, and had one Remembrancer, who was chosen by lot. There were also delegates (called πυλαγόροι) who spoke but could not vote. Athens sent three at each meeting. See Aeschines, *Crown*, 115 ff.

should not be penalized. 'But if,' I declared, 'you go to the length of using force to confirm Theban misdeeds, you will get no thanks for your assistance. You could not confer a greater benefit on them than Athens once did, and they have no recollection of that.[68] And it will be an injustice to the people you leave stranded, whom you will turn into still more bitter enemies instead of friends.'

I don't want to weary you with too precise an account of what was said on that occasion, so I will close with a summary of the whole thing. It was chance and Philip who were responsible for what happened. I was responsible only for my loyalty and for my words. What I said was in accord with justice and with the interest of Athens. But in the event our prayers went unfulfilled, and Philip's actions decided the day. Which, then, deserves your credit, a man who showed no eagerness for the good of Athens or one who left no stone unturned for it? At the moment I omit a good deal which time does not allow.

Demosthenes declared[69] that I made a false statement that within a few days Thebes would be humbled, and that I alarmed the people of Euboea and thus led the country to groundless hopes. But please realize, gentlemen, what he is doing. I reported to you the claim made in Philip's presence, that Thebes ought by rights to be part of Boeotia, not Boeotia subject to Thebes. This he describes not as a report but as an undertaking. But I told this court that Cleochares of Chalcis said he was astonished at the sudden agreement between Philip and Athens, particularly in view of our instructions to 'do what we could' to improve things. Small states like his own were frightened by the secret agreement of the big ones. Demosthenes' statement is not that I related this story but that I undertook to surrender Euboea. But I had merely supposed that deliberations about the whole Greek world ought to be continued while any Greek view remained unheard.

Again he made the false claim[70] – this was another divided

---

68. The Phocian control of Delphi prevented an Amphictyonic meeting, and Aeschines maintains that Philip should have occupied the place to ensure the rights of the Amphictyons instead of Athens supporting Phocis, which would hinder them. Assistance to Thebes would be as unrewarding to Philip as it was to Athens at the time of the Spartan hegemony.

69. See Demosthenes, *Treaty*, 21–3 and 74 (p. 62 ff. and 75).

70. See Demosthenes, *Treaty*, 23.

accusation – that he was prevented by Philochares and myself from making the true report he intended. Now I should like to ask you whether there was ever anyone in Athens who was sent out as a member of a delegation and was prevented from making an official report on his mission, and after this had happened, and he had been discredited in this way by his colleagues, then proposed a vote of thanks to them and an invitation to a banquet. Well, when Demosthenes returned from the last conference, in which he asserts that the Greek world was disrupted, he not only commended us in the decree, but after my report to the Assembly of my disquisition about the Amphictyonic Council and Boeotia, which was not a hasty summary like this but given to the best of my ability in full and in detail, and enthusiastically received by the Assembly, he was called by me with the other delegates and asked the question whether this was a true account and corresponded with what I had said before Philip. Then amidst the general protestations of approval from the other delegates he rose in addition to the others, and said that my speech had not been the same on both occasions, but the original had been twice as good. Gentlemen of the jury, you are about to vote on this case, and you are my witnesses of this. Yet what better opportunity could we have had to disprove at once any deceptive statement I had made? (*To Demosthenes:*) You assert that on the first occasion you failed to realize the plot I had hatched against Athens, but on the second you grasped it, though that was the meeting at which you are shown to have supported me. That was the occasion over which you deny the attack you are actually making, and claim to direct it against the conference of ratification. Yet, if your criticism is against the peace, it was you who proposed to include an alliance. If Philip misled Athens, his deception was aimed to secure the peace, which was in his interest. So the earlier conference had this aim before it, the second was based on its achievement.

The deception Demosthenes practised – because that is what the trickster does – should be realized in the light of his statements. He says I went down the Loedias in a skiff at night to visit Philip[71] and composed for him the letter which arrived here. Leosthenes,

71. This incident does not appear in Demosthenes' speech as we have it. See Introduction, p. 15.

who was forced into banishment from Athens by false accusations, is supposed to have been unable to word the letter neatly enough, though he is named without hesitation in some quarters as the most capable of Greek speakers after Callistratus of Aphidnae. Even Philip himself, against whom Demosthenes proved unable to speak for the delegation, or Pytho of Byzantium who so prided himself on his command of words, were not his equal. But apparently the job needed my assistance. You assert that I frequently held tête-à-tête conversations with Philip in the day time. You accuse me of going down by river, so vital was the need of this nocturnal epistle. But there is no truth in your statements, as is proved by the evidence of my companions at table, Aglaocreon of Tenedos and Iatrocles son of Pasiphon, in whose company I spent the evening continually throughout the time, and who know that I was never away from them a single night or any part of it. I am also prepared to bring the servants and subject them to torture on the point. If the plaintiff agrees, I will break off my speech at this point. We can get the prison officer and apply the torture in your presence, if you demand it. But it can be done in the remaining part of the day. My case is allowed eleven amphorae of water in the day's programme.[72] And if they state that I slept apart from these companions of mine at any time, allow me no lenience, gentlemen. Just conclude the sitting and impose the death penalty. But if *you* are convicted of perjury, Demosthenes, here is your penalty. Confess in this court that you are more a woman than a man. Now call the slaves to the platform, and read the evidence of my colleagues.

(The evidence and the judicial summons are read.)

Well, as he refuses to accept the summons, and maintains that it is not a matter of putting men to torture, take this letter written by Philip. It is obvious that it must be full of misleading fallacies for us to have sat up at night writing it.

72. The reference is to the *clepsydra* or water clock. Apparently Aeschines reflects, on second thoughts, that it would be better not to interrupt his speech.

(The letter is read.)

You hear what he says, gentlemen: 'I have given my oath to your representatives.' Then he writes down by name those of his own allies who were there, giving their own names and those of their states, and declares that he will send those who arrive late. Don't you think Philip could have written that much by day without my assistance?

But really it seems to me that Demosthenes' only idea is to win credit when he is speaking, and he just doesn't care whether next moment his reputation may sink to the depths. Who could feel confidence in a man who took upon himself to assert that Philip's appearance at Thermopylae was not due to his military achievements but to my public utterances? He actually gave you a calendar of events,[73] according to which I made a report on the conference, and the runners employed by Phalaecus, tyrant of Phocis, passed the news on from here, so that Phocis accepted Philip inside the pass and so caused the destruction of her own cities.

This was all fabricated by my accuser. The collapse of the fortunes of Phocis was due partly to the universal control of chance, partly to the ten years' length of the war.[74] The factor which raised the fortunes of the Phocian tyranny also brought it down. It rose to power by the audacity of laying hands on the sacred treasure, and used mercenary troops to change the constitution. But failure was due to lack of funds, when their resources were exhausted by payment for the army. A third cause of disaster was that normal concomitant of underpaid forces, internal strife, and a fourth was Phalaecus's failure to see the probable future. The coming campaign of Philip and Thessaly was plain to see, and not long before the conclusion of the pact between Athens and Phocis, representatives were sent here from Phocis demanding Athenian aid and undertaking to surrender Alponus, Thronius and Nicaea, which command the pass of Thermopylae.[75] A decree was passed in Athens that Phocis should hand these places to Proxenus, and that

73. See Demosthenes, *Treaty*, 57–60 (p. 71).
74. i.e. the Third Sacred War (356–346 B.C.). See Introduction, p. 22 ff.
75. Just east of and commanding the pass.

fifty ships should be manned by the under-forty age class. But instead of handing these places to Proxenus, the Phocian tyrants arrested their representatives who had made the undertaking to surrender the key points, and Phocis was the only state which refused to take part in the sacred truce for the conduct of the mysteries.[76] Again, when Archidamus of Sparta was prepared to take over these key points and protect them, they did not agree. They replied that they were afraid of the dangers occasioned by Sparta rather than what they had themselves. And at that time no agreement had been reached between Athens and Philip. The discussions about peace were in progress when the letter from Proxenus was delivered with the information that Phocis had not handed over the key points. The same day the proclamation of the mysteries showed that Phocis was the only Greek state which had not accepted the truce, and had gone to the length of arresting the representatives who had arrived there. In proof of my statement call the heralds who inaugurated the truce and the delegation from Proxenus to Phocis, Callicrates and Metagenes, and then listen to the letter from Proxenus.

(The depositions and the letter are read.)

Gentlemen, you have the relative dates as shown by the public records, and the depositions to corroborate them in proving that, before my appointment to the delegation, Phalaecus, tyrant of Phocis, already distrusted Athens and Sparta and trusted Philip. But was his the only failure of foresight? What was the public position of Athens in the matter? Was it not the general expectation that Philip would humiliate Thebes in the realization of her self-assurance and a dislike of increasing the power of a people he distrusted? Was not the attitude of the Spartan delegation[77] in agreement with ours against Thebes, ending in an open clash in Macedonia, followed by threats? Did not the Theban representatives themselves betray uncertainty and apprehension? Again, did not the Thessalians laugh at all the rest and claim that the expedition was for their benefit? Did not some of Philip's associ-

76. On these events see Demosthenes, *Treaty*, 50, note 23.

77. Aeschines is evidently still talking about the visit of the second delegation to Macedonia (346 B.C.).

ates tell some of ours in so many words that it was Philip's intention to re-establish Boeotia?[78] Indeed, in their anxiety Thebes had ordered full mobilization; on which Philip sent a message to Athens to move in full force in the support of right. And did not the present war party, who call peace cowardice, prevent action even at a time of peace and alliance with Philip, on the score of the danger of Athenian soldiers being taken as hostages by him? (*To Demosthenes:*) Was it I, then, who prevented Athens from following the example of her ancestors, or your conspiracy against the interest of Athens? And which situation was safer or more honourable for an Athenian intervention: the first, when Phocis was at the height of her insane career and at war with Philip, and still in command of Alponus and Nicaea which Phalaecus had not handed over to Macedonia, when our protégés were refusing to accept the truce for the mysteries, and we had Thebes in our rear; or the later occasion, when we came by Philip's invitation with a sworn alliance already made, and with Thessaly and the other Amphictyonic powers on the march? Was not the latter moment much more to the credit of Athens? Yet it was then that your cowardice and jealousy forced Athenians to move their property from the country districts,[79] at a time when I was already on the third delegation[80] concerned with the position of the Amphictyons, on which you dare assert that I went without being elected, though even your hostility has never yet led you to accuse me of misconduct in regard to it. It is certainly not that you have grudged the infliction of personal penalties against me.

Therefore it was at a time when Theban representatives were at Philip's elbow, making requests to him, when you had brought Athens to a state of disquiet and there was no Athenian force available,[81] when Thessaly was linked with Thebes by your mismanagement and the dislike of Phocis which had existed in Thessaly from early times, since Phocis had seized their representatives and

78. See above 116 (p. 170) and Demosthenes, *Treaty*, 20–21 (p. 62) and note.

79. See Demosthenes, *Treaty*, 86 (p. 73).

80. The reference is to the second expedition of the third delegation, which had returned without completing its task on the news of the surrender of Phocis, but was compelled to return again to finish it.

81. i.e. in response to Philip's request; see above, 137.

beaten them, when Phalaecus had departed by agreement before my arrival and that of Dercylus and Stephanus and the other delegates, when Orchomenus[82] was in panic and had demanded guarantees of personal safety for their citizens to leave Boeotia, when Theban representatives were still at hand and Philip's hostility towards Thebes and Thessaly was manifest – then it was that disaster came, not on my account, but because of your treachery and your attachment to Thebes.[83] I think there is important evidence to show this. Had there been a word of truth in your statements, I should have been accused by Boeotian and Phocian exiles[84] whose expulsion I had brought about or whose return I had prevented. As it is, Boeotian exiles have had no thought for the past, but have accepted my friendship and collected to choose speakers to support me, while representatives have arrived from the cities of Phocis, whom I rescued during the third conference, which dealt with the Amphictyonic League. There was an attempt emanating from Oeta[85] to maintain that Phocians of military age should be thrown from the cliff, and I led them to the Amphictyonic assembly and secured them the right of defence. Phalaecus had been allowed to leave under agreement, but the innocent who were faced with death were reprieved by my sponsorship. To prove the truth of this statement, please call Mnason of Phocis and his colleagues, and the Boeotian exiles who were selected. Come up here, Liparus and Pythion, and do me the same kindness to secure my safety as I did for you.

82. Orchomenus had gone over to the support of Phocis; see Demosthenes, *Treaty*, 112 (p. 83) and 325 (p. 135).

83. It was not the practice of Greek cities to maintain one of their own citizens as a resident ambassador in another city, but to appoint a citizen of the other city to represent their interests as *proxenos*. This term, or the equivalent abstract *proxenia*, appears at Aeschines, *Treaty*, 89, 172, and *Crown*, 42, 138, as well as the present passage, and is rendered 'representative' or 'consular agency', etc. In most cases reference is to the specific appointment of Athenians to act in Athens. The present instance, however, appears from the context to have a more general implication, and may need to be seen in relation to other rather broader uses of the word.

84. i.e. those who fled from the prospect of renewed Theban domination at the fall of Phocis.

85. One of the twelve Amphictyonic tribes listed above, 116 (p. 170). Mt Oeta is west of the pass of Thermopylae.

(The testimony of Boeotian and Phocian witnesses is read.)

Could it be anything but scandalous if I were found guilty on the accusation of Demosthenes, the friend of Thebes and the most unprincipled man in Greece, when I had the support of Phocian and Boeotian speakers?

He had the temerity to say that I am hoist with the petard of my own quotation. He states that during my prosecution of Timarchus I said that the story of obscene practices was generally maintained against him, and that the lines of Hesiod,

> No word is for ever lost that the multitudes
> Report: the power of god is in it,[86]

are to be applauded, and that the same god now comes to accuse me; because the story of bribery by Philip is generally maintained against me. But you are quite well aware, gentlemen, that there is all the difference in the world between a story and a misrepresentation. A story has no connotation of slander, which is blood brother to misrepresentation. But I will give a precise definition of each of them. It is a story when the majority of people say without prompting or pretext that some event has taken place. It is misrepresentation when a single individual insinuates in the mind of the majority an accusation which he repeats in every assembly of the Council, to defame another individual. We regard 'storied fame' as a value to worship, but misrepresentation as a crime to prosecute. So you must not confuse good with evil.

A good many of his accusations have enraged me, particularly when he charged me as a traitor. These charges have put me in the position of an inhuman creature, a character devoid of feeling and guilty of numerous other forms of evil dealing. My life and my daily conduct of it are, I think, sufficiently open to your own judgement. But what are commonly harder to detect, but of greater importance to men of high character, qualities which are both numerous and of high value from a legal point of view, these I hope to put before you, to show what I left in deposit at home, when I went to Macedonia on the delegation. This was a fabri-

86. See Demosthenes, *Treaty*, 243 (p. 113), quoting Aeschines, *Against Timarchus*, 129.

cation of yours against me, Demosthenes. Mine was an honest upbringing, and my account of it will be equally honest. Here is my father, Atrometus, who is one of the oldest of Athenian citizens. He is now ninety-four. When he was young, before he lost his money in the war, he was an athlete, but he was banished under the Thirty and fought in the army in Asia, showing great bravery on active service. By birth he was of a phratry[87] which shared the same religious observances as the Eteobutadae, and from which comes the priestess of Athena Polias. And as I said before he took part in the restoration of democracy.[88]

My relatives on my mother's side are all in fact free too. She now appears in my mind's eye, distraught with anxiety for my safety. Yet, Demosthenes, my mother shared my father's exile to Corinth, and took her part in that time of political troubles. But you, who lay claim to be a man – I wouldn't go as far as to say you are one – were charged with desertion,[89] but escaped by bribing your prosecutor, Nicodemus of Aphidnae, whom later you helped Aristarchus to assassinate. By this act you are still contaminated, and your presence in the market-place is an invasion. Here, now, is Philochares, the eldest brother in the family. He has not spent his days in dishonourable pursuits, as you libellously assert,[90] but at the gymnasium. He fought under Iphicrates and has now been a *strategus* for over two years. He has come here to beg for my acquittal. Here too is Aphobetus, my youngest brother. He performed a valuable service for the country as a delegate to the King of Persia. He has superintended the public revenues with honour and justice when he was elected to the office of finance. He then became a father of children in a legal fashion, not by providing his wife with another lover, as you did with Knosion. He is here too to express his contempt for your abuse, because slander goes no further than the hearing. You even went so far as to say things about

87. The phratries or brotherhoods were divisions of the ancient Ionian tribes in Athens, and subsisted only for religious proceedings and as the mechanism for the formal admission of a child as a member of the state.

88. In 403 B.C. See above 78, p. 161.

89. See 79 above. Aristarchus was a friend of Demosthenes, but accusations that Demosthenes was concerned in his murder of Nicodemus were never substantiated.

90. See Demosthenes, *Treaty*, 237, 287 (pp. 112, 127).

my in-laws. You are so shameless, so deeply uncharitable, that you have no feeling, no respect for Philodemus, the father of Philo and Epicrates, by whose agency you were enrolled in your deme,[91] as is known to the older men of Paeania. But I am staggered at your daring to abuse Philo, and to do it before an audience of the best men in Athens, men who have come here to give their verdict with a view to the greatest good of Athens, and who look more to our lives than to what we say. Which do you suppose that they would prefer to have, ten thousand soldiers like Philo, with his characteristics of physique and character, or thirty thousand degenerates like you? You also take his brother Epicrates' good character, and drag it in the dirt. No one ever saw him misconduct himself either by day, as you assert, at the Dionysiac procession, or at night either. You can't say this went unnoticed. He was well enough known. Gentlemen, I have three children by the daughter of Philo and sister of Epicrates, a girl and two boys. I have brought them here with the others, to answer one question to the jury which I shall now put to them. I ask, gentlemen, whether you think it likely that I would add to the betrayal of my country, my life with my friends, and my right to worship and to be buried with my fathers, and betray to Philip the people whom I love best in the world, these children, and set greater store by his friendship than their safety.[92] What vice have I been subject to, what disgrace have I incurred for the sake of gain? It is not Macedon which can make a man evil or good. It is his nature. We are not different men who have returned from the conference. We are the same men you sent to it.

I have become involved in politics with a deceiver who cannot speak the truth even by accident. The first thing that happens, when he is lying, is the oath which is uttered without a flicker of the eyes, and he tells you not only that what is untrue is true, but the date on which, according to him, it happened, adding the name

91. Another reference to Demosthenes' foreign blood: see above, note 11. Philo and Epicrates were Aeschines' brothers-in-law (see 152 below); Philo served on the delegations to Philip in 346 B.C.; Epicrates was the man nicknamed Cyrebion in Demosthenes, *Treaty*, 287 (p. 126).

92. Such *ad misericordiam* appeals were familiar to Athenian lawsuits; cf. Aristophanes, *Wasps*, 568 ff.

of a witness, which he has fabricated to complete an imitation of true statement. But we who are innocent have one advantage, that the swindler's method and the addition of the names are not accompanied by intelligence. Observe the folly and the naïveté of a man who invented a story against me like the one about the Olynthian woman,[93] which you cut short in the middle. His slanders were as inapplicable to the victim as they were incredible to his hearers. But think how far he went in preparation for this accusation. There is an Olynthian called Aristophanes who is resident in Athens. Demosthenes was brought into contact with him by someone, and found he was a capable speaker. So he paid him excessive attention and compliments, till he induced him to make false allegations against me in this court. He promised him five hundred drachmae to appear with a protest and declare that it was his own wife, then reduced to captivity, on whom I made a drunken attack, and five hundred more when the false evidence was given. But he replied, according to his own account, that it was a very good guess Demosthenes had made of his exile and his present difficulties, but not of his character. He wouldn't do that sort of thing. In proof of the truth of my statement I will bring Aristophanes himself into the witness box. Please call Aristophanes of Olynthus and read his testimony, also those who heard his story and reported it to me, Dercylus son of Autocles of Hagnus, and Aristides son of Euphiletus of Cephisia.

(The evidence is read.)

You hear the evidence, duly sworn and witnessed. But do you remember that unspeakable verbal trickery which Demosthenes offers to the young and is now using against me, how he mourned and wept for Greece, and sang the praises of the comic actor Satyrus[94] for asking Philip, at a party, for some friends of his whom he found in captivity digging Philip's vineyard in chains; and then after the preamble he went on at the top of his harsh,

93. See Demosthenes, *Treaty*, 196 ff., and note 1 above.
94. On Satyrus' exchanges with Philip see Demosthenes, *Treaty*, 193–5. But Demosthenes' observations quoted here by Aeschines are not in the published edition. Satyrus often took slave parts, e.g. those of Carion in Aristophanes' *Plutus* and Xanthias in the *Frogs*.

unpleasant voice to the effect that it was appalling that the actor of parts like Carion and Xanthias should show such breeding and such nobility, while I who represented the greatest of all cities and preached sermons to thousands in Arcadia could not control my violence, got drunk and quarrelsome when Xenodocus, one of Philip's friends, gave us a party, and dragged a girl who was a prisoner off by the hair and beat her with a strap?[95] If you had believed him, or Aristophanes had backed the libel, a charge like that would have been the end of me. Can you allow such guilt – its author's, not the country's – to remain at large? Can you purify the Assembly's meetings,[96] and yet in the decrees utter prayers by his instrumentality and send out forces on land and sea? It is Hesiod who says:

> Often the whole state suffers for one bad man
> Who is a sinner and works wickedness;[97]

There is one thing I want to add to what I have said. If there is any wickedness in mankind and I have failed to show Demosthenes' pre-eminence in it, I accept the death penalty. But there are many troubles, it seems to me, that dog the footsteps of a defendant. Danger calls back his spirit from indignation to safer subjects and sets him to argument for fear he may neglect any of the charges. So for your benefit and my own I want to return and recall the charges. Ask yourselves the question, gentlemen, what proposal of mine leads to my indictment, what law I have broken or frustrated, what agreement I have made in the country's name, what decision of peace I have rescinded or what addition I have made to it which was not approved.[98] There may be some speakers who are displeased with the peace. Then should they not have made their objection at the time instead of prosecuting me now? There may be some who have been profiteering out of war contributions and revenues, and have ceased to do so. Peace does not feed the idle.

95. See again note 93 above.
96. Meetings of the Assembly began with a sacrifice of purification and a prayer.
97. *Works and Days*, 240–1.
98. Demosthenes specifically warned the jury (*Treaty*, 93 ff., p. 80) that his charge was not against the fact of making peace but the terms on which it was made. But the distinction is less clear than he would like to make it.

Then are those people who are not the victims but the perpetrators of wrong to descend on the advocate of peace[99] – are the profit-makers to leave public spirit stranded? I joined in the jubilations after the destruction of the walls of Phocis, according to my accuser. What evidence could there be to give conclusive proof of that? I was invited to the banquet with my fellow delegates. The number of guests who took part on that occasion, including delegates from the other Greek states, was at least two hundred. In this crowd I was apparently conspicuous for not remaining silent but joining in the celebrations,[100] so Demosthenes tells you, though he was not there himself and has produced no evidence from anyone who was. What made me conspicuous, unless I was a sort of chorus leader? So if I remained silent, the charge is false. But if our city still stood with her people uninjured, and I joined the other delegates in a song of victory in circumstances in which honour was done to the god and no dishonour to Athens, it was an act of piety, not of injury, deserving a verdict of acquittal. Am I, then, a heartless monster, and you a hero for bringing accusations against men who said grace and sat at table with you?

You charged me with political irresponsibility[101] in first taking part in the delegation to Philip after rousing antagonism to him in the Greek states. But this accusation will amount equally to a public criticism of Athenian activity. Athens was at war with Sparta, but after the catastrophe of Leuctra turned to her assistance. She helped to recall Theban exiles, and then went to war with Thebes at Mantinea.[102] She conducted a campaign against Themison and Eretria,[103] and subsequently rescued her. There are dozens of other instances of such behaviour to the Greek states on the part of Athens. Adaptability to circumstances to the best effect is required of an individual and a state alike. What is the statesman's real duty? Presumably the ideal adaptation of policy to existing circumstances. And what about the bad politician? He will obscure the true situation and make accusations against actual practice.

99. i.e. Philocrates, who had anticipated condemnation by voluntary exile earlier in 343 B.C.

100. See Demosthenes, *Treaty*, 128 (p. 87).

101. See Demosthenes, *Treaty*, 9 ff. (p. 59 ff.)

102. On Leuctra and Mantinea see Introduction, p. 16.

103. In 357 B.C. See Demosthenes, *Treaty*, 75 (p. 75).

And the out-and-out traitor? He will use the treatment you have accorded to the associates who have trusted you, and accept payment for the composition of speeches for them, which are then disclosed to their opponents.[104] You accepted payment for a speech on behalf of Phormio, the banker. You then revealed it to Apollodorus, who was plaintiff against Phormio on a capital charge. You were introduced to a happy household, that of Aristarchus[105] son of Moschus, and brought it down in ruin. You exacted an advance of three talents from Aristarchus, depriving him of the resources for his exile, without any compunction at the reputation you earned of being a competitor for the favours of an attractive young man. Your conduct was not based on genuine feeling. The affection of integrity does not admit of the immoral. This and the like is the traitor's way of conduct.

He had something to say, I fancy, about military service, and spoke of me as 'that splendid soldier'. But it is not his libellous remarks but my present danger which induces sufficient foresight to mention a subject which I think is inoffensive. What time or place, what audience can I have for it except the present moment? After my boyhood's days I spent two years on patrol of Athenian territory, and I can call my fellow cadets[106] and the officers to attest this. I was first on active service with the sections, as they are called,[107] when with my age group I was attached to Alcibiades' troops on the convoy to Phlius, and we were under fire near the so-called Nemean ravine.[108] I conducted myself on that occasion to the outspoken satisfaction of my superiors. Other expeditions I took part in were among the age classes and sections. I took part in the battle of Mantinea without disgracing myself or Athens. I was on the expeditions against Euboea and at the battle of

104. Aeschines enlarges on the accusation in *Crown*, 173 (p. 238).

105. See above 148 (p. 179).

106. An Athenian youth acquired citizenship at his eighteenth birthday, after which those of hoplite census did two years' military service as *epheboi* in the garrisons of Peiraeus and of border forts before being enrolled in the hoplite ranks.

107. i.e. part of the body of hoplites called up for service in a particular year.

108. Phlius was fifteen miles south-west of Corinth and a little way north-west of the vale of Nemea. This engagement took place in 363 B.C. and is described by Xenophon, *Hellenica*, VII, ii, 17 ff.

Tamynae,[109] where I was in the special division and met the danger in a way which led to the award of a decoration, both on the field and at home from the people on my return. I brought in news of the Athenian victory, and Temenides, the commander of the Pandionid tribe, shared the dispatch with me from the army and brought information about the character of the fighting. In proof of the truth of this statement take this decree, and call Temenides and the others who took part in these actions for Athens, with their commander Phocion[110] – but not to make him support my cause at present, if members of the jury agree, but as a witness who must answer for it to a libellous prosecutor if he subscribes to any misrepresentation.

(The decree and evidence are read.)

On that occasion I brought you the first news of victory and of the success of your sons, and accordingly I ask a first favour of you, when I beg for the preservation of my life. I am no opponent of democracy, as my accuser says I am, but of villainy. I do not stand against following in the footsteps of Demosthenes' ancestors.[111] He has none. I call upon all who value right conduct and the preservation of Athens. Now let me go back into the past and deal a little more clearly with this point.[112]

In days gone by the city of Athens earned high fame after the naval victory against Persia at Salamis. The walls had fallen before the foreigner, but we were at peace with Sparta, and democratic government remained to us. Then there were days of trouble brought upon us from certain sources, and there came war with Sparta, and after numerous blows sustained and inflicted by us, at the instance of Miltiades son of Cimon, who was representative of

109. The battle of Mantinea was fought in 362 B.C. See Introduction p. 16. The expeditions to Euboea were in 357 and 349–348 B.C., the battle of Tamynae being the critical engagement of the latter campaign.

110. Phocion is called later in the speech (see 184, p. 188) to support Aeschines' plea for acquittal.

111. See Demosthenes, *Treaty*, 16 (p. 60).

112. This passage (172–6) bears strong resemblances to another in Andocides (*On the Peace*, 3 ff.), but whether or not it derives from it the two passages are alike in giving a travesty of Greek history of the fifth century. It is not worth the trouble of emendation, but stands, as Adams (Loeb) points out,

Sparta at Athens, we made a fifty-year truce, which we maintained for thirteen years. During this time we fortified the Peiraeus and built the northern wall, extended our existing fleet by the building of a hundred warships, made an addition to our forces of three hundred cavalry, purchased three hundred Scythians[113] and securely maintained the democracy. But our state suffered an intrusion of people who did not pursue political freedom or moderate methods, and we again went to war with Sparta on the score of Aegina. Here we suffered considerable damage, and in the desire for peace we sent a delegation under Andocides to Sparta, and maintained a peace for thirty years, which raised our democracy to great heights. We paid a thousand talents in specie into the Acropolis, commissioned a hundred more warships, built dockyards, and established a force of 1,200 cavalry and an equal number of archers. The southern wall was also fortified. And no attempt was made to subvert the democracy. We were then induced to go to war again, in connection with Megara. We left our land open to devastation, and after numerous deprivations we sought peace, which was concluded through the agency of Nicias son of Niceratus. Once again we paid seven thousand talents into the Acropolis during this period of peace, we acquired no fewer than three hundred seaworthy and fully equipped warships, and enjoyed an income from tribute of more than 1,200 talents a year. We held the Chersonese, Naxos and Euboea, and in that period we sent out a large number of colonies. Despite the numerous assets we had at that time we again undertook a war with Sparta, this time on the persuasion of Argos, and eventually as the result of rhetorical rivalry[114] we were reduced to accepting a garrison in Athens, to undergoing the episode of the Four Hundred and to subjection to the infamous Thirty. We had not agreed to peace, but had been compelled to it by the orders of others. We returned to reasonable government, when democracy was restored by the exiles from Phyle under the leadership of

---

as interesting evidence of the rapidity and the extent to which past history could become blurred. Accordingly no further comment will be made in these notes on the details.

113. These Scythians were used as police. cf. Aristophanes, *Thesmophoriazusae*, 1018.

114. See Appendix, p. 331.

Archinous and Thrasybulus, who imposed the rule of amnesty on the country to the great credit of Athenian wisdom. Then democratic government grew to a fresh beginning of power. But illegal additions were made to the register of citizens, men who attracted the weakest elements in the state and pursued a policy of continual wars. In time of peace they claimed to foretell danger and roused patriotism and jingoism to the heights, while in war they never touched a weapon, but appeared as auditors and service organizers in charge of equipment. They are people who get mistresses to bear their children and earn disgrace as informers, and they bring a state to the utmost peril by giving lip service instead of loyalty to democracy, while they undermine the very basis of it, peace, and make common cause with the enemies who destroy it.

These are the people who collect in a gang against me, and who assert that Philip bought his peace with bribes, was always a step in advance of us in the conclusion of terms, and when he had got a peace to suit his requirements proceeded to break it. I am not being brought into court as a negotiator, but as giving a guarantee for Philip and for the peace. I was responsible for the discussion, but I am being made responsible for the results expected. I give proof of receiving at the hands of the same person official commendation and legal prosecution. I was a member of a delegation of ten, but I alone am subjected to examination.

My supporters in asking for the favour of the court are my father, who begs not to be deprived of hope in his old age, my brothers, who would have no desire to live in separation from me, my relatives and these little children, who have no comprehension of my perils but deserve pity if I am to suffer. For them I beg and beseech you to exercise consideration, and not to give them up to my enemies, to the violence of an effeminate, unmanly temper. I urge and beg for the protection first of the gods, and then of you yourselves who hold the decision in your hands. To you I have made my defence against every item of the accusation, so far as my recollection goes. I beg you to preserve me in safety from one who is a mere speech writer, and a Scythian too. I beg all of you who have children or younger brothers whom you have much at heart to recall that I made a memorable plea for decent living in the case against Timarchus, and I beg all of you to whom I have given no ground for offence in my life as an ordinary citizen like the most moderate of yourselves, while in the stress of politics I am alone in having made no conspiracy against you, I beg you to give me my life. I performed a delegate's duties with all loyalty to Athens, I stood unaided against the clamours of false accusation, which has often broken the spirit of splendid fighters. Death has no terrors, but death with ignominy is horrifying. It is surely pitiable to have in our eyes the face of a derisive enemy, and in our ears the sound of reprobation. Yet I have faced it. My life has been put in jeopardy. Among you I was brought up, and your ways of living have been mine. None of you has been the worse for pleasure of mine, nor been robbed of his right by my accusation at the voting on the registers,[115] or been in danger on the examination of his tenure of office.

I have little to add before I sit down. It was in my hands, gentlemen, to avoid injury to Athens. To avoid accusation was in the hands of chance, who went into partnership with a slanderer who is not a Greek, who had no thought for the sanctity of ceremony or the bond of a common board, but intimidated any intended opposition to him and has now come here with a false accusation framed against me. If, therefore, it is your wish to preserve the men who helped to champion your peace and security, there will be a host of helpers to preserve the interests of Athens, ready to face danger at your side.

I call on the support of a wise politician in Eubulus, and one of the board of *strategi* in Phocion, who is outstanding for high character, and among my own friends and contemporaries I call on Nausicles[116] and all the others with whom I have shared companionship and common pursuits. My speech is finished, and my person is given into your hands by my act and by the law.

115. i.e. lists of citizens.
116. See Demosthenes, *Crown*, 114 (p. 284).

THE CROWN

I. THE PROSECUTION: AESCHINES

Summary of the Speech

I. Preamble. 1–8.

II. The legal issue. 9–48.

The case against the illegal proposal of honours (9–16). Sophistries to be avoided (17–23). Demosthenes' liability to examination (24–31). Proclamation in the Theatre illegal (32–48).

III. Demosthenes' career and policies. 49–177.

Introduction (49–53). Division into four periods (54–61). *First Period – To the Peace of Philocrates* (62–78): proposal and trial of Philocrates and his association with Demosthenes (62–3); Demosthenes' aim at peace for Athens alone, (a) up to (64–8) and (b) after the City Dionysia (69–70); proceedings at the two meetings (71–8). *Second Period – The Peace* (79–105): impeachment of Philocrates (79–83); Euboea and the story of Callias of Chalcis (84–98); Demosthenes' methods and bribes (99–105). *Third Period – To Chaeronea* (106–58): the affair of Amphissa (106–29); general condemnation of Demosthenes – three main charges: (a) the agreement with Thebes (141), (b) strategical demands (145), (c) responsibility for war (148); peroration (149–58). *Fourth Period – After Chaeronea* (159–76): Demosthenes and Alexander (159–67); Demosthenes as a man of the people (169–76).

IV. General considerations and recapitulation. 178–229.

Crowns and rewards, and the greatness of the past (178–89). Reversion to emphasis on illegality (190–212). Ctesiphon (213–4). Demosthenes' attacks on Aeschines. Further attacks on Demosthenes (215–29).

V. Summary. 230–end.

Equity (230–32). Power in the hands of the people (233–5). Deserts of the protagonists (236–54). Peroration (255–end).

You observe the preparations that have been made, the dispositions that have been worked out, the public appeals that have been resorted to in some quarters, to prevent moderation and established custom from prevailing in Athens. I stand here with my confidence set first in the divine will and secondly in the power of law and of this court, in the belief that there can be no intrigue which can have greater force than the law and justice. I could wish, gentlemen, that the Council of Five Hundred and the meetings of the Assembly were satisfactorily controlled by the authorities who preside over them, and that the code established by Solon for the proper behaviour of speakers held good, and that two things in particular could be relied on. It would then be possible first for a senior statesman to address the meeting in the proper fashion intended by the law, and give the country the sound advice his experience implied, and after that others at will could offer their view of any subject in accordance with their age.

This I think, would promote good government with a minimum of litigation. But as it is, all previous assumptions about good methods have been abandoned, and illegal proposals[1] are made without any compunction and put to the vote in defiance of the principle by which the office of president is assigned by lot. Instead parties sit together by design, and any other member of the Council who may be allotted the office and duly announce his election by the votes declared is threatened with prosecution by a party which is not democratic but autocratic, whose members reduce the private voter to impotence to secure power for themselves. They have put an end to judgements depending on law and carry decisions by decree on a basis of party feeling. Consequently we hear no more of the question, 'Who wishes to address the

1. i.e. proposals inconsistent with the laws of the city; see Introduction, pp. 46–7.

House? Over fifty years old first', and then, 'any other Athenian citizen'. The undisciplined behaviour of speakers is beyond the control either of law or of the Prytaneis, of the presiding magistrates or the presiding tribe, which represents a tenth of the state.[2] Such is the situation, such the political circumstances as you yourselves understand them. There therefore remains one constitutional expedient, if I grasp the position, namely the prosecution for illegality.[3] If this is also to go by the board or its attackers allowed the whip hand, I foretell you will find you have surrendered the constitution piecemeal to individuals.

You fully realize, gentlemen, that the human race is capable of only three kinds of constitution: tyranny, oligarchy and democracy. In tyranny and oligarchy government depends on the whims of power, but democratic government depends on stated law. Every one of you must realize, must never forget, that on the day on which he enters this court as a member of the jury on a bill of illegality he enters it to vote on his own freedom. Thus our great lawgiver laid down as the first essential of the juridical oath the declaration 'I will vote in accordance with the law'. He fully understood that the maintenance of law in our community is the salvation of her democracy. You must keep this in mind, and feel a detestation of illegal proposals. You must not regard it as in any sense a trivial offence, but of the highest importance in every instance. This is a right which you must not allow any man to take from you, any conspiracy of *strategi* who have long been hand in glove with certain political speakers to the damage of the country, any appeal from abroad, which is often introduced as a reason for escape from the courts by men who are pursuing a political career of illegality. Every one of you would be ashamed to abandon his post in war.

2. The Council of 500 was drawn equally from the ten tribes. Each tribal contingent of 50 (the Prytaneis) formed the full-time executive sub-committee of the Council for one month of the Attic year. The *proedroi* (presidents) were nine selected by the president of the Prytaneis from one of the other tribal contingents to preside at each meeting of the Council or Assembly. It appears from Aeschines, *Timarchus*, 33, that the tribe which supplied the presidents used to sit together in the front block of seats to support the presidents and enforce their decisions, and that this is a practice which, Aeschines complains, was falling into abeyance.

3. See Introduction, pp. 46–7.

You must feel equal shame today to abandon your stated constitutional post in defence of democracy. One more thing you must keep in mind, that the citizen body of Athens have today transferred to your keeping the city and its constitution. They set their trust in you, whether they are here to witness this case, or absent in pursuit of their own business. You must feel respect for them, and retain your recollection of the oaths you have sworn and of the laws. And if I prove the illegality, the falsehood and the undesirability of Ctesiphon's proposal, put an end, gentlemen, to illegal views, give strength to the democracy of Athens, and punish political action which is in opposition to law and expediency. If this is the spirit in which you follow the words which are to be spoken here, I am quite sure your decision will be consistent with justice and with your oath, and with the true interest of yourselves and of all Athens.

As far as concerns the accusation as a whole, I hope that is adequate by way of preamble. But the actual laws on the subject of the examination of office, which are in fact contravened by Ctesiphon's proposal, demand a short reference. In the past, holders of the highest offices who controlled public money, and feathered their nests on every occasion, secured the services of speakers in the Council and in the Assembly, and prejudiced the examination in advance with a flood of eulogies and proclamations of honours. At the examination of holders of such offices this put accusers, and still more the jury, into great difficulty. Here was a whole crowd of men subject to examination, who could be convicted on their own showing of embezzlement of public funds, but who now escaped justice. It was understandable, because members of juries felt some compunction that one and the same man, in the same city and possibly in the same year,[4] should first be proclaimed at the festivals as having been awarded a gold crown for his integrity and justice, and next moment be found emerging from the courts with a conviction for embezzlement. So juries were compelled to accommodate their verdict not to the offence but to popular feeling. In view of this an enactment of a praiseworthy nature was passed to prevent the proposal of a crown to a man still *sub judice*.[5] Since

---

4. See Appendix, p. 331.

5. i.e. a man who had not yet submitted the necessary accounts of his office and had them passed.

this valuable legal provision, formulae have been contrived to defeat the law, and if they are not pointed out you may fail to realize that you have been misled. Some illegal proposals of honours to *sub judice* officials have a certain initial good sense on their side, if there can be good sense in illegal proposals. At any rate a face-saving pretext is adopted by the addition to a decree of the clause that the recipient is to be crowned 'when he has completed the submission of his office to legal examination'. The state is subjected to the same injury by the eulogies and proposed honours which prejudice the examination. But the proposer puts on an act to his audience of coupling an illegal proposal with a certain compunction for the offence. Ctesiphon, however, has side-stepped the law about officials who are *sub judice*, and brushed aside the pretext I have just warned you of, by proposing a crown for Demosthenes before any accounts or examination have been required, in the middle of his term of office.

There is yet another argument, gentlemen, which will be put forward, and is the opposite of the one I mentioned. It is claimed that the actions of a man elected in accordance with a decree do not constitute an office, but are a form of 'superintendence' or 'service', while the word 'office' covers only posts allocated by the Thesmothetae[6] at the Theseum, or normally voted by the people, while the other kind depends on a special decree in the course of administration. In opposition to such contentions I will proffer the law passed by the state to set aside pretexts of this kind. Here explicit reference is made to 'elected offices', which are all specified under the same phrase, the term 'office' being applied to all posts elected by the people, including 'superintendence of public works'. The construction of the city walls constitutes in fact the superintendence of the most important of public works, and the enactment goes on to refer to 'all who direct public activities over a period of more than thirty days or who have courts of law under their direction'. And every superintendent of public works is allowed the direction of a court.[7] What, then, are such men instructed to do? Not to perform a service, but to hold office after an inaugural test in a court of law, because even offices appointed by lot are not

6. The six junior archons. Their duties were mainly judicial.
7. i.e. to decide disputes within his own department.

immune from an inaugural test, but are subjected to it before holding office, and required to enter an account to the Recorder and auditors.[8] In proof of this you shall hear the actual text of the relevant laws.

(The laws are recited.)

Well, gentlemen, when what are called 'offices' by the framer of the law are given the appellation of 'business' or 'superintendence' by people like those, it is up to you to recall the law and set it squarely against such unjustifiable proceedings, by laying down the fact that you will not accept a dishonest sophistry designed to use words to undermine the law, and that the more illegality is supported by ingenious special pleading the more enraged you will be. The orator and the law ought to speak the same language. When they are out of tune with each other the verdict must be given to the just voice of law, not to the blatant tones of oratory.

As to the 'irrefutable argument' mentioned by Demosthenes, I want to say a few words in advance. He will say, 'I am in charge of the walls, I agree. But I contributed 100 minae of my own to public funds, and have improved the construction. So what am I under examination for? Unless there is an examination of public spirit.' In reply to this pretext I have an answer which is in the interests of both justice and expediency. In this great and ancient city of ours no one is immune from responsibility for any approach to public life. I support my point first of all from the least obvious instances. Priests and priestesses, for example, are under the law of examination both collectively and separately as individuals. These are people who only receive gifts of privilege for their service of prayer to the gods on our behalf. This applies not only in private, but communally to different denominations. Eumolpidae, Keryces[9] and the rest. Again, take the trierarchy.[10] Men who undertake it are put under examination. They don't control public money, nor make large inroads on it for small productivity; they don't

8. The public accountants who inspected the accounts of outgoing magistrates.

9. The Eumolpidae and Keryces were ancient clans in which the office of hierophant and torch-bearer at the mysteries were respectively hereditary.

10. i.e. the system by which the building and equipment of triremes was undertaken by private individuals. See Demosthenes, *Crown*, 103 and note 45.

claim extra expenses when they are giving the public what they got from it. They are admittedly contributing their own wealth for patriotic purposes. Yet it is not only the trierarchy but all the principal public bodies who are brought under the courts. First and foremost the Council of the Areopagus[11] is compelled by law to submit an account to the auditors and undergo an examination, and that most severe tribunal of the highest instance is subjected to the verdict of this court. Can they not, then, be awarded a crown? No, it is not traditional. Do they not show patriotic feeling? Of course, but they are not complacent at mere impeccability in their members, and they punish any misdemeanour. They do not have it all their own way like your orators. Again, the Council of Five Hundred is put under legal examination. And the law has such a healthy distrust of officials who are *sub judice* that as a prelude to the text of the law it enacts that a man who is *sub judice* shall not leave the country. 'Good heavens!' one might say, 'not go abroad because of a term of office?' No, to make sure you do not turn public money or public action to your advantage and then run away. Then a man who is *sub judice* cannot commit property to sacred funds or make a dedication[12] of it or an adoption, or make special disposition of it, and there are other similar restrictions. In a word the property of such a man is held in trust until he has rendered account of his office to the state. Yes, but there exists the man who has neither received nor spent public money, but has simply had some access to public activity. He too is legally bound to render account to the auditors. What account can be rendered by a man who has not received or spent anything? This again is laid down by the text of the law, which compels him to make a *nil* return. No public activity at all is exempt from examination, audit, or verification. In proof of this listen to the relevant laws.

11. The Council of the Areopagus, originally the body of nobles who ruled the city, had lost political power by 462 B.C. but continued to enjoy prestige and veneration, and retained authority in cases of homicide and certain religious matters.

12. 'An official who caused himself to be adopted into some family poorer than his own might thus diminish the security which the state would hold in case of his misconduct in office' (Adams, Loeb).

(The laws are read.)

So when Demosthenes confidently boasts that his extra payment exempts him from examination, just point this out to him, and say, 'That means, Demosthenes, that you should allow the announcer of the auditors to give the traditional and legal proclamation, "Who desires to make an accusation?" You must allow any citizen who wishes to dispute the existence of your contribution and claim that you have only laid out a small portion of the large sum you were allotted for the construction of the walls, since you received ten talents for it. You must not steal the credit, nor take the decision out of the hands of the auditors. You must not put yourself above the laws. Your political action must be subservient to them. That is the foundation of democracy.'

To the empty pretexts put forward by my opponents that will be sufficient response. The next point is that in actual fact Demosthenes was *sub judice* at the time when Ctesiphon moved this decree, because he held two offices, as a member of the board of the Theoric Fund and of that for the construction of the walls, for neither of which has he so far rendered any account or undergone any examination, and I shall endeavour to prove this by reference to the public records. Read me the names, please, of the archon of the year, of the month and the day, and of the meeting of the Assembly at which Demosthenes was appointed to the board of the Theoric Fund.[13]

(The decree is read.)

So if I could prove nothing more than that, it would still be valid for Ctesiphon's conviction. He is proved guilty not by my accusation but by the public records.

In the past, gentlemen, there was a publicly appointed Accountant General, who made a public computation of the revenue of the state at each prytany. But confidence in Eubulus led to a position in which men elected to the board of the Theoric Fund also commanded the office, until the law of Hegemon was passed, of

13. See Demosthenes, *Treaty* 291, note 111, p. 127 above.

the Accountant General and of the checking clerks,[14] also the Docks and the Office of Works. They were also city surveyors, and they controlled practically the whole administration of Athens. I do not say this in accusation or criticism of them, but merely to demonstrate that the law does not allow a crown to any man who is under examination for a single office, however small, until he has given an account of it and has submitted to an examination; while in the case of Demosthenes, whose office has been the virtual control of the whole of Athens, Ctesiphon makes no bones about proposing a crown for him.

Now to prove that he held the office of controller of operations on the walls at the time of Ctesiphon's decree, and administered public money, imposed fines like the holders of other offices, and had the direction of courts of law, I shall use Demosthenes' own evidence. It was in the year of Chaerondas' archonship, 22 May, that an assembly was held at which Demosthenes moved meetings of the Tribes for the second and third of June, and enacted the election from each of the Tribes of superintendents of works on the walls, and also of paymasters, very rightly, with the object of securing for the state persons from whom he intended to exact accounts of expenditure.

(The decree is read.)

His retort at once takes another twist to the effect that it was neither the lot nor election which gave him the commission over the walls. This is a theme on which Demosthenes and Ctesiphon have a lot to say, though the law is succinct and clear, and puts a summary end to such devices. But I want to say a word about it before I go further. The holders of office fall into three classes, the first and most conspicuous consisting of appointments by lot or by vote, the second of appointments to some public service for more than thirty days and superintendents of public works, and the third is described in the law as 'any others who have been selected and direct jury courts', and these also have to submit to a test after holding office. Take away officials elected by the people

14. The ten annually appointed officials who were responsible for receiving payments due to the state, granting receipts and reporting defaulters to the Council.

and those allotted to office, and there remain those selected by Tribes, *trittyes*[15] and demes, out of their own number, to command public money. This comes about when, as now, a man is given command over the Tribes for either digging trenches or building ships. You can gather the truth of my statement from the text of the law itself.

(The law is read.)

So please recall the laws I have mentioned, and reflect that first of all the law requires that appointments from the Tribes shall be made after a test in court, secondly that it was the Pandionid tribe which appointed Demosthenes superintendent of the walls, and that he has little short of ten talents for the execution of the job, thirdly that there is a further law which forbids the award of a crown to a man who is *sub judice*, fourthly that you have sworn to vote in accordance with the laws, fifthly that your orator has proposed a crown for a man who is *sub judice* without the addition of the clause 'after the submission and examination of an account', and finally that I prove the illegality on the evidence of the laws and the decrees of my opponents. Could any man have more transparent proof of extreme illegality?

I shall go on to show that there is also illegality in the citation of the award in the decree. The law expressly orders that a crown if conferred by the Council shall be proclaimed in the Council Chamber, if by the People, in the Assembly, and there is no third alternative. Read this law, please.

(The law is read.)

This is an admirable law, gentlemen. The enactment shows a distaste for public display on the part of the proposer, but is content that an honour conferred by Athens should be proclaimed in Athens without making a profit out of the proclamation. This was the original aim. And what about Ctesiphon? Now read his decree.

15. To prevent the disunity caused within the state by local loyalties, Cleisthenes in 508 B.C. grouped the demes into thirty *trittyes*, ten in each of the three regions of city, coast and plain, and then took one *trittys* from each region to constitute each of his ten new tribes.

(The decree is read.)

You see, gentlemen, that the enactment requires a proclamation to the People in the Assembly on the Pnyx for the award of a crown by the People, and allows no alternative. But Ctesiphon puts it in the Theatre. This is not merely a contravention of law, but a change of venue. It is not to be at a meeting of the Assembly, but a new sort of stage performance, not in the presence of the People, but of the Greek states,[16] to enable *them* to share in the realization of the character of the recipient. This is a patently illegal proposal in which Ctesiphon joins forces with Demosthenes to bring artifice into action against law. I intend to make this clear and forewarn you not to let yourselves be taken in.[17] They will not be in any position to deny that the law forbids the proclamation of an award from the People except in the Assembly. But they will cite in defence the law for the Theatre of Dionysus, part of which they will make use of to delude your ears, by putting forward a law which is irrelevant to this proposal. They will claim that there are two laws valid in Athens on the subject of proclamations, one of which I have just presented, which expressly forbids the proclamation of a crown awarded by the People except in the Assembly, and another, they will claim, which says the opposite and authorizes the proclamation of a crown to actors in the Theatre, subject to the vote of the People. This then is the law they will claim is being invoked by Ctesiphon.

Against these decrees of theirs I present in my support the laws of Athens, and this is my constant aim throughout this case. If this is true, if this is the way of thinking which has made its way into your constitution, so that invalid laws are drafted alongside valid ones, and two opposite ones exist on a single practice, can one call it a constitution at all, if the same actions are both enjoined and forbidden by law? But it is not so. I hope you will never be brought to such legal incoherence. Indeed there is no

16. i.e. at the City Dionysia, when representatives of the Greek states were present at the festival.

17. On this section see the note on Demosthenes, *Crown*, 83 (note 34, p. 277 below); and Goodwin (*Demosthenes, De Corona*, p. 263), where it is suggested that this passage has been inserted by Aeschines after Demosthenes' speech was delivered.

neglect here on the part of the code which established Athenian democracy. There is explicit provision that the Thesmothetae shall make an annual revision of the laws with special examination into any inconsistency which may have arisen, any intrusion of invalid enactments among the valid, or any duplication of enactments on the same subject. Any instance of this sort is to be set out in writing on boards to be exhibited in front of the statues of the Eponymi,[18] and the Prytaneis are to call an assembly specifically for a legislative committee to consider it, and the chairman of the presiding officials is to put the question to the vote, so as to abolish one enactment and retain the other on the statute book, and to leave one law on the subject and not more. Read me these enactments.

(The enactments are read.)

So if my opponents' argument were true, and there were two laws about these proclamations on the books, it follows, I fancy, that the Thesmothetae would have discovered the fact, and the Prytaneis would have given them the task of deleting one of the two, either the one which authorized the right or the one which made it illegal. As neither has happened, it is clear proof of the falsity of their claim. I will tell you the origin of these misrepresentations with a foreword on the reason for the existence of laws about proclamation in the Theatre. When plays were given in Athens, the habit grew up of proclamations, made without the permission of the People, that such and such persons were awarded a crown by members of a Tribe or of a deme. Or after an announcement liberty was conferred on the servants of some person, who called the evidence of the Greeks to that effect. What was the most invidious of all was that an Athenian who had been awarded a consulate[19] in another Greek state secured an announcement that he had been granted a crown by the people of, let us say, Rhodes or Chios or somewhere for his high character and bene-

18. i.e. statues in the *agora* of the heroes after whom Cleisthenes named the ten tribes. The legislative committee was a special commission chosen by lot from the jurors of the year, which might be set up in any year by vote of the Assembly to review the existing laws.

10. See Aeschines, *Treaty*, 141, note 83.

ficence. This was not done in the manner of awards of honours by the Council or People, after a request and by means of a decree secured by a claim of high service to Athens. These men took the decision themselves without a word to authorize it. The result of this proceeding was to give annoyance to spectators, *choregi* and performers alike, while the subjects of proclamations in the Theatre were accorded greater honour than men awarded a crown by the People of Athens. These had had a place given them, the Assembly, in which it was proper that a crown should be awarded which was forbidden anywhere else. The others made their announcement in front of all the Greeks. In the first case the announcement was accompanied by a decree which indicated permission, in the other there was no such decree.

In realization of this a law was made which had nothing in common with that regarding the award of crowns by the People, and did not rescind it either. It was not the Assembly which suffered annoyance, but the Theatre. Nor was it in opposition to existing laws, which is not permissible. But in regard to awards made by Tribes and demes without an official decree, and to grants of freedom to slaves and awards from non-Athenians, it specifically forbids the liberation of slaves in the Theatre or the proclamation of a crown awarded by a Tribe or deme or any other person, to quote the text, on pain of loss of citizenship to the herald officiating. So when the enactment lays down the Council Chamber as the place for the proclamation of awards made by the Council, and the Assembly for those made by the People, and denies the right of proclamation at performances in the Theatre, to prevent the acquisition of prestige by the collection of awards and false proclamations, and adds a clause against their proclamation[20] by any other person to the exclusion of Council, People, Tribes and demes – when, as I say, all these are excluded, what remains except awards by non-Athenians? I will offer a strong indication of the truth of this from the actual text of the law. The actual gold crown, when proclaimed in the Theatre of Athens, is put down by official enactment as consecrated to Athena, and removed from the recipient of the award. But how could anyone in Athens tolerate the imputation to the People of Athens

20. See Appendix, p. 331.

of such ungenerous conduct? No city, but I will go further and say no single individual, could sink so low as to award a crown which is in one breath proclaimed and withheld. I imagine it is because it is a non-Athenian gift that its consecration is enjoined, to prevent setting a higher value on gratification from abroad than at home, which might lead to a diminution of loyal feeling. There is no consecration of a crown proclaimed in the Assembly. The recipient can keep it, to ensure that not only he himself, but his descendants who retain it at home as a memorial, shall not be guilty of disloyalty to the People. The reason for the law against the proclamation of a crown from abroad in the Theatre, without the authority of the People's decree, was to ensure that any city desiring to confer an award on an Athenian should send her representatives and request the People's permission, and so the recipient of the award should feel greater gratitude to the People for their permission than to the donors. In proof of the truth of this I ask you to listen to the text of the laws.

(The laws are read.)

So when they mislead you by saying that an additional clause in the law allows the practice, if authorized by decree of the People, remember to reply, 'Yes, if you receive a crown from another state. But if it is Athens, the place for it is laid down, and proclamation outside the Assembly is forbidden. The phrase, "nowhere else" can be explained till the cows come home. But you will never prove the practice legal.'

There remains that part of the accusation on which I feel most strongly. This is the basic claim which enables him to justify the award of the crown. According to the wording of the decree, 'the herald is to proclaim in the Theatre to the Greeks that the crown is presented to him by the People for merit and high character', and most striking of all, 'because in word and in action he continually promotes the best interest of the People of Athens'. The rest of the argument is simple, and when you have heard it your decision presents no difficulty. As the accuser my task is to prove to you that the eulogy of Demosthenes is false, that in word he never began and in action he does not continue to promote the best interest of the People. If I succeed in proving this, justice dictates the defeat of Ctesiphon's proposal. Every law forbids any false proposal in a public decree. The defence need to prove the opposite, and the justice of the case lies in your hands.

I look at it like this. I consider it an indescribably long task to investigate Demosthenes' whole life. What point is there now in discussing the action about his injury, when he indicted his cousin Demomeles[21] of Paeania before the Areopagus, and the cut on his head? Or the business about Cephisodotus'[22] year as General and the voyage to the Hellespont, when Demosthenes was one of the trierarchs, and had the admiral on board, and after sharing his table and the day-to-day ceremony which it entails, which was a privilege due to his being a relative of his father's, he found it reasonable to impeach him on a capital charge and act as his accuser? Then there was the case of Meidias[23] and the rough treatment he got in the orchestra, when he was *choregus*, and the fact of his accepting thirty minae for the violence done to him and for the official censure passed against Meidias in the Theatre. I think I can pass over all this and more of the same sort without doing less than justice to you, or allowing an unjustifiable compromise of the action. My fear is that the result as far as concerns you may be the impression that I am telling a story which is true, but belongs to the remote and well-known past. However, Ctesiphon, in a case where the most disgraceful episodes are such common knowledge and so familiar to the audience that the accuser gives no appearance of falsity, but offers a story which is old and admitted fact, should the offender be awarded a gold crown, or censured? It is you who have dared to make a false and illegal proposal. Should you treat the court with contempt, or submit to official punishment?

As regards his misconduct of public affairs I will try to give you the facts more clearly. I learn that when Demosthenes' turn comes to speak he intends to specify four divisions of the period of his

21. See on Aeschines, *Treaty*, 93, note 55, and Demosthenes, *Crown*, 223, p. 307.

22. The generalship of Cephisodotus was in 360–359 B.C., his trial soon after.

23. See Demosthenes' speech against Meidias (Demosthenes XXI) in a case in which Demosthenes accepted a settlement for which there is no need to impute unworthy motives.

concern with affairs of state.[24] The first, I gather, is reckoned as that of the Athenian war for Amphipolis, which he concludes with the peace and alliance proposed by Philocrates of Hagnus, a move to which he himself was a party, as I shall show. The second he lays down as the period of the peace, evidently down to the moment of the breach of peace for Athens by the same orator and his proposal of war. The third is the conduct of the war down to Chaeronea, and the fourth the present period. After enumerating these periods he proposes, I hear, to call me into the box and ask which of these periods is the subject of my accusation, and when it was that, in my view, his policy was not in the interest of Athens. And if I avoid a reply and cover up or run away, he will come up and expose me, drag me to the platform and compel a reply. So to prevent bluster on his part, and to secure some foreknowledge on yours and enable my own reply to proceed, I give you your answer, Demosthenes, before the members of the jury, before other Athenian citizens in the circle of the court, and before other Greeks, who are making a point of listening to this case – I observe that their numbers are not small, in fact greater than anyone can remember in a public case – and my answer is that my accusation concerns all four periods which you enumerate. And if I have the goodwill of heaven, if the jury are prepared to give me an impartial hearing, and my memory suffices to match my knowledge, I most certainly expect to give a demonstration that the authors of Athenian welfare have been the gods in company with the great men who have shown goodwill and moderation in their treatment of Athens,[25] and that our misfortunes have all been due to Demosthenes. I shall take the arrangement of the subject matter which I gather he intends, and shall begin with the first period, continue with the second, then with the third, and finally with the present situation. Accordingly I will now go back to the peace proposed by Philocrates and yourself.

It would have been in our power, gentlemen, to have made the previous peace[26] at a general meeting of the Greek states, had we

24. Not to be found in the speech of Demosthenes.

25. i.e. Philip after his victory at Chaeronea and Alexander after the unsuccessful revolt of Thebes in 335 B.C.; see Introduction, pp. 45, 48.

26. i.e. the Peace of Philocrates (346 B.C.).

been allowed to await the delegations[27] sent to Greece on that occasion to urge them against Philip, and in course of time Athens would have assumed the leadership of the Greek world. She was deprived of this opportunity by Demosthenes and Philocrates and the corrupt proceedings which they conspired to institute against the Athenian community. Now, if on a first hearing any of you find this statement a little difficult to accept, the attitude in which you should approach the rest of the hearing is this. When one sits down to accounts of expenses after a long interval, one starts out, very likely, with wrong impressions. But when the total is totted up, no one is contumacious enough not to admit the truth of the arithmetic. That is the spirit in which you should carry out this hearing. If any of you start out with the idea derived from earlier days that Demosthenes has never spoken a word on Philip's behalf in collaboration with Philocrates, I ask anyone with that attitude of mind not to have anything to do with acquittals and condemnations till he has heard the facts. So much justice demands. But when I have given you a brief recapitulation of the events, and presented the decrees proposed by Demosthenes and Philocrates, if after that the true reckoning convicts Demosthenes of making a greater number of proposals than Philocrates on the subject of the original peace and alliance, of going to shameful extremes of servility towards Philip and his representatives, and of being responsible to the People for removing the peace negotiations outside the general assembly of the Greek states, and for making over to Philip's control Cersobleptes,[28] King of Thrace, who was a staunch ally of Athens – if I can give you clear proof of this, I shall make one small request. Agree, I beg you, that in the first of these four periods Demosthenes' policy was not as it should have been. I will put it in a form which you can easily follow.

27. See Aeschines, *Treaty*, 57–62 (pp. 155 ff.), and Introduction, pp. 28–9.
28. Cersobleptes had conducted negotiations with Athens in 356 B.C. for the control of the Chersonese (see Demosthenes, *Treaty*, note 66), had then been reduced by Macedon, but had revolted and was engaged against Macedon at the time of the Peace of Philocrates, when his inclusion in the peace terms as an ally of Athens became a subject of controversy; see Aeschines, *Treaty*, 81 ff. (pp. 161 ff.), and *Crown*, 74 (p. 212 below).

Philocrates proposed[29] that Philip should be permitted to send a herald and a delegation to discuss peace terms. The proposal was indicted for illegality. The stated date for the trial arrived. The accuser was Lycinus, who had lodged the indictment, and the defendant was Philocrates,[30] supported by Demosthenes, and Philocrates was acquitted. Next came the year of Themistocles' archonship,[31] when Demosthenes appeared as a member of the Council without having been allotted the place or succeeded to a vacancy, but having bribed[32] his way in by design, with the aim of seconding Philocrates in word and action, as is proved by the outcome. Philocrates carried another measure,[33] for the election of a delegation of ten, to approach Philip and ask him to send representatives with full powers to negotiate for peace. Demosthenes was among their number. On his return he was an advocate of the peace, his report tallied with the views of the other delegates, and he was alone in the Council in proposing a safe conduct for Philip.[34] In this he followed Philocrates, who had proposed free permission for sending a herald and representatives, while it was Demosthenes who entered into relations with the Macedonian delegation when they came.

Now please pay careful attention to what happened next. Negotiations took place not with the majority of the delegation, who were misrepresented afterwards by Demosthenes time after time, but only with Philocrates and Demosthenes. This was understandable. They were on the delegation, they had made the proposals: first of all, not to await[35] the representatives sent out to urge a movement against Philip, so that peace should not be made in common with the Greek states, but privately with Athens;

29. In 348 B.C.; see Aeschines, *Treaty*, 13 (p. 146), and Introduction, p. 26.

30. In *Treaty*, 14, Aeschines says that Philocrates was ill.

31. The year beginning midsummer 347 B.C.

32. The assertion that Demosthenes' membership of the Council was due to bribery is not corroborated. He is marked as an influential member of it in 347 by his being appointed to certain minor posts of dignity (Pickard-Cambridge, *Demosthenes*, p. 236), and it is hard to see how bribery could have secured his election.

33. See Aeschines, *Treaty*, 18 (p. 146).

34. See in more detail Aeschines, *Treaty*, 47–54 (pp. 153 ff.), where Aeschines had Demosthenes' proposals read as evidence.

35. See especially Aeschines, *Treaty*, 61, p. 156.

secondly that not peace alone but an alliance should be made with Philip, so that any states which had an eye to the People of Athens should be reduced to despair at the realization that Athens was summoning them to war, and at the same time had herself accepted not merely peace but an alliance; and thirdly that the Thracian king, Cersobleptes, should not be included in the oath or have any part in either alliance or peace. In fact a campaign was already being raised against him. The buyer in this deal committed no offence. No oaths had been sworn, no agreements made, and there was no reason for censure against him for being out for his own interests. But the sellers, who conspired to barter away the strength of Athens's position, deserve our deepest indignation. Demosthenes, the enemy of Alexander as he now calls himself, as once he called himself the enemy of Philip, who charges me with friendship for Alexander, proposed a decree to undermine the interests of Athens, demanded a meeting of the Assembly on the eighth of March, on the day for the sacrifice to Asclepius and the preliminary to the festival, on the sacred day,[36] a thing unprecedented within living memory. And what was the pretext for this? The importance, according to him, in the event of Philip's representatives arriving, of as immediate a debate as possible on relations with Macedon. For this he made an arrangement in advance for a delegation which had not yet arrived, cutting down the normal programme to hurry this on, to prevent the possibility of the Athenian representatives returning from the Greek states, and so peace being made in concert with the Greeks instead of by Athens alone. After this, gentlemen, Philip's representatives arrived. Yours were still away on their mission to Greece against Philip. At this point Demosthenes carried another decree,[37] concerned not only with peace, but alliance. This was moved without waiting for the delegation abroad, immediately after the City Dionysia, on the eighteenth and nineteenth of the month. In proof of this I ask you to read the relevant decrees.

36. i.e. the City Dionysia. The preliminary day was one of ceremonial preceding the contests. In his earlier speech Aeschines does not mention this proposal of Demosthenes about a meeting of the Assembly before the Dionysia.

37. See Aeschines, *Treaty*, 61 (p. 156).

(The decrees are read.)

After the festival, when the meetings took place, a general resolution of the allies[38] was read, the headings of which I will summarize in advance. First they voted that we should negotiate only about peace. They passed over the word 'alliance', not because they had overlooked it but in the belief that even peace was a matter more of necessity than of honour. Next they countered Demosthenes' corrupt action by adding as a sovereign remedy the decision that any Greek state which so desired should be allowed within three months to have their name inscribed on the same stone with Athens, and become a party to the oaths binding the agreement. They made two great strides, the first by securing the three-month interval which was enough to enable Greek delegations to arrive in Athens, the second by ensuring good feeling among the Greek states towards Athens by allowing a general congress, so that if the provisions of the treaty were contravened we should not go to war without support or viable equipment, which was the position to which we had now been reduced by Demosthenes. The truth of this will be proved by the text of the resolutions.

(The resolution is read.)

I admit I supported this resolution, as did all the speakers at the first of the two meetings. The people left under some such impression as this, that peace would be made (though it would be better not to discuss alliance in view of the appeal to the Greeks) and that it would include all the Greek states. There was a night between the debates, and we met again in the Assembly next day. Demosthenes now took first stand on the platform, and allowed no one else to get there.[39] He declared that the arguments of the day before were now useless if Philip's representatives were not going to agree, nor could he accept peace without alliance. He maintained that one should not – I remember the word because, like the speaker, it was so unattractive – that one should not split the

38. i.e. the members of the naval Confederacy. Aeschines does not mention this resolution in *Treaty*. On its practicability see Introduction, p. 30.

39. i.e. on 15 Elaphebolion, 18 April. But see Aeschines, *Treaty*, 65–7 (pp. 157 ff.), where Aeschines declares that there was no speaking on this occasion.

alliance from the peace, nor wait for dilly-dallying Greek states, but either go to war on our own or make peace. Finally he called Antipater[40] up and put a question, after first telling him what the question was to be and instructing him what answer to give to ensure the injury of Athens. Eventually the proposal won the day. Demosthenes' rhetoric forced it through, and Philocrates worded the terms. What remained for them to do was the betrayal of Cersobleptes and Thrace. They brought this about on 26 March, before the start of Demosthenes on the last delegation to administer the oaths. Your fine speaker, who was such an enemy of Alexander and Philip, went on two delegations to Macedonia, when he need not have accepted either, though he now calls for defiance of Macedon. It was he who on the 26th took the position of President of the Assembly by a piece of chicanery as a member of the Council, and with Philocrates' assistance betrayed Cersobleptes. Philocrates slipped a clause into the rest of the decree and Demosthenes put it to the vote, and they got away with it. It was a provision that 'the oaths be sworn to Philip's representatives by the members of the Synod of the allies'. But there was no member to represent Cersobleptes. By providing that the oaths be sworn by the members of the Synod he excluded Cersobleptes,[41] who was not a member. In proof of this read the statement identifying the proposer and the chairman who put the decree to the vote.

(The statement is read.)

It is a splendid thing, gentlemen, the maintenance of public records. They are irremovable, they don't change with political turncoats, but provide the state with a clear view of people who have been traitors for years, and then turn round and claim to be noble characters.

My remaining task is to describe his servility. Demosthenes, gentlemen, after a year on the Council had never, apparently, invited a delegation to the President's seat.[42] This was the one and

40. Philip's delegate and subsequently Alexander's general and regent in Macedonia and Greece.

41. Despite Aeschines' indignation it is almost certain that it had been agreed with Philip's delegates that the treaty was limited to Athens's allies within the naval Confederacy, and that Aeschines was well aware of this fact at the time.

42. In the Theatre.

only occasion. On this occasion he issued the summons to the Presidential seat, he placed cushions for them, he spread red carpets, and during the day ushered the delegates to the Theatre, and was hooted for his vulgar ostentation. And when they left, he hired three teams of mules, escorted them to Thebes, and made Athens ridiculous. But to enable me to stick to my point, bring the decree about the Presidential seats.

(The decree is read.)

Well, gentlemen, our great expert in the art of flattery was the first to learn, through Charidemus'[43] intelligence service, of Philip's death. So he announced a fictitious dream, which he claimed to have had from the gods, that this information, instead of coming from Charidemus, emanated from Zeus and Athena – whom he desecrated with false oaths in the day time, and claimed as prophets at night. It was the seventh day after the death of his daughter, but without mourning her with normal decency he put on a crown and a white robe and conducted sacrifice, in defiance of law, though the unfeeling brute had lost the one and only child who ever called him her father. It is not that I hold his misfortune against him, only his reaction to it. A bad father who is not interested in his children will never make a good statesman, and a man who is wanting in affection for his nearest and dearest will never set much store by people like you who are not related, nor will a bad character in private turn into a good one in public any more than a despicable person at home could ever have been an honourable one in Macedonia. He only changed his habitat, not his habits.

How was it, then, that this change came over his politics – because we have now reached the second period – and what is the reason why Philocrates has moved from the same political position as Demosthenes into exile after impeachment,[44] while Demosthenes

---

43. Charidemus, a mercenary captain and adventurer, at one time supporter and brother-in-law of Cersobleptes, later entered Athenian service, and was stationed at the time in northern Greece. The reference is to the actual time of Philip's death in 336 B.C.

44. In 343 B.C. Philocrates was accused by Hyperides of corruption as an ambassador and went into exile before being condemned to death, shortly before Demosthenes' accusation of Aeschines on the same charge.

took the lead in accusing the rest, and how has this damnable twister plunged Athens into disaster? This is a story of outstanding interest. As soon as Philip was inside the pass of Thermopylae, he turned on Phocis against all expectation[45] and devastated it, and, as was then felt in Athens, went further in adding to Theban power than was consistent with the circumstances or the interests of Athens, so that alarm spread in Athens, and property was moved from the country into the city.[46] Immense indignation then descended on the delegates responsible for the peace, particularly on Philocrates and Demosthenes, who had not merely been on the delegation but moved the decrees; and some difference arose between Demosthenes and Philocrates at this juncture for a reason which was soon suspected. In this general atmosphere of disturbance Demosthenes deliberated with the reactions endemic in the man, cowardice and jealous rivalry with Philocrates for his bribe. He came to the conclusion that, if he appeared as the accuser of his fellows on the delegation and of Philip, it would obviously be the end of Philocrates and a great danger to the delegates, but *his* reputation would gain; by betraying his friends and abandoning his principles he could be made to appear a true patriot. He was taken up by the enemies of peace in Athens, who eagerly haled him to the platform and called him the only honest man in Athens. He duly appeared, and provided them with the seeds of hostility and discord. It was he, gentlemen, who first discovered the fort of Serrium and Doriscus, Ergiske and Myrtiske, Ganus and Ganias, places we had never previously heard the names of.[47] He brought things to a see-saw position, whereby if Philip did not send representatives it was contempt of Athens, and if he did they were spies instead of ambassadors. On the other hand, if he wanted to refer his complaints to the arbitration of an unprejudiced and equivalent third party,[48]

45. According to Demosthenes, *Treaty*, 19–22, 44–7 (pp. 61 ff., 67 ff.), Aeschines above all encouraged public misapprehensions at Athens.

46. For Demosthenes' account of this episode, see *Treaty*, 86 (p. 78), where he had the decree authorizing the evacuation read out.

47. Serrium and Doriscus are several times mentioned by Demosthenes (e.g. in *Chersonese*, 64), and Ergiske and Myrtenum in *Crown*, 27, as places taken by Philip between the voting of the treaty and its ratification. Aeschines indulges in a parody of the names.

48. It is not known that Philip ever did make such a proposal.

we were told there could be no equivalent to Athens and Philip. Philip offered us Halonnesus,[49] but Demosthenes forebade acceptance of it, if Philip said 'give' instead of 'give back'. This was a pure verbal quibble. Finally he awarded crowns to Aristodemus' delegates to Thessaly and Magnesia, whose mission was a contravention of the peace terms, and so put an end to the peace and precipitated the disaster and the war.

Yes, but he gave us walls of bronze and adamant, according to his account, to defend our country, in the shape of the alliance with Euboea and Thebes.[50] But this, gentlemen, is precisely the point upon which the deepest wrong has been done you, the darkest ignorance imposed. However, despite my eagerness to deal with that magnificent Theban alliance. I will maintain the order of events, and mention Euboea first.

This country was subjected to much seriously unjustifiable treatment, gentlemen, at the hands of Mnesarchus of Chalcis, father of Callias and Taurosthenes, a family whom Demosthenes, having taken his bribe from them, now has the presumption to propose as Athenian citizens. The same applies to Themison of Eretria, who in time of peace took Oropus[51] from Athens. We deliberately let all this be forgotten, and, when Thebes made a raid on Euboea in an attempt to enslave these cities,[52] we sent a naval and military force within five days, and before the end of thirty we let the Theban force go on terms, masters ourselves of the whole of Euboea. We then rightly and properly restored the cities themselves and their previous constitutions, which had been entrusted to us, in the view that we ought not to recall past grievances when we were in a position of trust. That was the treatment Chalcis had from Athens, but she did not return like for like. When we crossed to Euboea to assist Plutarchus,[53] admittedly a pretence of friendship was made to

49. The island of Halonnesus (near Sciathus) had passed into Philip's possession after the expulsion of pirates there. In 342 Philip offered to give it to Athens, but Athens claimed ownership of it, and demanded a form of gift which recognized the claim.

50. With Euboea in 341, Thebes in 339; see Introduction, pp. 41 ff., and Demosthenes, *Crown*, 87 (p. 278) and 179 (p. 298).

51. In 366 B.C.

52. In 357 B.C., when hostilities took place between rival groups in Euboea.

53. During Philip's siege of Olynthus, probably in 349 B.C.

start with. But as soon as we arrived at Tamynae,[54] and passed what is called Mount Cotylaeum, Callias of Chalcis – the object of Demosthenes' bribery and his compliments – observed that the Athenian force was shut in a dangerously unfavourable position from which, short of a successful battle, there was no way of retreat and no hope of assistance, military or naval. He therefore collected a force from all over Euboea and sent to Philip for troops to add to it, and with his brother Taurosthenes, who nowadays greets everyone with smiles, brought over the mercenaries from Phocis and advanced to annihilate us. Had the force not been rescued by the hand of heaven and the valour of our troops, infantry and cavalry alike, which enabled us to meet the enemy by the race-course at Tamynae and defeat them, Athens would have been in danger of disgrace and disaster. Not that a military reverse is the greatest of calamities, but to be put to the point of danger by unworthy opponents and fail makes a doubly disastrous day.

None the less after this experience we still came to terms with them. And after receiving such generosity from Athens,[55] Callias of Chalcis returned after only a short interval to his characteristic attitude. While ostensibly collecting a Euboean congress at Chalcis, he actually contrived to create a strong Euboea against Athens, securing the special prize of a tyranny for himself. After that, in the hope of getting Philip as coadjutor, he went off to Macedonia, where he went about with Philip and got the title of one of his 'companions'. However he fell foul of Philip and ran away from there as well, and offered his humble services to Thebes. He left there too, showing himself more of a twister than his native Euripus, and falling between the two stools of Theban and Macedonian dislike. At his wits' end what to do, with an expedition being raised against him, he saw only one hope of safety left to him, to get a sworn promise from the People of Athens, whom he described as his ally, to assist him if he were attacked, which was obviously his fate if we didn't prevent it. With this in view he sent Glaucetes, Empedon and

54. See Aeschines, *Treaty*, 169 (p. 185), for this battle, in which he took part himself.

55. Aeschines is here suggesting that after 348 Athens retained control of Euboea (which is not the case) and lost it only when Demosthenes abandoned it in 341 (below 92, p. 217).

Diodorus, the one-time runner, to represent him, with the offer of vain hopes to the People, and a bribe to Demosthenes and his friends.

There were three things he was paying for: first of all, success in getting his Athenian alliance – there was no middle course, if the People were to recall his past offences and refuse the alliance, but the certainty of exile from Chalcis or death, with such formidable forces as Philip and Thebes on his track; secondly, the money for the proposer of the alliance was to prevent Chalcis joining the congress at Athens;[56] and thirdly, to ensure that she should not pay contributions to the League. In every one of these aims Callias succeeded, while our anti-autocratic Demosthenes, as he styles himself, our patriotic orator, according to Ctesiphon, sold up the interests of Athens, and proposed his decree for Athenian assistance to Chalcis according to the terms of the alliance. He accepted one thing in exchange for all this, but it was a mere matter of words, to make it look well, when he included the clause that Chalcis should give aid to Athens in the event of attack on her. The demand for inclusion in the congress and the payment of contributions, which were the source of strength in the war, were frankly granted for bribes, by using fine words to cover disgraceful practices. He led us on by mere talk, to the effect that Athens should come forward to render assistance to Greek states who asked for it, and that alliance came after benefaction. To convince you of the truth of what I say, please bring the alliance voted to Callias. Read the decree.

(The decree is read.)

But this sale of Athenian interests, Athenian congress rights and Athenian contributions is not the worst I have to tell you. I have much more in store. Callias' outrageous appropriations and the corruption of Ctesiphon's hero, Demosthenes, reached such a pitch that the contributions from Oreus and Eretria, a matter of ten talents, were fiddled away. We were not blind nor half-witted. We looked on and failed to notice it. As for their congress members, they had them removed and sent back to Chalcis to the *soi-disant* congress of Euboea. The methods and the illicit machinations involved make a tale to listen to. Callias arrived in person; he didn't

56. i.e. to the naval Confederacy; see note 38 above.

use intermediaries. He appeared in the Assembly,[57] where he made a speech put together by Demosthenes. He stated that he had just returned from the Peloponnese, where he had arranged contributions of up to a hundred talents for the war against Philip, and made a calculation of the amount due from each state, sixty talents from Achaea and Megara, and forty from the Euboean states. These supplies would provide a fleet and a land force. There were numerous other states, he said, who wanted to join in the contributions, so that there would be no shortage of men or money. This was all on the table, but there were other secret transactions going on, he continued, which could be vouched for by actual Athenian citizens. Eventually he called on Demosthenes by name, and asked him to verify it.

Demosthenes made an imposing appearance, uttered fulsome eulogies of Callias, and claimed knowledge of the great secret in reference to the delegation to the Peloponnese, in which he had taken part, and that to Acarnania. These he wanted to report. The gist of his speech was that the whole Peloponnese and the whole of Acarnania were solid against Philip, that the money contribution was designed to man a hundred quick-sailing ships and provide ten thousand infantry and a thousand cavalry, and they would have the additional asset of the citizen troops, more than two thousand heavy infantry from the Peloponnese, and as many again from Acarnania. The command of the whole force was to be in Athenian hands, and the whole was not to be a long-term operation, but was scheduled for 17 February. He had in fact sent word to the cities concerned that all were to attend a congress[58] at Athens at the full moon. This was in Demosthenes' personal and individual style. Most swindlers who want to pull a fast one try to produce vague, indefinite statements for fear of being caught out. But when Demosthenes does it, first of all he tells his lies on oath, invoking destruction on himself, and secondly, with a prediction which he knows is false, he has the nerve to give the date at which it will occur, and in referring to people he has never seen in person he will give names with actual details and a counterfeit story to back the false one. This earns him

57. Early in 340 B.C.
58. This does not refer to the naval Confederacy, but to a new alignment against Macedon.

well-merited dislike, as a crook who even casts discredit on honest men's means of expression. After giving these details he presents the herald with a decree as long as the *Iliad* and emptier than the speeches he is in the habit of delivering or the life he has himself lived, full of hopes which are never to be fulfilled and armies which are never to be raised. He leads you away from the deception, poises you on the brink of expectation, after which he makes a curt proposal to select a delegation to Eretria to ask them (because they had to be asked) for the withdrawal of the five-talent contribution to Athens and payment of it to Callias, and then another delegation to Oreus to ask them to identify themselves with the Athenian line in regard to foreign relations. He then makes it clear that the whole business is part of his plot by the proposal that Oreus should also be expected to pay their contribution to Callias instead of to Athens. To prove the truth of my claim, cut out the eyewash, the triremes and all the flummery, and read out the passage beginning with the surreptitious fraud devised by that outrageous and unscrupulous person declared by Ctesiphon in respect of this decree to have been continuously pursuing the best interests of Athens.

(The decree is read.)

Well, you have heard the spoken word – the warships, the infantry, the full moon, the members of the congress – but the concrete benefit of the contributions from the allies, those ten talents, are what you have lost.

It remains for me to state that it was for bribes of three talents that Demosthenes proposed this motion, a talent from Chalcis given by Callias, a talent from Eretria given by Cleitarchus, the tyrant there, and a talent from Oreus, which showed the business up, because Oreus is a democracy and all transactions require a decree. The state was exhausted in the war and reduced to poverty, so they sent Gnosidemus, the son of Charigenes, once a power in Oreus, with the request that he would waive the talent, and with the promise of a bronze statue to be erected to him in Oreus. He replied to Gnosidemus that he had next to no use for bronze, and, through Callias, continued to exact the talent. As the people of Oreus were compelled to pay but were short of money, they provided a mortgage on the public revenues for the talent, and gave Demosthenes interest, a drachma per mina per month,[59] on his bribe until they had paid off the capital. This was put through by a decree of the people. In proof of my statement bring the decree of the people of Oreus.

(The decree is read.)

This decree, gentlemen, is a disgrace to Athens. It unmasks Demosthenes' policy and provides a manifest condemnation of Ctesiphon. A man who descends to such bribery cannot have become an estimable citizen, as Ctesiphon had the audacity to call him in the decree.

We now come to the third period,[60] or rather that bitterest time of all during which Demosthenes brought ruin on the affairs of Greece and of Athens. In it he committed sacrilege on the shrine of Delphi, and brought about an unjustifiable and unjust alliance with Thebes. I will begin with his misdeeds against the gods.

You know of the plain and harbour of Cirrha, nowadays laid down as unholy and accursed. The district was in time past inhabited by Cirrhaeans and Cragalidae, who were the most lawless of peoples, and were guilty of sacrilege in respect of the sanctuary at Delphi and the offerings there, and of misconduct against the Amphictyonic states.[61] There was indignation at their proceedings, particularly, it is said, on the part of your ancestors, but the other Amphictyons as well, and they asked for an oracular reply at the shrine to the question what punishment should be visited on these people. The answer given was that war be made against the Cirrhaeans and Cragalidae by day and night to ravage their land and sack their city and enslave them, and to make offering of it to Pythian Apollo, Artemis, Latona and Athena of the Forecourt,[62] and the soil of it should not be cultivated. On receiving the oracle the Amphictyons voted, on the proposal of Solon of Athens, on the strength of his capacity as a law-giver and his experience in poetry and philosophy, to make an expedition against the accursed in accordance with the oracle of Apollo. They collected a con-

---

59. i.e. 12 per cent, not an exorbitant rate.

60. 340–338 B.C. Demosthenes in his defence also treats these events at length (*Crown*, 140 ff., pp. 291 ff.).

61. See Demosthenes, *Treaty*, note 10.

62. See Appendix, p. 332.

siderable force from the Amphictyonic states, enslaved the inhabitants of Cirrha,[63] razed its city and harbour to the ground, and
dedicated the territory in accordance with the oracle. In connection
with this they swore a binding oath that they would never themselves work the consecrated soil nor allow others to do so, but
would aid the god and the consecrated land with foot and hand and
voice and with all their power. This oath was not enough for them.
They made a solemn invocation and added a powerful curse to
preserve it. The curse contained the words, 'if there be any breach
of it by any city or any man or nation, let it be accursed of Apollo
and Artemis and Latona and Athena of the Forecourt'. It further
invokes upon them that their land bring forth no fruit, their women
no children like their fathers, but monsters, and their flocks no
offspring of like nature, but that they meet with defeat in war, in
court and in the market-place, and that they be utterly destroyed,
themselves and their households and their people. 'And may they
never do guiltless sacrifice to Apollo nor Artemis nor Latona nor
Athena of the Forecourt, nor these receive their gifts'. In proof of
this read the oracle of Apollo. Then hear the curses, and recall the
oaths sworn by your ancestors in company with the Amphictyons.[64]

(The oracle, the curses and the oaths are read.)

This curse, these sworn oaths and the oracle were still there in the
inscription, when the Locrians of Amphissa, or rather their leaders,
in complete defiance of law began the cultivation of the plain and
harbour on which the solemn curse had been invoked. They rebuilt
the place and inhabited it, imposed taxes on all who put in there,
bribing some of the Amphictyonic delegates[65] who arrived at
Delphi, one of whom was Demosthenes. He was elected from
Athens to the Amphictyonic assembly, and accepted two thousand
drachmae from Amphissa to avoid mention of their activities among
the Council. It was also agreed that a further sum of twenty minae
a year should be sent him at Athens out of money from the site on

63. The so-called First Sacred War, *c.* 590 B.C.

64. Aeschines speaks at length about the curse because it provides justification for his action in demanding vengeance on Amphissa (see below 118–21,
pp. 223–4 for which he was later blamed since it contributed to the events
leading to the defeat at Chaeronea in 338 B.C.

65. See Aeschines, *Treaty*, note 67.

which the curse was solemnly pronounced on condition of his assisting Amphissa at Athens by every means in his power. It has thus come about even more markedly than before that he has enclosed everyone he has had contact with, individual rulers or free states alike, in a net of irreparable disaster. Now consider how destiny and chance rose above the irreligion of Amphissa. In the archonship of Theophrastus,[66] the year Diognetus of Anaphlystus was Remembrancer, the selected Amphictyonic delegates were Meidias[67] of Anagyrus – for many reasons I wish he were still alive – Thrasycles from Oeum, and thirdly myself. It so happened that soon after our arrival at Delphi Diognetus, the Remembrancer, caught a fever, and then Meidias also went down with it. The rest of the council were in session. Notification was given us from sources desirous of showing favour to Athens that the people of Amphissa, who were in a state of lamentable subservience to Thebes at the time, intended asking for a judgment imposing a fine of fifty talents against the People of Athens, because we had dedicated gold shields[68] at the new temple before its consecration, and inscribed the words which belonged to them, 'Offered by the People of Athens, spoils taken from the Persians and the Thebans when they fought against the Greeks'. The Remembrancer sent for me and asked me to go to the meeting of the Amphictyons and address them on behalf of Athens, as I had intended to do myself.

As I was beginning my speech, after entering the meeting with perhaps excessive haste, when the elected delegates had withdrawn, a man from Amphissa, an utterly uneducated brute, I thought, unless he was led by some demonic power to do wrong, shouted, 'If you were sensible, men of Greece, Athens would be an unspoken name these days. They are a people accursed, and you should shut them out of the Holy Place'. He then reminded them of the

66. The year beginning midsummer 340 B.C. See also Aeschines, *Treaty*, 116 (p. 170).

67. See 52, p. 206 above.

68. The shields had been part of the Athenian spoils at Plataea in 479 B.C., and had been rededicated after a fire which damaged the temple at Delphi in 373. The complaint was that these shields, which gave great offence to Thebes, had been rehung without waiting for the consecration of the restored temple.

Phocian[69] alliance proposed by our friend, the 'Big Wig',[70] adding a number of insults against Athens which I found intolerable at the time and still dislike recollecting. I was more enraged at this than I have ever been in my life. I can pass over much of what I said, but it then occurred to me to refer to the sacrilege of Amphissa in regard to the sacred land, and I stood up there and then and replied by pointing to it. The plain of Cirrha lies below the sanctuary, clearly in sight. So I said to the Amphictyons: 'You see the plain, gentlemen. It is under cultivation by the people of Amphissa, there are potteries built on it and cottages. You can see with your own eyes that the harbour under curse and interdict has been built up. You know yourselves without any need of further evidence that these people have sold harbour dues and derived money from the harbour which is sacred.' I at once gave orders to read them the oracle of Apollo, the oath sworn by our ancestors, and the curse which had been imposed, and I proclaimed, 'On behalf of the People of Athens, in defence of my own life and my children and my household, in accordance with that oath I stand as champion of Apollo and the sacred land with hand and foot and voice and all my powers, and so I clear my city of guilt before the gods. You must decide for yourselves. The offering has been begun and the sacrifice stands ready, and you are about to ask the benefits of heaven upon all and each. Ask yourselves how you can find the voice, the spirit, the face, the audacity to make your supplication if you let these men go unpunished, men who stand under the curse of heaven. There are no doubts, the words are clear about the guilty and their punishment, and about all who have condoned their guilt, and the last words of the curse are these, "For men who do not punish them, be there no guiltless sacrifice to Apollo and Artemis and Latona and Athena of the Forecourt, and may they never receive their gifts." '

I said a good deal more in elaboration of the theme, and when I finished and stood down there was a storm of shouts from the members. There was no more talk of the shields we had dedicated. It was all for retribution on Amphissa. As it was late in the evening,

69. The enemies of the Amphictyons in the recent Third Sacred War, 356–346 B.C.

70. A nickname given to Hegesippus from a novel hair style. On Hegesippus see Demosthenes, *Treaty*, 72 (p. 74) and 331 (p. 136).

the herald rose and announced that all adult Delphians, slave or free, should come in the morning with shovels and mattocks to the Thyteum, as it is called. The same herald made a second announcement that the Remembrancers and members of the Council should come to the same rendezvous 'to render aid to the god and the sacred land, and any city which shall not appear, shall be debarred from the sanctuary and shall be accursed and under imprecation'.

Next day we arrived at the stated place at dawn, descended to the plain of Cirrha, pulled down the harbour, set fire to the houses and returned. While we were doing this, the Locrians of Amphissa, who lived sixty stades away, descended on us under arms in a body. We had to run for it back to Delphi, or we should have been in danger of our lives. Next day Cottyphus, who was chairman of the meeting, called an assembly of the Amphictyons. It is called an assembly when it is not only the Remembrancers and members who are convened, but all who are offering sacrifice or consulting the oracle. Here numerous accusations against the people of Amphissa were made, and numerous eulogies of Athens. The end of it all was a decree that before the next regular meeting[71] at a stated date the Remembrancers should proceed to Thermopylae with a judgment in accordance with which punishment should be meted to Amphissa for her offences against the god and the sacred land and the Amphictyonic Council. In proof of this please read the decree.

(The decree is read.)

This judgment was put on record by us in the Council and again in the Assembly. The People accepted what we had done and the whole city agreed to the course of piety. To honour the pledge he had given at Amphissa, Demosthenes opposed it.[72] I made a clear refutation of his claim in the Assembly. So, as the man had failed to mislead Athens by open means, he went to the Council, brushed aside non-members, and by gaining assistance from an inexperienced proposer produced a resolution to go to the Assembly. He

71. Meetings were held twice yearly in spring and autumn. The next would have been that of spring 339.

72. The charge of bribery is presumably factious. Demosthenes no doubt foresaw the possibility that Aeschines' attack on Amphissa might lead to dangerous developments.

contrived to get this resolution put before the Assembly and made a decree of the People at a time when the Assembly stood adjourned, when I had left, or I would never have allowed it, and the majority of citizens had dispersed. The gist of it is that 'the Remembrancer of Athens and the existing members of the Amphictyonic Council shall proceed to Thermopylae and to Delphi at the times laid down by previous generations'. So far, so good, nominally. But actually it was a disgrace, because it forbade attendance at the meeting at Thermopylae dictated by the emergency for an earlier date than the regular one. The same decree also contains a clearer and more antagonistic passage which enacts that 'the Remembrancer of Athens and existing members of the Amphictyonic Council shall not participate in the meeting there in word or deed, decision or action'. What does this non-participation amount to? Am I to give the true answer or the most palatable? I shall give the true one. It was addiction to the palatable that brought Athens into this position. The decree forbids any recollection of the oaths sworn by our ancestors, or of the curse or the oracle of the god.

We stayed therefore, gentlemen, because of this decree, while the other Amphictyonic states assembled at Thermopylae, with one exception, which I will not name and whose fate I hope will not be paralleled in any Greek state.[73] At their meeting they voted an expedition against Amphissa, and elected Cottyphus of Pharsalus, the Amphictyonic chairman, to command it. Philip was not at home in Macedonia at the time, nor contemplating any move against Greece. He was far away in Scythia.[74] Yet you will be told in a few minutes in Demosthenes' shameless fashion that it was I who brought him in against Greece. On the first expedition to Amphissa they treated her very leniently. She had committed outrageous offences, but they imposed a fine and allotted a time interval by which to pay it into the sanctuary, and expelled the guilty who were under the curse, recalling the party who had suffered exile for their attitude of reverence. But as they not merely failed to pay the fine, but restored the guilty party and again expelled the innocent who had been recalled by the Amphictyons, this led to a second expedition against Amphissa. This was some time later,

73. i.e. Thebes, destroyed by Alexander in 335 B.C.
74. i.e. beyond the Danube.

after the return of Philip from his Scythian expedition, when the leadership in the ranks of religion had been given to us by the gods, but Demosthenes' bribery had stood in the way of the gift.

Did the gods give no warning, no prophecy, to urge precautions? Why, it was almost uttered in human language. I have never seen a clearer case of a state that was preserved by heavenly guidance and destroyed by a group of rhetoricians. Was no adequate warning found in the portent at the mysteries and the death of the initiates?[75] Was it not in this connection that Ameiniades foretold the need for caution and for a request for instructions from Delphi? The suggestion was vetoed by Demosthenes, who declared that the oracle was 'pro-Philip', which showed his crudity and the appetite, the infection of the power he had been given. And eventually did he not neglect unsuccessful and unpropitious sacrifice and send our forces out into manifest danger? Yet the other day[76] he had the audacity to say that what prevented Philip from entering our territory was that his sacrifices had not been propitious. What then is the penalty you deserve? You are indeed the curse of Greece. If the conqueror keeps clear of conquered territory for lack of favourable sacrifice while your ignorance of future probability allowed you to forgo favourable sacrifice when you sent your men into battle, do you deserve a crown for the disasters of Athens, or exile long since from her borders?

That is the reason for our fate, a fate beyond forecast or expectation. For it is no life, no human way of living, that has been ours. It is our destiny to provide a tale of wonder for generations to come. Was it not the Persian king who divided Athos with a channel, who bridged the Hellespont,[77] who demanded earth and water from the peoples of Greece on the ground of his mastery of all mankind from the rising to the setting of the sun? And is not that monarch now[78] fighting not for the supremacy of the world, but to preserve his life? And in the same hands now lies all the glory of

75. The reference is apparently to an occasion when some initiates were killed by a shark during their ceremonial bathe in the sea.

76. After his victory at Chaeronea, 338 B.C.

77. These two feats were carried out on Xerxes' orders in preparation for his invasion of Greece in 480 B.C.

78. The King of Persia had already been killed when this speech was delivered, but the news had not reached Athens.

that enterprise and the leadership against Persia as those which set free the shrine of Delphi. And Thebes, Thebes, our neighbour city, after a single day has been seized away from the very midst of the land of Greece; just though it may have been – for her conduct of Greek policy was wrong – yet her madness was no human folly, but the visitation of heaven.[79] And the wretched people of Sparta, whose only contact with these events was in connection with the seizing of the temple, once proud leaders of Greece, are now forced to send hostages and, to witness their calamity, are to be sent to Alexander, their country and themselves at Alexander's mercy, to undergo a sentence which depends on the moderation of the conqueror they have provoked.[80] And our own city, the one refuge of all Greece, to which in the past came the representatives of every state in turn to seek preservation, now no longer struggles in quest of the leadership of the Greek states but of the very basic existence of her own country. This has been our fate since Demosthenes came into control of politics. There are some fine words of the poet Hesiod on such a theme as this. In one place, where he is instructing the masses and giving advice to states, he bids us exclude unprincipled orators. I will repeat the lines, because I think this is the reason why, as children, we learn poetry by heart, so that we can turn it to account in later years.

> Often the whole state suffers for one bad man
> Who is a sinner and works wickedness;
> And Zeus brings great ill against her from heaven
> Famine and plague together, and the people fall.
> Or he brings ruin on their broad-set army
> Or on their wall, or on the ships in the sea
> He takes vengeance, far-searching Zeus.[81]

If you strip off the poetical metre and look for the thought, I think it will cease to appear as lines of Hesiod and become a clearly

79. The destruction of Thebes by Alexander in 335 B.C.

80. A revolt of Greek subject states against Macedonian power had been led by the previously unconquered Spartans but was crushed in 330 B.C., just before Aeschines' speech was delivered. Aeschines describes Demosthenes' reactions to the revolt below, 165–7 (p. 236.). Athens took no part in it.

81. Hesiod, *Works and Days*, 240–5. Aeschines has already quoted the first two lines in *Treaty*, 158, p. 182.

oracular account of the policy of Demosthenes. Fleet, army and cities have been totally extirpated as a result of that policy.

I do not think Phrynondas or Eurybatus[82] or any of the villains of olden days can have been such a lying impostor as Demosthenes. I call upon all powers in heaven and earth, human or superhuman, that love truth to witness the audacity with which he could look us in the face and declare that the Theban alliance was due, not to circumstances, not to the terror that faced them, not to the reputation of Athens, but to the speeches of Demosthenes. Yet numerous representations had been made to Thebes before his time by her well-wishers,[83] first by Thrasybulus of Collytus, in whom the closest trust was held in Thebes, secondly by Thrason of Erchia, who was Theban representative in Athens, by Leodamas of Acharnae, as good a speaker as Demosthenes and more attractive in my view, by Archedemus of Pelekes, an able speaker who had run into political dangers on account of Thebes, by Aristophon of Azenia, who was long subjected to the charge of pro-Theban sympathies, by Pyrrhander of Anaphlystus, who is still alive now. Yet not one of them, gentlemen, had been able to induce them to friendship with Athens. The reason is one which I know, but have no wish to enlarge on after the disasters of Thebes. But in fact it was when Philip had taken Nicaea from Thebes and given it to Thessaly, when the war he previously directed away from Theban territory was now brought back through Phocis to the gates of Thebes, when, finally, he had captured Elatea[84] and fortified it and placed a garrison there, it was then, when they were at grips with disaster, that

82. Eurybatus was a proverbial villain; cf. Plato, *Protagoras*, 327 D.

83. Thrasybulus of Collytus was a supporter of the famous Thrasybulus of Stiria (see below 195, p. 244, and Demosthenes, *Treaty*, 280, p. 124), the leader of the Athenian democrats who took refuge at Thebes from the Thirty Tyrants in 404 B.C. He was sent to Thebes with Pyrrhander on some mission at the time of the founding of the Second Athenian Confederacy (377 B.C.). Thrason was a patron of exiled Theban democrats during the Spartan occupation of Thebes (382–379 B.C.), Aristophon a leading Athenian politician after 365 B.C. (see below 194, p. 243, and Demosthenes, *Treaty*, 297, p. 128); the occasions of their diplomatic missions to Thebes are unknown, as are those of the other missions mentioned here.

84. Philip by now (autumn 339) had been appointed by the Amphictyonic Council to take charge of the war against Amphissa. The appointment enabled him to enter central Greece. Nicaea was at the eastern end of the pass of

they called for Athens and we came to their aid and entered Thebes under arms, horse and foot, before a syllable of any proposal of alliance by Demosthenes. We were led to Thebes by circumstances, by fear, by the need of alliance, not by Demosthenes.

In regard to these events there are three principal instances of wrong action on the part of Demosthenes. The first is that at a time when Philip, though nominally at war with Athens, showed much greater dislike of Thebes – this is proved by the facts,[85] and one need say no more – Demosthenes concealed a fact of such great importance, and pretended that the coming alliance was due, not to circumstance, but to his diplomacy, and thus induced the People to abandon the question of terms and accept the alliance itself. By gaining this point, he put the whole of Boeotia into the hands of Thebes[86] through his wording of the decree with the provision that in the event of any secession from Thebes Athenian aid would be given to the Boeotians in Thebes. This piece of dishonest verbal manipulation, typical of him, assumed that Boeotia was in fact in trouble and would accept Demosthenes' form of words instead of feeling resentment at being unjustifiably treated. Secondly, he put down two thirds of the war budget to Athens, whose danger was more remote, and one third to Thebes, accepting bribes in every instance, while the naval leadership was equally divided, though the cost lay wholly with Athens, and the military command, in any sane account, was handed over, lock, stock and barrel, to Thebes.[87] The result was that when war came the Athenian general Stratocles had not the power to consider the safety of his troops. This is no personal accusation of mine, omitted by others. I am voicing criticisms made by everyone and known to yourselves. And yet you show no resentment. This is the result of dealing with Demosthenes. You are so inured to news of his misconduct that it

Thermopylae, and Elatea a little farther south. The news of his seizure of Elatea created consternation at Athens, vividly described by Demosthenes, *Crown*, 168 ff., pp. 296 ff. See Introduction, p. 44.

85. i.e. the comparative moderation of Philip and Alexander towards Athens.

86. On Thebes' attempts to dominate all Boeotia see Demosthenes, *Treaty*, 20, note 11.

87. We have no other evidence by which to judge Aeschines' version of the terms of this alliance. It would not be surprising if they were liberal towards Thebes. See Demosthenes, *Crown*, 238 (p. 310).

brings no surprise. But this is wrong. Resentment and retribution should follow, if the future is to be what it should.

The second and much more serious offence committed by Demosthenes is that of removing the Athenian Council and her democracy without advertising the fact, and planting it in Thebes at the Cadmeia, where he allowed the Boeotians participation in it.[88] The personal power he assumed was such that he actually appeared on the platform and said that he proposed to conduct negotiations with any state he chose irrespective of mandate, and if there were any opposition on the part of the generals, he would propose a dispute between the platform speakers and the board of generals, because Athens would get more benefit from him on the platform than from generals on the board. Then he made money out of pay for absentees, and played other tricks with military pay, and by hiring ten thousand mercenaries[89] to Amphissa, in spite of protests and objections from me at meetings of the Assembly, on the removal of these mercenaries he brought the whole danger on Athens totally unprepared. What do you suppose would have been Philip's prayer at this stage? Surely to divide the political opposition and the mercenary opposition at Amphissa and meet them separately, and to find Greece in despondency at such an initial blow. These were the ills for which Demosthenes was responsible, and yet he is not content with eluding punishment. He actually resents being deprived of a gold crown. It is not enough to receive a public proclamation of it. He is aggrieved if it is not made before the assembled Greeks. This, apparently is the extent to which a depraved character possessed of great power can work public disaster.

I now go on to the third and greatest of my charges against Demosthenes. Philip did not underestimate the Greek states. He was astute enough to realize that in a matter of hours his whole position would be at stake, and therefore he was anxious for peace

88. This charge is obviously highly coloured and of the sort made by opponents of any important international engagement entered into by their nation at a time when union is clearly needed at the expense, if need be, of separatist loyalties.

89. In the campaign of Chaeronea a quarter of the whole allied force was placed at Amphissa, some way from the main scene of operations. This, Aeschines complains, was the proposal of Demosthenes. It is to this charge that Demosthenes replies at *Crown*, 245 (p. 312).

and prepared to negotiate. The Theban government were terrified
of the danger which faced them, not unnaturally. Their ideas were
not derived from a general whose experience of warfare was confined to desertion.[90] They had ten years of the Phocian War to give
them a lesson they were not likely to forget. Demosthenes understood the situation and, suspecting that Thebes might make a
separate peace and get money from Philip without his being a party
to it, and regarding it as intolerable that he should be left out of any of
the bribery, he jumped up in the Assembly before any opinion had
been voiced either for or against peace with Philip, and gave what
he took for a warning to the Theban government to credit him
with his share of the takings. In the name of Athena, whose image
apparently Pheidias made expressly for jobbery and perjury on the
part of Demosthenes, he swore that anyone who advocated peace
with Philip should be hauled off to prison by the hair. It was like
the proceedings of Cleophon,[91] who destroyed Athens, we are told,
at the time of the Peloponnesian War. But as the government at
Thebes did not accede to him but actually reversed the movement
of Athenian troops to secure a consideration of peace, he became
absolutely distraught, got up on the platform, called the Theban
government traitors to the cause of Greece, and declared that he
would move a resolution – a man who had never looked an enemy
in the face – to send an Athenian deputation to Thebes demanding
free access through their territory for an attack on Philip. The
Theban government, overcome with shame at the idea of really
seeming to be traitors to Greece, abandoned peace and at once
mobilized.

At this point it is right to recall those brave men whom on a
basis of sacrifices not made or not favourable Demosthenes sent
into obvious danger of death, and then, himself the deserter who
had run away from battle, set foot on the burial place of the dead and
dared to speak in praise of their courage.[92] In face of great deeds

90. See Aeschines, *Treaty*, 79, note 49, p. 161.

91. Cleophon was the Athenian demagogue who led the restored democracy
after the oligarchic coup of 411 B.C. He prevented Athens from seeking terms
from Sparta for several months after the decisive defeat of 405 B.C.

92. Demosthenes was appointed to deliver the funeral oration over those
who fell at Chaeronea. See Demosthenes *Crown*, 285, p. 321.

and noble action you are of all men the most despicable, though in words your brazen audacity is astonishing. And will you in a few minutes undertake to look members of the jury in the face and declare it to be right that you should receive a crown for your part in the disasters of Athens? And if he does, gentlemen, can you tolerate it, can you accept that with the death of the fallen shall die also your memory of them? Imagine yourselves for a moment in the Theatre instead of in this court. Imagine the herald's procession, the proclamation now to be made in accordance with the decree, and ask yourselves whether you think the relatives of the fallen will shed more tears over the fate of heroes in the tragedies to be performed than over Athens's lack of thought and feeling. What Greek, what human being bred to freedom would not be grief-stricken at the reminder, if no more, that on this day in the past, when, as now, the tragedies were soon to be performed, at a time when in Athens life and leadership were better, the herald would advance and present the orphans of the dead in battle, young men in full armour, and would pronounce that most glorious and most stirring proclamation that these are the young sons of fathers who bravely fell in battle, and have been brought up by the state till they were men, and now are thus equipped as soldiers and allowed with every good wish to go their way, and here are called to seats of honour? That was the old proclamation, not the present one.

Now he presents the man who made them orphans, and what proclamation, what utterance will he pronounce? Even if he follows the actual words of the proclamation, the dishonour which the truth holds will not rest undeclared. The words of the proclamation will carry the opposite meaning, and declare that this man, if man he is, is crowned by the People of Athens for virtue but is the vilest of men, is honoured for bravery but is a coward and a deserter. I most solemnly beg you, gentlemen, in heaven's name, not to make the orchestra of the Theatre of Dionysus the scene of a trophy to your own defeat, not to convict the people of Athens of insanity before all Greece, not to recall miseries that are beyond remedy or redress to the memory of the unhappy people of Thebes, who were driven from their country by him and received in Athens, whose sacred places, whose children, whose graves were destroyed by the bribery of Demosthenes and by Persian gold.[93] You were not there in person, but in imagination have regard, I beg, to their calamities. Watch the capture of their city, the destruction of their walls, the burning houses, the captive women, the children in slavery, the old, men and women alike, forced to learn late in life the loss of freedom, their tears, their supplications to you, their anger, not at their punishment but at the men who caused it, their cry to you not to crown the curse of Greece, but to take guard against his star, against the fortune which dogs his steps. For no city, no individual citizen ever came well out of taking the advice of Demosthenes. When a law was passed on the ferrymen of Salamis that any man of them who by error capsized a boat on the crossing should be a ferryman no more, to avoid their learning their craft at the expense of Greek lives, are you not ashamed that a man who utterly capsized the state of Athens should be allowed to steer her voyages again?

In embarking on the fourth period, the present position, I want to remind you that Demosthenes was not only a military but also a political deserter, when he seized an Athenian warship and went off collecting money from the Greek states.[94] When the unexpected preservation of Athens brought him back, to begin with he was a trembling creature. He appeared on the platform, half dead, and urged his appointment as 'guardian of the peace'. He was not so much as given permission for his name to be inscribed on the decree,

93. Thebes was humbled by Philip after Chaeronea, and his political opponents took refuge in Athens. Aeschines wishes to attribute the whole of the Theban disaster to Demosthenes, including the sack of the city by Alexander in 335 B.C. In her final revolt Thebes was promised help from Persia, who sent 300 talents to Athens. The money was refused, but Aeschines claimed that 70 talents were left in Demothenes' hands for use against Macedon. To this charge Demosthenes implicitly replies in *Crown*, 298 (p. 324).

94. i.e. after Chaeronea, when Demosthenes seems to have been absent from Athens at the time of the peace negotiations, which were carried out by Demades. His absence may have been due to an attempt to raise money abroad. Aeschines implies that it was only because of Philip's unexpected clemency that he returned. But see Demosthenes, *Crown*, 248 (p. 312), for his defence against these charges. Nausicles had commanded the Athenian force sent by sea to Thermopylae in 352 B.C. (see Demosthenes, *Treaty*, 84, and *Crown*, 114, pp. 77 and 284). He later became a member of the first delegation for peace negotiations under the decree of Philocrates in 346, and himself proposed Aeschines as a member.

which was assigned to Nausicles. And now he claims a crown. After the death of Philip and the accession of Alexander he returned to braggadocio and instituted a cult of Pausanias,[95] which led to an accusation of the Council for instituting a sacrifice on the score of good news. He gave Alexander the nickname of 'Margites', and went so far as to say that he would never disturb himself to leave Macedonia, he'd be content with peripatetic movements at Pella inspecting the omens.[96] He did not give this as guesswork but as certain knowledge, because blood was the price of courage. The fact was that he himself has no blood in him, and his view of Alexander was not derived from Alexander's character, but from his own cowardice. On the Thessalian decision to move against Athens[97] the young man was at first in a violent rage, and at a time when the army was near Thebes Demosthenes was appointed an Athenian representative, but rushed home when he was half-way over Cithaeron and showed himself as useless in peace as in war. Worst of all, though you did not betray him or allow him to be charged at the Greek congress, he has now betrayed you, if report is true. According to the crew of the *Paralus*[98] and the delegation which met Alexander, and to reasonable accounts, there is a man of Plataean citizenship[99] called Aristion, son of Aristobulus, a chemist, in case he is known to any of you. This young man was exceptionally good-looking, and lived for some time in Demosthenes' house. Accounts vary as to what lay behind it or what his occupation was, and discussion of the affair is of doubtful propriety. According to the story I heard no one knew who he was or what

95. Pausanias was the killer of Philip.

96. *Margites*, 'madman', was the title of a poem ascribed to Homer by Aristotle (*Poetics*, 1448b), apparently a mock-heroic parody of Achilles. The participle translated as 'peripatetic' perhaps glances at Aristotle's Peripatetic school of philosophy, and so at his tuition of Alexander.

97. This again refers to the events of 335 B.C. before and after the destruction of Thebes by Alexander with assistance from Thessaly. The surrender of Demosthenes together with others of his party was afterwards demanded by Alexander, though not ultimately exacted.

98. The Athenian state galley, used for official missions.

99. Athenian citizenship was conferred on Plataea, as a faithful ally, after its overthrow by Sparta in 427 B.C., and this form of honorary citizenship took its name from that award. But this story of Aristion, put about by Demosthenes' enemies, is very doubtful.

his business was, but he got himself into Alexander's good graces and associated with him. Through him Demosthenes has had communication with Alexander, and secured his own safety and relations with him by means of a great deal of flattery.

Now observe how the facts bear out the story. If Demosthenes' attitude towards Alexander had been one of hostility, as he maintains, he has had three admirable chances without making use of any of them.[100] The first was before Alexander had been long in power or his personal position had been consolidated, and he crossed into Asia when the Persian power was at its height in respect of ships, men and money, and urgent danger would have made him glad to include Athens in the alliance. Did you say a word at all at that point, Demosthenes, or propose any motion? Shall I put it that you were frightened, and displayed your normal reactions? But a country's opportunity does not wait for the timorous orator. Again when Darius advanced to the coast in full strength, and Alexander was cut off in Cilicia and totally unprovided, or so you said, and was on the point, according to you, of being trampled down by the Persian cavalry, while Athens could hardly tolerate your unpleasant behaviour and all the letters strung from your fingers, as you went round pointing to my expression and saying how horrified and miserable it was, and how I was set for the garland and the gold horn[101] if anything happened to Alexander – even then you did nothing. You put it off for some better occasion. Well, I will pass over all this to the immediate present. Sparta and her mercenary force won a victory, and destroyed Corrhagus' army. They were joined by Elis and the whole of Achaea except Pellene, and the whole of Arcadia except Megalopolis, which was under siege and seemed likely to fall any day. Alexander had moved to the extreme north, almost off the globe, while Antipater was taking a long time collecting a force, and the future was quite uncertain. Now give us an indication,

100. These occasions were in 334, late 333 and 330 B.C. The second opportunity was very fleeting and cannot in fact have been appreciated in Greece until long after it had passed. Darius' thrust to the coast behind Alexander's army was followed directly by Alexander's decisive victory at Issus. On the third occasion see above 133 (p. 227) and note 80.

101. The gold horn and the garland are the decorations of the animal to be sacrificed.

Demosthenes, what you did or said at that juncture. I resign the platform to you, if you like, until you've said it. As you say nothing, I sympathize with you in your difficulty, but what you said then I will now reveal. Don't you remember his appalling unbelievable expressions? It needed an impenetrable hide to stand up to the sound of them when he got up and said, 'The vine of Athens is being pruned, the vine-shoots of the people have been lopped, the sinews of our affairs have been hamstrung, we are being pierced with bodkins, we are being brought to sore straits with needle-stabs.'[102] What are we to call this obscene language – words or enormities? Then again you staggered round in circles on the platform, and claimed opposition to Alexander by saying, 'I admit I caused a Spartan rising, I admit I caused a revolt in Thessaly and Perrhaebia.'[103] You, cause a Thessalian revolt? Could you ever cause a revolt in a village? Could you approach – we won't say a city, but a house which offered any kind of danger? If money is being paid out anywhere, you will sit and wait, but without acting like a man. If a piece of luck occurs, you will pretend it is your doing, and put your name on the achievement afterwards. If there's anything to be afraid of you'll run away, but if there's reason for confidence you'll demand presentations and gold crowns.

Yes, but he's a man of the people. So if you concentrate on impressive language you will be deceived again, as before. But if you look at his character, if you go to the truth, you will not. Let that be your attitude to the account you demand of him. I will help you in the estimate of the initial characteristics needed in a sensible, democratic character, and make a comparison with the expected nature of the despicable, oligarchic type. You shall set one against the other, and consider which category he is to be placed in, not by his statements but by the life he lives. I think you would all agree to these as characteristics indispensable to the man of the people: first he must be free-born on both his father's

102. Aeschines had a turn for parody (cf. 82, p. 214 above), but the metaphors to which he objects and the improvisations in which they are expressed in Greek are not to be found in Demosthenes. It is also interesting that Aeschines seems to have found them shocking rather than laughable; see also 72, p. 211 above.

103. In the western part of Macedonia.

and his mother's side, so as not to inherit any antagonism to law, which is the preserver of democracy, and secondly there must be some benefit conferred by his forebears on the people, or at the very least no antagonism, so that he shall not be concerned to right their wrongs and try to injure his city. Thirdly, he must be naturally reasonable and moderate in his way of life, to prevent ungoverned expenditure from leading him to accept bribes at the expense of the people. Fourth, he must have good sense and ability as a speaker; right principle should lead him to good choice of policy, and right training and style to the persuasion of his audience; failing which, good sense must take precedence over style. Fifth, he must have a courageous spirit, so as not to leave the people stranded in time of trouble and danger. But your oligarchic character must be supposed the reverse in every respect.

Now consider which character applies to Demosthenes. Let us have a fair reckoning all the way through. His father was Demosthenes of Paeania and a free man – one must not tamper with the truth. But the position on his mother's side and her father's must be made clear. There was a man called Gylon from Ceramea, who betrayed Nymphaeum in Pontus to the enemy, when it belonged to Athens. Gylon was impeached and exiled from Athens. He made no defence, and went to the Bosporus.[104] Here he was presented by the tyrant there with a site called 'The Gardens' and married a wife who was well off, we gather, and brought him a lot of money, but was a Scythian by birth. By her he had three daughters, whom he sent here to Athens with large dowries. He married the first to a husband who shall be nameless, to avoid widespread ill-feeling. The second was married regardless of Athenian law[105] to Demosthenes of Paeania, and the son of the marriage was our lying busy-

104. i.e. the Cimmerian Bosporus, the strait leading to the modern Sea of Azov. Nymphaeum was one of several Greek foundations in the Tauric Chersonese (Crimea), the chief being Panticapaeum.

105. In 403 B.C. the restored democracy reaffirmed Pericles' citizenship law, thus disqualifying from the citizenship those subsequently born from parents who were not both citizens. The facts of this case are obscure. It is not certain that Demosthenes' mother was born of a Thracian mother, or that she was born after 403; indeed Demosthenes' own birth is usually put in 384 B.C. Aeschines had already brought up this point at *Treaty*, 22 (p. 148) and 93 (p. 165).

body, Demosthenes. Thus on his grandfather's side he is an enemy to Athens, since she condemned him to death, and on his mother's he is a Scythian, a foreigner, Greek only in speech. So even his bad character is not indigenous.

What about his day-to-day way of life? After a trierarchy he turned up as a speech-writer,[106] having made a ridiculous hash of his father's money. But he wasn't to be trusted in that either. He got a reputation for tipping off his opponents. So he jumped up on the platform. But though he made a lot of money out of politics, he saved very little. Now, however, he has been refloated by means of Persian gold,[107] but even that won't be enough. Wealth has never yet got over bad character. In short he never lives on his own resources, but out of risks run by the state. How does he stand on the score of good sense and power of speech? Clever in speech, vicious in life. His abuse of his physical powers I prefer not to describe, because I have known ill-feeling arise from excessive criticism of a neighbour's shortcomings. What, then, about his effect on Athens? Fine speeches and contemptible action. On the score of bravery there is a word to be said. If he denied his cowardice,[108] or if you were not aware of it, the subject would have demanded more length. But as he admits it in public and you are quite conscious of it, it remains to recall the existing laws which bear on it. The old Solonian law regarded avoidance of service, desertion and cowardice as liable to the same penalties, and there exist means of indictment for cowardice. You might be surprised at the existence of indictment for natural failings. But there are such means. What for? To ensure that everyone shall be more afraid of legal punishment than of the enemy, and so be a better fighter for his country. The law thus puts avoidance, cowardice and desertion outside the scope of the lustral cleansing of the market-place,[109] and therefore forbids a crown, and forbids

106. i.e. a man who wrote speeches to be delivered by clients, a relatively degraded occupation. The story in Demosthenes' own first speech (*Against Aphobus*, c. 364 B.C.) is that his guardians squandered his father's property.

107. On Persian gold, see 156 above, p. 233.

108. On Demosthenes' alleged flight from Chaeronea see 152 and 159, pp. 231 and 233 above.

109. i.e. they are excluded from the ceremonial absolution of the citizen body.

entry to public ceremonies. And you, Ctesiphon, instruct us to crown a character legally debarred from it, you use a decree of your own to invite an ineligible person among the performers in the orchestra, and to introduce to the sanctuary of Dionysus a coward who has forfeited all sanctity.

But I do not wish to distract you from the main subject. So remember this when he claims to be a democrat. Have regard not to his statements but to his life, not to what he claims to be but to what he is.

While I am on the subject of crowns and presentations, before I forget, let me forewarn you, gentlemen, that unless you put an end to these unrestricted presentations and the random award of crowns the recipients will not thank you, nor will the position of the country be redeemed. You will certainly not change bad characters for the better. You will merely bring the good to the depths of despondency. I think I can bring powerful proof of this. If you were asked whether the reputation of Athens stood higher at the present time than in that of past generations, the answer would be universally admitted, in the past. And were the men of that generation the more admirable, or of this? The past were outstanding, the present are greatly inferior. And how about awards of crowns, proclamations, dinners in the Prytaneum? Were there more of them than there are now? In the old days the moments of glory were few and the honours of virtue high. Now the whole thing has been diluted, and crowns are a matter of habit, not of careful thought. So isn't it extraordinary, if you think of it like that, that presentations should be more frequent now, though Athenian affairs were stronger then, and that the quality of the men should now be lower, whereas then it was higher? I will attempt to explain it. Do you suppose, gentlemen, that there would have been any desire to train for the Olympics, or any other competition which carried a crown, if instead of being awarded on merit the crown had been given as the result of intrigue? None of course. As it is, the rarity of it, the competition, the distinction and the lasting fame induce people to accept the physical strain and the extreme exertion of the attempt. Assume, then, that you are yourselves the organizers of competition in the field of civic virtue, and reflect that, if you grant the awards to a few worthy winners and do it with respect for law, you will have a wide field for the display of virtue, but if you look for the gratification of the chance comer and the schemer you will corrupt genuine character as well. I want to give a somewhat clearer proof of my point. Which do you regard as the finer character, Themistocles, who commanded in the naval victory over the Persians at Salamis, or Demosthenes, who ran away recently? Miltiades, the victor over the foreigner at Marathon, or Demosthenes? Or the heroes of the return from exile at Phyle?[110] Or Aristides the Just, who enjoys the opposite appellation to Demosthenes? Heavens above! I would not so much as mention this creature in the same day and hour as those great men. Let Demosthenes prove that any of them was ever granted a crown. Were the people of Athens ungrateful? No, they were high-minded, and the great men were worthy of them; they did not deign to seek written inscriptions to honour themselves, but only to live in the memory of the men they saved. And that memory remains for ever. But the rewards they did receive are worth recalling.

There were some in those days who underwent great hardship and great danger, to defeat the Persian by the river Strymon.[111] When they returned to Athens, they asked a reward of the People, who granted them what then seemed the highest honour, three stone Hermae in the Colonnade of the Hermae, with the imposed condition that their names should not be inscribed, but the inscription allowed to stand in the name of the People, not of the commanders. The truth of this can be vouched for by the actual verse inscribed. On the first is written,

> They too were stout-hearted who at Eion
> By the waters of Strymon brought on the Medes
> The fire of hunger and the violence of battle
> And first tested the foe beyond his strength.

And on the second,

> To their leaders Athens gave this reward
> For noble deeds and high courage.

110. In 404 B.C.

111. Probably 477 B.C. at the siege of a garrison left at Eion by Persian forces in retreat from Greece.

> Later ages who see it will be the more able
> To endure toil for their common welfare.

And on the third,

> Menestheus was leader of this city
> With the Atridae on the sacred plain of Troy,
> Whom Homer declared to be the first of all
> When he marshalled the bronze-clad Greeks in battle.
> Thus it is not amiss to say of the Athenians
> That they order the array in war and prowess.

Do the names of the generals appear? Nowhere. Only that of the People.

Go a little farther in your mind's eye – to the Painted Portico.[112] Every great achievement of Athens has its memorial there in the market-place. What are the particular occasions I mean? The battle of Marathon is depicted there. Who was the general? If you were asked the question, you would all reply, Miltiades. But his name does not appear. Why? Did he not ask for this reward? He asked for it, but the People did not grant it. Instead of the inscription of a name they granted that his figure should be foremost in the painting, urging on his men. In the temple of Cybele is to be seen the reward that was given to the men who restored the democracy at Phyle. The man who secured the passing of the decree was Archinus from Coele, one of those who took part in the restoration. His first clause was for the provision of a thousand drachmae for sacrifices and offerings. This is less than ten drachmae per head. He next proposed that each of them should be crowned with olive shoots, not gold, because in those days the olive crown was held in honour, while nowadays even the crown of gold has been brought into contempt. Even this was to be no haphazard decoration, but to be made only after a careful examination by the Council into the question who had been under siege at Phyle, when the Spartan force and the Thirty attacked the force in control of it – not the question who ran away from the enemy's

---

112. The famous Stoa Poikilē in the Agora at Athens contained frescoes of gods and benefactors, and was later famed as the place where Zeno taught and the birthplace of Stoicism.

attack at Chaeronea.[113] To prove the truth of my statements the decree shall be read.

(The decree on the reward to the men at Phyle is read.)

Now for comparison read the decree proposed by Ctesiphon for Demosthenes, the source of our greatest disasters.

(The decree is read.)

The restoration decree is nullified by this one. If this is praise-worthy, that is the reverse. If the honour for the restoration is deserved, Demosthenes' coronation is undeserved.

Now I gather he intends to maintain that it is unfair to compare the achievements of past generations with his. Philammon,[114] the Olympic boxer, he will point out, did not receive the crown for a victory over the ancient boxer Glaucus, but over the competitors of his own time – as though you failed to realize that boxers compete with each other, while claimants to a crown are set against virtue itself. That is what the crown is for. The herald must speak the truth in his citation in the Theatre before the Greeks. So don't enlarge to us on the superiority of your policy to that of Pataecion, but when you have attained to high merit, ask for the gratitude of the People, and not till then.

But to avoid distraction from the subject, the clerk shall read the verse inscribed for the restorers of the democracy at Phyle.

> *These for their courage the ancient city,*
> *Athens, adorned with crowns, for they first*
> *Checked the rule of wrongful ordinances,*
> *And carried the danger on their own shoulders.*

It is to their abolition of illegal rule that the poet attributes their honour. It was still fresh in memory that the time of the overthrow of democracy was the time of the destruction of indict-ment for illegality.[115] As I learnt from my father, who died at the age of ninety-five after living through all the troubles of Athens,

---

113. See again on 175, p. 238 above.

114. Philammon is said to have been victorious in 360 B.C. Pataecion is unknown. On this passage see on Demosthenes, *Crown*, 319, note 126, p. 328.

115. On this indictment see Introduction, pp. 46–7.

and often told me the story in calmer days, in the period just after the restoration of the democracy, whenever a writ of illegality was entered the mere word was tantamount to its execution. What greater iniquity could there be than illegality in word or deed? The hearing, according to his account, was not carried out in the same way as it is now. Juries were much more severe on illegal proposals than the prosecutor himself. They often recalled the clerk, and made him read laws and decrees over again, and proposers of illegal motions were condemned, not merely if they broke all the laws in the register, but for a contravention of a single syllable. What happens nowadays is ridiculous beyond words. The clerk reads the illegality, and it is as though the jury were listening to some quite irrelevant mumbo jumbo, and they give their view on something different. Nowadays Demosthenes' devices have introduced a reprehensible habit in the courts. The proper proceedings have been turned upside down, and the prosecution conduct a defence, while the defendant acts as accuser, and juries sometimes forget the case they are adjudicating, and are compelled to pass votes on subjects outside their scope. If the defendant ever touches the subject at issue, he does not claim that his proposal is legal but that a similar proposal has been made in the past and allowed. This I gather is a claim which Ctesiphon is making capital out of now.

At one time the well-known Aristophon of Azenia[116] used to boast in this court of having been charged and acquitted of illegality on seventy-five occasions. It was different with the old jurist, Cephalus,[117] who was reckoned a pillar of democracy, who derived satisfaction from the opposite achievement. He said he had been the proposer of more decrees than anyone else, and had never been defendant in an indictment for illegality. This was a fine boast, in my opinion. Indictments for illegality used to be brought not only by political rivals, but between friends, if any injury to the state was involved. Here is evidence of this. Archinus of Coele brought an indictment for illegality against Thrasybulus of Steiria, one of the democrats of the restoration, and won his case,

116. See above, 139, p. 228, and Demosthenes, *Treaty*, 297, p. 128.

117. One of the leaders of the democratic opposition to the Thirty Tyrants in 404–403 B.C.

just after Thrasybulus's achievements for Athens; the jury did not count these in the reckoning on the view that, even if Thrasybulus had restored them from exile, it was tantamount to expelling them again to make an illegal proposal. This is not true now. Just the opposite. Good generals, in some cases men who have been awarded maintenance in the Prytaneum, come and demand acquittals for others in cases of illegality.[118] You might well regard this as ingratitude. If anyone who has been honoured by a democracy, a form of state which has divine as well as legal protection, lends assistance to illegal proposals, he is undoing the constitution which has honoured him.

The argument which is open to a reasonable petitioner, I will point out. In a case of illegality the time is divided into three parts. The first division[119] is allotted to the prosecution, that is to law and democracy. The second is given to the defendant and to relevant discussion of the case. Then, when the first vote has decided the issue of illegality, the third division is taken up on the assessment of damages and the degree of official disapproval. So to ask for your vote on this assessment is to ask you for extenuation of your disapproval. To ask it on the first vote is to demand an appropriation of the rights that reside in your oath, in law and democracy, which is a demand as unjustifiable to make as to grant. So you must tell them to allow the court to take the first vote in accordance with law, and to meet it on the assessment. In effect I would almost go so far as to say that there should be a law in connection with indictments for illegality, forbidding assistance in support of either prosecutor or defendant. Justice is not elastic, but controlled by the laws you maintain. Carpentry applies a rule to determine what is right and what is wrong. Equally indictments for illegality preserve a rule of right and wrong in the shape of the inscribed decree and the parallel columns of the law.[120] Show that they tally with your proposal, Ctesiphon, and sit down. No need to appeal to Demosthenes. When you overstep the bounds of

118. On the importance of the *graphê paranomôn* and the likelihood of large juries attracting attendance on the part of the well-to-do to influence verdicts, see A. H. M. Jones, *Athenian Democracy*, pp. 36–7.

119. In Greek ὕδωρ, the water in the water clock.

120. The passage of the decree objected to and the corresponding passage of the law claimed to have been violated were posted side by side.

reasonable defence to call in a dishonest person and a professional manipulator of words, you distort the hearing, you do injury to Athens, you undermine democracy.

I will offer you a suggestion of what means you have of countering this kind of argument. When Ctesiphon stands up here and delivers the prearranged prelude, and enlarges on it without any defence, remind him gently to get hold of the panel and read the laws it contains in comparison with the decree. If he pretends not to hear you, don't listen to him either. You are not here to listen to evasions of justifiable defence, but to acceptance of it. If he sidesteps genuine defence and calls on Demosthenes, I hope you will not acquiesce in a sophistic attempt to use words to undermine law, and I hope too that it will not be counted as a virtue if Ctesiphon's repeated question whether he shall call Demosthenes is greeted by a cry of 'yes'. It will be a cry directed against its author, against law, against democracy. If you do decide to give him a hearing, demand from Demosthenes a plea similar to mine. What was the character of mine? Let me remind you. I did not start by describing Demosthenes' private life, nor by mentioning the iniquities of his public career, though I had copious enough material for it. If I had done so, I must be totally ineffectual. The first thing I did was to point to the law as forbidding a crown to a man still *sub judice*. Next I brought home the point that the orator was proposing a crown while Demosthenes was still *sub judice*, and without the additional prelude, 'when I have passed the accounts', in total defiance of this court of law. I also mentioned the pretexts likely to be put forward, which I must ask you to recall. In the second place I enlarged on the laws dealing with proclamations, which expressly preclude proclamation of a crown awarded by the People anywhere except in the Assembly. But the orator who is defendant in the suit has not only contravened the laws, but the regulations of time and place for the proclamation, by the enactment that it should take place in the Theatre instead of the Assembly, as a prelude to a tragic performance instead of at a meeting of the People. It was after this that I said a very little on matters of a private nature, and a good deal on his public misconduct.

This is the line of approach you should demand of Demosthenes in his defence, that he shall first deal with the law relating to a man who is *sub judice*, secondly with that on proclamations, thirdly with the most important claim, that he is not deserving of the award. If he asks you to make an arrangement about the order of his speech, with an understanding to deal with the point of illegality at the end, do not agree to it. You must not fail to realize this is a piece of forensic trickery. He will not be prepared to take up the point later on. He has no reasonable defence to offer, and hopes to include some irrelevant matter to make you forget it. In the ring you see boxers sparring for position. You must do the same in the interests of Athens. You must contend against him on this point of order, and not allow him to get round the issue of illegality. You must block the way to it, obstruct the hearing, and drive him into the question of illegality, and keep watch on his habit of eluding the point. But if you conduct the hearing on his lines, I am entitled to warn you of the result. Ctesiphon will introduce this dishonest pickpocket, who has torn the constitution to ribbons. He is more given to tears than most men are to laughter, and readier than anyone to break his word. I should not be surprised if he changed his ground and started abusing bystanders at the back of the court, and maintaining that on an absolutely truthful count it is oligarchic sympathizers who take the side of the prosecution, and democrats that of the defence. When he takes this line, meet his factious contentions with the reply, 'Demosthenes, if the men who restored the exiled democracy at Phyle had been like you, the democracy would never have come back into being. As it was they rescued the city from the depths of disaster with the finest slogan of enlightenment, "Forgive and forget". You, however, open new wounds, and are more concerned with the contention of the moment than the good of Athens.'

But when he turns from contempt of oaths to take refuge in their sanctity, he needs one of two assets which he does not possess – either different gods or a different audience. As to his tearful high-pitched voice, when he asks the question, 'What resort have I, gentlemen, when you hem me in like this? I've no line of flight at all', counter him with the question, 'What resort have the people of Athens, Demosthenes? Where can they find alliances or finance to help them? What line of defence have your policies left them? We can all see your personal precautions. You've got out of Athens, and the pretext of living at the Peiraeus is merely a means for you to weigh anchor and leave, with money provided as a protection for your cowardice in the shape of Persian gold and Athenian bribery. But in any case what are all the tears for, and all the noise and the high voice? Isn't Ctesiphon the defendant? The case is to be settled in court[121] and your property isn't at stake, is it, nor your life nor your rights.' What *is* he so concerned about? About things like a gold crown and its illegal proclamation in the Theatre. If the People were mad enough, or oblivious enough of established practice, to want to crown him in spite of the circumstances, he ought to stand up in the assembly and say, 'Gentlemen, I accept the crown, but I regret the occasion on which the proclamation is made. It is wrong that an occasion of grief and mourning for Athens should bring a crown to me.' But of course those are words which would arise from a life of genuine high principle. Yours would be the utterance of a squalid imitation of it. I am absolutely certain that none of you gentlemen will feel the smallest apprehension that a high-minded soldier like Demosthenes, if deprived of the highest glory, will go home and take his own life. He is so contemptuous of civic ambitions that this infernal head of his, itself *sub judice*, which Ctesiphon has proposed to crown in contravention of every law in the list, has had strips cut in it by his own hand over and over again for the financial profits to be made out of deliberately bringing suits for violence.[122] It has been knocked about enough, I should think, for the traces of Meidias'[123] fists to be still visible. What Demosthenes has on him is not a head, but a source of revenue.

As regards Ctesiphon, who put his name to this proposal, I have just a little to say. I shall omit the greater part of it so as to test whether you can distinguish a bad character without being told. I will mention only what is to the discredit of both of them equally. They both go about the market-place with true stories of arguments against each other. There is not a word that is false. Ctesiphon declares he has nothing to fear on his own account, but the corrup-

121. As opposed to a case in which a fixed penalty was laid down.
122. See Aeschines, *Treaty*, 93, p. 165.
123. See above, 52, p. 206.

tion of Demosthenes' public affairs, his violent manner and his cowardice are another matter. Demosthenes says that as far as he is concerned he is perfectly confident, but Ctesiphon's low character and bad morals make him very apprehensive. So when they accuse one another, you, as their judges, should not discount any of their accusations.

But I offer a little warning on his personal attacks on myself. I understand that Demosthenes intends to say that Athens has received great value from him and great damage from me, and to bring up the names of Philip and Alexander and put their strictures to my account. He is apparently such an ingenious adept in the art of words that it is not enough in reference to public affairs of mine to attack speeches I may have made. He has to misinterpret my peaceable habits of life, and inveigh against my silences, so as to leave no space free of misrepresentation. He casts aspersions on my association with younger men in the gymnasium, and right at the opening of his speech he criticizes proceedings in this court with the statement that my motives for bringing the indictment were not patriotic ones, but an attempt to make an impression on Alexander in view of his enmity towards him.[124] Indeed I understand he intends to ask why I condemn his policy as a whole when I did not attempt to prevent or take proceedings against it in detail, why I left an interval and made no continuous attack on it before bringing this indictment. Actually I have never emulated Demosthenes' way of life, nor felt ashamed of my own. I should not wish unsaid the words I have spoken here, and I would rather die than speak in the same sense as he has. My silence, Demosthenes, has been the outcome of a life of moderation. I am content with little, and have no desire of more at the cost of disgrace. So I speak, or say nothing, by intention, not under the compulsion of a congenital extravagance.

Your method, I fancy, has been silence when you are in funds, and clamour when you've spent them. The moment and the

---

124. Nothing corresponding to these two charges appears in Demosthenes' speech as we have it. It may have been revised to suit Aeschines' prosecution. What is more remarkable is the implication that Aeschines could have had access to the speech before making his own. He may merely be enlarging on hearsay.

subject of your utterances do not depend on your decision, but on the instructions of your pay-packet. And you are not ashamed to give vent to pretentions which are immediately proved false. The indictment of this decree, which according to him I did not bring for the benefit of Athens, but to impress Alexander, was in fact brought in Philip's lifetime, before Alexander came to power, and before the date of your dream about Pausanias or your night's conversation with Athena and Hera.[125] So how could I have made a previous attempt to impress Alexander? Unless I had the same dream as Demosthenes.

You criticize me for leaving an interval before approaching the People instead of doing so at once. You imagine people fail to realize that yours is an idea which in origin is not democratic, but something else. It is under oligarchy that public speaking, instead of being at the will of the speaker, is controlled by power. Under democracy the subject and the occasion are the speaker's choice. An interval before speaking is an indication of political activity depending upon circumstances and upon expedience. The lack of an interval suggests jobbery and corruption. As to the claim that you have never before had an indictment from me, or undergone the consequences of your misconduct – when you resort to this sort of argument, you must either think your audience has a short memory or else you deceive yourself. Your sacrilege in regard to Amphissa and your corruption in regard to Euboea were both clearly exposed by me.[126] After the lapse of time perhaps you imagine Athens has forgotten them. But your depredations in regard to the warships and their commissioners are something no lapse of time can conceal. After your enactment about the Three Hundred,[127] when you induced Athens to appoint you in charge of the Navy, you were convicted by me of having abstracted sixty-five commissioners of cruisers from the list, of spiriting away more of the Athenian fleet than the force that won the battle of Naxos[128]

125. See 77 above, p. 213.
126. See 113 and 85 above, pp. 221 and 215.
127. The Three Hundred here, as in Demosthenes, *Crown*, 171 (p. 296), are to be identified with the rich. See below on Demosthenes, *Crown*, 102 ff. (p. 282). But Aeschines' charges are not intelligible here.
128. The battle of Naxos was in 376 B.C.

against the Spartans under Pollis. Your accusations so far succeeded in blocking the way to your due punishment that the danger came to lie not with you, the guilty man, but with your attackers. You had a great deal to say about Philip and Alexander in your invectives, and brought accusations in certain quarters of impeding the interests of Athens, while your undertakings for tomorrow constantly brought disaster today. Then, when you were on the point of impeachment at my hands, did you not contrive the seizure of Anaxinus of Oreus, who was purchasing goods for Olympias?[129] You twice personally put him on the rack, and then proposed the death penalty for him. After staying with him at Oreus, after eating and drinking with him and sharing his libation ceremony, after putting your hand in his and treating him as a friend and a host, you did him to death. I made your guilt clear all over Athens and called you the murderer of your host, and you did not deny your sacrilege. You made a reply which produced a loud protest from the Assembly and from any foreigners who were standing about there. You said you set the claims of Athens above those of personal hospitality. I say nothing of the lying letters you wrote, of the arrests for espionage you had visited with the rack on non-existent charges of a revolutionary conspiracy between me and other Athenians.

And then, according to my information, he proposes to ask me what sort of a doctor it is who gives no advice to the patient when he is ill, and then goes to the funeral and dilates to his friends on the treatment that might have saved him. You don't put the opposite question to yourself, what sort of a statesman it is who can flatter the people and throw away the opportunities for their preservation, can use defamation to prevent the assistance of their well-wishers, can run away from danger, involve his city in irreparable disaster and then claim a crown of valour, though his value to it has been negligible and the damage he has caused all-embracing, can ask the dupes of his policy on the occasions when salvation could have been attained, why they failed to prevent his mistakes, and can conceal the last misfortune of all, the fact that after the battle there was no time to attend to retribution because we were

129. See Demosthenes, *Crown*, 137, p. 290 below. The purchase for Olympias (the wife of Philip) may have been a pretext for going to Athens.

negotiating for the safety of Athens. But as you were not content to have escaped punishment, and proceeded to demand rewards to the extent of making Athens a laughing stock in the Greek world, I was here to act, and therefore brought this indictment.

Now I most emphatically declare that there is not a single item among the claims which I gather Demosthenes intends to make which annoys me more than this. He draws a comparison between my character and that of the Sirens, who brought destruction, he says, to their hearers, which is the reason for the discredit which attaches to the music of the Sirens.[130] In the same way, according to him, my oratorical flow acted to the detriment of my audience. But I maintain that it is entirely improper for anyone to make such a statement about me. It is disreputable to make a charge which cannot be substantiated. If the charge had to be made, it should not have been made by Demosthenes, but by a military expert credited with the highest service to Athens, but lacking in oratorical skill and therefore jealous of his rival's capacity, conscious of his inability to put any of his achievements across and of his opponent's ability actually to give the audience an unfounded impression of non-existent successes. But when an individual who depends purely on words, and words of gratuitous acrimony, then takes his stand on simplicity and fact, it is surely intolerable. Take his tongue away, and he'll be no more use than an instrument with no one to play it.

I must say, gentlemen, I wonder what consideration could lead you to reject this indictment. The legality of the decree? Its illegality is unparalleled. The idea that the proposer does not deserve punishment? It is an end of the rendering of any account of a way of life, if Ctesiphon is to be acquitted. It is a matter of pain and grief, if in the past the orchestra used to be filled with the gold crowns presented by the Greek states in honour of the People of Athens, because that was the day devoted to the presentation of crowns from abroad, while the policies of Demosthenes bring the People no crown, no proclamation, but this is only for himself. If any tragic poet in a future production introduced the presentation by the Greeks of a crown to Thersites, it would never be tolerated because of Homer's description of him

130. Again not to be found in Demosthenes' speech.

as a coward and a fraud.[131] Do you imagine that a presentation to a man like this could fail to be hissed off every platform in Greece? It was the custom in previous generations to attribute great and distinguished achievements to the People, while low or contemptible proceedings were put down to inadequate advisers. But Ctesiphon imagines it is your duty to divest Demosthenes of disgrace and place it on the shoulders of the People. We call ourselves fortunate, and I am happy to say we are. Are you, then, to vote that it is fortune that has let us down, and Demosthenes who has put us right? Most unreasonable of all, when you punish a conviction for bribery with disfranchisement, are you to honour a known receiver of political bribery with a crown? You penalize the judges of the cyclic choruses at the Dionysia for any unfair judgement.[132] You yourselves are the judges, not of choruses, but of law and political right and wrong. Instead of presenting the rewards in accordance with law to the deserving few, are you to give them for dubious intrigue?

Secondly, that sort of judge will leave the court with his own power diminished and the orator's increased. A private citizen under a democracy owes his power to law and to his vote. When he hands this last to someone else, he impairs his own position. Further, the oath which he has sworn on taking his place in court dogs his spirit and harasses him, because it is this which lies behind his misconduct, while the gratification he confers is unknown to its recipient, because the ballot is secret. It seems to me, gentlemen, that our political success and our political dangers are alike due to lack of control. The fact that in times like these the majority surrenders the reins of democratic power to the minority is a fact to be condemned. The fact that we have not been faced with a whole crop of unrestrained and unprincipled speakers is our good fortune. There was a time in the past when public affairs did produce such characters, who made short work of democracy. Democracy enjoyed the sunshine of flattery, and was then annihilated not by a party she feared but by one she had trusted. Some of its members joined the Thirty, who were responsible for the death of more than

131. In *Iliad*, II, 231 ff.

132. On judges at the Dionysia see A. W. Pickard-Cambridge, *The Dramatic Festivals of Athens* (2nd edition, 1968), pp. 95 ff.

fifteen hundred Athenian citizens untried and ignorant of the charge to which they owed their death. Even attendance at the funerals of the dead was banned. Are you then to lose control of public affairs? Can you forbear to humiliate triumphant self-satisfaction? Can you forget the fact that never has there been an attempt to overturn democracy until the rise of a power stronger than the courts?

I should like in your presence, gentlemen, to come to a reckoning with the proposer of the decree, and estimate the good services which make Demosthenes deserving of a crown. If, Ctesiphon, you are to maintain, as you did in the preamble to the decree, that it is because Demosthenes made a good job of the trenches round the walls, I am greatly surprised. The success of this piece of work is overshadowed by the charge of having made it necessary.[133] It is not the erection of defensive lines nor the destruction of public burial places which justify an orator's demand for recognition, but his part in a valuable service to Athens. If, however, you take your stand on the second part of the decree, on the outrageous claim that he is an honour to Athens and that his proposals and actions were consistently of the highest value to her People, then cut out the extravagant braggadocio in the decree and come down to the facts, give us a clear indication of your meaning. The bribery in connection with Amphissa and Euboea I omit. But when you ascribe to Demosthenes responsibility for the Theban alliance, it amounts to deception of the ignorant and an affront to all who know and grasp the truth. You take the event out of its context and omit the high repute of Athenian citizens, which lay behind the alliance, and imagine that you can get away with the claim to invest Demosthenes with the reputation of Athens. The degree of humbug involved in this I shall endeavour to mark by a most telling indication. Not long before Alexander crossed into Asia the King of Persia sent a dispatch in a hectoring tone quite alien to Greek ideas, which among other crudities concluded with the words, 'I shall give you no money. Don't ask for it, as you won't get it.' However, when caught in the net of his present misfortunes,[134] without any demand

---

133. This is a false implication by confusion between the hasty erection of fortifications after Chaeronea referred to by Lycurgus (*Against Leocrates*) and the later operation carried out under Demosthenes.

134. See 132, note 78.

from Athens this monarch spontaneously sent three hundred talents to the People of Athens, which we had the good sense to refuse. What lay behind this present was circumstances, fear and the lack of allies. This was the cause at work in the case of the Theban alliance. You distract us, Demosthenes, by continually introducing references to Thebes and to this unhappy alliance. But you keep rather quiet about the seventy talents you took as an advance on Persian largesse and got away with it.[135] Was it not shortage of money, the lack of five talents, which saved the mercenaries[136] from surrendering the citadel to Thebes? Was it not for lack of nine talents that the expedition of all Arcadia, which was ready to march, came to nothing?[137] You, meanwhile, live in wealth. You do service to your own self-indulgence. In fact Demosthenes gets the Persian gold, and we get the dangers.

It is also worth observing their crude manners. If Ctesiphon has the face to introduce Demosthenes to the court, and he to pronounce a eulogy on himself, it will be worse to listen to than the actuality was to undergo. When we cannot tolerate self-adulation from genuine heroes whose greatness we realize, who can be expected to endure the recital of self-praise from an individual who is a disgrace to the state? You will steer clear of this unsavoury business if you are wise, Ctesiphon, and make your defence on your own. You will not presumably claim inability as a speaker. It would be very extraordinary after allowing yourself to be chosen to make an address of condolence to Philip's daughter Cleopatra, on the death of Alexander,[138] king of the Molossians, if you are now going to say that you are no speaker. Apparently you can console a foreign princess in her grief, but are incapable of making a defence for a corrupt proposal. Or is it that your proposed decoration is for a

---

135. See 156, p. 233 above.

136. i.e. Alexander's mercenaries, who still held Thebes after the revolt in 335 B.C.

137. This expedition is alleged by Deinarchus in the speech against Demosthenes to have advanced to the Isthmus at the time of the insurrection of Sparta under Agis, but to have withdrawn on Demosthenes' refusal to supply ten talents for it. On the complicated question of Athenian support to Agis see A. W. Pickard-Cambridge, *Demosthenes*, pp. 425 ff.

138. Brother of Philip's wife, Olympias. He married Cleopatra, Philip's daughter, and was killed in Italy just before Aeschines' speech.

man who without outside support would be unknown to the people he has served? Ask members of the jury whether they know of Chabrias, Iphicrates and Timotheus. Ask them why they conferred honours on them and erected statues of them. They will answer universally that in Chabrias' case it was for the naval victory of Naxos, in that of Iphicrates for the defeat of a Spartan division, in that of Timotheus for the voyage to Corcyra, and for other war services of distinction.[139] And then ask for the reasons in Demosthenes' case. For being a corrupt, cowardly deserter? Will you be conferring honour on him or bringing dishonour on yourselves and the dead in battle on your behalf? It is they whose indignation you must suppose you are witnessing if he is to be crowned. If we cast away pieces of wood, stone and iron,[140] the dumb unthinking agents of death to a man they fall on, if in the case of a suicide we bury the guilty hand apart from the body, it would be outrageous, gentlemen, to treat Demosthenes with honour. It is an insult to the dead and a discouragement to the living to see that the prize of merit is death and its memory is transitory.

Most of all the question before the younger generation is what example to set themselves in life. You well know, gentlemen, that it is not solely in the gymnasium, or in the classroom, or in artistic pursuits that the young receive their education. Much more is it from public decrees. Suppose the proclamation is announced in the Theatre of a crown for high character and patriotic merit to a man of low moral standards. Knowledge of this is corruption of the young. Suppose a despicable and immoral creature like Ctesiphon is punished. This contributes to the education of the rest. The man whose vote is opposed to nobility and justice, who returns home and gives instruction to his son, who reasonably enough rejects it, gives admonition which rightly earns the name of vexatious. When you vote, you are not merely making a judgment. You are under

139. The exploit of Chabrias belongs to 376 B.C. (see above, 222, p. 249), that of Iphicrates to 390 during the Corinthian War, and that of Timotheus to 375, when he took a fleet round the Peloponnese, won over Corcyra, Cephallenia and Acarnania to the Second Athenian Confederacy and defeated a Spartan fleet off Acarnania.

140. The instrument of death is ceremonially thrown away as a form of purification.

observation, and may need a defence to offer to citizens who are not
here but will ask what decision you made. You must know,
gentlemen, that the character of the city will be equated with that of
her proclaimed hero. And it is a disgrace to be compared not with
your fathers, but with the cowardice of Demosthenes.

How is this disgrace to be avoided? By taking precautions against
the class of people who are quick to seize upon expressions of
popular connotation, though their own character is unreliable.
Patriotism and democracy are titles in common currency, but the
first to take refuge in them are often the most remote from their
real nature. So when you find an orator with an eager desire for
crowns and proclamations, make him refer back, as is legally
obligatory in regard to a title to property, to the guarantee of an
estimable life and a character of principle. Anyone who cannot show
evidence of this must not be credited with any title to eulogy. Think
of democracy, and remember how it can slip out of your hands.
Does it not seem a scandal that Assembly and Council should be by-
passed, and correspondence and official visits should be addressed to
private individuals not from random sources but from outstanding
leaders of Europe and Asia? Conduct legally punishable with death
is not denied, but publicly admitted, while official correspondence
on it is openly read and compared, and in some cases we are urged
to look towards the men in question as protectors of democracy,
while others demand presentations as saviours of Athens. And the
people are in despair. It is as though old age had paralysed their
powers or their wits, and they only assume the name of democracy
and leave the action to others. The Assembly is adjourned without
a meeting, nothing but distribution of the leavings from a sort of
supper party. This is no exaggeration. Look at this sample. At the
time of a certain misfortune to Athens, which I hate to recall, a
private individual who had done no more than attempt to sail to
Samos was there and then executed by the Areopagus as a traitor to
his country. Another who had sailed to Rhodes was recently indicted for cowardice in the face of danger, and, had there been a
single change in the voting, would have been exiled from Athens.[141]

141. This refers to Leocrates, recently prosecuted by Lycurgus in a speech
which is still extant. The other mentioned above is unknown. Lycurgus
(*Leocrates*, 52) says that several men were executed on such charges.

Compare what happens now. An orator responsible for all our disasters abandoned his post in the army, and ran away from Athens.[142] This is the man who claims a crown and imagines he deserves a proclamation. Cast him out as he deserves. He is the ruin of all Greece alike. Or arrest him and punish him. He is a robber who has stolen our prosperity as he sails on his wordy course through our politics. And do not forget the occasion on which you are making your vote. It is not long before the Pythian festival, when the congress of the Greeks takes place. The policies of Demosthenes have brought disrepute to Athens for these events. If you crown him, it will seem that you are in agreement with the breach of the Common Peace of the Greek states. If you do the opposite, you will free the People of Athens of responsibility.[143]

The city in whose interest you are deliberating is no foreign one, but your own. The honours concerned must not be easily distributed, but jealously judged. The presentations must be made to better persons, worthier men. Not your hearing only, but your vision must be directed to yourselves in your deliberations, and you must consider which of you will be the people to assist Demosthenes, his fellows in the hunting field or in the gymnasium. But I assure you that his life has not been spent in pursuit of the wild boar, or of physical fitness, but in devising schemes against the possessors of property. You must have an eye to the humbug involved in his claim that by his action as ambassador he snatched Byzantium out of Philip's hands, that he caused the insurrection in Acarnania,[144] that he fired Thebes with his speeches. He imagines you are simple-minded enough to believe all this, as though your protégé were the goddess Persuasion, instead of a figure of mendacity. And when at the end of the case he calls on his accomplices in bribery to support him, you must imagine that on this platform on which I now stand to speak you see ranged against their wicked dealing the great benefactors of Athens; that you see Solon, the author of the noblest of laws to adorn democracy, philosopher and

142. See 159 (p. 233) above.

143. i.e. in particular for the insurrection of Greek states led by Sparta in 330 B.C., which broke the Common Peace organized by Philip in 338–337.

144. In 341 Demosthenes had led a delegation to Byzantium, which subsequently withstood a siege by Philip in 340–339 B.C. Athens had sent a force to protect Acarnania against Philip in 343 B.C.

poet of rectitude, demanding soberly according to his duty that you shall never rate Demosthenes' speeches higher than law and your oath; that you see Aristides,[145] the assessor of tribute for the Greeks, at whose death the People allotted a dowry to his daughters – that you see him in indignation at the abuse of justice, demanding whether you are not ashamed, whether it can be true that, when your ancestors found Arthmius of Zelea,[146] the bearer of gold from Persia, on a visit to Athens, whose guest he was, they were within an ace of executing him and proclaimed him an outcast from Athens and from every city of her empire; and yet, when you yourselves found Demosthenes not as the bearer but as the receiver of Persian gold, which he still has in his possession, you intend to award him a gold crown. Themistocles, too, and the dead at Marathon and Plataea, and the very tombs of your ancestors – do you not suppose they will lament that a confessed opponent of Greece in the service of Persia should be crowned?

I call upon Earth and Sun, upon virtue and intelligence and that learning which enables us to distinguish good and evil. I have come to the support of right, I have said my say. If my duty as accuser has been well and truly done, it has been all I wished. If it has fallen short, it has been all I could. You must take note both of the spoken and the unspoken word, and make your vote in accordance with justice and the good of Athens.

145. Aristides, known as the Just, assessed the ability of Athens's allies to provide ships and men or money to the fleet of the new Athenian alliance against Persia, the Delian League, in 478–477 B.C.

146. The decree of Arthmius is referred to also in Demosthenes, *Philippic*, III, 43, and in *Treaty*, 271, note 102.

II. THE DEFENCE: DEMOSTHENES

Summary of the Speech

I. Preamble. The request for a favourable reception. 1–8.

II. Matters outside the indictment. 9–52.

Introduction on relevance (9–17). Events of Aeschines' *First Period* (18–52).

III. Reply on the indictment. 53–125.

Introduction (53–9). Demosthenes' public life. Aeschines' *Second Period* (60–109). The charge that Demosthenes was still *sub judice* (110–19). On the proclamation of the award in the Theatre (120–1). Conclusion (121–5).

IV. Attack on Aeschines' private and public character. 126–59.

Private matters (126–31). Public affairs (132–9). The war with Amphissa (140–59).

V. Demosthenes' public career, including Aeschines' *Third Period.* 160–251.

Policy after Amphissa and before Chaeronea (160–92). The Athenian resistance in general and her spirit of nobility in the cause of honour (193–210). Further details of the alliance with Thebes (211–17). Demosthenes as an orator deserving of reward in the circumstances in which he was placed (218–51).

VI. Replies to further accusations. 252–96.

The taunt of Demosthenes' 'unlucky star'. The comparison with Aeschines and further personalities (252–67). Recapitulation of this theme (268–75). The charge of political deceitfulness rebutted (276–84). The claim that Athens has already given her verdict on Demosthenes by his appointment to speak the funeral oration

(285–90) and by the sympathy of her feelings in contrast with the traitors (291–6).

VII. Peroration. 297–end.

Defences provided by Demosthenes (297–300). Methods put into operation (301–5). The good and the bad statesman (306–13). Comparison with the great men of the past, and conclusion (313–end).

The text of the speech on the *Crown* includes a number of documents decrees, letters and the like, purporting to be those referred to in the speech. This applies to all such documents mentioned as read in the course of the speech up to and including the long decree in 181–7 (p. 299). But since their analysis by Droysen in 1839 it has been clear that the great majority of them cannot be accepted as genuine on grounds of inaccuracy and sometimes irrelevance to their purpose. Accordingly, though included in the Greek text of the Oxford and other recent editions, they are omitted here.

FIRST, gentlemen, I beg you by every pledge that we hold sacred
that the warmth of heart which I have never ceased to feel towards
Athens may be equalled from the start by your feeling towards me
at the opening of this case, and secondly that in accordance with
your best interests, your respect for religion and your high reputation you may be inspired from above with the determination not to
listen to my opponent on the question of the hearing you are to give
to me – which would be abominable – but to law and to your oath.[1]
Here in its enactments it is laid down that an equal hearing be given
to both contestants. This is not merely a matter of freedom from
prejudice, or of extending goodwill to both alike. It implies that
each shall be allowed to organize the order of his defence according
to his own desire and intention.

There are several respects in which Aeschines has the advantage
of me in regard to this case, and two of them, gentlemen, are important. One is that the issue at stake is not the same for us both. It is
not an equal loss for me to be deprived of your sympathy and for
him to fail in his prosecution. For me – but I do not wish to start
with unpleasant implications,[2] so suffice it to say that he has the
advantage over me. The other is the common fact of human nature
that, while an audience will listen with relish to abuse and vituperation, it will be irritated by self-praise. Of these two parts the
enjoyable one is reserved for him, while I am left with what is
almost always tiresome. If in my caution to elude this pitfall I avoid
describing my own achievements, it will appear that I have too little
material to rebut the charges or demonstrate my reasons for claiming
the award. If I pass to the subject of my actions and policies, I shall
frequently be compelled to talk of myself. I shall try to do this with

1. A reply to Aeschines, *Crown*, 202 ff., p. 245.
2. The implication is that for himself the loss would be fatal.

all moderation. But where the case makes it necessary, the blame ought to lie at Aeschines' door for instituting these proceedings.

I think you would all agree, gentlemen, that this case is shared by Ctesiphon and myself in common, and of the two I have at least equal reason for strong interest in it. Any deprivation is painful and regrettable, especially if it is inflicted by an enemy, and most of all deprivation of happy and kindly relations with Athens, in so far as it is the greatest of privileges to win them. But since this is the issue in the present case, I hope I am justified in asking you all alike to listen to my just defence, which accords with the enactments of the law, whose author, Solon, out of his feeling for Athens and her people, regarded them as needing the validity not only of written form but of an oath on the part of the jury. This was not from distrust of you, gentlemen, as I see it, but from the understanding that accusation and misrepresentation, which are the strength of the prosecutor from his position as opener, can only be overcome if every member of the jury maintains his religious duty, adopts a feeling of friendliness as he awaits the second speaker, and becomes an unprejudiced and unbiased hearer before making his final decision.

But as I am apparently to render account today for the whole of my private life as well as my public policies, I want to invoke divine aid, and I pray once again that the warmth of heart which I have never ceased to feel towards Athens may be equalled from the start by your feeling towards myself in regard to this case, and secondly that heaven may put it in your hearts today to make a decision which is in accord both collectively with the honour of the city and individually with the conscience of every man in it.

Now had Aeschines confined his accusations to the subject of the prosecution, I would at once have made my defence to the terms of the bill prepared. But as he has devoted so much space to the discussion of other things, involving numbers of false statements at my expense, it is in accord with justice to speak a few words on this subject, in the hope that no one of you will be led by irrelevance to a harsher view of the bill itself.

As regards the personal abuse and misrepresentation which the prosecutor has produced against me, just consider the straightforward and proper reply which I offer. If you know me for the kind of person described by the prosecution – all my life has been spent among you here – don't listen to me for a moment, even if my political success has been overwhelming. Just stand up and give your verdict against me. But if the character you know has been far higher and comes of higher breeding, if – I don't want to be tiresome – if you have found me and mine up to the average of reasonable people, then don't trust Aeschines on this or any other subject – it is obvious that it is all fabrication – but show me the same goodwill you have shown throughout in numerous other cases in the past.[3] In the blackness of your heart, Aeschines, it appears as a strange innocence to have imagined that I was likely to pass over facts and policies and turn to your abuse of me. I shall not do that. I am less deluded than you suppose. I shall examine your lying misrepresentations of my political career, and make some mention later of your unbridled and scurrilous abuse, if the jury so desire.

The charges are numerous and in some cases liable by law to great, indeed extreme penalties. But the essence of the present case is this. It involves rancour, violence, vituperation and abuse, everything of this kind. Yet for the accusations made in it, supposing them proved, the state could not exact anything like adequate penalties. It is not legitimate to deprive a man of access to the People[4] and a reasoned judgement, nor to do it in a spirit of envy and rancour, which is neither good sense nor good politics nor good conduct. Any offence which he could see on my part against the state, if it equalled the histrionic[5] account he has given of it, he should have met with the legal penalties at the time it was committed. If it was a matter for impeachment, he should have impeached[6] me, and used that method of bringing me to justice. If I were guilty of illegality, he should have brought an indictment for that offence. He can hardly be bringing an indictment against Ctesiphon because of me

---

3. On Demosthenes' frequent trials after the defeat at Chaeronea see 249-50, pp. 312 ff. below.

4. Demosthenes' point is apparently to protest against the unfairness of making the attack through Ctesiphon and after a long interval, so as to deprive him of a genuine confrontation.

5. In the word 'histrionic' we have the first of many references to Aeschines' profession as an actor.

6. 'Impeach' is the nearest English equivalent of the special Athenian practice in dealing with crimes not covered by normal judicial means, i.e. trial before Council or Assembly.

which he would not have brought against myself, had he thought he could succeed. Indeed, if he knew for true any of his long, libellous statements against me, or any other misconduct of mine, they are all covered by the law, with prescribed punishments, with forms of trial and stated judgments involving severe and painful penalties. All these he could have deployed. As soon as it was clear that he was doing so, that he was employing any such method in his dealings with me, the prosecution would have been in agreement with his proceedings. As it is, he has abandoned the path of right and justice, he has avoided criticism at the time of the actual offences, and after all this long interval he now puts on an act with his accumulation of charges, abuse and parody. Then he accuses me, but brings Ctesiphon to court. Throughout the case he puts his hostility to me in the forefront, yet he never faces me on this issue, but makes an open attempt to deprive another man of his rights. Yet whatever else can be said for Ctesiphon, this can be added, it seems to me, that justice demanded that the test should be made on the basis of the hostility between Aeschines and myself. We are the protagonists, and this fact ought not to have been shirked in quest of someone else to penalize. That is the height of iniquity.

All the charges alike are thus proved devoid of justice or veracity. But I want to examine them separately, particularly his mendacious account of the peace and the delegation,[7] in which he made me responsible for activities which he concerted with Philocrates. It therefore becomes both necessary and right to recall the state of affairs at that time, to enable you to view it in the light of circumstances contemporary with it.

At the outset of the Phocian War – which was not my responsibility (I was not yet in politics) – our attitude was a hope for the success of Phocis, although we realized that her activities were unjustified, and jubilation at anything detrimental to Thebes, against whom we were irrationally and wrongfully incensed because of her immoderate exploitation of the victory at Leuctra.[8] The Pelopon-

7. i.e. the events of 346 B.C., see Aeschines, *Crown*, 58–76, pp. 207 ff.
8. At this distance of time Demosthenes takes a more dispassionate view than in earlier speeches of the Third Sacred War (355–346 B.C.). Athens had been the ally of Phocis but had done little to help her except defend Thermopylae in 352. On this and on the history of Theban hegemony and of the Peloponnese after the battle of Leuctra (371 B.C.) see Introduction, pp. 16 ff, 22 ff.

nese was in a state of division. The opponents of Sparta had not the power to destroy her, and the rulers she had established were no longer in control. Both sides were in a state of confused and inde-cisive conflict. Realizing this – which was obvious – Philip paid out money to the traitors on both sides in an attempt to foster general confusion and antagonism between them. Their mistakes and dis-loyalties secured him his ends and his growth at their expense. The once overbearing, now most unhappy people of Thebes were in distress at the length of the war, and it was obvious that Thebes would be compelled to resort to Athenian aid. To prevent this *rapprochement* between the two cities, Philip offered peace to Athens and assistance to Thebes. What contributed to our falling victim virtually without resistance to his deception ? The attitude of the Greek states, whether one is to call it cowardice or unintellig-ence or both. We were engaged in a long, continuous war in de-fence of the general interest, as the event has made clear, but they brought neither men nor money nor anything else to our support.[9] In our proper and justifiable exasperation at this we readily acceded to Philip. The peace agreed as a result, not by my doing, as Aes-chines alleges, was then negotiated. It was the corrupt and unjusti-fiable practices of my opponents at that time which any proper examination will show was responsible for all our troubles. I can give all this as a precisely detailed account. Whatever degree of guilt may be supposed to attach to these proceedings, none of it attaches to me.

The first mention of peace was made by Aristodemus, the actor. The man who took up the suggestion and made the proposal was Philocrates of Hagnus, your associate, Aeschines, and not mine, even if you lie till you are black in the face. The supporters of the peace, for whatever reason – I pass that over for the present – were Eubulus and Cephisophon.[10] I was not concerned in it at all.

9. A fair charge; see Introduction, p. 25.

10. On Aristodemus see Demosthenes, *Treaty*, 12, and Aeschines, *Treaty*, 15–19, where a different analysis of his political support is given. In his speech against Timarchus (174) Aeschines had claimed the credit of negotiating the peace for himself and Philocrates. For Eubulus see Introduction, pp. 22 ff. Cephisophon, whose role in the negotiations is unknown, was prosecuted by Aeschines according to Demosthenes, *Treaty*, 293 (p. 128 above).

None the less, though this was proved to be the truth of the matter, Aeschines was brazen enough to assert that besides being responsible for the peace I prevented Athens from making it in the general congress of the Greeks. Then, you – what name can I give you? – was there ever an occasion when you saw Athens deprived by me of such negotiation and alliance as you describe, and expressed indignation, or got up and gave substance and detail to your present accusations? If I accepted a price from Philip for obstructing the Greek community, it rested with you to burst out into loud protest instead of saying nothing, and point it out. You never did so. You were never heard to say a word of the kind. In fact no delegation was sent to any of the Greek states at the time.[11] They were all tried and proved useless, and Aeschines' statement has not a word of truth in it. Apart from this, his lying account constitutes a defamation of Athens. If we issued a summons to war from the Greek states while at the same time sending a peace delegation to Philip, it was an outrage, not the conduct of statesmanship, or of common honesty either. But it is totally untrue. What would have been the object of a summons to them at that point? To secure peace? They all had it already. To declare war? But we were negotiating peace. It will thus be clear that I was neither an initiator of peace nor responsible for it, and that none of his other mendacious statements is true.

After the conclusion of peace by Athens observe the line taken by each of us. This will show you who it was who was hand in glove with Philip throughout, and who was concerned to act in the interest of city and people. I made the proposal in the Council[12] that the delegates should sail at once wherever they learnt of Philip's presence, and administer the oaths. They refused to do this even after my proposal. What did this mean, gentlemen? I will tell you. It was in Philip's interest to secure as long an interval as possible before the oath, and in ours that it should be as short as possible. Why? In our case it was not the administration of the oaths but our own hopes of peace that put an end to our war preparations. But in his case it was the delay which was an object of intrigue all the time,

---

11. This is Demosthenes' answer to Aeschines' elaborate arguments of *Crown*, 64–70 (pp. 209 ff.). cf. *Treaty*, 57–62, and see Introduction, pp. 28 ff.
12. See, at greater length, Demosthenes, *Treaty*, 150–57 (pp. 92 ff.).

because he rightly supposed that any gains he could make in advance, before the oaths were administered, would be safely in his pocket. No one was likely to abandon the peace on their account. I foresaw this, gentlemen, and my anticipation of it led to my proposal to sail wherever Philip was and administer the oaths at once, so that it could be done while your allies in Thrace still held the places which Aeschines has been pouring scorn on, Serrium, Myrtenum and Ergiske,[13] and Philip should not get a hold on the positions of advantage, and gain the mastery over Thrace, nor use the advantage he would gain there in men and money to get an easier control of the rest. Aeschines does not read out or refer to this decree. But he makes unfair capital out of the fact that I proposed in the Council the introduction of the Macedonian delegates.[14] What should I have done? Propose the exclusion of the delegates who had come expressly for talks with us? Or order the manager to assign them no seats in the Theatre? They could have sat in the two-obol seats without my decree. Or should I have kept a jealous guard on minor public expenses, while subjecting the state as a whole to bribery, as they did? Surely not. Now take and read the decree, which Aeschines obviously knew, though he failed to mention it.

(The decree of Demosthenes is read.)

That was my decree at that time. My aim was to secure the interests of Athens, not those of Philip. Our admirable delegates hardly gave it a thought. They sat inactive in Macedonia for three whole months, till Philip arrived back from Thrace in complete control. They could have been at the Hellespont in ten days, possibly[15] even in three or four, and saved the key points by exchanging the oaths before Philip could capture the places. He would never have laid hands on them in our presence; or we should have refused to swear and he would have failed to secure the peace. He could never have had both that and the strategic points.

Such was the first piece of robbery on Philip's part and of bribery of these unprincipled people. In respect of it I agree that both then and now and always I was opposed to them. Now observe another,

13. See Aeschines, *Crown*, 82, p. 214.
14. See Aeschines, *Crown*, 76, p. 213.
15. See Appendix, p. 332.

greater wrong action in succession to the first. When Philip had sworn the peace after stealing a march on us in Thrace because of the refusal of these people to follow my decree, he next bribed them into an assurance that we delegates should not leave Macedonia till he could make arrangements for his campaign against Phocis. This was to prevent our announcing his intentions and his plans to march, in case of an Athenian expedition and a voyage with warships to Thermopylae, to bar the way like the previous one.[16] Then at the moment when we gave the news he would be inside the pass, and we should be helpless. Yet Philip was in such an agony of apprehension lest even after his success a decision to march on our part before Phocis was destroyed might mean that the position would slip through his fingers that he hired this contemptible accomplice, this time not with all the rest of the delegation but privately on his own, to give you the assurances and the information[17] which caused the disaster.

It is my earnest request, gentlemen, that you will remember throughout this case that had Aeschines brought no charge outside the indictment I would not have gone outside it either. But in view of all the accusations and misrepresentations which he has combined together in it, I cannot avoid a few words in answer to each of them. What, then, were the arguments then put forward by him, which occasioned the disaster? The statement that: 'There is no cause for alarm at Philip's appearance inside the pass. All your wishes are going to be realized, and in two or three days you will hear the news that his former hostilities have changed to friendships and vice versa.' It was not words, he said in impressive tones, that cemented friendly relations, but community of interest; and the interest of Philip, Phocis and Athens alike demanded an end of the unthinking intransigence of Thebes. This was welcomed in some quarters because of the existing unpopularity of Thebes. What followed – immediately, not later on? The abolition of Phocis and the destruction of her towns, without Athens lifting a finger. Instead, Aeschines' advice meant moving in our possessions from the country districts, while he got well paid for it. Add to this that the unpopularity of Thebes and Thessaly was now attached to this

16. In 352 B.C.
17. See Demosthenes, *Treaty*, 17–24 (pp. 60 ff.).

country, while the gratitude for the whole proceeding went to Philip. In corroboration of my statement please read the decree of Callisthenes and Philip's letter. Both will make clear the whole story.

(The decree is read.)

Were these the hopes on which the peace was based? And were these the assurances given by Aeschines?

Now read Philip's subsequent letter.

(The letter is read.)

Observe how clearly Philip demonstrates and lays down to his allies in the letter to Athens that, 'I have done this against the will and to the regret of Athens, so that, if you in Thebes and Thessaly are sensible, you will treat them as your enemies and put your trust in me.' He does not say this in so many words, but he makes his intention clear. Thus he deluded them into a total lack of foresight about the future and into allowing him to keep the whole situation under his control. This has led to all these disasters for those unhappy people. And the accomplice who was hand in glove with him in these acts of bad faith, the man who told the lying story to Athens which deceived us, was Aeschines, who now laments the fate of Thebes and describes her sufferings and miseries when he himself is the cause of it all, both of this and of the horrors of Phocis and all the sufferings of Greece. Of course, Aeschines, you must be deeply grieved at it all, and filled with pity for the people of Thebes. You have property in Boeotia and farm Boeotian land, whereas I of course am delighted, since it was I whose surrender was demanded at once by the perpetrator of it.[18]

However, I have been led to deal with subjects which will be suitable at a later stage. I will return to the proof that it was the misconduct of Aeschines which was responsible for the present state of affairs.

18. Demosthenes is ironical at the contrast: Aeschines, he claims, acquired land in Boeotia from Alexander, while the surrender of Demosthenes and other anti-Macedonian orators at Athens was demanded after the destruction of Thebes in 335 B.C. This demand, however, was not pressed. See Aeschines, *Crown*, 161, note 97, p 234.

After the deception practised on us by Philip by means of members of the delegations whose corruption distorted the account they gave, and the deception practised on the unfortunate people of Phocis which led to the destruction of their towns, what happened? The despicable creatures of Thessaly and the insensitive dullards in Thebes thought Philip their friend, benefactor and saviour. He was everything to them, and they wouldn't hear a word of any other view one tried to express. We felt suspicious and discontented, but maintained the peace. There was nothing else to be done. The other Greek states, who had been equally hoodwinked, and had failed to secure their aims, were still glad to keep the peace. They also had been the victims of war from a distance. When Philip went about the country, reducing either Illyrian or Triballian tribes,[19] or sometimes a Greek state, and often adding considerable fresh power to his resources, when individuals from various cities used the liberty of peace to go to Macedonia and receive bribes – Aeschines was one of them – everyone against whose interests these steps were taken was in fact a victim of war. If they were unaware of it, that is another matter, and not my concern. I foretold all this with great emphasis both in Athens and wherever I was sent.[20] But the cities were in a poor way. There was corruption in politics and public life, there were people receiving bribes. Private citizens to a large extent failed to foresee the future, or they were lured by the inertia and the leisure of everyday existence. This sort of thing happened to everyone, except that no one thought the worst would happen to him. Everyone imagined that other people would suffer, and he himself would be all right.

The result for the majority, it seems to me, has been to compensate for their vast, untimely lethargy by losing their liberty, and for the leaders, who expected to sell everything except themselves, the discovery that they were themselves the first victims. Instead of the title of friends and guests, which they enjoyed in the days of

19. The victory over the Illyrians was in 344 B.C. according to Diodorus. The Triballi lived near the Lower Danube; Philip's only known encounter with them was on his Scythian campaign in 339 B.C., when he was not victorious.

20. In *Philippic*, II, 19–26 (*Greek Political Oratory*, pp. 231 ff.), Demosthenes describes a visit he made as ambassador to Messene in 344 B.C. He also visited Argos at that time.

bribery, they are now called damnable bootlickers and other appropriate terms. No one spends money in the interest of a betrayer, and no one after paying his price asks for advice from the traitor. Otherwise the traitor's lot would be the happiest of all. But of course it is not. How could it be? Anything but! Once the seeker of power is in control of the situation, he is master of the people who sold it to him. He knows their low character, and that is when he begins to hate, distrust and abuse them. Just think. Even if the critical moment is past, good sense can always catch the moment for recognition of the truth. Lasthenes was called a friend up to his betrayal of Olynthus, Timolaus up to the destruction of Thebes, Eudicus and Simus of Larissa until they made over Thessaly to Philip.[21] Now they and their like have been driven out and treated with insolence and violence of every sort all over the world. What about Aristratus at Sicyon and Perillus at Megara? They have been expelled. It is clear proof that a jealous guard on one's country and opposition to traitors is the best way to provide mercenary betrayers like you, Aeschines, with the means to get your bribes. It is because of the number of honest citizens who oppose your wishes that you yourselves are alive and paid your wages, when by yourselves you would long ago have come to ruin.

There is much I could say on the events of this period, and yet I think I have said more than enough. The fault lies with Aeschines for trying to give me a drenching – in the dregs of his own low practices and misconduct. Before a jury too young to remember the facts I needed to clear myself. But it may have been a tiresome irrelevance to people who without a word from me know the whole story of his corruption. He refers to it as friendship and hospitality. He talked just now about 'charging him with friendship to Alex-

21. On Lasthenes' betrayal of Olynthus (348 B.C.) cf. Demosthenes, *Chersonese*, 40, and *Philippic*, III, 56 (*Greek Political Oratory*, pp. 241 and 259). Timolaus and Perillus appear in the list of Greek traitors in 295 below (p. 323). Timolaus is thought to have caused Philip's intervention over Amphissa in 339 B.C. and the surrender of Thebes to Philip after the battle of Chaeronea in 338. Perillus almost succeeded in handing Megara over to Philip in 344–343 B.C. It is uncertain whether Eudicus as well as Simus was from Larissa; Simus probably belonged to the Aleuadae family, which called in Philip in 352 B.C. Aristratus was a tyrant of Sicyon, where Philip's only known intervention was after Chaeronea.

ander'. Friendship with Alexander! Where did you get it, or how were you supposed to deserve it? I would not call you a friend to either Philip or Alexander. I am not such a fool. Unless one is to call casual labourers who can pick up a wage for any job friends of their employers! I do call you a hired employee first of Philip and now of Alexander. So does everyone here. If you don't believe it, ask them, or, better, I'll do it myself. Do you gentlemen think that Aeschines is a hired employee of Alexander's, or his friend? You hear their answer.

So now I want to make my defence on the indictment itself. I want to narrate my political career, so that, well though he knows it already, Aeschines may hear the reasons for my claim to deserve not only the awards mentioned in the resolution of the Council but much more besides. Please read the indictment.

(The indictment is read.)

These, gentlemen, are the accusations made against the decree. I think I can use the same material to prove to you that my defence will be justified. I shall keep the same order of subjects and go through each in turn without intentionally omitting anything. The claim that my words and actions throughout maintained the best interests of the people of Athens, the mention of my eagerness to do all I could to further it, and the vote of thanks accorded me belong, I consider, to the subject of political activity. The examination of these claims will show whether Ctesiphon's proposal about me was true and appropriate, or false. That the proposal of a crown did not add the words 'after passing the accounts', and included proclamation in the Theatre, is also, I think, concerned with political events and the question whether I deserve a crown and the proclamation proposed, or not. At the same time I think I need to show the enactments enabling Ctesiphon to make this proposal. Thus I intend to make my defence in all justice and simplicity. I shall advance immediately to the subject of my public career. But it must not be supposed that I am making a separation between this account and the indictment, if I proceed to the subject of Greek affairs. The action of the prosecutor in attacking the words of the decree to the effect that my words and actions were praiseworthy, and denying their truth, is itself responsible for making the question of my public career relevant and necessary to discussion of the indictment. There are numerous departments of public life, and I chose that of Greek affairs, so that I am justified in drawing my evidence from this.

Philip's depredations and appropriations before the outset of my political career I will omit. I do not think any of them concern me. The restrictions he underwent from the first day of my entry into public life are what I shall recall and render account of, after making this preliminary point. There was one advantage, gentlemen, which lay in Philip's hands. Among the Greek states, not in isolated instances but everywhere, there came into existence a crop of corrupt, abominable traitors beyond all previous memory. With them as accomplices and collaborators he worked on the deteriorating condition of the Greeks and their internal dissensions, and made these worse. He used deception or offers of money or wholesale corruption, and divided them into numerous parties, when their interests were one and the same – to curb his rising power. Now at a time when the Greek states were in this condition, gentlemen, and still failed to understand the gathering disease that was growing among them, what conduct, what course of action was it proper for Athens to adopt? This is the question before you of which you should demand an account from me, because the man who took his political stand at this point was myself. Should she have abandoned her spirit and pride, Aeschines, and ranked herself with Thessaly and Dolopia[22] in helping Philip to acquire the command of Greece at the expense of all that was good and great in past generations? Or should she have shunned this appalling prospect, but have looked on at what she could long foretell would happen, if no one stood in the way, and let it go on? I should like to ask critics of our policy which party they would have preferred Athens to join, the party of collaboration in the ruin and dishonour of Greece, in which one would include Thessaly and her associates, or the party which turned a blind eye to all that for the sake of private advantage, like Arcadia, Messenia and Argos. Yet many or all of these came out of it worse than we did. If after his success Philip had at once left Greece and made no mischief thereafter, if he had

22. Philip had subdued Thessaly in 352 B.C. and the Dolopians, who lived in the mountains west of Thessaly, at about the same time.

done nothing to damage any of his own allies or the other Greeks,[23] there would have been some reason to criticize and censure the opponents of his measures. But if he was concerned to circumscribe the repute, the pre-eminence, the liberty of every state, indeed I might add their constitution, where he could, how can it have been anything but our most honourable course that we pursued at my instance?

But, to return, what should have been the policy of Athens, Aeschines, in view of Philip's continued machinations to secure a tyrant's control of the Greek world? What should the statesman have advocated or proposed at Athens – this is the important question – who knew in his heart, as I did right up to the moment of my appearance on the platform, that our country has always striven to be first in the world's honour and distinction, has spent more in men and money for glory and the common welfare of Greece than all the Greek states individually for their own, who could see Philip, our antagonist, sustain in search of power and supremacy the loss of an eye, a broken collar-bone, an injured arm or leg,[24] the sacrifice of any part of his body chance might seize from him, in the hope that with the rest of it intact he might live in glory and renown. And yet no one would dare to breathe the idea that it was fitting that a man born and bred in a small and mean city like Pella, as it then was, should have in him such greatness of spirit as to set in his heart the desire and ambition of power over Greece, while we Athenians, who every day in every word we speak, in every spectacle we look on, keep in our minds the memory of noble ancestors, should have in us a spirit so demeaned as by our own offer, our own will, to cede to Philip the place of liberty. It is unthinkable. The only remaining course, therefore, and the course of necessity, was righteous opposition to every unjustifiable action of his against us. That is what Athens did from the beginning, naturally and with justice, and that was the policy I proposed and advised throughout my public career. I own it. What should I have done? I put the

23. Though Philip treated Athens well, he was severe on Thebes, and intervened in the Peloponnesian cities and established permanent garrisons in various places. See Introduction, p. 45.

24. According to the scholiast Philip lost an eye at Methone (353 B.C.), had his collar-bone broken in the Illyrian campaign, and sustained the leg and hand injuries when fighting the Scythians (339 B.C.).

question to you without reference to Amphipolis, Pydna, Potidaea, Halonnesus. I cast them out of memory. As to Serrium, Doriscus, the sack of Peparethus[25] and all else that Athens underwent, I ignore their very existence. Yet you asserted that it was my speeches about these that brought enmity between Philip and Athens, though Eubulus, Aristophon and Diopeithes[26] were the authors of these decrees. You would assert anything in that blandly irresponsible manner. However, even now I make no mention of them. But when you have a man who appropriated Euboea and engineered a fortification there to threaten Attica, who made an attempt on Megara, who captured Oreus[27] and destroyed Porthmus, establishing Philistides as tyrant on Oreus and Cleitarchus in Eretria, who besieged Byzantium and razed Greek cities or restored their exiles, do these actions constitute unjustifiable breaches of agreement and contraventions of the peace, or do they not? And was it right that someone in the Greek world should have appeared to prevent it, or not? If not, if it was right that Greece should be seen as a proverbial 'booty from Mysia',[28] while Athenians still lived, then I have wasted my time in dealing with the subject, and Athens has wasted her time in following me, and all that she has done must go for wrong and folly of mine. But if it was right that a stand should be made against all this, what other people should make it but Athens? Such was my political career. I saw the whole world enslaved by

25. Amphipolis, Pydna and Potidaea were taken by Philip, the two latter from Athens in 357-356 B.C.; see Introduction, pp. 19-20. It is not known when he took Halonnesus, an island north of Euboea, but he offered to return it to Athens in 343-342. Serrium and Doriscus (see Aeschines, *Crown*, 82, p. 214) were taken by Philip in the period between the peace agreement and its ratification in 346; Peparethus, another island near Halonnesus, was sacked by Philip in 341-340, after its people had taken Halonnesus from him.

26. On Eubulus see Introduction, pp. 22 ff; on Aristophon see Aeschines, *Crown*, 139 and 194 (pp. 228 and 243), and Demosthenes, *Treaty*, 297 (p. 128). Diopeithes is probably not the general whose alleged infringements of the treaty Demosthenes defended in *Chersonese*. The occasions and purport of the various decrees referred to here and read below are unknown.

27. Oreus was at the north-western tip of Euboea, Porthmus the port of Eretria in the south facing Attica and only thirty miles north of Athens. Philip helped to overthrow democracy at Eretria and to establish Cleitarchus as tyrant in 342 B.C.; his attempt on Megara was in 343. His unsuccessful siege of Byzantium (see below 87-9, p. 278) was in 340 B.C.

28. i.e. unresisting prey, a proverbial expression.

Philip, and stood against him. I gave continual warning and admonition not to allow it. The peace was broken by Philip's capture of the ships,[29] not by Athens, Aeschines.

Now please bring the actual decrees and Philip's letter, and read them in succession. This will give clear indication of the responsibility.

(The decree is read.)

This decree was proposed by Eubulus and not by me, and the succeeding ones by Aristophon, then Hegesippus, then Aristophon again, then Philocrates and finally Cephisophon[30] and others. I was not the proposer of any. Continue.

(The subsequent decrees are read.)

As I produce the decrees, Aeschines, please point out which one I proposed so as to have been responsible for the war. You won't be able to. If you could, there is nothing you would be quicker to put forward. Even Philip has no accusation of me in respect of war. He puts the blame elsewhere. Please read Philip's letter.

(The letter is read.)

Here he never mentions the name of Demosthenes. He makes no charge against me. Why, amidst all the complaints he has of others, is there no mention of activities of mine? Because it would have involved recalling his own unjustifiable conduct. I took a firm hold on this, and set all my power against it. I first proposed a delegation to the Peloponnese[31] after his surreptitious inroad there, then to Euboea, when he got his hands on it, then the expedition to Oreus which was no longer a mere delegation, then to Eretria, when he

29. This incident is not precisely identifiable, but was the excuse for the final declaration of war by Athens (see below, 139, p. 290). It must have been in late 340 B.C.

30. On Hegesippus see on Demosthenes, *Treaty*, 72 and 331 (pp. 74 and 136); on Cephisophon see above, 21, note 10.

31. On the mission to the Peloponnese see above, 45 note 20; the mission to Euboea was in 342 B.C., when Philip was establishing tyrants in Oreus and Eretria (see above, 71), the expeditions which suppressed them being in 341 B.C. See Introduction, p. 40.

established tyrants in the cities there. After this I was responsible for the sending of the forces which saved the Chersonese and Byzantium and our allies there.[32] The result of this for Athens was all that is most estimable, eulogies, high repute, honour, awards and gratitude for benefits conferred. For Philip's victims who accepted Athenian advice the gain was survival, while those who neglected it were rewarded with the constant recollection of warnings given them, and with the opinion not merely of Athenian goodwill, but good sense and foresight, when all these warnings were justified. What Philistides would have given to hold Oreus, or Cleitarchus to hold Euboea, or Philip himself to maintain these positions against Athens without being exposed or taken to task for his other unjustified actions, is known to all, to you as much as anyone. Representatives here from Cleitarchus and Philistides stayed with you, Aeschines. You sponsored them. Athens regarded them as enemies whose claims were as far from her interest as from justice, but they were your friends. None of their proposals was carried out, despite your libellous attacks to the effect that I say nothing when my pocket is full and protest when it is empty.[33] Anyhow that is not your way. You protest all the time and will never come to an end, unless you are put out of court by a condemnation today. So the city awarded me the crown for all this on that prior occasion, when Aristonicus made a proposal which was word for word the same as that of Ctesiphon now, and the award was proclaimed in the Theatre, so that this is now the second announcement of it.[34] Yet at the time Aeschines made no opposition in person, nor brought any indictment against the proposer. Please read the decree.

(The decree of Aristonicus is read.)

Does anyone know of any slur which this decree brought on Athens, any contempt or ridicule, which is what Aeschines asserts

32. These operations were in 341–340 B.C.

33. See Aeschines, *Crown*, 218, p. 248.

34. Demosthenes appears to say that this was the second occasion on which he was publicly crowned. He mentions a third occasion at 222–3 below (pp. 307 ff.), when a crowning was proposed by Demomeles and Hyperides, but this was perhaps not carried out because of the defeat at Chaeronea. At 120 below (p. 285) he speaks of his numerous earlier crownings.

will be the result of a crown awarded to me? It is when actions are newly promulgated and universally known that they come in for gratitude if they are good, or, if otherwise, for retribution. Well, it seems that what I came in for on that occasion was gratitude, not criticism or retribution.

Thus up to the time when these transactions took place the benefit to Athens of my administration has been admitted by the success of my suggestions and proposals in your deliberations, by the execution of the measures proposed; by the award of crowns as a result both to the city and myself and everyone concerned, and by the performance of sacrifice to the gods and thanksgiving processions in honour of their value.

So when Philip was expelled from Euboea by armed force on the part of Athens and as a result of statesmanship and measures of mine – even if my opponents deny it to the point of apoplexy – he looked for another territory to threaten Athens. Observing that we depend more than anyone on imported corn, for the purpose of controlling the corn trade he moved into Thrace, and opened dealings with his allies at Byzantium. He first asked for their assistance in the war against Athens. They refused with the justifiable claim that this was not the object of the alliance. He then raised a stockade, brought up artillery and laid siege to the city. I will not ask what was the duty of Athens at this juncture, because it is obvious to everyone. But where did assistance and rescue for Byzantium come from? Who prevented the Hellespont falling into alien hands at that moment? You yourselves, gentlemen, by which I mean the city of Athens. And who was it who addressed the city,[35] made proposals, took action, and in a word gave himself unsparingly to the task? I myself. The value of this to the world does not need words of mine for proof. Practical experience proves it. The war which then broke out, apart from adding to our reputation, kept us in a higher and cheaper general standard of living than the peace of today, which is carefully maintained by our admirable

35. The extant *Chersonese* and *Third Philippic* were two of Demosthenes' speeches at this time. There is no means of judging the claim to improvement in the standard of living. It is possible that Athenian operations round Byzantium led to an increase of confidence among traders and a reduction in the price of corn.

friends to the detriment of Athens on the basis of future wishes. I hope these will be unfulfilled. I hope these people will participate in what all well-wishers of Athens pray for, and will not impose the results of their own chosen policy. Now please read the list of the crowns bestowed on Athens by Byzantium and Perinthus[36] in recognition of these affairs.

(The decree of Byzantium is read.)

Now the crowns from the Chersonese.

(The decree from the Chersonese is read.)

Thus it was not only the rescue of the Chersonese and Byzantium, nor the preservation of the Hellespont from control by Philip, nor the resulting honour to Athens that was achieved by my public actions and policy, but the universal demonstration of the uprightness of Athens and the dishonesty of Philip. He was publicly exposed in the siege he laid to his own allies at Byzantium, which was as scandalous an outrage as you could find. Athens, on the other hand, might have had much to say against Byzantium for her lack of consideration towards us in the past.[37] Yet not merely did she nurse no grievances; she refused to abandon a maltreated city, appeared as a rescuer, and won glory and goodwill for it in all quarters. The number of crowns awarded by Athens to political leaders is common knowledge. But no one could point to another statesman and orator except myself who has been responsible for a crown conferred on Athens.

Now I want to show that the slanderous statements Aeschines made against Euboea and Byzantium[38] by recalling anything they had done to displease Athens were pure misrepresentation, not solely in being untrue, which I fancy you knew all the time, but also

36. Perinthus, on the north shore of the Propontis (Sea of Marmora), successfully resisted Philip's siege in 340 B.C. before he moved against Byzantium.

37. i.e. the conduct of Byzantium in the Social War (357–355 B.C.). Byzantium had defected from the Second Athenian Confederacy during the Theban naval campaign of 364 B.C., and later assisted the other secessionist allies in the Social War.

38. For Aeschines' attack on leaders in Euboea see *Crown*, 85–93 (pp. 215 ff.). There is no trace in the extant version of an attack on those at Byzantium.

in the fact that however true they might have been my political course was the right one. I therefore propose to describe, quite briefly, one or two of the noble actions of our city. An individual in private and a city in its public capacity are alike, and should always try to follow the noblest path. At a time, then, gentlemen, when Sparta was in command of sea and land alike, and points all round Attica were held by harmosts[39] and garrisons, Euboea, Tanagra, all Boeotia, Megara, Aegina, Ceos[40] and the other islands, when Athens itself was devoid of ships and fortifications, your countrymen made an expedition to Haliartus,[41] and another not much later to Corinth. They might have had strong reasons for a grievance against Corinth and Thebes for the events of the campaign at Decelea.[42] But they did not. Very far from it. On both occasions it was not action taken in aid of benefactors, nor action obviously free from danger. That did not make them abandon the appeal for assistance. For the sake of honour and glory they desired to offer themselves in the face of danger, and it was a right and a noble decision. Beyond life stands death for every man, shut himself as he may in a little cabin to preserve it. And great men should always set themselves to noble action with good hope before them, but endure with nobility what God gives. Such was the action of your ancestors. Such too was that of the oldest of our own generation, who after the Theban victory over Sparta at Leuctra and the threat to destroy her, though Sparta was no friend or benefactor to Athens, but had done her frequent and grievous wrong, yet stood in the way of Thebes.[43] They were unafraid of Theban strength and reputation at that time, unconcerned at the past policies of the men they were befriending at their peril. Indeed these events made it clear to all Greece that in any case of wrong action against Athens

39. After the defeat of Athens in 404 B.C. Sparta, now in control of Greece, suppressed democratic constitutions in favour of narrow oligarchies, which they supported with garrisons and a Spartan governor or 'harmost'.

40. See Appendix, p. 332.

41. The battle of Haliartus in Boeotia (395 B.C.) was the first engagement of the Corinthian War; an invading Spartan army was defeated and its commander, Lysander, killed.

42. The last phase of the Peloponnesian War, from the Spartan fortification of Decelea in Attica (413 B.C.).

43. On the Theban invasion of Laconia in 370–369 B.C. Athens made an alliance with Sparta. The claim to have saved her, however, is exaggerated.

she may in principle retain her resentment at it, but if the wrong-doer is overtaken by danger to life or freedom, Athens will nurse no grievance, take no account of the past.

This was not the only occasion of such an attitude. Again, when Thebes attempted to appropriate Euboea,[44] Athens refused to countenance it. She showed no recollection of the misconduct of Themison and Theodorus in connection with Oropus, but sent assistance to them too, and this was the first instance of volunteer trierarchs, of whom I was one. But of this more later. It was a credit to Athens to have saved Euboea, and a far greater credit that, when she had their lives and their cities in her power, she restored them in accordance with justice to those who had wronged her without reference to the wrong committed, because trust had been placed in her. There are numerous other instances which I omit, campaigns by sea and land both in the past and in our own time carried out by our city for the sake of the life and freedom of the Greek world. When, therefore, in all these events I could see how Athens set out to fight for the interests of others, when it was with her, virtually, that my concern lay, what orders, what advice was I to give her? To remember her grievances and reject the call for help? To look for reasons for betraying the whole position? Every man could rightly have called for my death if I had so much as said a word to tarnish the city's existing honour. No one could have carried it into action, I am sure. Had there been the will to do so, what was there to prevent it? It was feasible, wasn't it? There was support for it in Aeschines and his friends.

I want, then, to return to the subject of my political career immediately after this. Ask yourselves in this context again what was the best course for Athens. I observed, gentlemen, that our navy was falling into decay, that the rich were getting tax immunity on the basis of small payments while owners of moderate or small incomes were losing their money, and in consequence Athens was unable to meet her opportunities. I therefore brought in an

44. In 357 B.C. an attack on Eretria by her neighbours, supported by Thebes, was repelled by Athenian forces under Diocles. In 366 Theodorus and Themison, tyrant of Eretria, had seized Oropus on the border between Attica and Boeotia, and gave it to Thebes. See Demosthenes, *Treaty*, 22 (p. 62), and Aeschines, *Crown*, 85 (p. 215).

act[45] compelling the first group, the rich, to fulfil their obligations, and relieving the troubles of the poor, and, most valuable of all, enabling the country to equip herself at the requisite time. I was met by an indictment of the same kind as this, and came before this court, but was acquitted, and my accuser failed to receive the minimum vote. Yet how much do you think I was offered by leaders of the committees, or members of them in second or third place, to refrain from proposing this law, or, failing that, to let it drop on an affidavit[46] of proceedings? I would hesitate to reveal the figure to you. It was natural on their side. The previous law allowed them to carry out their service as one of a committee of sixteen, involving little or no payment on their part, while they ground the payment out of the poorer citizens. By my law they were required to pay an amount proportionate to property. A man might find himself responsible for two ships, who had previously contributed only a sixteenth part of one, because they were no longer referred to as trierarchs but as contributors. There was no limit to what they were prepared to offer to avoid this enactment and the compulsion to carry out their just obligations. Please read first the decree by which I was brought to court for the indictment, then the rolls of service[47] according to the previous law and according to mine.

(The decree is read.)

Now the old[48] service roll.

(The roll is read.)

Now in comparison with it the roll as it appears in my act.

45. The war tax (*eisphora*), and, since 357 B.C., the trierarchy (see Aeschines, *Crown*, 19, p. 197 and note) had been organized on a system of committees (symmories), whose richer members (leaders) paid the tax, recouping themselves advantageously by exaction from the poorer. In 354 Demosthenes' extant speech *On the Symmories* had proposed a reform, but it was rejected. In 340, when Greece was on the verge of war, he succeeded in passing a new measure for payment in proportion to property assessment. Demosthenes (312 below, p. 327) accuses the rich of bribing Aeschines to oppose this measure. See also Aeschines, *Crown*, 222 (p. 249), and 171 (p. 296) below.

46. The 'affidavit' is a sworn statement of the intention to bring an indictment for illegality.

47. The 'service rolls' presumably showed liability for duty in the trierarchy, whether or not they also showed property assessments.

48. See Appendix, p. 332.

(The roll is read.)

You cannot think it any insignificant assistance that I gave to the poorer citizens, or any insignificant sum the rich would have given to evade their duty. It is not merely on having refused to compromise this issue that I congratulate myself, nor on my acquittal in court, but on having made the law effective and proved it in a test case. Throughout the war naval expeditions were organized in accordance with my law, without any appeal[49] by a trierarch on a claim of excessive exaction in either Athens or Munichia, without an arrest by the supervisory board, without a single ship being either abandoned at sea and lost to the state, or left behind at home as unseaworthy, all of which had happened under the old law. The reason was that then the service depended on the poor, which made for all sorts of difficulties. I made the change from the poor to the rich, and all went well. Indeed, this is another fact meriting praise for me; that my public policy was one which added to the honour and glory and the power of Athens. No policy of mine was ever characterized by malice, antagonism or ill will, nor by any indignity which could demean the city. This is the character which can be shown to have typified my policies both at home and in foreign affairs. At home I did not attempt to secure the wishes of the rich at the expense of the rights of the poor, and abroad I did not pursue enrichment and good relations with Philip at the expense of the common interests of Greece.

It now remains, I think, to discuss the proclamation and the matter of the accounts.[50] The claim to have furthered the interests of Athens, and to have been unfailing and strong in patriotic feeling, has, I think, been sufficiently substantiated in what I have said. And yet the most important item of my political career and achievements I omit in the belief first that I should go straight on to the other arguments on the subject of the actual illegality, and secondly that even if the later part of my career is omitted I shall have behind me the knowledge which exists in the heart of each one of you.

The remarks on the subject of the parallel versions[51] of the law

49. In the form of a suppliant branch on the altar.

50. Demosthenes turns to the specific accusations of illegal procedure made by Aeschines in *Crown*, 11-21 (pp. 195 ff.).

51. See Aeschines, *Crown*, 200, p. 244.

which my opponent brought to such elaborate confusion are of a kind which I really doubt if you could take in. I could not understand most of them myself. But I shall discuss them in a simple and straightforward fashion. I am so far removed from maintaining that I am exempt from an account,[52] as he mendaciously alleged, that I confess I have been subject to it all my life for my administration and policy in Athens. On the other hand for what I have promised and given to the people from my own property I declare that I am not for one moment liable to account – you hear, Aeschines? – nor is anyone else, even if he happens to be one of the nine archons. Has there ever been a law so totally lacking in equity or sympathy that when a man is the donor of a free gift in an act of spontaneous generosity it first deprives him of gratitude, and then brings him before a board of malicious busybodies and gives them a right to exact an account of his gifts? Never. If Aeschines claims that there is, let him prove it, and I will accept it and say no more. But there is no such thing, gentlemen. It is mere malice on the part of Aeschines, because I was in control of the Theoric Fund[53] when I made the gift, so he says, 'Ctesiphon paid him compliments when he was *sub judice*'. The compliments did not refer to matters for which I was *sub judice*, but to the gift I had made. It was pure malice. Then he says I was also commissioner for the repair of the walls. This was another justifiable subject of eulogy, in that I waived my expenses and made no charge for them. The arithmetic of the accounts requires auditors, but a free gift is a right subject for praise. This is the reason for the phrase in Ctesiphon's proposal. That this is a principle established not merely in the law, but in the character of Athens, I can prove from a variety of evidence. First of all Nausicles[54]

52. See Aeschines, *Crown*, 11 and 17, pp. 196 and 197.

53. See on Demosthenes, *Treaty*, 291, p. 127.

54. On Nausicles see Aeschines, *Crown*, 159 (p. 234). Charidemus (see also Aeschines, *Crown*, 77, p. 213) was an adopted Athenian and a leader of mercenaries in the service of Cersobleptes and then of Athens. He and Diotimus are said to have been among the Athenians whose surrender was demanded by Alexander in 335 B.C. Neoptolemus (not the actor of Demosthenes, *Peace*, 6–7, *Greek Political Oratory*, p. 224) is mentioned as a rich man in Demosthenes' speech against Meidias, 215. Frequent proclamations of this sort, including one in honour of Neoptolemus, Charidemus and Nausicles, are corroborated by inscriptions, and, whatever the law, they formed strong precedents.

has often, as general, been crowned for sacrifices he made from his own property. Secondly the presentation of shields by Diotimus, and again by Charidemus, was rewarded with the proposal of a crown. Again, as supervisor of a number of public works, Neoptolemus has been commended for his generosity. It would be intolerable that the holder of office should be forbidden to present his own property to the state for the purposes of his office, or that instead of winning gratitude for his gift he should be subject to an account of it. In proof of the truth of my statement please read the actual text of the decrees passed in these instances.

(The decrees are read.)

Each of these, Aeschines, was subject to an account for the office he held, but not for action which had won him a crown. Therefore the same applies to me. Presumably justice demands the same for me in the same circumstances as theirs. I made the gift, and I win praise for it, because I am not subject to account for it. I also held office and I have undergone an account for that, but not for the gifts I made. Perhaps I am supposed to have misconducted the office. In that case why did you not make the accusation when the auditors dealt with the case?

Now to prove to you that he himself affords me evidence that the crown has been awarded me for actions which are not subject to account, please take the whole decree of the award, and read it. Those items in the text which he did not indict will prove the vexatious nature of the charges he does bring.

(The decree is read.)

So the gifts I made are not included in the indictment, but the reward the council saw fit to make for them is what you sue me for. You admit the legality of receiving what is given one, but gratitude for it you indict for illegality. I ask you, where is one to find an example of thoroughgoing unpleasantness and intolerable malice, if not in a man like Aeschines?

As regards the proclamation in the Theatre I say nothing of the hundreds of previous instances of such proclamations, and of a number made to me.[55] But I do ask you, Aeschines, if you are really

55. See on 83 above, p. 277, and note.

so devoid of feeling and understanding as to be unable to grasp that for the recipient a crown brings the same satisfaction wherever it is proclaimed and it is for the benefit of the makers of the presentation that it takes place in the Theatre. Everyone in the audience is stimulated to patriotic action, and is more concerned to acclaim the givers than the receiver of the award. That is why our city has enacted this law. Read the text of the law, please.

(The law is read.)

You hear the words of the law, Aeschines, which state quite clearly: 'Except in the case of any decree of the People or of the Council. For these the proclamation may be made.' So why did you go on with this malicious prosecution, with these fabrications? What you need is a dose of hellebore.[56] Are you not ashamed of entering a suit on a basis of spite instead of for any kind of offence committed, and manipulating laws and obliterating parts of them, when they ought to be read in their entirety in view of the jury's oath to vote in accordance with the law?

Then after this you give a description of the character of the popular statesman, as though you had made a contract for a statue and failed to receive all the items contracted for, or as though popular statesmen were to be recognized by a specification instead of by action and policy. And then you let out a string of vociferations, proper and improper, as if you were on a cart at the festival, in a style appropriate to you and your kind, but not to me.[57] However, I may add, gentlemen, that I make this distinction between accusation and vituperation: accusation concerns offences for which the law assigns penalties, while vituperation is a matter of abuse uttered by personal enemies in accordance with the chance dictates of nature. I take it that these courts were built by our ancestors not to enable us to use unspeakable language in private

---

56. Goodwin argues (pp. 313–16) that this contemptuous trump card from Demosthenes cannot be a reply to the tortuous argument of Aeschines, *Crown*, 34–48 (pp. 202 ff.), and suggests that the latter is an addition in Aeschines' published version designed to counter this claim by Demosthenes. See Introduction, p. 15. Hellebore was supposed to cure madness.

57. On the popular statesman see Aeschines, *Crown*, 168 ff., pp. 236 ff. Ribald abuse was a feature of some of the festival processions.

dealings, but to convict the guilty of misconduct against the state. Aeschines knows this as well as I do, but none the less preferred abuse to accusation. All the same, even here he does not deserve to get away with less than he gave. I shall go on to this later, with just one question for the moment. Are you supposed, Aeschines, to be an enemy to myself or to the state? Obviously to myself. Why then do you leave aside the verdict which, if I were in the wrong, you could get against me over this affair by means of the accounts, the normal forms of indictment or other procedures? Yet you attack me where I am entirely impregnable by reason of the law, of the lapse of time and the statute of limitations,[58] and because I have undergone frequent judgment before without a single conviction for any offence against the state, while, on the contrary, it has been more or less inevitable that the state has shared the reputation of actions which have been public policy. So you may well prove to be the enemy of the state, and only masquerading as mine.

However, the way of religion and justice towards the vote in this case has been clearly indicated, and, much as I dislike abuse, I am compelled by the misrepresentations made by Aeschines to counter a large quantity of lies by including the bare truth about him, and to make clear the character and the origins of a man who enters so lightly on evil language in his attack on certain expressions of mine, although he has given vent to so much himself which no decent person would utter for the world. If the accuser were Aeacus, Rhadamanthys or Minos[59] instead of a miserable gossiping pen-pusher, a mere hack of the market-place, I don't think he would use such language or so offensive a vocabulary as Aeschines does with his theatrical exclamations to 'earth and sun and virtue', his invocation of 'intelligence and education, which enables us to distinguish good from evil'. No doubt you heard that remark of his. What has such scum as this to do with virtue, he or his like? What distinction can he draw between such things as good and bad? What criterion can he lay claim to? What right has he to talk about education? Anyone really in possession of it would not use such expressions about himself, but blush to hear them on the lips of others,

58. After a stated lapse of time a defendant was no longer liable to an action.
59. The judges of the dead. See e.g. Plato, *Gorgias*, 523 e. On Aeschines' exclamations see *Crown*, 260, p. 258.

though the kind of people who have never had it, like him, but lay crude claim to it, finish only by agonizing their audience when they speak, instead of appearing educated.

I have no shortage of material[60] to use about you, Aeschines. I only hesitate where to begin – with the fact that your father, Tromes, was a slave in the service of Elpias, the schoolmaster by the Theseum, and was to be seen in shackles and a wooden collar? Or how your mother practised the rites of union at all times of day in the hut next to the bone-setter's, and brought you up, her picture of perfection, to become a born third actor? Everyone knows this, whether I mention it or not. Or how she was saved from this distinguished profession by Phormio, the bosun slave of Dio of Phrearrii? But I give you my word I am afraid that in describing you as you deserve I may give the impression of choosing a subject that is beneath me. I will leave it, and embark on that of his own way of life, which was no ordinary proceeding but one to merit official condemnation. Somewhat late in the day – indeed only recently – he had become an Athenian and an orator, and by adding a couple of syllables turned his father from Tromes to Atrometus, while he gave his mother the imposing name of Glaucothea, though everyone knew she was referred to as Empusa,[61] an appellation obviously derived from an unlimited variety of experiences, active and passive. This must be its origin. However, you are so ungrateful, so naturally depraved, that despite your transformation by the gentlemen of this court from slave to free, and from poor to rich, you were so far from thanking them as to hire yourself for political activity against them. The occasions which afford him a possible claim of having spoken in support of Athens I pass over, and recall those actions by which he is clearly proved to have served her enemies.

60. For detailed scholarship on these obscure vituperations students should consult the editors of the speech. It is enough here to point out the contrasts between Demosthenes' account here of Aeschines' father and mother, the account he gave in 343 B.C. (*Treaty*, 199, 249, pp. 104 and 116) when they were still alive, and the account given by Aeschines (*Treaty*, 147, *Crown*, 191, pp. 147 and 242) to see the effects of allowing irrelevant and personal considerations to carry weight in a suit of this kind.

61. A hobgoblin remarkable for assuming various shapes (see Aristophanes, *Frogs*, 288 ff.).

Everyone knows the story of Antiphon, who was struck off the citizen roll,[62] made Philip an undertaking to set fire to the docks, and arrived in Athens for the purpose. I caught him in hiding at the Peiraeus and brought him before the Assembly, but Aeschines out of sheer malice set up a loud outcry about my scandalous and undemocratic conduct in maltreating citizens who had fallen on evil days, and invading their houses without a warrant, and got him released. Had not the Areopagus got wind of the affair and realized how regrettable the general ignorance about it was, and so made a search for the man and brought him back into court, an individual like that would have been whisked away by our impressive orator, and would have slipped out of the hands of justice and escaped. As it was, he was put on the rack and executed, which should have been the fate of Aeschines as well. The Areopagus realized the fault had been his, and when the vote for a speaker at the temple of Delos[63] was given to him by the sort of unintelligence which has so often dogged public affairs, as they were appointed to control the festival, they dismissed him as a traitor, and allotted the honour to Hyperides. This was done by a vote from the altar, and this disreputable individual was not awarded a single vote. Please call the witnesses to attest the truth of this.

(The witnesses are called.)

Thus by dismissing him from speaking, and entrusting the task to someone else, the Council exposed him as a traitor and an enemy. There is one of our hero's political achievements. It resembles his accusations against me, doesn't it? Let me remind you of another. When Philip sent Pytho of Byzantium to Athens[64] together with a Macedonian delegation with the aim of bringing discredit on Athens and putting us in the wrong, Pytho put on a confident performance, and was in full flow attacking us when I refused to tolerate it, and

62. Probably at the general revision of the citizen lists carried out at Athens in 346–345 B.C.

63. In 343 B.C. Delos contested the claim of Athens to the temple of Apollo at Delos, and Aeschines' election to speak for Athens in the ensuing case before the Amphictyonic Council was set aside in favour of Hyperides, who won the case.

64. This mission, also in 343 B.C., was intended to assure Athens of Philip's friendship. See Introduction, pp. 38–9.

stood up and spoke in opposition instead of betraying the rights of Athens. I proved Philip so clearly in the wrong that his own allies rose and agreed. Aeschines, on the other hand, took Philip's part and put forward evidence against Athens, and false evidence at that.

Even that was not enough. Again later he was caught in an assignation with a spy, Anaxinus,[65] at Thraso's house. A man who had a secret meeting and conversation with a spy sent by the enemy was proved in his own character a spy and an enemy to his country. Please call the evidence to the truth of my statement.

(The evidence is read.)

There are thousands of other incidents about him which I could mention, but which I leave out. The fact is that there are numerous occasions which I could point to at that period, when he was discovered aiding the enemy and bringing malicious attacks against me. These things are not retained accurately in the memory, or treated with the indignation they deserve. You have a bad habit of allowing a lot of licence to attempts to trip up or misrepresent anyone who speaks in the interest of Athens. You enjoy the amusement occasioned by abuse in exchange for maintaining the interest of the country. This is the reason why it is easier and safer to earn pay in the service of the enemy than to take a stand in the ranks of patriotism.

Open association with Philip before the war was, heaven knows, a sufficiently damnable means of attack on this country. But allow him that, if you like, let it be. But after the open plunder of the ships,[66] when the ravage of the Chersonese was in progress and Philip was moving against Attica, and the position admitted of no doubt that war had begun, neither malice nor a diet of tragic verse can show a single thing he ever did for Athens. There is not a single decree in the Athenian interest in the name of Aeschines. If he claims any, let him display it, and use my time allowance. But there is none. He is in a dilemma. Either it is because he had no criticism to make of my actions that he made no contrary proposals, or it is because he was acting in the interest of the enemy that he offered nothing better.

65. See Aeschines, *Crown*, 223, p. 250.
66. See above, 72, p. 276.

When he had mischief afoot, he proposed no motions. Are we to suppose he made no speeches either? By no means. No one else could get in a word. To some extent, apparently, Athens tolerated it, and his actions went unnoticed. But there was one crowning act, gentlemen, which put the cap on all the rest, when he expended a vast amount of oratory in discussing the decrees of Amphissa,[67] in an attempt to distort the truth. But this occasion was beyond him. He will never obliterate that story. No words will do that.

I call upon every pledge most sacred to Athens, I call also upon our patron god, Pythian Apollo, and pray that if I speak the truth to you, and spoke it there and then to the People immediately I saw what this abominable character was up to – I grasped it, I grasped it soon enough – they will accord me good fortune and success; but if enmity or private rivalry induces me to lay a false charge against him, I may be left without benefit of all their bounty. What is the object of this invocation and of all the intensity with which I make it? The reason is that, although I have documentary proof in the public records and though I know you remember the facts, I am afraid that Aeschines may be thought incapable of the damage he inflicted on Athens. That is what happened before, when he caused the destruction of the unhappy people of Phocis by giving false information here. As to the war in Amphissa, which led to Philip's entry to Elatea[68] and to the appointment as leader of the Amphictyons of the man who overthrew the whole of Greece, it was Aeschines who contrived it, and caused greater disasters than any individual has ever caused. I at once protested in the Assembly[69] with all the power in my lungs: 'It means war in Attica, Aeschines, a war of all the Amphictyonic states.' But his packed supporters refused to allow me to speak, while others were astonished and assumed that it was an empty accusation based on personal enmity on my part. The real character of the affair, and the reason why, and the way in which it was contrived, is what I want you to listen to,

67. On the affair of Amphissa see Aeschines, *Crown*, 106–31 (pp. 220 ff.).
68. On the importance of Elatea see Aeschines, *Crown*, 140 ff. (pp. 228 ff.).
69. Aeschines' version of this meeting, which is very different, is at *Crown*, 125–6 (pp. 224 ff.). It seems that after Aeschines had received a favourable hearing Demosthenes persuaded the Assembly to send no representatives to the additional Amphictyonic meeting at Thermopylae, the implications of which he realized.

since you were prevented from doing so then. You will see it as a deliberately organized business, and it will aid your understanding of public affairs, when you contemplate the cleverness of Philip.

Philip could see no end or escape from war with Athens unless he could bring Thebes and Thessaly into conflict with her. However unfortunate or unskilful Athenian generals proved against him,[70] the war itself and the privateers did him considerable damage. He was not getting exports out from his country, nor obtaining necessary imports. He had not supremacy over Athens at sea, and could not approach Attica, unless he was either reinforced from Thessaly or allowed through by Thebes. The result was that though he was successful in the war against our generals – such as they were, but I say nothing about that – the geographical and the general situation on either side caused him considerable distress. Thus if he could help to induce Thessaly or Thebes to move against Athens for reasons of their own, he reckoned to avoid general attention. And if he could use pretexts of their making to get himself put at the head of affairs, it would be easier to use deception or persuasion as the case might be. So what did he do? He attempted[71] – you can see how successfully – to engineer a war among the Amphictyonic states, and confusion in connection with the meeting at Thermopylae. This was the situation which would put them in the most immediate need of his assistance.

Now if this were introduced by his own Remembrancers[72] or those of any of his allies, it would rouse suspicion in Thebes and Thessaly who would be on their guard, but if the responsibility could lie with an Athenian and an opponent of his, it would be easy to conceal – which is what happened. How did he manage it? He bribed Aeschines. No one, I imagine, foresaw what was happening, or took any precautions. That is the normal way at Athens. Aeschines was proposed as a member of the Amphictyonic as-

70. i.e. in 340 B.C. Inscriptions show Chares in command of a fleet in 341–340 and Phocion in 340–339, and both are connected by the literary sources with the defence of Byzantium in 340–339. It is not clear where Athenian commanders subsequently engaged Philip's forces.

71. Demosthenes' analysis of Philip's policy and motives is probably based on nothing more than his observation of what actually happened. See Introduction, pp. 43–4.

72. See Aeschines, *Treaty*, 116, note 67.

sembly, three or four hands went up, and he was elected. As soon as he was invested with the dignity of Athens and joined the assembly, he let everything else go by the board and proceeded to the business he had been hired to perform. He had only to put together a few plausible arguments and stories[73] about the consecration of the plain of Cirrha and dwell on them to persuade an inexperienced, unthinking body like the Remembrancers to vote a formal circuit of the territory which the people of Amphissa claimed to be farming as their own land, but Aeschines declared was sacred. Locris had no summons against us, nor anything to accord with Aeschines' pretext,[74] which is untrue. Here is the evidence. Locris was not in a position to proceed against us without serving a summons. Well, who witnessed it? Before what authority was it done? Tell me who knows the answer, and let's see him. You cannot, you are making an empty, false pretence. Anyhow, the Amphictyons went ahead with their circuit under the leadership of Aeschines, until the Locrians fell on them and were within an ace of shooting them down, and did actually arrest some of the Remembrancers. Complaints arose from the incident, and first of all Cottyphus[75] raised an army from the Amphictyonic states. But as some of them did not appear, and others, who did, took no action, a vote was at once passed by men of established bad character from Thessaly and elsewhere, who had been organized for the purpose, that Philip should be accorded the leadership at the next meeting of the League. They offered plausible pretexts. Either war contributions must be paid, mercenaries hired, and any failure to do so penalized, or else Philip must be elected. To cut a long story short, he was elected as a result. After that he at once collected a force and made a pretence of marching[76] to the plain of Cirrha, but then abandoned all concern with Cirrha and Locris, and seized Elatea. Had there not been a change of heart in Thebes at this in favour of Athens, the whole torrent would have descended on this country. As it was, Thebes exercised a momentary check, for which, gentlemen, we have principally the will of heaven to thank for favour towards Athens; but in addition, if

73. See Aeschines, *Crown*, 118–21 (p. 223).
74. i.e. at *Crown*, 117 and 123 ff. (pp. 222 and 224).
75. See Aeschines, *Crown*, 124 (p. 224).
76. i.e. try the route west of Thermopylae. See Introduction, p. 44.

credit can be given to any single individual it is to me. Please produce the Amphictyonic decrees and the list of dates of these events, as an indication of the extent of the trouble stirred up by this unprincipled person without his being penalized for it. Read them.

(Decrees of the Amphictyons are read.)

Now read the list of dates of these events. They cover the period of Aeschines' membership of the Amphictyonic congress.

(The dates are read.)

Now give us the letter sent by Philip to his allies in the Peloponnese,[77] when Thebes refused to submit. This will help to show clearly how the true facts (that his actions were designed against Greece and against Thebes and Athens) were masked by the pretext of a general decision of the Amphictyonic states. And the man who provided Philip with the means to this and the pretext for it was Aeschines. Read it, please.

(The letter is read.)

You observe that he avoids offering personal pretexts, and takes refuge in those arising from Amphictyonic affairs. Well, who was it who helped him produce them? Who provided these pretexts? Who is the prime cause of all the disasters that took place? It is Aeschines. Don't go about with the story that it is at one man's door[78] alone that all the miseries of Greece are to be laid. Not one, but many have been the traitors in every state, heaven knows. But he is one of them, and if one is to speak the truth without caution, I would not hesitate to put him down as the common plague which has infected all that has since been ruined, men, districts and cities. The sower of the seed must be blamed for the crop. How Athens failed to turn from him at the first glance I greatly wonder. Except that there seems to be a thick haze between her and the truth.

In touching on his activities against Athens I now find it relevant to mention my own action in opposition to them. There are many reasons to urge you to listen to this, and particularly, gentlemen, the slur it would be, when I have the labour of action on your

77. Probably Messene, Elis and Argos.
78. i.e. Philip's.

behalf, that you should refuse to tolerate the account of it. I observed that Thebes and to some extent Athens herself were being induced by Philip's supporters, and by the victims of his corruption in both states, to overlook the principal cause of alarm, Philip's unhampered expansion, which called for strong precautions in both cities. Instead of any such precautions, both were ready to turn to mutual hostility and conflict. I therefore continued to guard against this situation. I did not depend solely on my own opinion for the view that this was valuable. I knew that Aristophon and Eubulus[79] desired throughout to bring about this friendship, and that, frequent as were their differences in other respects, they were always at one in this. In their lifetime you followed them with your flattery, like the reptile you are, but after their death you attacked them unwittingly; for your criticism of me on the subject of Thebes is a far greater criticism of them, since their approval of the alliance was earlier than mine. But, to return, my point is that as soon as, the war over, Amphissa had been provoked by Aeschines, and his accomplices had helped to fan our antagonism against Thebes, what happened next was Philip's attack on us, which had been the object of bringing the two states into enmity. And if we had not roused ourselves in time, we could never have recovered. This was the point to which things had been brought. The feeling that existed between the two cities can be judged from these decrees and replies. Take them and read them, please.

(The decrees are read.)
Now read the replies.

(The replies are read.)

Such were the relations to which Philip brought the Greek cities. These were his assistants, and it was these decrees and replies which spurred him to action. He came down in force and seized Elatea on the assumption that whatever happened there would never be accord between Athens and Thebes. The commotion which then

79. Aristophon is said by Aeschines (*Crown*, 139, p. 228) to have led a diplomatic mission to Thebes; on Eubulus see Introduction, p. 22 ff. The friendship here referred to is that between Athens and Thebes during the supremacy of Sparta, 378–371 B.C.

took place in Athens is something you all remember. But I would like you to hear the barest outline of it.

It was evening you remember. Suddenly news was brought to the Prytaneis[80] of the capture of Elatea. At this they got up in the middle of dinner, and started at once to drive people away from the stalls in the market-place and open the wicker fences. Others proposed to summon the strategi and called for the herald. The city was in chaos. At dawn next day the Prytaneis called the Council to the Chamber, and citizens moved into the Assembly, where, before the Council could conclude their business and prepare a draft, the whole People was already seated on the hill. The Council appeared, announced the news they had received, and brought forward their informant to repeat it. The herald then voiced the question, 'Who desires to speak?' No one moved. The question was repeated several times without a man standing up, though all the strategi were there, all the orators, and the voice of Athens called for a word to save her. For the voice of the herald, uttered in accordance with law, must be regarded as the voice of the country. Yet if the response should have come from all who wish for the safety of Athens, every man of you, every Athenian would have risen and moved to the platform. You all desired her safety, I know. If it was a call to the wealthy, it should have been to the Three Hundred.[81] If the call was both to patriotism and to wealth, it should have been to those people who later made large extra contributions, which was proof of patriotism and of wealth. But it appeared that that moment and occasion demanded not merely patriotic feeling and wealth, but familiarity with public affairs from the beginning and a right judgement of Philip's aims and motives. Without that knowledge, without that deep study, even patriotism and wealth were no more likely to know what policy to take and what advice to give. I therefore was

80. The Prytaneis (see Demosthenes, *Treaty*, 190, p. 102, and Aeschines, *Crown*, 4, note 2, p. 194) would have been the first to receive the news. They dined together in the so-called Tholos. Their immediate aim seems to have been to clear the way from the market-place to the Pnyx. This accords with a scholiast's note on Aristophanes, *Acharnians*, 22, which deals with measures to bring people into the Assembly on important occasions. But see Appendix, p. 332.

81. The Three Hundred are the richer members of the state. See Aeschines, *Crown*, 222, note 127, and Demosthenes, *Crown*, 102–4, note 45 above.

the man who showed such capacity that day. I came forward and addressed the Assembly. And for two reasons I want you to listen with attention to what I said. The first is that you should realize that of all the speakers and politicians I alone refused to abandon the ranks of patriotism in the hour of danger. In what I said and the motions I proposed I was proved right in pursuing the country's interest at the moment of peril. The second reason is my hope that without spending much time you may take a long step forward in knowledge of the whole range of politics for the future.

What I said was this.[82] 'This extreme commotion in the belief that Thebes is firmly in Philip's camp is, I believe, a misapprehension. I am quite sure that if this were in fact the case the news would not be of his capture of Elatea but of his presence on our borders. That he has come to arrange Theban affairs to his liking, I am quite certain. But let me tell you the true position,' I said. 'He has already secured to himself every man in Thebes he could bribe or mislead. The party originally in opposition to him are still against him, and he cannot overcome this. What is his aim, then? What is the object of his capture of Elatea? By a display of his force close at hand, and a demonstration of his power, he aims to rouse his friends to martial eagerness, and intimidate his opponents into making or being forced to make concessions they do not want. If then,' I said, 'our policy at this moment is to keep in our memory anything done by Thebes to cause us irritation, and to distrust her people and rank them with our enemies, first of all we shall be answering Philip's prayers, and secondly I am afraid that he will be accepted by his present opponents, who will join his party with one accord, and both groups will descend alike upon Attica. If you follow my advice, however, and apply yourselves to the question without seeking to make debating points, I think it will appear that my proposal is right and will serve to disperse our impending danger. What then is the proposal? First a relaxation of your present fears, then a change to fear for the people of Thebes. They are far nearer than we are to danger. It threatens them first. I further

---

82. This may be an actual quotation from a published speech which we no longer have. The practice of publishing speeches made in the Assembly was perhaps begun by Demosthenes. See George Kennedy, *The Art of Persuasion in Greece*, p. 205.

urge a march to Eleusis of all men of military age, together with
cavalry, as a general demonstration that we are mobilized. It will
allow our supporters at Thebes freedom to speak their minds in
defence of right, because they will see that, though the traitors who
sold their country to Philip have a force to back them at Elatea, yet
the cause of freedom has in you ready helpers against aggression.
Next I urge the appointment of ten representatives to share with
the generals the decision of the moment to move and of the march
itself. As to the proceedings of these representatives on reaching
Thebes, please take careful note. They must make no demands of
Thebes – honour forbids this – but an offer to come to their aid at
command, since in their extreme danger our provision has been
better than theirs. Then if they accept and accede to our proposal,
we shall have accomplished our aims, and acted in a manner to
maintain the honour of Athens. If we are denied success, they will
have themselves to blame for the mistake they will be making, and
this country will have no action to her name which can dishonour
or demean her.'

This, in effect, was what I said. I then sat down. There was universal applause, not a sound of dissent. And I did not speak without
proposing a motion. I did not propose a motion and decline to
serve as a delegate. I did not take part in the delegation and fail to
win Thebes to my view. I went straight on from start to finish,
giving myself entirely to the service of Athens in her hour of
besetting danger. Now please bring me the decree which was then
passed.

I ask you, Aeschines, what figure you would assign to yourself
on that day, and what to me. You would like to give me the title of
your insulting and abusive tongue, the word 'pansy',[83] and yourself
that of a hero, but no ordinary one, a stage hero, Cresphontes or
Creon or the one you murdered in such lamentable fashion at
Collytus, Oenomaus. Well, on that occasion the pansy of Paeania
was proved of greater worth to his country than the Oenomaus of

83. For this see Aeschines, *Treaty*, 99, and Appendix, p. 331. Cresphontes
was the name of a play by Euripides; see Aristotle, *Poetics*, 1445. On Creon
see Demosthenes, *Treaty*, 247 (p. 114). Oenomaus is the name part in a
play of Sophocles; Aeschines is supposed to have fallen on the stage in
performing it (see also below, 242, p. 311). Plays were performed in the deme
Collytus in the lesser Dionysia festival.

Cothocidae. You were of no value in any respect. I did all that a citizen should. Read the decree, please.

(The decree of Demosthenes is read.)[84]

Such was the beginning and the basis of that association with Thebes, since previous relations had been undermined and reduced to dislike and distrust by Aeschines' party. This decree caused the cloud of danger which hung over this country to pass away. It now became the duty of a good citizen to indicate any improvement he could offer – instead of adverse criticism. The true and the false politician are distinct enough in other respects, but their difference is greatest of all in this. The first gives his view before the event, and makes himself responsible to his supporters, to chance, to the trend of circumstance, to all and sundry. The other says nothing when words are needed, and makes the most of any untoward occurrence. That was an occasion for thought in the interests of Athens and of right. And I go to this length, that, if any man can now point to a better course, indeed if any alternative policy to mine existed, I will own myself wrong. If any course has now become apparent which would have been better, I declare that I ought not to have failed to find it. But if there neither is nor was nor could be such a course which anyone could suggest even today, what was the duty of our true statesman? Was it not his duty to see what lay open to him, what was feasible, and choose the best he could? That is what I did. The herald's question, Aeschines, was, 'Who desires to speak?' not 'Who desires to make accusations about the past?' or, 'Who desires to give guarantees of the future?' You sat silent in the Assembly on those occasions, while I rose and spoke. However, point to the truth now, since you refused before. Tell us what idea which should have been forthcoming, what valuable opportunity for Athens I left untried. What alliance, what negotiation was there to which I should have pointed the way?

However, the past is always finished and done with, and no one wants deliberations about it. It is the future and the present which demand the statesman's part. On that occasion part of the danger

84. The long decree included in the text at this point and now known to be a forgery can only be considered in the light of what Demosthenes says above (178 ff., pp. 298 ff.) and Aeschines' criticism in *Crown*, 141 ff. (pp. 229 ff.).

belonged to the future, as it then appeared, part to the immediate present. Those are the realms in regard to which you must consider my policy, instead of complaining of the past. The end is the will of destiny in every case. It is the policy in itself which shows the mind of the statesman. Do not put it down to my fault that victory in the battle fell to Philip. The conclusion was in the gods' hands, not mine. But failure to try all human possibilities and to carry them out to the full with all due care and energy even beyond my strength, failure to initiate actions that were to the honour and credit of Athens – that is what you have to prove against me, and only after that to bring accusations. If the tornado which then arose proved too much not only for us, but for the whole of Greece, what help have we? It is as though a ship's owner who has taken all precautions for the safety of his ship and equipped her against all foreseeable risk should then, when he has run into a storm and had his gear dislocated or smashed to pieces, be accused of the shipwreck. 'I was not at the wheel,' he would say, just as I too did not command in the field, 'and I did not rule fortune, but she was ruler of all.'

Consider a further point. If despite the alliance of Theban arms with ours fate ordained that we should fare as we did in the struggle, what could have been expected, had we had no such assistance, had it gone to swell the ranks of Philip, in whose behalf all Aeschines' oratory was expended? Again, if after a battle at three days' distance from Attica such peril and such panic beset Athens, what could have been expected if this disaster had fallen somewhere in Attica itself? Do you realize, Aeschines, that, as it was, those three days gave Athens time to stand, to rally, to breathe, a great deal of the means to safety, but otherwise – one cannot describe events which were saved from happening by providence and by the shield of this alliance which you condemn.

All this, all these long discussions, are addressed to you, gentlemen of the jury, and to the audience outside the bar of the court.[85] So far as concerns this despicable individual, I could be content with one short, clear argument. If, Aeschines, the future was clear

85. Spectators were allowed to attend outside the wooden barriers (cf. Aristophanes, *Wasps*, 552), and there would have been a great many there for a case of this importance. See Aeschines, *Crown*, 56, p. 207.

to you alone when these affairs were under discussion in Athens, you should have enunciated it at the time. If you did not foresee it, you can be charged with the same failure as everyone else. So why should you accuse me rather than I you? I have proved a better citizen of Athens than you in regard to this affair – I go no further than that for the moment – in so far as I gave myself to the country's interest without flinching at personal danger or giving it a thought, while you had no better policy to offer – or we should not have followed mine – nor any useful action to pursue in regard to it, but instead you were convicted by the facts of taking the way of bitterest hostility and damage to Athens. At one and the same moment Aristratus in Naxos and Aristolaus in Thasos,[86] the out-and-out enemies of Athens, bring her friends to judgment, and at Athens Aeschines accuses Demosthenes. But a man who made capital out of the misfortunes of Greece to increase his fame should be rewarded with his own death rather than bring accusation on others. And a man whose best opportunities of success have always coincided with those of his country's enemies cannot be a patriot. You are betrayed by your life, your actions, your policy – and your lack of policy. Is some activity beneficial to Athens in progress? Not a word from Aeschines. Is there some obstruction, something that has gone amiss? At once Aeschines is to the fore. He is like an old fracture or a sprain, which is affected in moments of illness anywhere in the body.

But as he lays such stress on past events, I want to say something paradoxical. I most solemnly assure you that I hope it will not seem an extreme statement designed merely to cause astonishment, but will be looked at with understanding. If anyone could have foreseen the future, if they had had foreknowledge of it, if you had foretold it, Aeschines, and protested with all the power in your lungs instead of not uttering a sound, it would still have been wrong for Athens to abandon this course, if she had any thought for her fame, for her ancestry, for the age to come. For the moment her fortunes stand low, which is the common fate of all men, when heaven so wills. But after her past claims to the leadership of Greece, had she abandoned them to Philip, she would have been open to the charge of having betrayed the world. Had she thrown

86. The facts here are unknown.

away her position without a struggle, the position for which her ancestors braved every danger, what man is there who would not have cast contempt – on you, not on Athens nor on me? And how, I ask, could we have borne to look in the face of newcomers to Athens if affairs had taken their present turn, if Philip had been elected to control all Greece,[87] and the struggle to prevent it had been in other hands than ours, when never in the past had Athens preferred safety with infamy to danger and glory? Is there a man in Greece or outside it who does not know that Thebes, or the previous power, Sparta, or the King of Persia would gladly and gratefully have granted Athens the bargain that she should take what she liked and keep her own possessions as the price of acquiescence in acknowledging another leader of the Greeks. But this was not in her blood, nor in her competence nor in her nature. None could ever persuade her at any time to join herself to the cause of strength without right, or gain safety at the cost of slavery. In the struggle for the highest crown of honour and glory she has lived with danger all her days. We regard this with such pride, we feel it as so fitting to the character of our country, that we heap the highest praise on the generations who maintained it. And that is right. Who could fail to admire the bravery of men who agreed to leave country and city and take to the ships, to avoid submission to another power, who gave the highest command to the author of this policy, Themistocles, and stoned Cyrsilus for the proposal to yield and obey? And not only he himself suffered this fate, but his wife too at the hands of Athenian women.[88] Athenians of that day looked for no speaker, no leader who should secure them slavery with comfort. They did not even ask for life, unless freedom could be coupled with it. Every man of them believed he was born not to his father and mother alone, but to his

87. The settlement of Greece organized by Philip after his victory at Chaeronea provided for a *synhedrion* to decide on action by the signatories in defence of the peace and for a *hegemon* to be appointed to lead in any action. Philip was then elected *hegemon*, and subsequently appointed commanding general of the Greek army which was to attack Persia (see Ryder, *Koine Eirene*, pp. 102 ff.).

88. It appears from Herodotus (IX, 4) that this story properly belongs to the period before the battle of Plataea in 479 B.C., although there the victim's name is Lycidas.

country. Where is the difference? It is in this, that one who believes himself born to parents alone waits for the death that is fated to come of itself, but one who is born to his country also will be willing to die to avoid seeing her in slavery, will think the insult and dishonour which follow of necessity with slavery more to be feared than death.

If I set out to say that I raised Athens to a spirit worthy of past generations, I should rightly incur universal disapproval. But in fact I am declaring that these policies have been her policies, I am pointing out that before my day this was her spirit, though the service of putting it into practice in public affairs is something in which I too have had a part. But Aeschines makes general accusations, and urges you to ill-feeling against me, as the cause of anxiety and danger to Athens, and in his desire to rend immediate honour from me will deprive you of the lasting eulogies of future generations. If you condemn Ctesiphon on the ground that my policies were ill conceived, it will be thought that you too are wrong-doers, not victims of the cruelty of fortune. But it is impossible, gentlemen, impossible that you were wrong in shouldering the dangers and protecting the safety and liberty of the Greek world. I call to memory the ancestors who faced danger before your day at Marathon, the men who fought at Plataea, the men who manned the ships at Salamis and Artemisium, and the many others who lie in places publicly dedicated to the heroic dead, whom our city thought deserving of the same honour, all of them alike, and gave them burial – not the successful or the victorious alone. And with justice. The work of noble men was done by all alike. But they met the fate which destiny allotted to each.

And you, Aeschines, who are nothing but a damned lawyer's clerk, you seek to wrest from me the honour and good wishes I have earned in Athens by talking about the victories and battles of past days. What have they to do with this present case? You were a performer, and a third-class one. I stood ready to advise the state on matters of supreme importance. When I spoke, what spirit should I have carried with me to the platform? That of an orator whose text would disgrace the country? If so, I should have deserved execution. Even you, gentlemen of the jury, should not adopt the same attitude of mind in your judgment of private cases as of public ones. You should consider the contracts of common life in the light of private enactments and actions, but for the principles of public policy you must regard the values set by your ancestors. With your staff and ticket of office[89] you should each of you feel that he carries with him the spirit of Athens, when you enter on cases of public import, if you believe it your duty to match your actions with them.

However, in entering upon the achievements of previous generations I have omitted certain decrees that were passed and actions that were taken. So I must return to the point from which I digressed.

When we arrived at Thebes, we found representatives from Philip, from Thessaly and his other allies already there. We found our supporters in a state of apprehension, theirs of confidence. But to prove that it is not my own advantage which leads me to make this point, please read the letter sent by our delegation. None the less, such is Aeschines' capacity for malicious accusation that anything valuable that was done is ascribed to circumstances, not to me, while everything of the opposite kind is put down to me and my unlucky star.[90] He thinks, apparently, that I, as adviser and spokesman, had no part in the effect of words and deliberations, but am wholly responsible for the failures of military action and strategy. Could anyone go further in sheer, cold-blooded, damnable misrepresentation? Read the letter.

(The letter is read.)

When the meeting was convened, they began by calling Philip's representatives, because they ranked as allies. Their speech contained a great deal of eulogy of Philip and indictment of Athens with reminders of every instance of Athenian opposition to Thebes. The sum of it all was a demand that Thebes should show gratitude for favours at Philip's hands and retaliate for wrongs suffered at ours, and either allow them to pass into Attica or themselves join in the invasion. It was by way of a demonstration that

89. The staff showed which court to go to, and the ticket entitled the juror to his day's pay.

90. See Aeschines, *Crown*, 157 (p. 233), and Demosthenes 252–5 below (pp. 313 ff.).

acceptance of their advice would lead to bringing cattle, slaves and other property from Attica to Boeotia, while ours would mean the destruction of Boeotian property in the war. There was a good deal more to the same effect. As to our reply, I would give my life to narrate the details, but I am afraid that the flowing river of time has washed away the past, and you may think such a narrative trouble for nothing. But listen to the conclusions to which we led them, and their reply. Take this document and read it.

(The Theban reply is read.)

After this they called the Athenian delegation and sent for the Athenian troops, who marched in and reinforced them – to omit the intervening details. The Theban welcome was such that, though their heavy infantry and their cavalry were stationed outside, the Athenian army was received into their houses and into their city,[91] and admitted among women and children and their most treasured possessions. Indeed that day the Thebans three times handsomely expressed their praise of the Athenian force, first for its bravery, then for its integrity, and finally for its restraint. Having elected to fight the battle at our side instead of against us, they gave their opinion that our courage was higher and our claim better than Philip's. And by putting in your power what they, like all men, seek most to protect, wives and children, they displayed their faith in our restraint. And in this, gentlemen, they showed their true knowledge of us. In the first place, when our army entered the city no complaint was made, however unjustified of its members, such restraint did they exercise. And after the two earlier battles, that at the river and the winter battle,[92] our men showed not only integrity, but extraordinary discipline, equipment and enthusiasm. From this they earned high praise in all quarters, and at home special sacrifices and services of thanksgiving. Indeed I should like to ask Aeschines, at the time when this was taking place, when Athens was overwhelmed by pride,

91. Though it has been disputed, this clearly means that the Theban forces were largely stationed outside, so that the Athenians were not merely complimented by being placed in the town but shown to be trusted.

92. These two earlier battles were apparently successes for the allies, and took place before 338 B.C. But no more is known of them.

delight and congratulation, whether he took part in the services and
joined in the general enthusiasm, or sat at home with groans of
misery and antagonism at the good news. If he was there, if he was
to be found in his place with everyone else, it is surely scandalous,
indeed impious, that he should first call heaven to witness a
magnificent success and next ask you for an opinion on your sacred
oath that it was the opposite. If he was not there, he surely deserves the death penalty many times over for lamenting an occurrence which brought rejoicing to everyone else. Now please read
these decrees.

(The decrees of public celebration are read.)

So we were engaged in celebrations at that time, and the people
of Thebes held the opinion that their rescue had been due to us.
There had been a change, and a country which had seemed in need
of assistance owing to my opponents' activities now brought
assistance to another owing to the view to which I had led them.
What sort of tune Philip was singing at that moment, and in what
difficulty he found himself in this situation, will be shown by the
letters he was sending to the Peloponnese. Please take these and
read them. They will show my perseverance, my constant movements, the hardships I underwent and the decrees I proposed, which
Aeschines was concerned to disparage,[93] and their effect.

There have been plenty of eminent and distinguished orators
before me, gentlemen, the renowned Callistratus, Aristophon,
Cephalus, Thrasybulus and numbers of others.[94] Yet none of them
devoted his whole time to any of the city's affairs. A man concerned
with proposals of legislation would not take part in delegation,
and vice versa. Each left himself a little leisure or a loophole in case
of accident. 'Well,' I shall be asked, 'was your strength and daring
so overwhelming as to enable you to do everything in person?' I
don't make that claim. But so great, in my conviction, was the
danger which had come upon Athens as to leave no room for so

93. Goodwin finds passages in Aeschines, *Crown*, to which to refer this
remark, especially 141–3.

94. On Callistratus, whose oratory had inspired Demosthenes in his early
years, see Demosthenes, *Treaty*, 297 (p. 128). On Aristophon see above, 70
(p. 275). On Cephalus see Aeschines, *Crown*, 194 (p. 243). This Thrasybulus
is probably Thrasybulus of Collytus (see Aeschines, *Crown*, 138, p. 228).

much as a thought of personal safety. One could be satisfied only with an unfailing performance of one's duty. On my own score I was convinced – perhaps stupidly, but convinced I was – that neither in the field of statesmanship nor of action nor of diplomacy had anyone the power to go farther than myself in positive and just proceedings. That was why I put myself in every field of activity. Read Philip's letters please.

(The letters are read.)

This was the point to which Philip was reduced by my policy, Aeschines. This is the tone of his words despite the long, confident utterances he used to address to Athens. It was for this that I was deservedly awarded a crown by the People, while you stood by without a word, and Diondas, who indicted me, failed to win the minimum support. Read me the decrees that were acquitted on that occasion and never indicted by Aeschines.

(The decrees are read.)

These are the same decrees, gentlemen, word for word and syllable for syllable, which were previously proposed by Aristonicus and now by Ctesiphon. Previously Aeschines neither prosecuted them in person nor supported the indictment that was made. Yet, if his accusations of me now are justified, it would have been more reasonable of him to accuse Demomeles and Hyperides for making the proposal than Ctesiphon.[95] Why? Because Ctesiphon is in a position to refer as precedents to their case, both to the court's decisions and to the failure of Aeschines to make any accusation against the same proposal as Ctesiphon's to the illegality of further prosecution in such instances and a good many other facts as well. The earlier case would have been judged on its merits without being prejudiced by any of these circumstances. However, it would not have been open to him, I fancy, to pursue his present course, and get hold of decrees and episodes belonging to the remote past, which no one foresaw or expected would be brought

95. On Aristonicus' proposal see 83, note 34 (p. 277) above. Demomeles was Demosthenes' cousin (see Aeschines, *Crown*, 51, p. 206). Hyperides, six of whose speeches are partially extant, was a leading anti-Macedonian politician.

up today,[96] and make numerous quotations from them for dishonest purposes, alter the dates and substitute false pretexts for true accounts of the facts, and so give a semblance of justification. That was impossible then. The discussion would have been based on truth, soon after the events, which gentlemen of the jury would have remembered and had virtually at their finger tips. That is why he has avoided an investigation at the time of the events, and come here now in the expectation, it seems, of a contest of rhetoric instead of an investigation of the facts of public policy; a judgement of oratory, not of the interests of Athens.

He then indulges in sophistry with the claim that you ought to neglect any opinion of me which you brought with you into court, and treat it as you would a case in which you expect a surplus, but, if the accounts balance even, you accept it.[97] So in this instance you should accede to the facts as they appear. Now I invite you to observe how anything dishonestly engineered falls to pieces of itself. This ingenious instance of his involves the admission that the judgement formed of us is that I am the spokesman of patriotism and he of Philip. He would not be trying to persuade you if this were not accepted as the underlying assumption about the two parties. That he is not justified in demanding a change of this opinion I can soon prove, not by means of accountancy, which is not the method in dealing with public affairs, but by a short recapitulation of the details, calling upon the audience as auditors and witnesses. By my policy, condemned by Aeschines, instead of Thebes being hurled into Attica in the train of Philip, as everyone expected, she was ranged with Athens in preventing his invasion. By my policy instead of war being fought in Attica, it was ninety miles away on the borders of Boeotia, and instead of our being ravaged by bandits from Euboea[98] Athens was at peace by sea; while instead of Philip capturing Byzantium and holding control of the Hellespont, Byzantium was in alliance with us against her. Does there appear any correspondence between this arithmetical

96. See Introduction, p. 14.

97. This refers to Aeschines, *Crown*, 59 ff. (pp. 208 ff.), which, however, is concerned only with the Peace of Philocrates.

98. A reference to the rescue of Oreus and Eretria from Philip's supporters. See 79 above (p. 276) and 87 (p. 278).

reckoning by counters and the reckoning which fact affords? Do you think it ought to be a matter of cancelling out instead of ensuring that the facts are recalled? It may be added that the savagery which can be seen every time Philip finally reduces any state has fallen elsewhere, while the benevolence[99] which he used to exude in his attempts to gain control of a situation is what we have fortunately secured for ourselves.

Here is another point I make without hesitation, that a genuine attempt to examine a speaker's character without misrepresentation would not lead to accusations of your kind with bogus examples and imitations of phrase and gesture.[100] According to this – surely you can see the point – Greek affairs depended on my use of this word instead of that, or on a wave of the hand this way or that. Actually it would require an estimate of the facts, of Athenian resources and capacities at the time of my rise to power as against those I acquired for her afterwards in my period of leadership, and of the position of our opponents. Then if I reduced her capacity, the fault would have been shown to lie with me. Or if I increased it, no misrepresentation would have been made. But as you avoided this course, I will take it. Observe gentlemen, whether my conduct of the argument is correct.

The power available to Athens consisted of the island states, and not all of them, only the weaker ones. Chios, Rhodes and Corcyra were not in our alliance.[101] There was an agreed money contribution of up to forty-five talents collected in advance. But apart from home forces there was no infantry or cavalry at all. And the most dangerous feature of the situation, which most of all favoured our

99. i.e. the moderate terms obtained by Athens after Chaeronea, which Demosthenes represents as the fruits of his firmness.

100. See Aeschines, *Crown*, 166 (p. 236.).

101. Chios and Rhodes (and Cos) had left the second Athenian Confederacy in 357 B.C., and successfully resisted Athenian coercion in the Social War (357–355 B.C.). Corcyra had seceded in *c.*360; its adherence was regained in the diplomacy of 341–340 (see 237, p. 310, below). The figure of 45 talents, compared to about 400 in Pericles' time, is an indication of the poverty to which Athens was now reduced, but regular annual payments had never been instituted in the Second Confederacy. On Euboea see especially Aeschines, *Crown*, 86–9 (pp. 216 ff.), Demosthenes, *Philippic III*, 57 (*Greek Political Oratory*, pp. 259–60), and *Crown*, 301 (p. 324). On Megara see Demosthenes, *Treaty*, 294–5 (p. 128).

enemies, was that Aeschines and his party had brought all our nearest neighbours closer to enmity than friendship, that is Megara, Thebes and Euboea. This was the position for Athens, and no one can add any further assets.

Now consider the situation of our great antagonist, Philip. First of all he had absolute power over all his following, which in warfare is the greatest asset of all. Secondly they were under arms continuously. Then again he had ample supplies of money, and could do what he liked, with no preliminary decrees, no open debates, no vexatious criticisms, no indictments for illegality, no responsibility for his actions to anyone. He was himself the complete and despotic controller of everything. I stood in opposition to him, and – I think this is a fair question – what had I in my control? Nothing. Public speaking first and foremost was my sole asset, and that was offered to Philip's corrupt supporters on an equal basis with myself. When they succeeded at my expense, which was frequent on one pretext or another, that meant one more decision in favour of the enemy. Yet in spite of disadvantages such as these I secured assistance for Athens from Euboea, Achaea, Corinth, Thebes, Megara, Leucas and Corcyra, and from these sources fifteen thousand mercenary troops were collected and two thousand cavalry apart from citizen forces. I also raised money contributions to the utmost of my ability. And if you talk[102] about parity with Thebes, or with Byzantium or Euboea, if you now talk of equality, first of all you fail to realize that in the past it was just as true, that of the total of three hundred warships which fought for Greece[103] Athens provided two hundred. She did not feel unfairly treated, she did not criticize the proposal, she was not found nursing some contemptible grievance about it, but feeling gratitude to heaven that at a time of universal peril in Greece she could provide double as much as the rest towards the safety of all. The favours you bestow on Athens by misrepresenting me are valueless. Why do you wait till now to pronounce on what should have been done? You were there, you were in Athens, but you made no such proposals – if the crisis of that time really allowed it, when we had to accept not what we liked but what circumstance

---

102. See Aeschines, *Crown*, 143 (p. 229).
103. At Salamis against the Persians in 480 B.C.

granted us. There was a rival bidder ready at hand who would receive anyone we drove away from our side, and pay them as well.

But if I am subjected to accusations as it is, what do you suppose would have happened if I had adopted a principle of exact calculation and all the states had gone off and joined Philip? What line would have been taken then by these unprincipled people? Wouldn't they have talked about surrender, about willing allies driven into the arms of the enemy? 'He has control of the Hellespont,' they'd have said, 'by winning Byzantium, he's in command of Greek corn supplies, he has brought a dangerous war to the borders of Attica because of Thebes, and pirates from Euboea make the sea routes impassable.' They'd have said all this and more. A wicked, wicked thing, gentlemen, is vexatious criticism, invariably malicious and destructive. This particular specimen is full of cunning. He has never in his life performed a sound or liberal action. He is a veritable ape of tragedy, a rustic Oenomaus,[104] a figure of oratorical fraud. What good has the country ever had of your cleverness? And now you dilate on the past. It is as though a doctor were to visit his patients when they are ill without giving them a word or any indication how to escape the disease, and then, as soon as one of them died and the funeral took place, were to follow the procession to the grave and give a lecture to the effect that, if he had done this and that, he wouldn't be dead. Lunatic, to say it at that stage!

So even the defeat, if you commit the outrage of gloating over that when you ought to be lamenting it, will not be found due to anything in my power. Regard it like this. Never yet have I returned worsted by Philip's representatives from any delegation on which I have been sent by this country, from Thessaly or Ambracia or Illyria, from the Thracian princes of Byzantium or anywhere else,[105] including the last occasion at Thebes. But where his representatives underwent a diplomatic defeat, he reduced his opponents by a military attack. This is what you

104. See 180, p. 298 above.

105. Little is known of these occasions. Demosthenes may have visited Ambracia in 343-342 B.C. (see *Philippic, III*, 72 *Greek Political Oratory*, p. 262) and Thracian princes when he went to Byzantium in 341. It is hard to see what success he can have obtained in Thessaly, which remained firmly under Philip.

demand of me. You are not ashamed to jeer at me for cowardice, and then you expect me to defeat single-handed the power of Philip. And by the spoken word at that. What other resource had I at command? I did not control every man's spirit, nor the fortune of the fighting forces, nor the strategy, of which you are naïve enough to demand an account of me. Gentlemen, you may make examination of anything for which an orator can be held responsible. I ask nothing less. What does that amount to? That he shall see events at their inception, that he shall foresee and foretell them to others. This I did. Further, wherever there is dilatory action, hesitation, ignorance, jealousy, which are the unavoidable political shortcomings of any state, he should reduce them to the smallest possible proportions, and instead lead all to unity, friendship and enthusiasm for their duty. All this too, I achieved, and no one can charge me with any deficiency in it. Ask whom you will what were the means by which most of all Philip secured his successes. Everyone will point to his army and the liberality with which he corrupted leading politicians. Well, the forces were never under my control or leadership, so that there is no argument in these fields which applies to me. In that of bribery and corruption I had the better of Philip. Bribery is a defeat for the man who accepts it, if it succeeds. On the other hand to refuse it is to defeat the offer. So here, so far as concerns me, Athens is undefeated.

My own contribution towards justifying the prosecutor's indictment was approximately this among much else. That of the people of Athens I will now describe. After the battle[106] in the knowledge and full view of all my proceedings and in the midst of extreme danger and anxiety, when some severe treatment of me would not have been surprising, the people first voted my proposals for the safety of Athens. All the precautionary measures that were being taken, the organization of defence forces, trench works, provision for maintenance of the walls, were embarked on in accordance with my proposals. Secondly, in electing a corn commissioner they appointed me out of the whole nation. After this a combination of all whose concern it was to injure me brought indictments, tests, impeachments against me, not in their own names in the first place, but under names which they supposed

106. i.e. Chaeronea.

would be unknown. Your own memories will recall that in those early days I was brought into court day after day, and even Sosicles' insane measures, Philocrates' false accusations, and the mad attempts of Diondas[107] and Melanthus did not go untried. In this situation the will of heaven, but also the Athenian people, including yourselves, were my salvation. And this was justified, both as right and proper conduct and as befitting juries which had sworn the oath and kept it in their verdicts. Thus on the occasions of my impeachment, when you acquitted me and refused my prosecutors the minimum vote, you gave your verdict on the excellence of my political conduct. On the occasions of my indictment I made proof of the legality of my proposals and speeches. On the occasions when you set the seal of approval on my accounts, you gave an added testimony of the justice of all my conduct and its freedom from corruption. This being so, what name did justice and propriety demand that Ctesiphon should apply to my achievements? Could it be other than that which he could see was applied by the people and by the sworn members of the jury, and confirmed in every instance by the facts?

'All the same,' he says, 'that was a fine claim of Cephalus', never to have suffered an indictment.'[108] Well, he was a lucky man. But why should greater blame attach to the man who has suffered numerous indictments but never a single conviction of misconduct? None the less so far as Aeschines is concerned I can claim the same proud boast. He never drew up an indictment against me nor carried it into court. So he has agreed that I am no worse a citizen than Cephalus.

Everything displays his malignity and illwill, not least his remarks about my 'star'. Personally when one human being condemns another on the score of fortune I regard it as folly. What an apparently successful man supposes to be excellent, but cannot tell whether it will last overnight, is something you cannot speak of nor hold up against another. But as Aeschines has added

107. Diondas is mentioned in 222 above (p. 307), Philocrates, who is not the Philocrates of the treaty, at Demosthenes XXV, 44. Sosicles and Melanthus are unknown.

108. See Aeschines, *Crown*, 194 (p. 243). Cephalus was an orator at the time of the restored democracy.

to his other sneers by giving a presumptuous turn to this subject, just consider and reflect, gentlemen, how much more true and more modest is the spirit in which I shall deal with the subject of fortune. I regard Athens as possessed of good fortune, and the same, I observe, is implied by the oracle of Zeus at Dodona,[109] but the mass of mankind I take to be of persistently harsh and evil fortune. Is there anyone in the Greek world or elsewhere who has not known numerous troubles in the present period? To have chosen the noble path, and to have risen higher than those Greeks who imagined that abandonment of Athens would mean prosperity, I take as instances of the good fortune of Athens. But the contretemps that have occurred, and the failures to get her way, must be regarded as the fair share of human misfortune which falls to her lot. As to my personal fortune and that of each of us, it is proper to count that among private matters. That is my view about fortune, which is right and proper in my opinion, and, I think, in yours. But Aeschines asserts that my personal fortune carries more weight than that of Athens, and puts what is small and insignificant above what is good and great. How can this be so?

Furthermore, if you set out in any case to examine my fortune, just consider your own. If you find that mine is better than yours, you can stop your abusive remarks. Look at it right from the beginning. No one should accuse me of want of feeling. I do not think there is any sense in putting poverty in the pillory, nor in self-congratulation on an affluent upbringing. It is Aeschines' harsh and malicious misrepresentation which is responsible for my dropping into arguments of this sort, and I will treat them with what moderation circumstances allow.

These are my foundations, Aeschines. As a boy I went to the best schools, and I had all I needed for one who was not to be brought to active disgrace by poverty. When I grew up, my course followed on from that, and I performed public services, became a trierarch, made my money contributions. I did not miss any opportunity of distinction, private or public, but sought to be of use to my city and my friends, and when I decided to enter on public affairs I chose policies which frequently brought me the

109. Referred to by Herodotus (I, 140 ff.) as the oldest of Greek oracles. See H. W. Parke, *Greek Oracles* (London, 1967), pp. 20 ff.

honour of a crown from Athens and from other states alike. And even you who are my enemies never attempted to maintain that my policies were at fault. That was the fortune that was my life. There is much more that I could say of it, but I refrain for fear of giving offence by the fact that I have my pride. Against this you, who display your own self-importance and your contempt of others, consider what fortune you enjoyed in comparison with mine. It led you in boyhood to considerable want, when you attended your father in the schoolroom, grinding the ink, dusting the benches and sweeping the waiting room, a slave's and not a free man's job.[110] And when you grew up, you used to read aloud from the rites your mother conducted, and help in the rest of the performance, busy at night with the fawn skins and the mixing bowl, purifying the candidates and cleansing them with the clay and the bran, and then concluding the ceremony by making them get up and recite, 'I have fled the evil and found the good', and priding yourself on giving the loudest cry ever heard in the rite. This I can believe. It can't be supposed that so penetrating a voice would have produced anything but an ear-splitting ceremonial cry. In the daytime you conducted your imposing companies of worshippers through the streets in their garlands of fennel and white poplar. You clasped brown snakes in your hands or waved them over your head, and shouted '*Euoi saboi*', or danced to the tune of 'Hyes Attes, Hyes Attes',[111] under titles like 'conductor', 'forerunner', 'ivy bearer' or 'fan bearer' which the old women gave you, and for which you were rewarded with sops and twists and little cakes, a real matter for self-congratulation and satisfaction on your fortune.

When you were enrolled a member of your deme, by whatever means – I leave that out – but when you *were* enrolled, you at once chose a most distinguished occupation as clerk or officeboy to the minor magistrates. Then on leaving that job, after doing yourself everything you had charged others with, you did not,

110. See above 129 ff. (pp. 288 ff.). The references to ritual initiations which follow are a contemptuous parody (Aristophanes, *Clouds*, 254 ff., perhaps offers another) of oriental religious practices which were becoming more prevalent in Athens.

111. Ancient mystic words whose significance is unknown.

of course, want to let your later career prove a come-down after your previous one. You got a job among the 'ranters', as they were called, Simycas and Socrates and their troupe, to whom you played third. You picked up your figs and olives and grapes like a thieving greengrocer,[112] and you made more out of that than out of the dramatic contests. Contests indeed they were, and you carried them on for very life in a war without quarter or mercy which you conducted against the spectators. Here you got as much as you gave, and could be justified for jeering at the cowardice of the uninitiated in such activities. However, I will pass over what could be ascribed to poverty and go on to actual points of character in you. You chose a policy – because this was another field which it occurred to you incidentally to enter – which meant that while the country was doing well you lived the life of a frightened rabbit, in fear and trembling of being beaten up for the offences you knew you had committed, while at times of general misfortune your confidence was universally observed. Yet when a man could display confidence after the death of thousands of his fellows,[113] what penalty does he deserve from the living? There are a great many more points I could make about him, but I will leave them, for the reason that I do not think all the blots I could point to in his character can be easily described. I am confined to those whose mention does not confer disgrace on myself.

Examine my life and yours, then, Aeschines, gently and without rancour. Invite members of the jury to say which of the two they would prefer. You were a teacher of reading and writing. I was a pupil. You performed initiations. I received them. You worked as a clerk, while I was in politics. You were on the stage playing third, while I was in the audience. You missed your lines, while I supplied the cat-calls. Your part in politics favoured the enemy, mine our own country. I go no further except about the present moment, when I am under consideration for the award of a crown, and have been agreed free of any offence, while you have an established reputation for malicious prosecution, and the question remaining

112. Editors differ as to the point of this. But it seems likely that the figs are thrown at him for his bad acting, and not that he is really robbing orchards as is suggested by some.
113. At Chaeronea.

is whether you pursue the practice or have now terminated it by failure to obtain the legal minimum of votes. A pleasant fortune, isn't it, that has governed your life and leads up to prosecution of me.

Now let me read to the jury the testimonies of public services which I have performed. You shall read me some lines to balance them, lines marred by your own performance of them.

> The pit of death and gates of darkness[114]
> Were my abode,

and

> No evil speaking is my desire,

and

> Foulest perdition,

which I hope may be your lot from providence in the first place, and then from members of the jury, for being as abominable a citizen as you were an actor. Read the testimonies.

(The testimonies are read.)

In public affairs, then, such is my character. In private ones, if you are not all aware of me as impartial, kindly disposed and a friend in need, then I say no more. I will not put forward any evidence on this score either of having ransomed prisoners from the enemy or helped with dowries or anything of that sort. My view is this. A beneficiary should bear the fact in mind at the time, and the benefactor should forget it, if the former is to show generosity and the latter magnanimity. A keen memory of private acts of generosity is virtually equivalent to a grievance. I am not going to harbour one. Nothing would induce me to do so. The opinion already formed of me is enough.

But I should like to leave private matters and say a little more about public affairs. If you can point, Aeschines, to any man under the sun, Greek or non-Greek, who is completely untouched by the power first of Philip, now of Alexander, I concede your point and agree that it was my fortune, or ill fortune, which you like, that has been responsible for all that has happened. But if

114. The first quotation is of Euripides, *Hecuba*, 1, the second unknown. The third is marked by the diction alone as tragic, but cannot be identified.

people who have never seen me or heard a word of mine have many of them undergone much that was disastrous, not individuals solely, but whole cities and peoples, how much more in accord with justice and truth is it to set the blame on human fortune, or some tide in human affairs which has been antagonistic or undesirable. But you neglect all this, to make accusations against me as a figure in Athenian politics, despite your knowledge that, if not all, at least a part of your slanderous abuse applies to all Athenians, and particularly to yourself. If I had had full and autocratic power to decide affairs, it would have been for you other speakers to bring accusation against me. But if you were all present at the meetings of the Assembly, every time the city laid it upon you to consult her interests, and if this policy was universally agreed to be the best, particularly by you yourself – it was certainly not friendliness towards me that made you withdraw from hopes and ambition and honour, all of which attached to my activities at the time, but you obviously succumbed to the truth and your own inability to do better – in that case is it not scandalously wrong to put the blame on Athenian citizens for what was beyond you to amend? Anywhere else I find that the rule is invariably laid down and predetermined. For deliberate wrong-doing, resentment and punishment. For unintentional error, forgiveness instead of punishment. It may be that without wrong-doing or error there is still submission to general policy which consequently shares in the common failure. If so, it is not a case for reproaches or abuse, but for sympathy. This is not a legal matter. Human nature dictates it in accordance with unwritten law and the character of mankind. It is Aeschines who in cruelty and malice so far exceeds the rest of men that he even puts down what he himself recalled as misfortune as ground for accusation.

Now in addition to everything else, with an air of simple good intention in everything he says he urges you to take careful precautions against me and against deceit and chicanery on my part. He adds appellations like dangerous, dishonest and crooked,[115] on the grounds that once the first speaker has attributed his own characteristics to another it immediately becomes the truth, and the audience have no further thought of the speaker's own char-

115. See Aeschines, *Crown*, 16 (p. 197), 207 (p. 246) etc.

acter. However, I am certain you all understand him, and will be far readier to think this of him than of me. I am also quite sure that my ability – however, let that pass. But I can see that the power of speakers is largely in the hands of their audiences. The reception you accord him, the degree of favour with which you view him, determines a speaker's apparent ability. In any case any such ability as exists in me will prove, you will find, to be exercised on behalf of Athens, never against her or for private ends, while in the case of Aeschines the opposite is true, not only in regard to speeches made on behalf of the enemy, but to his attacks on any who have annoyed him or come into conflict with him. He has never used his abilities in accordance with justice or in the interests of Athens. It is not resentment or hostility or any other such feeling that an honest citizen should expect a jury in the public interest to confirm for him. He should not go to court for any such purpose. For preference he should not entertain such feelings, but if he cannot help it he should keep them within mild and reasonable limits.

In what circumstances, then, is violent feeling permissible in a politician or speaker? Where a wide danger threatens the state, and where it has to deal with enemies. In these circumstances a good and honourable statesman may entertain such feelings. When no public wrong is involved – and I would add no private one either – for him to see fit to demand penalties from me without public or private interest at stake, and to come with a manufactured charge against a decoration and commendation accorded me, and to go to such length on the subject, is an indication of personal animosity in a petty mind and nothing else. Then to abandon the quarrel against me and turn to Ctesiphon shows the depth of infamy. On this evidence it seems to me, Aeschines, that it was a display of vocal execution you aimed at in bringing this suit, and not satisfaction for anyone's misconduct. It is not a speaker's words nor the modulations of his voice in which the value lies, but his political agreement with the people, the accord of his likes and dislikes with those of his country. A mind of this sort will give words based on goodwill. But to cultivate persons from whom the state anticipates some danger is to anchor one's boat away from popular feeling and to abandon the expectation of the same secure harbour.

Observe my case. I took a line which accords with the people's view. I have done nothing individual or exclusive. Does the same apply to you? Very much the reverse. Immediately after the battle you went on a delegation to Philip, though you were well known to have refused this mission throughout the preceding period. Then who is it who practises the greatest deception on the state? The insincere statesman. Who is it who rightly incurs the execration of the herald?[116] The same. What greater political wrong could be found in a speaker than inconsistency between thought and word? This is the character that is found in you. Can you open your lips, do you dare to look gentlemen of the jury in the face? Do you suppose they are unaware of your true character? Or that they are so drowsed, so oblivious as not to remember your public utterances in the war, when you swore under oath that there was nothing between you and Philip, and brought the same charge against me out of private ill feeling despite its falsity? But as soon as news came of the battle these thoughts vanished, and you at once admitted, indeed boasted of, the friendship and association which existed between you, giving a new title to your role of hired servant. On what genuine pretext could association or friendship or familiarity be claimed between Philip and Aeschines, the son of Glaucothea, the priestess with the drums? I see none. You were the servant hired to damage the interests of Athenians. None the less, though so clearly detected as a traitor, though your own audience convicted you on reference to the facts, you cast abuse and bring these charges on me, by whom they are less merited than by any man living.

There were a great many actions of moment, Aeschines, which Athens determined on and successfully achieved through my agency, and which she did not forget. Here is proof of it. When the people appointed a speaker to give the oration for the dead immediately after the event,[117] your name was put forward by the Council, but you were not selected, in spite of your vocal qualities. Nor was Demades who had just made the peace, nor Hegemon, nor any of the rest of you, but I was. You and Pythocles spoke in an un-

116. Meetings of Council and Assembly began with a solemn curse called down on wilful deception.

117. i.e. Chaeronea. The funeral oration found among Demosthenes' speeches (No. LX) is certainly spurious. Demades had been taken prisoner at Chaeronea, but after ingratiating himself with Philip was sent by him as a messenger to Athens. He was then sent back with Aeschines and probably

believably savage and unrestrained tone, with the same accusations against me as yours today, but I was all the more firmly selected The reason is one you are aware of, but I will tell you none the less. Two considerations were known to them, the patriotic enthusiasm with which I had conducted affairs and your own dishonesty. Facts which you had denied on oath in the days of public prosperity you admitted in those of disaster. And men who had been led by the country's misfortune to gain impunity for their ideas had long been her enemies, and now, they thought, it was proved. So the orator who was to speak the funeral oration and do honour to the bravery of the dead should not be one who had shared the same roof and the same table with men who had served against them, should not have joined there in the revels and the triumph at the disasters of Greece with the men whose hands had struck them down, and then come here and receive honour, or give a vocal pretence of lamentation at their fate instead of the true grief of the heart. They found this last in themselves and in me, but not in you. Hence they elected me and not you. It is not that this view was held by the people and a different one by the fathers and sons of the fallen who were selected to attend the ceremony. These had to hold the feast supposed to be given by the nearest relatives of the dead in accordance with custom, and they held it at my house. This was right. Though by birth each had his own relatives closer to them than I was, yet no one came nearer to them all together. The man to whom it meant most that they should survive and succeed was also touched most of all by the grief and the wish that they could have been spared.

Now read this epigram, chosen by the city to inscribe over their memorial. It will give you further demonstration, Aeschines, of your own cruel, malicious, hateful character.

(The epigram is read.)

> For their country they came to strife of arms
> And scattered the violence of the enemy.

Phocion, to negotiate peace terms. He subsequently proposed Athens' adherence to Philip's Common Peace Treaty, and was instrumental in the fall of Demosthenes and Hyperides in 322 B.C. before being executed in Macedon (319 B.C.). Hegemon and Pythocles were later executed with Phocion and others, in 317 B.C.

Courage and fear lay before their fighting,
But unsparing they made death the umpire
For Greece's sake, to keep the yoke from their neck
And the degradation of slavery from their shoulders.
The Fatherland now takes the wearied body
In her arms. This is Zeus' judgement for men.
God's gift in life is right judgement unerring,
But escape from fate he grants to none.[118]

You hear, Aeschines? 'God's gift in life is right judgement unerring.' The poet does not ascribe to the statesman the power to
grant success to the combatants. It belongs to the gods. How then
can you bring your damnable vituperation on me for this? We hope
heaven may turn it on your head and your supporters'.

Well, gentlemen, after all the mendacious accusations he has
made against me, I was most of all astonished when, recalling as he
did the fate of Athens at that time, he did not react like a sympathetic
and right-minded citizen, nor did he show regrets or display any
other mental attitude of the kind. He raised his voice in throaty
expressions of delight, which he evidently took for accusations
against me but which actually amounted to a demonstration against
himself that he had no reaction to share with others at events of so
painful a kind. Yet to profess, as Aeschines does, a concern for law
and the constitution ought to mean, if nothing else, that he can
sympathize with others in their joys and griefs, and will not follow
a general policy which is in line with the enemy's. This is what you
are proved to have done when you assert that I am responsible for
everything, and the cause of all the troubles of Athens. It was not
my political policy which led Athens to begin assistance to the
Greek states. As far as I am concerned, if it were acknowledged by
gentlemen of the jury that it was by my doing that Athens opposed
the despotism being practised against the Greek states it would be a
greater bounty than you have ever made to others. But I would not
claim it. It would do less than honour to Athenian citizens. And I
am sure you would not concede it. And if Aeschines' proceedings
were justifiable, he would not have made his malice against me a

118. This epigram has too many textual difficulties and too little merit to
be regarded as genuine, except for the last couplet which Demosthenes quotes.

reason for doing injury and dishonour to the greatest distinction the nation possesses.

But why concern oneself with such criticisms, when he has brought far more outrageous accusations which are equally false? Good Heavens! A man who can accuse me of support for Philip would make any imaginable assertion. I declare on any oath you like, if we are to set aside mendacious and malicious attacks and make a true investigation of the names of the men upon whose shoulders by general and reasonable agreement the real cause of our disasters would rest, you would find in every city men of his stamp, but not of mine, men who when Philip's affairs were at their lowest ebb of weakness, in spite of warnings and exhortations on our part, yet cast aside the interest of Greece for their own dishonest gain, by misleading and corrupting their own cities in each case, till they brought them down to slavery. I can name Daochus, Cineas and Thrasydaus in Thessaly, Cercidas, Hieronymus and Eucampidas in Arcadia, Myrtis, Teledamus and Mnaseas in Argos, Euxitheus, Cleotimus and Aristaechmus in Elis, and in Messenia the sons of the unspeakable Philiades, Neon and Thrasylochus. There were Aristratus and Epichares at Sicyon, Deinarchus and Demaretus at Corinth, and Ptoeodorus, Helixus and Perillus at Megara, while Thebes had Timolaus, Theogeiton and Anemoetas, and Euboea, Hipparchus, Cleitarchus and Sosistratus.[119] I could go on all day with the names of the traitors. These were all of the same proclivities in their particular states as Aeschines and his associates in Athens, abominable, insinuating and villainous men, who have crippled their own countries, who have squandered their freedom first to Philip, then to Alexander. Their stomach and their lower instincts are their gauge of happiness, and they have overturned liberty and independence, which for earlier Greeks were the be-all and end-all of value.

This notorious concatenation of evil and disgraceful influences, or rather, gentlemen, to avoid mere empty words, this betrayal of the liberty of Greece, is something of which our country stands

119. cf. the list of traitors at 48 above (p. 271). Otherwise Hieronymus is mentioned in Demosthenes, *Treaty*, 11 (p. 59), and Ptoeodorus ibid., 295 (p. 128), Cleitarchus in 71, 81 above. Little or nothing is known of the rest.

guiltless before the world after my political career, and I before yourselves. Then, Aeschines, you ask what quality I claim, to demand such honour. My reply is that when all the politicians in Greece were corrupted beginning with yourself, I was the man whom no political occasion, no fair speeches, no exaggerated undertakings, no hopes or fears or anything else could induce or lure into a moment's betrayal of the claims of justice and patriotism, and that in all the political recommendations I have made the scale has never been tipped, as it was with you, in the direction of personal aims. It has always depended on true judgement, undeviating and uncorrupt. I was the leader in greater events than any man of my time, and in all of them my political conduct has been based on equity and right dealing. That is the ground of my claim. As to this matter of defence works and entrenchments, which you have used to attack me, I do of course regard it as matter for credit and commendation. But I reckon it as far removed from the question of my policies. My defence of Athens was not one of stone and brick. That is not my principal ground for satisfaction. If you want to make a just assessment of the defences I erected, you will include in it arms, cities, districts, harbours, ships, cavalry and men to defend Athens. These were the bulwarks I brought for the protection of Attica, to the greatest extent of which human thought was capable. They were defences for the district, not just for the circle of city and Peiraeus. Nor were my calculations proved inferior to Philip's by any means, nor the provisions I made. It was the strategy and the resources of the allies that were brought down by fortune. What proof is there of this? It is clear as daylight. All the same consider the question.

What was the right course for the patriotic citizen, for the man of forethought, activity and right intent in political affairs on his country's behalf?[120] Was it not to use Euboea as a defence for Attica on the sea, Boeotia on the mainland, and on the side of the Peloponnese her neighbours there? Was it not to take steps for the maintenance of the corn route along friendly coasts to the Peiraeus?

120. Here Demosthenes refers again to the diplomatic activity he led in 341–340 B.C. See 234–43 above (pp. 309 ff.). Proconnesus, an island in the Propontis (Sea of Marmora) allied to Athens, and Tenedos, an island near the southern end of the Hellespont and a member of the Confederacy since the beginning, were garrisoned at that time, and Abydos, on the Asiatic shore of the Hellespont, won over.

To preserve some existing assets by the dispatch of expeditions, by speeches, proposals and so on, Proconnesus for instance, the Chersonese and Tenedos, and to maintain the friendly alliance of others, Byzantium, Abydos and Euboea? To deprive our enemy of his main sources of power and to fill the gaps in our country's? All this was done by the decrees I passed and the policy I carried out. And an unprejudiced investigation will find that it was based on true assumptions and executed by right methods, that the due occasion in each case was not missed by neglect, by ignorance or abandonment of the cause on my part. Everything open to the powers and calculations of a single man was carried out without fail. If the agency of destiny or chance, the failure of strategy or the malevolence of the betrayers of Greece, or all these forces together did damage to the outcome of affairs and eventually overturned them, where lies the fault of Demosthenes? If in each of the Greek states there had been one single man who had taken the same stand as I did in Athens, or rather, had Thessaly, had Arcadia contained a single man who thought as I did, no state outside the pass or inside it would have been subjected to the sufferings they underwent.[121] All would have been free and independent states maintaining their own territories in complete security, safety and happiness, and feeling gratitude on my account to you and all Athens for these great benefits. To convince you that I am enough afraid of envy to use words that fall far short of the facts, please read the list of instances of expeditions sent in accordance with my proposals.

(The list is read.)

These and their like, Aeschines, formed the path of duty for the honourable citizen. Their success would have made us beyond dispute the greatest of nations and, one could add, justly so. Failure still gives room for honour, still leaves the city and her policy free from blame, and casts it upon the fortune which so ordained. It did not lie in that path to turn your back on the good of Athens, and

121. Demosthenes makes a valid point. Without the adherence of Thessaly Philip could not have extended his power southwards, and his friends in Thessaly were an important factor in his success there. Similarly the activities of his supporters in Arcadia largely prevented the Peloponnese providing much assistance to the central Greek states.

take pay from her opponents, to cultivate the chances of her enemies rather than her own, nor to defame a man who had the courage to make his words and his measures worthy of Athens, and to remain in this resolution. It was no part of it to keep watch for any private irritation that may arise, and harbour it, or to conduct an unhealthy and malignant silence, as you often do. Silence, I assure you, can be right and expedient, when it is maintained in simplicity by the majority of the citizen body. That is not the silence that Aeschines maintains, very far from it. When he sees fit, as he often does, he abstains from active politics and waits for a moment when the Assembly is wearied with some frequent speaker, or when chance has brought some reverse or other untoward occurrence, which are common in human affairs. At this point his silence breaks into a sudden cyclone of speech. He gets his voice into trim and makes a collection of phrases and words, which he strings off loudly without taking breath. They are of no value or benefit to anyone. They merely damage someone in the citizen body, and embarrass everyone. Yet all this thoughtful attention, Aeschines, had it been the outcome of heartfelt sincerity in the interest of the country, should have brought a harvest of genuine benefits of universal value, alliances between states, financial resources, commercial expansion, useful legislation, setbacks for our established adversaries. In past days all these fields provided opportunities for a man to prove himself, and the old days offered many chances of distinction to one of high standing. But you will never appear in that category, not in the first, second, third, fourth, fifth, sixth class, not in any class at all, at any rate in any field of Athenian success. What alliance of your making appeared on Athenian records? What expedition which secured good relations or repute? What delegation or public service which contributed to the distinction of Athens? What deficiency in home affairs, or those of Greek or other states under your control has ever been made good? What have warships, armaments, dockyards, defences ever owed to you? What value have you had in any field? What have you contributed to rich or poor in the way of patriotic and generous assistance? Nothing. 'But without that,' you say, 'one can claim a strong and patriotic feeling.' Where or when has it appeared? You are farther from right dealing than any man alive, when everyone who has ever given utterance on the platform made some contribution[122] for our safety, ending with Aristonicus who gave the sum collected for the payment of his fine, and even then you neither appeared nor made any contribution whatever. It was not out of poverty obviously, as you inherited over five talents from your father-in-law, Philo, and you had a present of two talents given you by the leaders of the committees[123] for ruining the law on the trierarchy. But I do not want to add argument to argument and lose sight of my theme, so I will leave this aside. But it proves that it was not poverty that prevented your contributions, but precautions against making any opposition to the party whose interest determines your policy. So on what occasions do you show your spirit, your true brilliance? When something is wanted to the detriment of Athenians. Then your vocal brilliance and your memory stand out, and you become the best of actors, a true tragic Theocrines.[124]

You next call to my remembrance the great men of the past. You are right to do so. But it is not right, gentlemen, to take advantage in this court of the feeling which exists permanently towards the dead in order to examine me, living as I do among you, and compare me with them. No one can be unaware that there is always an undercurrent, deep or shallow, of envy towards the living, while the dead are immune from the dislike even of their enemies. In view, then, of the character of these gentlemen, am I now to be judged and assessed in comparison with my predecessors? I hope not. Justice and equity alike forbid it, Aeschines. The standard must be you yourself, or any other person still living who shared your policies. Here is another point. Is it more to the credit and distinction of Athens in view of the services rendered by past generations, which are beyond comparison and beyond description, to cast ingratitude and abuse upon those which are being rendered by the present generation, or that any who act in the spirit of patriotism should

122. Contributions of this sort were made after Chaeronea and after Alexander's destruction of Thebes (335 B.C.). Aristonicus, probably the one mentioned in 83, 223 above (pp. 277 and 307), had presumably failed to pay a fine, and had accordingly lost his rights. Instead of paying it and getting himself reinstated he gave the money to the state.

123. On the committees, see 102 (p. 282), note 45 above.

124. Information on this name is largely conjectural.

have their part in the honour and good feeling of all? Indeed, if this again is a subject I should discuss, my political principles and policy will be found on consideration the same in character and intention as those of the most highly extolled of earlier statesmen, while yours resemble their detractors. It is clear that in those times too there was a class which tended to condemn the existing generation in favour of their forerunners with malicious intent parallel to your own. And then you declare, do you, that I am unlike that earlier generation. Are you more like them? And what about your brother?[125] Or some other orator of the present day? Personally I would deny it of any of them. It is with the living, with his own generation that my honourable friend, to pass over other epithets, should compare the living, as in any other field, of drama, poetry or athletics. Philammon[126] did not go uncrowned at the Olympics because of his inferiority to Glaucus of Carystus and one or two other athletes of the past. He was superior to competitors of his year, and consequently earned his crown and his proclamation.

Similarly you should compare me with present-day orators, yourself or any of them you like. I exclude no one. When the time came for the country to choose her best policy, when true patriotism was the common goal for the emulation of all, it was proved that the ideas I expressed were the best, the decrees and enactments and diplomatic relations I advocated were made the basis of administration, while none of you came into the picture, except to make attacks on my activities. But when the lamentable disaster came, when the demand was not for statesmanship, but subservience to orders and readiness to accept the wages of a traitor and flatter a different leader, that was when you and each one of your party paraded in the splendour of wealthy resources, while I was, I own, feeble, though my feeling for Athens was higher.

There are two things, gentlemen – to speak of myself in the least invidious manner I can – which for the instinctively reasonable

125. Probably Philochares, who had been *strategus* at Athens. See Demosthenes, *Treaty*, 237, (p. 112).

126. Philammon was a recent Athenian, Glaucus a celebrated boxer of an earlier age, in whose honour Simonides wrote an ode (see Bergk, Fragment 8). The present reference to Philammon is 'anticipated' by Aeschines, *Crown*, 189 (p. 242), which presumably indicates that Aeschines has acquired knowledge of Demosthenes' speech before delivering his own.

politician are essential, that in positions of authority he shall retain for the city the policy of generosity and pre-eminence, and that in every crisis, in every action he shall maintain his loyalty. This is governed by his character, while power and strength depend on other things. And character is something you will find has remained unchanged in me. Look at the actual story. When my extradition was demanded,[127] when I was summoned before the Amphictyons, assailed by threats and promises, or when I was confronted by the savage attacks of these inhuman creatures who now oppose me, never have I betrayed my loyalty to Athens. From the very start I chose the true and just path in politics, to seek for the honours, the powers, the distinction my country offered, to increase them and to stand or fall with them. It is not my way to receive foreign successes with a face of joy, and walk delightedly about the market-place with hand outstretched to tell the good news to anyone I think will pass it on, and to listen with horror to Athenian good fortune, and bow to the ground in despondency like these wicked traitors, who defame Athens as though this were not at once to defame themselves, who cast their gaze abroad and find the detriment of Athens and the benefit of a foreigner a matter for jubilation and a circumstance to preserve with care for all time. It is my prayer that there be no power in heaven to grant them this, that, if it may be, a better heart and mind may be implanted even in them; but that, if they are obdurate beyond remedy, they may be brought to ruin utter and complete by land and sea, and that we who are left may be given with all speed deliverance from the fears they have contrived and lasting preservation.

127. Demosthenes is probably referring here to more than one occasion when his surrender was demanded or proposed, not only to Alexander's demand after the destruction of Thebes in 335 B.C., but to some other occasion, possibly during the war over Amphissa in 340–338 B.C. See Ryder, *Koine Eirene*, p. 162.

APPENDIX

Notes on passages in which the translation departs from the text accepted (Oxford text of Demosthenes, Teubner text of Aeschines), or in which other points of textual interest occur.

The numbers are those of the footnotes in the translation. *LSJ* – Liddell & Scott's Lexicon.

Demosthenes: Treaty

46. It seems unnecessary to excise this sentence, as the Oxford text does on the ground of its appearance again in 279 (p. 124).

52. The emendation of C. R. Kennedy, οἵ' ἄν, seems needed here.

58. An incomplete sentence appears here in the MSS. I have omitted it, following many editors.

81. Weil pointed out that the MS. text requires an awkward change of subject, and seems to need τὴν πόλιν, as object instead of subject. εὖ θέσθαι might do in place of εὐθενεῖσθαι and I have gone on that assumption.

95. The text is incomplete and perhaps corrupt. See Bergk, *Lyrici Graeci*, II, vi, 4.

101. I prefer to read with Weil οὐκ ἐπεῖχεν ὑπακούων and to keep εἶχεν after οὐδέ.

Aeschines: Treaty

59. Anyone interested in these appellations should see Aeschines, *Timarchus*, 126, 131, Demosthenes, *Crown*, 180, and *LSJ*, s.v. βάταλος. There seems little ground for rendering this word 'stammerer' as though by derivation from βατταρίζω.

114. *LSJ* renders ἀψιμαχίας as 'altercation', but Adams (Loeb) may be right in giving 'eagerness of public men for war'. It is Aeschines' theme.

Aeschines: Crown

4. Blass unnecessarily omits this clause, presumably because it does not apply to Demosthenes' case.

20. I omit the clause ἐὰν μὴ ψηφίσηται ὁ δῆμος which Blass adds here from 47.

Appendix

62. This title depends on the emendation προναίᾳ for προνοία, to accord with the ancient title of the temple of Athena at Delphi.

Demosthenes: Crown

15. Reading ἴσως with Blass.
40. 'Ceos' is an emendation generally accepted. The MSS. have 'Cleonae'.
48. The text has καλόν, which editors take as ironical. But the irony seems rather lost, and the, perhaps humourless, emendation πάλαι or παλαιὸν may have something in its favour.
80. The MSS. have τὰ γέρρ' ἐνεπίμπρασαν ('set fire to the wicker work'). It is possible that beacons were lit to signal the emergency, as Goodwin thinks. But to start a fire in the market-place seems a most improbable proceeding. Accordingly I have preferred the emendation ἀνεπετάννυσαν, 'spread open', which is approved in the apparatus of the Oxford text.

CHRONOLOGICAL TABLE

B.C.

404 Surrender of Athens to Sparta. Thirty Tyrants established in power at Athens.

403 Overthrow of Thirty; restoration of democracy.

395 Confederation of Athens, Thebes, Corinth and Argos against Sparta. Beginning of Corinthian War.

387–386 End of Corinthian War: the King's Peace (Peace of Antalcidas).

382 Spartan seizure of Thebes and attack on Olynthus.

379 Fall of Olynthus.

379–378 Liberation of Thebes.

378–377 Formation of Second Athenian Confederacy, to fight with Thebes against Sparta.

375–374 Short-lived renewal of Common Peace.

371 Common Peace agreed. Thebes excluded by Spartans. Spartans defeated by Thebans at Leuctra.

370–369 Theban invasions of Peloponnese. Messenia liberated from Sparta. Athenian alliance with Sparta.

367 Failure of Thebans to impose Common Peace.

362–361 Battle of Mantinea. End of Theban supremacy. Common Peace agreed.

359 Philip regent of Macedon.

357 Amphipolis taken by Philip. Social War between Athens and some leading allies.

356 Outbreak of Sacred War; Phocian seizure of Delphi.

355 End of Social War; secessionist allies independent.

353 Philip defeated in Thessaly by Phocians.

352 Philip victorious in Thessaly, blocked at Thermopylae by Athenians.

351 Demosthenes' *First Philippic*.

349 Philip's attack on Olynthus. Demosthenes' *Olynthiac* speeches.

348 Fall of Olynthus. Philip's first peace-feelers. Philocrates' proposal to negotiate blocked by accusation of illegality.

347 Philocrates defended by Demosthenes. Negotiations opened.

346 First Athenian delegation to Macedon (February–March). Debate

on peace terms at Athens (April). Second delegation to Macedon (May–June). Phocian surrender to Philip (July). Demosthenes' *On the Peace*. Philip at Pythian Games (September).

345 Timarchus prosecuted by Aeschines.

344 Demosthenes in Peloponnese. *Second Philippic*. Python's mission to Athens.

343 Failure of Hegesippus's mission to Macedon. Philip thought to be intriguing in Megara. Philocrates condemned and exiled. Aeschines acquitted on charge of misconduct on second delegation of 346; speeches of Demosthenes and Aeschines *On the Treaty*.

342 Hegesippus's *On Halonnesus*. Philip in Epirus. Demosthenes in Ambracia and Peloponnese. Macedonian intervention in Euboea.

341 Demosthenes' *On the Chersonese* and *Third Philippic*. Euboea freed. Demosthenes and Callias in Peloponnese. Demosthenes at Byzantium.

340 Demosthenes publicly crowned. Philip in Thrace. War declared by Philip and by Athens. Failure of Philip's attacks on Perinthus and Byzantium.

339 Sacred War declared on Amphissa by Amphictyons. Philip called on to lead Amphictyons; occupation of Elatea (September). Alliance between Athens and Thebes negotiated by Demosthenes.

338 Demosthenes publicly crowned. Battle of Chaeronea. Peace of Demades between Athens and Philip.

338–337 Common Peace Treaty organized by Philip.

337 Demosthenes commissioner for walls and for Theoric Fund.

336 Ctesiphon's proposal that Demosthenes be publicly crowned, blocked by Aeschines' accusation of illegality. Philip's invasion of Asia begun. Assassination of Philip (July), succession of Alexander.

335 Revolt of Thebes, its destruction by Alexander. Alexander's demand for surrender of Demosthenes and other orators not pressed.

334 Alexander's invasion of Asia.

333 Alexander's victory at Issus.

331 Spartan attempt to raise Greece against Macedon, not supported by Athens. Alexander's victory at Gaugamela (Arbela).

330 Spartans defeated. Aeschines' accusation of Ctesiphon tried; Ctesiphon acquitted, Aeschines leaves Athens.

324 Harpalus affair. Trial and exile of Demosthenes.

323 Death of Alexander. Rising of Athenians and other Greeks against Macedon (Lamian War).

322 Defeat of Greeks. Death of Demosthenes.

BIBLIOGRAPHY

I. Editions of the speeches:

Greek texts only of both Demosthenes' speeches in Oxford Classical Texts *Demosthenis Orationes*, vol. I (1903), and in the Teubner *Demosthenis Orationes* (Leipzig, 1928); Greek text with introductions and translation in Loeb Classical Library *Demosthenes de Corona, de Falsa Legatione* (by C. A. and J. H. Vince, London, 1926).

Greek texts only of both Aeschines' speeches in the Teubner *Aeschinis Orationes* (Leipzig, 1908); Greek text with introduction and translation in Loeb Classical Library *The Speeches of Aeschines* (by C. D. Adams, London, 1948).

Greek text with introduction, notes and appendices to both Crown speeches: G. A. and W. H. Simcox, *The Orations of Demosthenes and Aeschines on the Crown* (Oxford, 1872).

Greek text with introduction, notes and appendices to Demosthenes' *Crown*: W. W. Goodwin, *Demosthenes de Corona* (Cambridge, 1901; shorter version, 1904).

Translations with brief introductions of the Demosthenes speeches in A. W. Pickard-Cambridge, *Demosthenes' Public Orations* (London, 1963).

II. On Demosthenes' career and policies:

The fullest and best documented books on Demosthenes in English are A. W. Pickard-Cambridge, *Demosthenes and the Last Days of Greek Freedom* in the 'Heroes of the Nations' series (New York and London, 1914), and Werner Jaeger's Sather Classical Lectures, *Demosthenes: The Origin and Growth of his Policy* (Cambridge, 1938). Goodwin's edition (see above) has a detailed historical sketch of the years 359–336 (on pp. 229–99). Essential for further study are a series of articles by G. L. Cawkwell:

'Aeschines and the Peace of Philocrates', *Revue des études grecques*, LXXIII (1960), pp. 416–38.

'Aeschines and the ruin of Phocis', *Revue des études grecques*, LXXV (1962), pp. 453–9.

Bibliography

'The defence of Olynthus', *Classical Quarterly*, N.S. XII (1962), pp. 122–40.

'Demosthenes after the Peace of Philocrates', *Classical Quarterly*, N.S. XIII (1963), pp. 120–38 and 200–13.

'The crowning of Demosthenes', *Classical Quarterly*, N.S. XIX (1969), pp. 163–80.

See also *Philip and Athens*, ed. S. Perlman in the 'Views and Controversies' series (Cambridge, 1973).

III. On Greek history in the fourth century B.C.:

Cambridge Ancient History, vol. VI (1927).

A. R. Burn, *The Pelican History of Greece* (Harmondsworth, 1966).

N. G. L. Hammond, *A History of Greece to 322 B.C.* (2nd edition, Oxford, 1967).

M. L. W. Laistner, *A History of the Greek World from 479 to 323 B.C.*, Methuen History of the Greek and Roman World (London, 1936).

T. T. B. Ryder, *Koine Eirene: General Peace and Local Independence in Ancient Greece* (Oxford, 1965).

IV. On Greek oratory:

G. Kennedy, *The Art of Persuasion in Greece* (Princeton and London, 1963).